Leper Priest of Moloka'i

Leper Priest of Moloka'i

The Father Damien Story

Richard Stewart

A Latitude 20 Book
University of Hawai'i Press
Honolulu

Library of Congress Cataloging-in-Publication Data

Stewart, Richard, 1926–
Leper priest of Moloka'i : the Father Damien story / Richard Stewart.
p.   cm.
Includes bibliographical references and index.
ISBN-13: 978-0-8248-2232-3 (hardcover : alk. paper) — ISBN-13: 978-0-8248-2322-1 (pbk. : alk. paper)
ISBN-10: 0-8248-2232-3 (hardcover : alk. paper) — ISBN-10: 0-8248-2322-2 (pbk. : alk. paper)
1. Damien, Father, 1840–1889.   2. Catholic Church—Hawaii—Clergy—Biography.   3.
Missionaries—Belgium—Biography.   4. Missionaries—Hawaii—Biography.   5. Missions to
lepers—Hawaii.   I. Title.

BX4705.D25 S74 2000
266'.2'092—dc21
[B]   00-020266

Designed by Nighthawk Design
Printed by the Maple-Vail Book Manufacturing Group

To the men and women who, like Father Damien
and Mother Marianne, strive "to seek excellence in the healing arts"

E'imi i ka po'okela o ka lapa'au 'ana.

Contents

Acknowledgments

THIS BIOGRAPHY WOULD NOT have been possible without the inestimable support I received from Mary Stewart, my loving wife of forty-seven years. Mary adroitly brushed aside the most formidable fact-finding obstacle by enlisting the aid of Sr. Mary Hester Valentine, her former professor at Mount Mary College, Milwaukee. This seventy-year-old sister journeyed to the Provincial Archives of the Congregation of the Sacred Hearts, Louvain, Belgium, and to the Vatican Library, Rome, to photocopy all of the Fr. Damien letters and correspondence, then translated over two hundred letters written in French and Flemish into English. She also arranged for me to meet with key historians of the Congregation of the Sacred Hearts in Louvain, Belgium; and Sister Mary Laurence Hanley, O.S.F., who permitted me to read the journals of sisters who had served at the leper settlement on Moloka'i, journals housed in the Archives of St. Anthony's Convent, the Mother House of the Third Franciscan Order Minor Conventual, Syracuse, New York.

I owe a debt of gratitude to Dr. Bert Lum, Chairman and Professor of the Department of Pharmacology, University of Hawai'i Medical School at Mānoa, who introduced me to the Fr. Damien saga and Robert Louis Stevenson's *Open Letter to the Reverend Doctor Hyde,* which awakened my interest in the controversy surrounding Fr. Damien's ministry.

Two other persons merit special mention. Professor James A. Sappenfield, Chairman of the Department of English, University of Wisconsin–Milwaukee, not only scrutinized my manuscript and made hundreds of suggestions for improvement, but enlisted the aid of four professors—Thomas Bontly, Andrew Martin, Joseph Chang, and Donna Van Wynsberghe—to critique the work. Pamela Kelley, Editor, University of Hawai'i Press, Honolulu, honed the manuscript with the elegant precision of a born editor, and with the skill of an obstetrician ushered it into the world. I will be forever grateful.

Author's Note

In Damien's time, the term "leprosy" was commonly used by physicians, scientists, and lay people to designate the disease caused by the bacterium *Mycobacterium leprae,* first identified in 1873 by Norwegian physician Dr. Gerhard A. Hansen. A victim of the disease was called a "leper." Dr. Hansen, Father Damien, and all health officials of the nineteenth century used the words "leprosy" and "leper" repeatedly in the documents and letters cited in this biography, and that usage has endured in the twentieth century. Both Albert Schweitzer and Mother Teresa used "leprosy" and "leper" when referring to contemporary patients.

In the United States, the negative connotations of the term have led to the use of a surrogate—Hansen's disease—among the general public. However, the accepted medical and scientific term continues to be leprosy. The half million people who contract leprosy each year are correctly informed that they have the disease, that it is curable, and that they can live normal lives with the proper treatment. The derogatory historical image of the leper as a contagious social outcast is vanishing.

Prologue

And Jesus said to him, "Go and do likewise."
—Luke 10:29–37

ON A RAIN-SWEPT SUNDAY in June, 1995, Pope John Paul II stood before a crowd of thirty thousand in Brussels, Belgium, and celebrated the Beatification Mass of Father Damien De Veuster, the leper priest of Moloka'i who had died at age 49 in 1889. Seated before the Pope in the front row was Mother Teresa, founder of the Missionaries of Charity and winner of the 1979 Nobel Peace Prize, the woman who had masterfully championed the cause of Father Damien. She had beseeched the Pope for a saint to guide and protect the sisters who were caring for the thousands of lepers in India, Yemen, Ethiopia, and Tanzania, and Damien was her choice.[1]

The key to understanding this choice and discovering what motivated this man to risk his life to serve the ostracized Hawaiian lepers on the island of Moloka'i is in a name—*Damien*—the name a young Belgian, Joseph De Veuster, chose when he became a Catholic priest. He first heard the name as a young child when his mother, Anne Catherine De Veuster, gathered her children around her before the open-hearth fireplace in the spacious kitchen of their Belgian farmhouse and read aloud the stories of the early Christian saints and martyrs.[2] These awe-inspiring tales of Christians whose faith allowed them to face danger and even death were the high point of the day, and each child had favorite heroes and heroines.

Young Joseph's favorites were Saint Damien and his brother, Saint Cosmas, two third-century physicians who practiced medicine in Aegea, Cilicia, in Asia Minor. Damien and Cosmas were unique. Like Jesus Christ, whose healing ministry they emulated, they refused all payment for their medical services. For this reason the brothers were called the *Anargyroi*, the "Silverless Ones." Their skill and dedication in caring for the sick, regardless of the person's religion, race, or affluence, was an example that attracted many to Christianity.

The medical practice of the physician brothers flourished and increased in popularity until Diocletian, the emperor of Rome, decided to eradicate Christianity. Those who refused to renounce the Christian God and worship the Roman gods were executed. Damien and Cosmas stood firm and refused to bow down to pagan idols. Diocletian had the brothers imprisoned, tortured, and then beheaded in A.D. 303—just ten years before Emperor Constantine granted religious tolerance to all Christians. By the middle of the fifth century, the intrepid lives of Damien and Cosmas had become legend, and churches were erected in their honor in several major cities, including Constantinople and Rome.

Spiritually desirous of emulating the careers of his boyhood heroes, Joseph De Veuster overcame major obstacles to become a Catholic priest and serve as a missionary in Hawai'i. To his spiritual ministry he added the practice of medicine and the skill of a master builder of chapels and churches. At age thirty-three, the same age as Jesus when he carried his cross to Golgotha, Damien began the trek to his Golgotha when he voluntarily stepped ashore at the leper settlement on Moloka'i in 1873 to become the first resident clergyman and part-time physician. This act was viewed by many as that of a heroic Christian martyr, because leprosy was as feared in the nineteenth century as AIDS in the twentieth.

The cause of leprosy was unknown. It was known that the disease was contagious and incurable. Over the centuries, mankind had learned that the *only* preventive measure of merit was the banishment of all lepers. To make direct physical contact with a leper was to risk a hideous death. Father Damien knowingly took this risk thousands of times.

What follows is the biography of the Belgian priest who was quite possibly the most courageous and resolute man of the nineteenth century.

1

Exile: Day One
Saturday, May 10, 1873

*Yea, though I walk through the valley of the shadow of death,
I will fear no evil; for Thou art with me; Thy rod and Thy staff,
they comfort me.*
—Psalm 23:4

SIX-FOOT WAVES HEAVED and tossed the Hawaiian interisland steamer *Kīlauea* as she plodded toward the northern coast of Moloka'i to disembark the lepers crouched on her main deck. There was no joy in the faces of these fifty men, women, and children as they approached the island where they would be incarcerated until death. They were the dreaded "untouchables," the "unclean," because the abominable leprosy ravaging their bodies was contagious and incurable.

To protect its population, the Kingdom of Hawai'i had ordered them to join 720 other lepers already confined on the isolated peninsula on the northern coast of Moloka'i that is known as Kalaupapa. Here on this tiny, triangular shelf of volcanic rock, they would spend the rest of their shortened lives witnessing the systematic mutilation of their bodies—first the skin, then nose, ears, eyes, fingers, and toes; and if they survived long enough, the obliteration of their internal organs. Isolated from loved ones in the primitive, eight-year-old leper settlement where there were no doctors or nurses, death would seize them within two to four years.

In front of the lepers on the main deck were a dozen wide-eyed steers swaying with each roll of the ship. These unhappy animals were part of the food supply being delivered to the Kingdom of Hawai'i's

3

leper settlement. The cattle and the lepers were being herded against their will to a desolate peninsula where they would die.

Standing at the side railing of the *Kīlauea*, well behind the lepers and the cattle, were two Catholic priests. They stood motionless and silent while the ocean breeze tugged at their broad-brimmed black hats and long, black cassocks. The taller of the two was Bishop Louis Maigret, a frail-appearing, sixty-nine-year-old priest who had directed the Congregation of Sacred Hearts' missionary endeavors in the Hawaiian Islands for twenty-six years.[1] The shorter, stocky priest was Father Damien De Veuster, a robust thirty-three-year-old Belgian, a ten-year missionary veteran in the Islands who had volunteered to become the leper settlement's first resident priest. Neither spoke as they watched the 3,000-foot-high sea cliffs that form Moloka'i's northern coast loom larger and more menacing.

Bishop Maigret's face was expressionless as he pondered the wisdom of permitting this young priest to go ashore for an extended period of time. Even if Father Damien took every known precaution, the risk of contracting leprosy was great; yet the facial expression of the younger priest betrayed no hint of fear nor of regret for the decision made. The determination in Damien's dark eyes and the set of his jaw reflected his intrepid resolve to proceed with the venture.

From the priests' vantage point that morning in May, the sheer beauty of Moloka'i's towering sea cliffs, the highest in the world—called *pali* by the Native Hawaiians—belied the misery of the 720 lepers exiled on the peninsula at its base.[2] In the sunlight, the fortresslike *pali* shimmered in tropical splendor. Its nearly vertical face was a vibrant green, having been washed by the morning rain, and large birds soared lazily beneath the mist and clouds that obscured its top.

The majesty of the moment vanished when the flat shelf of land where the lepers lived came into view. There were few trees to be seen, vegetation was sparse, and the mounds of black volcanic rock that formed the shoreline of the 3,500-acre Kalaupapa Peninsula were under continuous assault by the turbulent surf, sending plumes of white spray high into the air. It was obvious to Father Damien why this drab shelf of volcanic rock had been chosen to sequester the lepers. The nearly vertical face of the *pali* served as a giant barrier to shield the island's two thousand "clean" inhabitants from any contact with the "unclean" on the tiny peninsula below, and the surf that pounded the shore was so overpowering that no small craft could safely launch and hope to escape to the open sea.

While serving the Kohala District on the Big Island of Hawai'i, Damien had become intensely interested in leprosy when, with increasing frequency, he began to recognize the early physical signs of the disease in members of his congregation. He had tried to treat the small, whitish spots on the skin and the tiny, emerging tumors on the face, arms, and legs with the various available medicinals, but to no avail. Once these lesions ulcerated and announced to the world that leprosy had attacked another victim, the unfortunate native was forced to surrender to the authorities and be exiled at the leper settlement.

Hawai'i's new king, William Lunalilo, had been informed unequivocally that leprosy was contagious. Like smallpox, measles, influenza, and cholera—diseases that had reduced the susceptible Native Hawaiian population from a high of between 200,000 to 400,000 people at the time of Captain Cook's discovery of the Islands in 1778 to an 1873 low of 52,000—leprosy would take an additional heavy toll.[3] The king needed subjects to rule. The greater the number, the more dependable the tax base. Also, the knowledge of the presence of the scourge in the island kingdom was proving harmful to foreign commerce, further jeopardizing the treasury. The king believed he had little choice but to enforce the 1863 Segregation Law with renewed vigor and order all lepers in his kingdom transported without delay to the leper settlement on Moloka'i, under armed guard if necessary. Consequently, the number of new lepers arriving in the first five months of his reign had more than doubled the population of the settlement, placing a severe strain on the facility's already limited resources.

The emotional impact on these family-oriented Hawaiians of a lifetime of separation from loved ones was universally catastrophic. They had many names for the offending disease. *Ma'i Pākē*, the "Chinese disease," was the most commonly used term as it was believed that Chinese laborers had introduced leprosy into the islands. Many, however, referred to leprosy as *ma'i ho'oka'awale 'ohana*, "the disease that tears families apart," or simply, "the separating sickness." The social isolation led to depression, drunken orgies, and crime—the settlement's omnipresent dark demons. While death erased the agonies of the disease, it usually occurred in the absence of a clergyman, and was followed by a hasty burial in a shallow grave. The prospect of such an ignominious end to life provoked an intense resistance to the government's renewed segregation efforts. To avoid arrest and incarceration, an estimated 10 to 20 percent of the Native Hawaiians with the disease fled and took refuge in remote areas of the islands, inadvertently initiating an effective, self-imposed segregation program. And there was some violence.[4] One Hawaiian, when informed that his daughter had been declared a leper and was about to be transported to Moloka'i, shot and killed the examining government physician; another Hawaiian leper shot to death the local sheriff who first attempted to bring him in, then killed two militiamen who attempted to arrest him. On Kaua'i, a leper named Ko'olau escaped after he had been arrested and fled to a remote valley where he successfully eluded the authorities for the rest of his life.

The sullen-faced men and women squatting on the spray-swept deck of the *Kīlauea* were passively complying with the Segregation Law, resigned to spending the remainder of their days at the leper settlement. They would never again embrace a spouse or delight in watching their children grow. A leper child would never again hear a parent say, *"Mea aloha, aloha 'oe"*—"Beloved, may you be loved." At best, a few of the young orphans would be cared for by the more benevolent resident lepers of Moloka'i because the flimsy structures designated as children's domiciles had no attendants. The leper settlement was an earthly hell plagued by a shortage of fresh water, food, clothing, and adequate housing. There was no law, no professional medical care, and no clergy. The only things present in abundance were wails of suffering and a guarantee of an early death.

About 75 yards from the landing wharf on the western side of the peninsula, the *Kīlauea* dropped anchor. The relentless incoming waves slammed the rough volcanic shoreline with such fury that it was impossible for the ship to venture closer. Above the rattle of the anchor chain, the fifty lepers heard the commanding voice of a crewman order them to gather their belongings and proceed to the longboats for transport to the landing wharf. Each leper had been given a blanket, one change of clothing, and some money for food. Each had been permitted to bring only those personal possessions he was capable of carrying, and in the bag each lifted from the open deck were extra clothing, a comb, hand tools, often a Bible, and food for a day.

Three longboats holding the fifty lepers and the two priests were lowered into the rough sea, and the apprehensive passengers clung tightly to their possessions as the wildly bobbing craft made slow progress toward the wooden landing wharf. Once the longboats were underway, crewmen shoved and prodded the balking cattle onto a plank that jutted out over the surging water. One by one the frightened, wide-eyed creatures were forced off the end of the plank to tumble with all legs kicking into the turbulent ocean for the long swim to shore. After a belly-smash landing, the terror-stricken beasts frantically churned the water with their legs to keep their heads above water. A lone longboat, like a sheepdog, patiently herded the bobbing heads toward the wharf.

Bishop Maigret and Father Damien were in the first longboat, seated in front of sixteen anxious lepers. The heaving surf gave the small craft a roller coaster-like ride to the wharf, where two hundred of the healthier resident lepers had gathered to welcome the new arrivals. Eighty to one hundred in the exuberant group were Catholics who ostentatiously waved their rosaries and clamored to make their needs known.

As the first longboat neared the wooden wharf, a crewman cast a line to a leper who still had ten fingers to grasp and secure it. When a second line secured the boat to the pier, the two priests stood up. *"Aloha kākou!"*—"Greetings, everyone!" the Bishop repeated several times, raising his right arm high overhead and waving it to emphasize his sincerity. *"Aloha! Aloha! Aloha!"* reverberated from the crowding lepers.

Father Damien was the first to exit the longboat and step onto the pier. Hands, some without five fingers, reached out to assist him. He turned and watched as his bishop stepped from the boat, assiduously avoiding the outstretched hands. Recognizing several of his former parishioners from the island of Hawai'i (the Big Island) who were now resident lepers, Damien forced a smile.[5] He tried not to appear shocked by the swollen, elongated ear lobes and ulcerated nose that disfigured a young girl, nor the limp of the former courier hobbled by an amputated foot, nor the fourteen-year-old former choir boy with a ruptured eyeball. More disturbing than the physical deformities was the disheveled appearance of the lepers—dirt-smudged hands and faces, matted hair, clothing that hadn't been washed for weeks—and the nauseating odor emanating from the open, pus-filled sores. Father

Damien swallowed hard and resorted to shallow breathing to repress the urge to vomit.[6]

From the grotesque, swollen faces with missing eyebrows, noses, and ears came a deluge of requests for the sacraments and for help with the dying and the bedfast. Hands with missing fingers beckoned insistently for the two priests to follow and attend to some special concern. In his former parish on the Big Island, Father Damien had witnessed the havoc that leprosy could inflict, but it had always been in the setting of an individual encounter. He had coped with the stench emanating from the pus-oozing, infected ulcers of a single leper by resorting to breath holding and shallow breathing, but the combined stench from the hundred or so who now crowded around the two priests was overpowering. This bedlam of noise, confusion, and odoriferous bodies with missing parts was a nightmare from which Damien knew he would not soon awaken.

After motioning for the lepers to stand back, Bishop Maigret raised both arms and signaled for silence. Dutifully, the lepers complied. When the crowd noise subsided, the Bishop smiled and in a friendly voice repeated his original greeting: *"Aloha kākou!"*

"Aloha! Aloha!" returned the lepers.

Then the bishop turned toward Damien and, speaking in Hawaiian, introduced him as the resident priest they had been requesting. "Here is Father Damien, who wishes to sacrifice himself for the salvation of your souls. He has not yet a house; we shall get him one as soon as possible."[7]

Cheers of thanksgiving erupted. The petition for a resident priest had finally been heeded. Again the bishop signaled for silence, and when he could be heard he invited everyone to proceed to St. Philomena Chapel in the leper village of Kalawao on the opposite side of the peninsula where he would celebrate Mass before returning to the *Kīlauea* for his return voyage to Honolulu. Following the Mass and his departure, the bishop assured the gathering, Father Damien would attend to the needs of the sick and the dying. Baptism of the dying, last rites, and burials would take precedence over confessions, communion, and marriages. The bishop beamed. With a Catholic priest in residence, the Kalaupapa leper settlement could become a respectable Christian community.

Fifty of the more affluent lepers who owned horses led the ragtag procession from the landing pier through the "clean" village of Kalaupapa with its five wooden buildings and cluster of thatched huts to the narrow trail at the base of the *pali* that led to Kalawao, the leper village. Standing silently beside their dwellings, observing the gala departure, was a group of forty or more of the healthy residents who lived on the more sheltered western side of the peninsula, Native Hawaiians who had stubbornly refused to relinquish their land—land that had been handed down from one generation to the next for hundreds of years.[8] This land was sacred and to abandon it, they felt, would be more grievous than being forced to share the peninsula with the lepers. Begrudgingly, these landowners tolerated the weekly intrusions into their village when a ship dropped anchor to disembark lepers or supplies for the settlement. They much preferred to have all incoming lepers and supplies for the settlement disembarked directly at Kalawao on the eastern shore of the peninsula, but the perpetually turbulent surf on that side generally precluded such hazardous landing attempts.

The two priests, riding on borrowed horses, trotted just behind the lead horsemen. The stragglers, a group of laughing, limping, singing lepers, followed those on horseback as best they could. Scattered along the 2.5-mile winding trail, the homeward-bound lepers passed an occasional frame house that the Board of Health had purchased from one of the previous healthy residents who had accepted the government's buy-out offer and vacated the peninsula. Predictably, the stronger or more affluent lepers had taken possession of these few more desirable houses, forcing the majority of incoming lepers to construct and live in the traditional thatched huts.

Kalawao, the leper village, was a collection of thatched huts situated on either side of the narrow dirt road that bisected the village.[9] The majority of the huts were small, generally not more than 8 to 10 feet long, 6 to 8 feet broad, and 4 to 6 feet high. They were constructed of a framework of branches from the indigenous *pū hala* or pandanus tree, lashed together with homemade twine and thatched with layers of *pili* grass or ti leaves. They were flimsy, drafty, damp, and had dirt floors. These suboptimal shelters were home for six hundred of the lepers and another hundred *kōkua*. *Kōkua* was the Hawaiian name for nonleper family members, healthy friends, or hired helpers who had been granted permanent resident status so they might attend to the needs of the lepers.[10]

In the center of the leper village, a picket fence enclosed a cluster of small wooden buildings. On one side of the picket fence enclosure stood the resident superintendent's house, the most substantial wooden structure in the village. Close by was the small schoolhouse and the two unstaffed dormitories for boys and girls that had been built under the direction of Donald Walsh, the settlement's second resident superintendent, now deceased. Two of the buildings, long, narrow structures, were the designated "hospitals" for the terminally ill—one for male lepers and the other for the women. Those interned were too weak to care for themselves, and they lay side by side on thin mats on the dirt floors. *Kōkua* paid by the government distributed the food to the patients and disposed of the bodily wastes. There were, of course, no doctors or nurses in attendance. The remaining wooden structures in the enclosure were an empty two-cell jailhouse, two wooden cookhouses, and three small dormitories for adults with advanced leprosy.[11]

A few hundred feet from the picket fence enclosure stood the two small rival churches. Siloama, the Congregational church, was the larger of the two, a sturdy, all-wood structure that had been built two years earlier. It boasted a steeple with a bell, and architecturally it resembled a small New England church. A Hawaiian Congregational deacon, Pastor Heulu, an incarcerated leper, served as the Protestant minister and conducted regular Sunday services. His disease severely limited his ministerial endeavors, so his board of deacons attended to the normal pastoral duties of visiting the sick and overseeing the Sunday School programs. Nevertheless, church attendance was poor.

One hundred ten feet away, beyond the reach of the shadow of the Congregational church, was the Catholic focal point, the St. Philomena Chapel, a boxlike structure with an unadorned, front-gabled roof. It had no steeple, no bell, and no cross pointing to the heavens.[12] The chapel could accommodate forty worshipers—fifty with crowding. It had been built the previous year by Victorin Bertrand, a brother of the Sacred Hearts and a printer by trade who had accomplished the task with $400 of materials contributed by Christians, both Catholic and Protestant, some from as far away as England.[13] Most of the time the chapel stood empty.

Bishop Maigret dismounted and led the procession into St. Philomena, followed by the first seventy lepers reaching the door who managed to squeeze into the sanctuary. There was standing room only. Disappointed stragglers huddled around the open door or peered in through one of the four side windows, jostling each other to catch a glimpse of the proceedings. Within minutes, the stench from the many bodies inside the chapel became offensive even to the lepers. In this jam-packed, malodorous setting, Bishop Maigret celebrated Mass.

After the bishop uttered the Benediction and rode off to the landing pier to reboard the *Kīlauea*, Father Damien announced that he would celebrate Mass each morning and conduct a vesper service each evening. Then, with his characteristic broad smile, he excused himself and devoted the remainder of the day attending to the dying and the many critically ill. While savoring the semitropical grandeur of Maui the previous week at the annual gathering of the Hawaiian mission, it had been an easy matter to volunteer to serve the lepers. Picturing himself as a true apostle to the lowliest of outcasts had given him a sense of intimacy with the Almighty, a feeling akin to the serenity of sunlight streaming through the beauty of stained glass windows in a silent cathedral. Now that he was face-to-face with the harsh reality of ministering to the lepers, the physical tasks and emotional stresses were dark clouds that blocked the celestial sunlight.

ON THAT SAME tenth day of May, the *Pacific Commercial Advertiser*, unaware of Damien's arrival at the leper settlement, published King Lunalilo's letter of April 20, "To My Dear Friends at Kalaupapa," expressing his sympathy for his segregated subjects and promising to assist them in every way possible.[14] The king had been prompted to write the letter because of the public's response to an article by Walter Murray Gibson, an American expatriate and the editor of the bilingual newspaper *Ka Nupepa Nuhou*, in which it was respectfully suggested that were King Lunalilo to make a visit to the leper settlement, it would have a "most consoling and inspiring effect" on his exiled subjects.[15] King Lunalilo had prudently declined to make the journey and risk physical contact with the lepers. Instead he had dispatched two members of his Board of Health to read his letter to the lepers.

In addition to the appeal to the king to visit the leper settlement, Gibson's April editorial had challenged the clergy to step forward and minister to the spiritual needs of the lepers. "And if a noble Christian priest, preacher or sister should be inspired to go and sacrifice a life to

console these poor wretches, that would be a royal soul to shine forever on a throne reared by human love." Gibson would later claim
that it was this editorial that had prompted Damien's heroic sacrifice.

AROUND MIDNIGHT OF that first day, an exhausted Father Damien
made his way through the darkness to the St. Philomena chapel for his
evening devotions.[16] Light from the moon bathed the tiny box-shaped
structure in silver and shadows. As he opened the wooden door, the
silence of the night was disturbed by the squeak of the hinges. He
paused in the doorway. The moonlight that was able to penetrate the
four dirt-streaked glass windows allowed him to make out the altar,
shrouded in blacks and grays at the end of the central aisle. From the
wooden stand inside the door he retrieved and lighted a candle, and
shielding the flame with a cupped hand he made his way to the altar
railing where he knelt in prayer.

It had been a day like no other—long, stressful, filled with the
horror of dying, disfigured people. Yet while ministering to these forlorn outcasts he had experienced an inner serenity. The words of
Jesus—"Truly, I say to you, as you did it to one of the least of these
my brethren, you did it to me"[17]—were a balm that lifted him above
the abject misery surrounding him. He lifted his bowed head. In the
flickering light he could just make out the figure of Christ on the cross
hanging above the altar. Silently he thanked his Lord for allowing him
to be an apostle in so desolate a setting.

His evening prayers completed, he picked up his bedroll from the
far corner of the sanctuary where he had placed his few belongings.
He extinguished the candle and walked out into the night. Heeding his
bishop's instruction never to sleep in a leper's dwelling, he spread out
his sleeping mat beneath the branches of the lone pandanus tree standing next to the chapel and slowly eased himself down onto the hard,
bumpy surface next to the ugly clump of slanting aerial roots that supported the base of the tree. As he attempted to relax, he may have been
aware of a disquieting irony. The delicate blossoms of the pandanus,
a tree the Hawaiians called *pū hala*, were seldom fashioned into a lei
because *hala* means "failure," and a lei of *pū hala* means 'oki, a "cut-
ting off," an "isolation," or even an "excommunication." The blossoms of the tree he had chosen for shelter symbolized the very sever-
ance from friends, family, and colleagues that had plagued him in the

Hawaiian mission, a loneliness and isolation that he had further intensified by stepping ashore at the leper settlement.

His first twelve hours on Moloka'i had been nightmarish.[18] A
macabre montage was indelibly etched in his memory: dirty hands
with stubs for fingers reaching out to him; children pressing to have
him bless them, their upturned faces with missing eyebrows, noses and
ears; last rites by flickering candlelight in tiny thatched huts; and the
ever-present odor—the suffocating smell of decomposing, putrefied
human flesh.[19]

While comforting the dying, he had stared into large ulcers on the
abdomen or legs that were filled with squirming maggots. He hadn't
been prepared to witness such scenes, and his first inclination had been
to scoop out and stomp the life from the offending maggots. But before
he could act, the other lepers stayed his hand. Maggots that fed on
dead flesh to keep open wounds clean were routinely used by the
kahuna lapa'au, the Native Hawaiian doctors who specialized in the
use of herbs and prayer to heal. He was politely informed that unless
he could offer a treatment of equal or superior efficacy, the maggots
would remain at their feast. Damien was appalled. He had been taught
that cleansing with water followed by the application of clean dressings was the treatment of choice, but clean water was in short supply
and dressings unavailable.

His Lord, Jesus Christ, had dealt mercifully and courageously
with lepers. Jesus had laid his hands on them and healed them. His
Lord hadn't flinched or vomited. He, Damien, was a failure on both
counts. With no medicines, dressings, or clean water with which to
cleanse the wounds, he was powerless to help the suffering outcasts;
and he was fearful that he would never become accustomed to the
putrid odor emanating from the wounds.

The burial service he had witnessed was grotesque—a rotting
corpse with arms and legs bound to the body with twine, lifted from
a dirty blanket, slid feet first into a small shallow hole in the volcanic
earth, and left doubled up in a seated position. When the hole was
filled, the head of the deceased was within a few inches of the surface.
To the bystanders his words of comfort and the assurance of life eternal were uttered against a backdrop of buzzing flies and the knowledge that after he had given the Benediction the wild pigs would come
to root up the body and feast.

Beneath the branches of the *pū hala* with its long, narrow, sharp-edged leaves silhouetted against the moon, Father Damien closed his eyes. He would need all of his strength to meet the challenges of the next day. After an early morning Mass he would spend most of the day visiting the sick, beginning with the forty most seriously ill who were housed in the two narrow hovels called "hospitals" where there was no medical care. To help these unfortunates, he would resume his practice of medicine. A dying leper couldn't contemplate the goodness and mercy of God when in the grip of a delirium from a high fever, or when doubled over with abdominal cramps from a bloody diarrhea. And with seven hundred lepers, how could he possibly find the time to be both a father confessor and a caring physician?

There was also the pressing problem of the inadequate water supply. Somehow he must find a way to harness one of the streams cascading down the face of the *pali* to provide water for wound cleansing, cooking, and bathing. And in his "free time" there was a rectory to build, a garden plot to be cleared and planted, and the stench in the chapel screamed out for a bucket of soapy water and a scrub brush. The tasks ahead seemed overwhelming.

Once he had lived in a more pleasant and simpler time, a time where God was near and love abounded, a time where the air he breathed carried the fragrance of spring flowers, new mown hay, or his mother's cooking. Laughter and joy had been his companions. He recalled a chill winter's day when he was ten years old, strapping on his ice skates to race his older brother down the frozen Dyle River south of their farm. Then he was called Jef. Damien was only a name that could be found in his favorite book. He remembered skating and winning and laughing. Life had been good in Tremeloo, Belgium. That was where it had all begun—in 1840 in a farmhouse in Tremeloo, where the air one breathed was clean and invigorating, and where he was surrounded by love—love and laughter—and the nearness of God.

He slept.

2

Birth, Childhood, and Beyond

And the child increased in wisdom and in stature,
and in favor with God and man.
—Luke 2:52

JOSEPH DE VEUSTER, the future Father Damien, was born on a chill January morning in 1840, in an upstairs bedroom of a two-story red brick farmhouse in Tremeloo, Belgium.[1] Like many of the houses with their steep, tiled roofs that made up the town of Tremeloo and sheltered its 1,600 inhabitants, the De Veuster house was nestled close to the snow-covered banks of the frozen Laah River. The scene was peaceful. A gentle wind wafted the wood smoke rising from the farmhouse's two chimneys into thin blue strands that crossed the morning sky.

In the upstairs birth room, Anne Catherine cuddled the seventh addition to the De Veuster family and tried to visualize the man that one day her son might become. Downstairs in the large kitchen, Frans De Veuster, the baby's proud father, seated himself at the head of the table. With a grateful smile, he nodded to his three sons, three daughters, and the revered middle-aged cousin who had joined the family for breakfast. With folded hands and a bowed head, Frans offered a prayer of thanksgiving for the successful birth. From the lips of each bowed head at the conclusion of the prayer came a reverent "Amen," and as the heads lifted, happy chatter filled the room.

The visiting cousin, Joseph Goovaerts, a retired soldier and prosperous grain merchant from Antwerp, was pleased that he had been asked to join the family gathering and become the baby's godfather.

15

He had accepted both the honor and the responsibility with the proviso that if the baby were a boy, he would be named Joseph, as he himself had been, in reverence of the earthly father of the Holy Family. Later that day the baby boy was baptized Joseph De Veuster.

Frans and Anne Catherine De Veuster were middle-class Roman Catholics. Frans was forty years old at the time of his son's birth; Anne Catherine was thirty-seven. Frans had courted and married Anne Catherine Waustere, the winsome daughter of a farmer from the nearby village of Haacht. In time the couple had eight children: Eugénie, Léonce, Gerard, Constance, Pauline, Auguste, Joseph, and Mary, who died when she was four.

In the early years of the marriage, Frans devoted most of his energies to managing the family farm. When his older sons reached an age at which they were able to relieve him of the physical labor, Frans turned his attention to the grain business that had made Joseph Goovaerts a prosperous merchant. In time, he too became a highly successful grain merchant who marketed his products in Louvain, Antwerp, Malines, and Brussels as well as in Tremeloo. This provided the De Veusters with the financial means to insure that each of their children received a good education.

The majority of the neighbors were farmers, and nearly everyone in Tremeloo was literate and embraced the Roman Catholic religion. Most of the children attended elementary and secondary schools until their parents judged it was time for the boys to work full time on the family farms and for the girls to marry. A few young men, destined to become teachers, priests, lawyers or doctors, continued their studies at the internationally famous University of Louvain, six miles distant.

Leopold I was king of the prosperous little country that only ten years earlier had declared itself independent of the Netherlands. Belgium was fortunate in that she was not viewed by her neighbors as a threat, nor was her land coveted. The biggest difficulty the new nation faced was overcoming the cultural intolerance resulting from the divisiveness of her two languages. Flemish was spoken in Flanders, the northern half of the country in which Tremeloo was located, while French was the official language of the people in Wallony, the southern half of Belgium.

YOUNG JOSEPH DE VEUSTER was "Jef" to family and friends. No one who knew him well called him Joseph. What little is known about

Jef's childhood and youth comes mainly from the reminiscences of his older brother Auguste, Father Pamphile, a Sacred Hearts' priest who, after Father Damien's death on April 15, 1889, wrote a detailed biographical essay that he made available to would-be biographers—along with a collection of his brother's letters.[2]

It is important to understand that Father Pamphile unabashedly loved and admired his younger brother. He had, however, broken his childhood promise to Jef that one day they would serve God side by side, brother priests, like Saints Damien and Cosmas, united in the service of their Lord. This breach of his word had always gnawed at Father Pamphile's conscience, and belatedly he wished to make amends. When newspaper accounts heralded the life of the "Hero of Moloka'i," and advanced the notion that the priest's life had been so exemplary that he quite possibly could become the Congregation of the Sacred Hearts' first saint, Father Pamphile knowingly applauded. Subsequently, the biographical information he released strongly supported the contention that his brother's life was indeed an example of extraordinary virtue, possibly deserving of sainthood. None of the remembered anecdotes he supplied the biographers detracted from nor tarnished Father Damien's saintly image. Dramatic episodes were crafted to suggest that on two occasions during Jef's childhood, Divine Intervention had saved his life—once when he had been run over by a horse cart[3] and a second time when he barely escaped falling through the ice and drowning.[4] Father Pamphile argued convincingly that God had a special plan for the life of Joseph De Veuster.

The career path for each of the eight De Veuster children was clearly defined and directed by their parents. Anne Catherine suggested and Frans concurred that Jef's oldest sister, Eugénie, the firstborn, should be encouraged to become an Ursuline Sister because she was virtuous, compassionate, and devout in prayer, three essential attributes for a nun. As it was proper for one of the older sons of a Catholic family to enter the priesthood, the opportunity to do so was offered first to Léonce and later to Gerard, but neither displayed the scholastic aptitude nor the spontaneous enthusiasm for the self-sacrificing life of a priest. On the other hand, Auguste, who was two years older than Jef, not only demonstrated superior scholarship, but he possessed both the demeanor and the sensitivity judged essential for success as a Catholic priest. Jef, the youngest son, like Léonce and Gerard, was groomed to become a farmer. The other girls, Pauline, Constance, and Mary, also were offered no options.

When Jef was three years old, Eugénie left home to enter the Ursuline convent at Thildonck, where she took her vows in October 1845. Her calling was to be a teacher, and she was teaching in elementary school in Uden, Holland, when a typhus epidemic ravaged the city in 1851.[5] Eugénie was among the first to experience the shaking chills and fever followed by the severe headache and the telltale pinkish red rash of typhus. After a brief illness, her body's defenses were overwhelmed and she died. The De Veusters were grief stricken. To assuage the grief, Pauline, the sister to whom Jef was most attached, pleaded to be allowed to take Eugénie's place when she came of age. For Frans and Anne Catherine to consent to Pauline's request meant losing a second cherished daughter, but since both believed that full-time service to God was life's highest calling, they somewhat reluctantly granted her request.

At age ten Jef received his first Communion in the parish church of Tremeloo. Father Pamphile remembered that at this young age, Jef already evidenced a love for solitude and contemplation. Classmates and companions dubbed him *le petit berger*—"the little shepherd"— for he loved to roam the fields in the silent company of a shepherd and his flock of sheep.[6] When given the opportunity he would frolic with the lambs, then stroll alone through the pastures for an hour or so until farm chores required that he return home.

Obediently but with enthusiasm, Jef learned the farming business: planting, harvesting, husbandry, and carpentry. Frans was pleased with his youngest son's progress. Not only was Jef industrious and quick to learn, but he possessed the physical prowess so essential for a farmer. By age thirteen, before Pauline left home for the convent and while Auguste was busy with his books, Jef was able to lift 100-kilogram (220.5 lbs.) bags of grain.[7] Jef's personal dream, however, was to become a priest, a secret goal he shared only with Auguste. If it were God's will, his older brother assured him, they would one day serve God, shoulder to shoulder as brother priests, like Saints Damien and Cosmas.

In August 1853, Auguste left home to enter the Minor Seminary at Malines. In religion he chose to be called Pamphile in remembrance of St. Pamphilus, who was acknowledged to be the greatest biblical scholar and Christian teacher of the third century. After a sterling education, the third-century Pamphilus sold all of his property, gave the proceeds to the poor, and entered the priesthood. Following his ordination he settled in Caesarea, where he established an outstanding theological school and housed his world-famous library. Four years after the executions of Damien and Cosmas, Emperor Diocletian had Pamphilus imprisoned, repeatedly tortured, and finally beheaded in A.D. 309. Auguste, who loved books, aspired to emulate the scholarly life of this famous biblical scholar and courageous Christian martyr.

With Auguste's departure, Jef lost his best friend and confidant, the one person who understood his intense desire to become a priest. Most of all he missed the philosophical discussions about the meaning of life and the proper worship of God through service to mankind the two shared in the quiet of the night after they had retired. Although Jef was unwilling to let the boyhood dream of a future Damien-Cosmas relationship with Auguste die, he was powerless to pursue it.

In an attempt to compensate for Auguste's absence, Jef sought additional ways to enhance his private worship of God. Covertly, he initiated a religious practice that made him feel that he, like the apostles, could demonstrate his devotion by engaging in the practice of mortification by sleeping on a hard surface: "Under his bed he hid a long board, which at night he placed in his bed and slept upon it. Each morning when he rose, he was careful to hide the board again, but one morning he forgot. When our mother discovered the plank, she was appalled and with a severe reprimand put an end to this practice."[8]

When Brother Pamphile returned home from the Sacred Hearts' seminary to celebrate the holiday season, Jef listened intently to just how fulfilling and joyous the religious life was. Under no circumstance, Pamphile counseled, was Jef to abandon his dream of becoming a priest. He must persevere; he must not lose faith. Nevertheless, there were two nearly insurmountable barriers that had to be overcome, foremost of which was the matter of Jef's scholastic deficiencies. Without a solid foundation in Latin, French, and the humanities, *no one* would be allowed to enter the Sacred Hearts' seminary. Jef had never studied a foreign language nor taken a course in philosophy, and there was no prospect for him to do so. The second obstacle was the predictable parental objection. The solution, his older brother counseled, was going to require prayer and quiet remedial action—prayer for divine guidance coupled with a plan he had devised to correct Jef's scholastic deficiencies by becoming his younger brother's personal tutor.

From Frans De Veuster's sage perspective, his youngest son was fortunate to have a choice of two, perhaps three vocations. Jef could become a farmer, but he would have to leave the family farm in order to pursue this option as there was a manpower surplus. Carpentry was the second option. For four years he had toiled under the full-time tutelage of his father and two older brothers and become highly proficient as a carpenter. Jef loved working with his hands, and he wasn't too old to become a carpenter's apprentice should he so desire.

A third, and the most attractive alternative, was the long-standing offer of Jef's godfather, Joseph Goovaerts, the grain merchant from Antwerp, to have Jef serve an apprenticeship in his firm with the prospect of becoming a junior partner. Then, too, Frans was fifty-eight, and in a few years he might consider turning his grain marketing business over to his youngest son. From Frans De Veuster's vantage point, the brightest future for Jef lay in the grain business.

There was, however, a problem with this attractive prospect. Jef spoke only Flemish, and without fluency in French, Belgium's business language, an apprenticeship in Antwerp was out of the question. The solution was obvious. Jef would be offered the opportunity to return to school and study French. French was not a difficult language, and while in school he could study modern bookkeeping methods and acquire other invaluable business skills as well. Since the family possessed the financial resources to afford the tuition, books, and room and board, all that was required of Jef was the motivation and the discipline to succeed. While in elementary school he had demonstrated a scholastic talent that rivaled that of his older brother, Auguste, so it was decided that following his eighteenth birthday, Jef would return to school.

Jef enrolled as a student boarder in the Cours Moyen College at Braine-le-Comte in Hainault.[9] This school offered two distinct advantages. The headmaster, M. Derue-L'Hoir, had a reputation for success with Flemish students; and the tuition and board were reasonable—one franc per day. However, the school was in Walloon country where only French was spoken, and where there was little tolerance for anyone who fumbled with the native tongue.

Jef's first day at Braine-le-Comte was traumatic. Teasing about his faulty French led to a scuffle with one of the Walloon classmates.

As a result, one of his two pair of trousers was torn at the knee, and in the fracas that followed Jef found that the surest way to silence his antagonists was to physically assault them wielding a heavy ruler.[10] By the end of the first week of classes, no Walloon dared snicker at the stocky lad from Flanders.

While at Braine-le-Comte, Jef took time to attend a religious retreat held by the Redemptorist Fathers. Following this moving experience, he returned to his studies with a strengthened resolve to become a priest. One of his cousins who was also a student at the school reported, "Joseph came home from the retreat evidently struck by something that had been said, for instead of retiring to bed, he began the habit of staying up a good part of the night, praying earnestly to God."[11]

Jef probably communicated the full impact of this religious experience to Auguste and reaffirmed his ardent desire to become a priest. Regrettably, none of the correspondence between the two brothers during this period has survived, but subsequent events indicate that Pamphile devised a plan to help his brother achieve his goal. Because he had demonstrated he was a superior scholar, he was granted permission to tutor Jef in the French language at the Formation House in Louvain during the upcoming summer period. Pamphile was confident that Frans and Anne Catherine wouldn't object to this, as the summer effort would reduce Jef's overall school expenses by shortening the time required for him to master the French language.

Auguste's offer to tutor his younger brother had obvious merit, and Frans and Anne Catherine granted Jef permission to spend the summer months at the Formation House.[12] This provided Jef with the opportunity to observe firsthand the active religious life of the postulates, brothers, and fathers. When Pamphile interrupted the fragmented teaching sessions to attend to his assigned studies and duties, Jef was free to wander about the Formation House and its grounds, to explore the gardens, and to meditate in the quiet of the chapel. In this setting he felt a nearness to God he had never before experienced, and by summer's end he was reluctant to return to the outside world.

Jef acknowledged that his academic deficiencies barred him from becoming a Scared Hearts' postulant, but there were other less demanding avenues to the priesthood. His ability to perform hard physical labor combined with his yearning for self-denial, solitude, meditation, and long prayer vigils convinced him that he had the requisite attributes to become a Trappist monk, as this order did not require a working knowledge of Latin, Greek, and French.[13] The Trappists were a severe and austere branch of the Cistercians whose members vowed to observe perpetual silence, perform hard manual labor, and engage in continual prayer.

Pamphile was vehemently opposed to this choice and urged his brother to reconsider the Congregation of the Sacred Hearts. In 1858 a postulant could be admitted to the Congregation either as a candidate for the priesthood or as a choir or missionary brother. Members of this order followed in Jesus' footsteps and imitated the dual aspects of his ministry—the silent adoration and prayer embraced by the Trappists; and equally important, an active ministry of service to mankind. Pamphile reminded Jef that the saints they most admired as boys were not cloistered monks like the Trappists, but men and women who dedicated their lives to the service of their fellow man. If he chose to do so, Jef could become a brother in the Congregation of the Sacred Hearts. A brother was not as high on the ecclesiastical ladder as a priest, but in the eyes of God he was a cherished servant. Christ himself had been a servant. While this wasn't exactly the dream the two had had as boys, life as a Sacred Hearts brother was certainly better than squandering a life in a cloistered silence.

Preferring to enter the priesthood on his own merits without the help of his brother, Jef boldly asked for an audience with the rector of the American College in Louvain. An interview was promptly granted, and at the scheduled time Jef walked through the doors of the American College and made his way to the rector's office. Standing hat in hand before the desk of Monsignor Jules De Becker, he was asked to answer "yes" or "no" to a series of intimidating questions that included, "Are you fluent in Latin and French? Which college or university have you attended?" He blurted out his desire to become a missionary priest and labor for God in North America among the Indians. The monsignor abruptly dismissed the youth and noted in the college record that an ignorant Flemish lad named "Jef" De Veuster had been refused admission because of the lad's "rudeness in manner and appearance and his gross ignorance of Latin or any other language."[14]

When Pamphile learned of Jef's humiliating rejection he renewed his efforts to convince his younger brother that the most promising career course to pursue was with the Congregation of the Sacred

Hearts. Since he sincerely believed that his younger brother merited a chance, Pamphile pleaded Jef's case with Father Wenceslaus Vincke, the superior of the House of Formation in Louvain. This wise old gentleman pondered the problem and offered a solution. Since Jef lacked the educational prerequisites for the priesthood, the Congregation would accept him as a choir brother.[15] Choir brother status did not automatically preclude him from pursuing other options. If Jef were as intelligent and motivated as Brother Pamphile believed him to be, there were ways to surmount the academic deficiencies. Were Pamphile willing to continue in the role of private tutor, and if Jef were physically and emotionally able to complete a grueling program of remedial study while attending to the full duties of a choir brother, the lad might still realize his dream of becoming a priest. Were the two De Veuster brothers to pursue this course, it was with the understanding that there would be no compromise with regard to satisfying every academic prerequisite required of a candidate for the priesthood. Not only might the joint effort fail to achieve Jef's goals, but the additional time Pamphile would have to devote to the endeavor might place his own academic career in jeopardy. Father Wenceslaus nodded thoughtfully. If it were God's will, it could be done. With Pamphile serving as the teacher and Jef as the student, the boyhood dream of two brothers becoming priests was still a possibility.

The brothers waited until Christmas Day, 1858, to unveil their plan.[16] To their immense relief, there was no parental objection. Anne Catherine and Frans had anticipated their son's announcement and enthusiastically encouraged the venture. In his New Year's greeting to his parents a few days later, Jef thanked his parents for giving their consent and blessing his plan to commence his religious training as a choir brother. "What a joy for me to tell you again today that I love you, and that my heart will never forget your goodness and kindness."[17]

ON A COLD JANUARY morning, Jef De Veuster, accompanied by his father, left Braine-le-Comte where he had been a student for seven months and traveled to the House of Formation of the Sacred Hearts for an admission interview with the same Father Wenceslaus Vincke who had offered this solution. The tenor of the session with the superior was in sharp contrast to that which Jef had experienced during his interview at the American College. Father Wenceslaus graciously received the young man from Tremeloo and invited him to be seated. Then he listened intently to the answers to his probing questions regarding both the lad's motivation and his aptitude to pursue a religious life as a member of the Congregation of the Sacred Hearts.

Jef listened gravely while Wenceslaus explained why his commercial education, which was grossly deficient in philosophy, theology, Latin, and Greek, precluded him from entering the order as a candidate for the priesthood. The older man acknowledged, however, that he did possess all of the essential attributes and talents that were required of a postulate for choir brother. Becoming a choir bother, Wenceslas explained, did not automatically rule out the possibility of one day becoming a priest. In the seclusion of the monastic environment a determined scholar could acquire the knowledge that he now lacked. A few others had done so; and if it were God's will, Damien's goal to become a priest was achievable. The interview concluded with Father Wenceslaus approving Joseph De Veuster's choice of the name *Damien*. To aspire to imitate the sterling qualities of Saint Damien the physician was a laudable ambition and, after a dedicatory prayer, Father Wenceslaus blessed "Brother Damien," the order's newest postulate.

There is no information as to why Jef De Veuster elected to remain at the House of Formation in Louvain following his acceptance rather than return home for the customary good-byes. All that is known is that a resigned Frans De Veuster journeyed home to Tremeloo alone.

3

The Sacred Hearts
of Jesus and Mary

You shall love the Lord your God with all your heart,
and with all your soul, and with all your mind. This is
the great and first commandment. And a second is like it,
You shall love your neighbor as yourself.
—Matthew 22:37–39

FEBRUARY 2, 1859, was the first day in the new life of Joseph De Veuster as a postulate in the House of Formation of the Congregation of the Sacred Hearts located in Louvain.[1] Without hesitation or regret, the nineteen-year-old lad closed the door on family, friends, and the material existence he had enjoyed in Tremeloo to commence the religious life he craved. When he did so he chose to replace his Christian baptismal name with *Damien*, and for the next four and a half years he would be known as Brother Damien.[2]

A choir brother took the same vows of poverty, chastity, and obedience as a priest. Like a priest he lived by the same rule, wore essentially the same habit, and fulfilled many of the duties of a priest—with the exception that he was never allowed to offer the sacraments. His responsibilities included the daily singing of the Holy Office, attendance at each of the scheduled church services, instruction and practice in cleaning and servicing chapels and churches, instruction in techniques for caring for the elderly and nursing the sick, and most importantly, participation in the Perpetual Adoration of the Most Blessed Sacrament of the Altar. This around-the-clock adoration by the Congregation mandated that each member engage in half an hour of daily adoration plus one hour of night

adoration each week. Damien consistently volunteered for the less popular hours, those after midnight, a practice he continued during his most
rigorous days at the leper settlement on Moloka'i.

A choir brother's day began before dawn, when a student brother
would walk through the dormitory corridors arousing the sleeping with
the exhortation "Benedicamus Domino"—"Let us bless the Lord," to
which the aroused would each reply, "Deo gratis"—"Thanks be to
God." The brothers then had twenty minutes to bathe, don their black
cassocks, tidy their quarters, and hurry to the chapel for meditation—
all in silence. This was a time for looking inward, to reflect on how to
make each new day better than the previous one, a time to improve
one's personal relationship with Christ.

After the morning meditation the members of the Congregation
seated themselves in the dining hall for a bland but substantial breakfast. In the short break between breakfast and the first of their scheduled duties, Damien and Pamphile planned the day's independent
study program. To facilitate the teaching, Pamphile arranged for
Damien to share his small room, and in this crowded setting the two
made optimum use of their free time together.

For Pamphile the task was a formidable one. The major obstacles were his brother's deficiencies in Latin, French, and Greek. While
Damien had acquired a modest command of the French language, his
working vocabulary was limited to words used in the field of business.
Until he learned the meanings and nuances of ten to fifteen thousand
additional French words, the literature of theology and philosophy—
literature every prospective priest was expected to know—remained
locked away in books.

The single biggest challenge, however, was Latin, and Pamphile
assigned it the top priority. A comprehensive command of Latin was essential for anyone preparing to enter the priesthood. In the seminary the
courses in philosophy and religion were taught in Latin, and most of the
litany used in church services was in Latin. Pamphile's plan was simple—
total immersion in the Latin language when the two were alone, except of
course for the brief intervals during which he tested Damien's expanding
French vocabulary or checked on his progress with the translation of the
New Testament from the Greek to French. Each day the two huddled in
the cramped quarters for as many minutes of instruction as their rigorous
daily schedules permitted. In the morning upon waking they greeted each

other in Latin, then prayed in Latin. In the snatches of time during the day and after evening prayers, while others were meditating before retiring, the brothers' main focus was on the Latin translation of *Cornelius Nepos*, the book that would be used to test Damien's proficiency.[3]

To Pamphile's delight, Damien exhibited a flair for languages and the progress was rapid. Within two months of initiating their marathon program, the De Veuster brothers realized that it was succeeding beyond their fondest expectations. The euphoria of accomplishment compensated for the fatigue induced by long hours of study and limited sleep. Then time became an issue. While the father superior had set no date for the completion of the remedial program, Pamphile learned that in six months he was to be reassigned to Paris, where he would continue his studies. To erase Damien's deficiencies in only six months would depend upon Damien's intellectual ability coupled with Pamphile's skill as a teacher. Minutes well used were an angelic gift. Minutes squandered were a sin.

Father Wenceslaus observed the intensity of the study program and nodded approvingly. In the Congregation of the Sacred Hearts there was a warmth, a camaraderie, a tolerance, a willingness to let God's will determine who would serve and in what capacity, a flexibility possible in a young order whose former superior general had set down as one of the Congregation's major objectives, "to give each member the opportunity of putting his talents to account."[4]

During his early months as a brother, Damien remained cheerful despite the additional stress imposed by the teaching assignments. To Pamphile's amazement and against his advice, Damien, who slept fewer than six hours a night, resumed his practice of mortification by sleeping on a hard surface. Pamphile recalled: "I awoke and saw a large bundle beside his bed. I went to see what it was. It was my brother who was sleeping on the floor as the nearest thing, no doubt, to a board like the one he used at Tremeloo."[5]

What the combination of Pamphile's skill as a teacher and Damien's innate ability to learn achieved in 1859 was remarkable. When examined by Father Wenceslaus, Damien demonstrated the competence of a fifth-year student of Latin as he translated at sight any part of *Cornelius Nepos*.[6] The seminary's superior was so impressed that he rewarded Damien's efforts by pronouncing him a fit candidate for the priesthood and directed him to commence his minor order studies at once.

Brother Damien successfully completed the prescribed curriculum, and he was sent to Issy, France, in June 1860, where novices trained elsewhere spent a mandatory three months before taking their vows.[7] At Issy it was emphasized that the members of the Congregation of the Sacred Hearts were pledged to imitate the four periods of their Lord's life, in harmony with the general aim of practicing and spreading devotion to the Sacred Heart of Jesus and the Immaculate Heart of Mary. To imitate the first period of Jesus' life, his childhood, a member was required to obtain a superior education. By the act of perpetual adoration one imitated the second period, Jesus' private life of prayer. By engaging in preaching and missionary work one imitated the third period, Jesus' apostolic life. And finally, by mortification and penance one imitated the fourth period of Jesus' life, his crucifixion.

Following the retreat at Issy, Damien journeyed to the Mother House at 31 Rue de Picpus in Paris to take his vows. This ceremony proved to be one of the most momentous of his life, an event whose spiritual significance he recounted numerous times throughout his ministry. The awesome affair took place on October 7, 1860, the Feast of Our Lady of the Holy Rosary, one of the holiest days on the ecclesiastical calendar. On this day the seminarians spoke the vows that would distance them from earthbound mortals and wed their souls to the Church. The setting for the ceremony was the darkened cathedral, dimly lighted by flickering candles. The novices, dressed in new black cassocks, entered in silence, and in a funeral-like procession solemnly approached the altar. No one smiled. There were no outward signs of joy as the young seminarians walked to the spot before the altar where they were to renounce all earthly ties and swear an allegiance to God and his eternal Kingdom. This voluntary act symbolized their earthly death. Once they had dedicated their lives to God by taking the vows of obedience, poverty, and celibacy, they would be aliens, exiled on earth where they would continue to worship God by serving mankind. The knowledge that at the end of their earthly exile they were guaranteed to be gloriously and permanently united with God in his heaven helped to ease the anxiety by instilling in each a heightened sense of serenity.

As the small group knelt before the altar, the *cerimoniere*—the master of ceremonies—read out their names in religion: "Holy Mother Church asks you to bless these men, our brothers, for service. . . . "

The fragrance of the incense and the shadows that shrouded the upturned faces of the celebrants merged to heighten the emotional tension of the moment.

"Do you judge them to be worthy?" intoned the *cerimoniere*.

Damien was living his dream. He did not judge himself to be worthy, but he vowed to live his life on earth imitating the life of Jesus, his Lord, as closely as was within his being to do so.

Along with the other novices, Damien prostrated himself before the altar, turning his head to rest a cheek against the cold stone floor of the cathedral. Dressed identically in black, the novices looked from above like a cluster of cocoons gathered by a child in the fall and scattered on a cold hearth. Each felt the chill from the stone floor penetrate the warmth of his cheek. The chill became a cold shiver as a black mortuary pall was drawn over each prostrate body, enveloping each one in darkness, isolating them from everything except the cold and the hard floor and their thoughts of God. Rhythmic breathing was the solitary sound in the black enclosures. Minutes passed. In the chill darkness the candidates felt suspended in time and place by an act that signified their earthly death. As the cheek of each became uncomfortably cold against the stone floor, each sensed that this was the opening phase of the remainder of his earthly life—publicly, he would smile as he embraced the Church—privately, the smile would vanish as he stood before the Church's altar and embraced loneliness.

Three steps above the candidates, Father Euthyme Rouchouze, the superior general of the Congregation, stood before the altar. In a slow-paced, resonate voice he began the celebration of the taking of the vows. The mortuary palls were removed and the candidates were asked for the final time about their dedication and readiness. Then they knelt, heads bowed, while the *cerimoniere* read out their names.

When a grave voice spoke, "Damien," the name echoed softly from the tall pillars reaching to the vaulted ceiling, and the young man from Tremeloo trembled as he pondered whether he would ever be worthy of answering to so extraordinary a name.

"Holy Mother Church asks you to ordain these men for service as our brothers," said a voice.

Another voice asked, "Do you judge them to be worthy?"

A third voice replied, "After inquiry among the people of Christ and upon recommendation of those concerned with their training, I testify that they have been found worthy."

As Damien knelt, the superior general placed his hands gently upon his head and blessed him. Each of the other officiating priests in turn blessed him with the laying on of hands. Those who had themselves already been touched by the hand of God now passed that sacred honor on to another. It was a way of saying, "We are all brothers now, exiles on earth, the servants of God and all mankind."

After the Prayer of Consecration was sung, the assisting priests vested the candidates with red stoles and chasubles. Like the butterfly that emerges transformed from the darkness of its cocoon after a long winter's sleep, the young men who had begun the ceremony prostrate beneath a mortuary pall had risen to begin life anew.

As he walked in the final procession down the central aisle, Damien saw his parents, guests, and friends—some in tears. The ceremony had been solemn; the postlude was joyous.

FOLLOWING HIS PROFESSION of vows, Damien remained in Paris one year to continue his theological studies. The major emphasis was on philosophy, with additional course work in both Latin and Greek. Then in the fall of 1861 Damien returned to the House of Formation in Louvain to begin the next phase of his preparation for the priesthood. Pamphile, who was quartered there, warmly welcomed his younger brother. This time there was more laughter. This time they each had their own room, their private conversations were in Flemish, not French, and Latin was reserved for church. This time the brothers, like St. Damien and St. Cosmas, were more equal in stature; however, their original goal to serve as missionaries in the same mission field had changed. Pamphile's burning desire was to emulate his patron saint and become a biblical scholar, while Damien was firmly committed to becoming a foreign missionary.

Damien, like Pamphile, matriculated at the world-famous University of Louvain, where he took the prescribed courses in theology and philosophy. To the amazement of his peers he requested and received permission to add an additional series of elective courses not required by the seminary. This astonished his less ambitious classmates since he managed to keep pace with them without appearing overburdened with work. A classmate observed that "study was his chief occupation" during his second sojourn at Louvain.[8] "The ease with which he grasped the meaning of every question, and the encouragement which his answers elicited from his professors made many believe that he was destined to have a brilliant career in teaching."[9]

In Father Pamphile's biographical manuscript there are some observations and anecdotes from the Louvain period that reveal the character of the emerging priest. "Fr. Wenceslas had preached a sermon one day in which he emphasized three points: Silence, Meditation, and Continual Prayer. My brother, as if writing the words on paper was not enough, wished to have them always before his eyes; so he took his knife and cut them into the wood of his desk."[10] The mandatory punishment that followed the mutilation of the desk was not disclosed by Pamphile, but the desktop bearing the words *Silence, Meditation, Prayer* has been preserved and is on display in the Damien Museum in Tremeloo.

Adjacent to the Formation House in Louvain stood St. Joseph's Chapel, which was being renovated. Originally dedicated to St. Anthony the Hermit, the five-hundred-year-old structure had been refurbished several times. Damien was so fascinated by the carpentry and the masonry techniques employed by the master tradesmen that he managed to spend an hour or so each day observing their labor. With the exception of an extremely tall and badly deteriorated chimney that was attached to the chapel, the renovation project progressed steadily. The decrepit chimney, however, was in such a state of disrepair that none of the masons was willing to risk a bad fall in an attempt to climb and dismantle it. Damien surprised everyone by volunteering to climb the teetering chimney and disassemble it brick by brick. Without hesitation the masons accepted his offer and quickly placed a long extension ladder against the swaying chimney. Two men steadied it while Damien calmly climbed to the top and, wielding a mason's hammer, patiently broke loose one brick after another until the hazardous portion of the structure had been removed.

No one who witnessed the stocky seminarian's bold act could have predicted that, forty-seven years after Father Damien's burial in the St. Philomena churchyard at the leper settlement, his body would be exhumed, returned to Louvain for burial, and in a quiet ceremony interred beneath a monument of black marble in the very chapel whose antiquated chimney he had helped dismantle.[11]

FEBRUARY 28, 1863, was a day of celebration for all of the De Veusters, for on that day Brother Pamphile was ordained as Father

Pamphile. The following day, Father Pamphile celebrated his first
Mass—and then waited patiently for his first permanent appointment.[12] In late summer he was notified that he had been chosen to
become a member of a missionary contingent of sixteen priests, brothers, and sisters destined for service in the Sandwich Islands (the Hawaiian Islands). The decision to send additional Catholic missionaries to
the Sandwich Islands was the result of a successful appeal to the superior general in Paris by Bishop Louis Desire Maigret, the vicar apostolic of the Hawaiian Islands, the veteran priest who was successfully
directing the Catholic Church's missionary program in Hawai'i.[13]
Were he given double the number of trained professionals, Bishop
Maigret believed he could lead the entire Hawaiian population to
God. The superior general concurred.

Pamphile viewed the missionary assignment as a major detour
from his academic pursuits, an unavoidable duty that he prayed would
be of short duration. He confided to Damien that he willingly accepted
the challenge, but not with great enthusiasm. Life as a foreign missionary in such a remote land would be difficult and threatening, the
missionary recruits were told. Not only were home leaves for reunions
with family and loved ones curtailed because of the great distances
involved, life in the hostile mission field meant adapting to primitive
living conditions and strange foods. Father Pamphile braced himself
for the cultural shock of a spartan life devoid of his beloved library.

OBLIVIOUS TO THE carefully laid plans of the Congregation of the
Sacred Hearts to send additional missionaries to the Hawaiian Islands,
a solitary louse bit a man in Louvain, and the consequences of that
random act dramatically altered the careers of the De Veuster brothers. The louse was sick and dying because the cells lining its intestinal
tract were lethally infected by *Rickettsia prowazekii*, the microbe
responsible for epidemic typhus in humans. When the infected louse
bit the man, it defecated, and in the tiny droplet of its fecal matter were
thousands of the infectious *R. prowazekii*. Later, when the man
scratched the bite site to relieve the itch, he scraped some of the contaminated fecal matter into the bite wound, inadvertently inoculating
himself with the deadly typhus microbes.

Once inside the man's body, the rickettsia moved with robot precision and invaded the delicate cells lining the blood vessels through-

out the body. The consequence of this assault was a high fever, headache, bloodshot eyes, and severe aching in the muscles of the back and legs. On the fifth day of the illness a pinkish red rash crept over his back and chest—the tiny fingerprints of epidemic typhus. A week later the man died, but not before other lice had fed on him, become infected, and jumped to feed on other humans. Lice carried in the robes of the parish priest and on the coat of the attending physician not only infected their hosts, but by the end of August twenty additional hapless persons watched as the pinkish red rash claimed them as victims as well.

The twenty cases swelled to sixty, and the physicians realized that they were witnessing the emergence of an epidemic. The majority of the new cases were in the poorer section of the city where entire families crowded into one-room dwellings, but no one recognized the sinister role the lice were playing. By mid-September more than a hundred persons were ill with typhus. Physicians and parish priests attending the sick were felled. When the shortage of parish priests became acute, the people of Louvain turned to the Sacred Hearts for assistance. Father Pamphile was one of the first to respond. He knew the danger. With the exception of malaria, typhus had killed more human beings since the dawn of recorded history than any other infectious disease. Typhus had killed his sister, Eugénie, the Ursuline nun in Uden, Holland. The danger was real. At the risk of his life, Father Pamphile ventured forth. His patron, St. Pamphile, hadn't flinched when facing an earthly death. Neither would he.

IGNORANT OF THE TYPHUS epidemic ravaging Louvain, Brother Damien received his minor orders at Malines on September 19, then boarded a stagecoach to return to the House of Formation. All that was required for him to be ordained a priest and become eligible for a missionary assignment was an additional three years of formal study. Upon his arrival in Louvain he was alarmed to discover that the usually bustling marketplace was deserted. The streets were empty; funeral wreaths hung on many doors. As he approached the House of Formation he observed a dozen persons dressed in black following a horse-drawn hearse. Once he entered the House of Formation he learned that Louvain was in the paralyzing grip of a deadly typhus epidemic, and that Pamphile was in the midst of the epidemic, ministering to the victims.

4

The Quest Begins: Hawai'i

And Jesus came and said to them, "Go therefore
and make disciples of all nations, baptizing them in the
name of the Father and of the Son and of the Holy Spirit,
teaching them to observe all that I have commanded you;
and lo, I am with you always, to the close of the age."
—Matthew 28:19–20

FOR TEN TEDIOUS DAYS in late September, Father Pamphile minis-
tered to the critically ill of Louvain, hearing deathbed confessions,
administering the Sacrament of Extreme Unction, and watching death
close the lids of the bloodshot eyes of the typhus victims. He dreaded
entering the crowded, lice- and rat-infested rooms of the dying poor.
Rats he could tolerate, but the itching following the bite of a louse was
a distraction of the devil. Throughout the daylight hours of his urban
ministry he scratched himself repeatedly, longing for the hush of night
so he could ease his body into a soothing bathtub and drown the pesky
little beasts. Each time he scratched, he unknowingly risked inoculating himself with the rickettsia in the feces of an infected louse, so it
was inevitable that typhus would claim another victim.[1]

Quite uncharacteristically, Father Pamphile failed to attend Mass
one morning. When he also failed to appear at breakfast an hour later,
Damien hurried to his brother's room to learn the reason for his
absence. There was no answer to his knock, so he entered the sparsely
furnished room where he found his brother in bed, shivering uncon-
trollably, blankets drawn up around his neck. Pamphile's face was
flushed, his forehead hot and dry, and the whites of his eyes looked
almost pink because of the engorged blood vessels. Battling through

the mental fog caused by the high fever, Pamphile blurted that he had typhus—for he had witnessed firsthand all of the manifestations of the illness during his short stint of ministering to the sick and dying. He whispered that he had the "worst ever" headache, and that all of his muscles ached, especially those in his back and legs. Squinting up at Damien through bloodshot eyes, he complained that the sunlight hurt his eyes and begged that the window curtain be drawn.

For ten days Father Pamphile languished, his body temperature ranging between 103 and 105 degrees F. Most of the time he slept; when awake he was either confused or delirious. The microscopic rickettsia were violating the delicate endothelial cells that lined the blood vessels of his brain, liver, muscles, and kidneys. Tiny blood clots formed in the damaged vessels, interrupting vital blood flow, which resulted in a cascade of tissue injury.

Damien spent his free time at his brother's bedside, helping to nurse him and praying almost continuously for his survival. Although twelve years had elapsed since his sister Eugenie's death from typhus, the memory was still painful. On the fifth day of the illness the sinister rash of typhus appeared—tiny pinkish red spots on the chest and back. By day seven only the skin of his face, palms, and soles were spared from the assault. Thousands of capillaries had hemorrhaged within Father Pamphile's body by day eight, injuring his liver, kidneys, muscles, and brain. His earthly life hung in the balance. On bended knee at bedside, Damien prayed that God would tip the scales in Pamphile's favor.

Father Pamphile did not die. As abruptly as typhus had seized him, it departed on the twelfth day. The high fever, the headache, and the muscle pain vanished, leaving the young priest so weak that he had difficulty assuming a sitting position. It would be weeks before his body could repair the extensive damage to his muscles and internal organs. Debilitation of this degree absolutely precluded extended travel aboard a ship, so Pamphile's name was removed from the roster of missionaries preparing for the October voyage to the Hawaiian Islands. Resigned to the prospect of a prolonged convalescence, Father Pamphile turned to his beloved books for solace.

Overjoyed that Pamphile had survived, but disappointed that his brother had been removed from the missionary contingent, Brother Damien conceived a plan to salvage the original missionary assignment.[2] He would simply join the missionary group as the replacement for his brother. In his mind this was a logical solution because the Sacred Hearts' manpower shortage was so acute that the superior general had been forced to assign two student priests to the missionary contingent. The strategy was to have the two complete an abbreviated curriculum following their arrival in the Islands. If two student priests were to complete their training in the mission field, why not a third? Pauline had replaced her older sister; why should not Damien replace his older brother? Pamphile voiced no opposition to the plan, but he warned that Father Wenceslas, their superior, would object strenuously.

Father Wenceslas was from the old school, which held that God demanded and deserved the best from his priests. To venture into the mission field required that a priest of the Congregation of the Sacred Hearts be fully trained and ordained. In Wenceslas' view, there could be no compromise and no shortcuts to the wearing of the clerical collar. A student priest in a foreign land attempting to complete his training under less than ideal conditions was a travesty to be avoided at all cost, and he disapproved of the superior general's assignment of two student priests from another seminary to the Hawaiian mission contingent.

There was, however, one possible avenue around Father Wenceslas' predictable refusal, and that was to forward the replacement request to a higher authority. The rules of the Congregation permitted a member to do just that, although this was an option rarely exercised. Thus Brother Damien wrote directly to the superior general in Paris, offering to take his brother's place. His letter has not survived, nor has the superior general's immediate response, which was delivered to Father Wenceslas to inform him that permission for Brother Damien to join the missionary group as the substitute for Father Pamphile had been granted. Surprised and annoyed by the directive, Wenceslas promptly confronted Damien. "It is rather silly of you to wish to go before you are a priest!"[3] Then he threw the letter at Damien, who calmly accepted his superior's admonition.

Once the older priest had left the room, Damien rushed to Pamphile's quarters, waving the letter over his head and shouting, "Yes! Yes, I am to go instead of you! I am to go instead of you!"[4] The letter instructed Damien to bid farewell to his family and immediately depart for Paris, where the missionary group was gathering for a three-day retreat prior to the departure for the long voyage to Hawai'i.

Damien did not wait for dinner that evening, but hurried the six miles to Tremeloo to inform his family of the good news and to say his good-byes. Missionary priests assigned to such remote outposts were rarely granted furloughs, so the emotional embraces of his father and brothers and the drying of his mother's tears were the acts of a final farewell. Once he reached his destination, his only contact with loved ones would be via the mail, often long delayed because commercial French ships did not regularly visit Hawai'i.

Before he walked away from his childhood home and waved a final good-bye, Damien invited his mother to join him at dawn the next morning at the Lady of Montaigu Shrine, located near Tremeloo. This shrine, one where he had worshiped on several occasions before entering the seminary, was the proper setting in which to bid good-bye to the special woman in his life who had led him to the Christ. Kneeling in prayer at her side, he could thank God for having chosen Anne Catherine De Veuster to be his mother.

Upon his return to the House of Formation, Damien invited several of the brothers to accompany him on the midnight pilgrimage to the shrine. In the quiet of the night they could enjoy a meditative, prayerful walk from Louvain to the shrine. After issuing the invitation he returned to his room to pack his few belongings. That task accomplished, he slipped into Pamphile's room and bid good-bye to the brother who had been so competent a teacher in the seminary and his spiritual guide throughout most of his life. From his brother's room, Damien went directly to St. Joseph's Chapel, adjacent to the House of Formation, the same chapel whose ancient chimney he had helped dismantle in 1861.[5] He entered through the tall doorway and walked down the central aisle to the altar where he lit a candle and knelt in prayer. He remained at the altar rail, in prayer, until midnight. Then he rose and left St. Joseph's.

Shortly after midnight, Damien and his companions departed for the Lady of Montaigu Shrine, walking slowly in complete silence, periodically pausing to bow their heads in prayer. At dawn the group reached the shrine where they found Anne Catherine, accompanied by Damien's sister-in-law, Marie, waiting. Anne Catherine was weeping. Damien embraced his mother, and the two knelt in prayer before the shrine. It was Anne Catherine who had loved him, nourished him, and inspired him to walk the path he was now following. When it came time to leave, a tearful Damien threw his arms around his mother for one final embrace. Unable to speak, he pointed with his hand to the image of Our Lady, then slowly walked away.[6] As the trio left the area, Damien paused and looked back one last time. "It's the last time I'll see this beloved shrine. Let me fill my eyes with it. I have asked our Blessed Mother to let me work in the missions for twelve years."[7]

Later that day Damien took the coach to Paris and joined the waiting missionaries. While attending the three-day retreat, Brother Damien had his photograph taken. In the photograph he is wearing a cassock and gripping a large crucifix in his right hand. He appears robust, a man of medium height with thick, curly dark hair, a muscular neck, and broad shoulders. His facial expression reveals neither joy nor sadness. His deep-set eyes look straight ahead through wire rim glasses and give the impression that he is a young man nurturing a solemn determination to succeed. In all probability his family and friends would never see him again, so he wished to be remembered, standing erect with a crucifix in his hand.[8]

On October 20, 1863, at the conclusion of the retreat, the missionaries—toting trunks, suitcases, and boxes—boarded the Paris-Cologne-Hamburg Express bound for Bremerhaven, Germany. The party was headed by Father Christian Willemsen and, in addition to Brother Damien, included ten Sacred Hearts sisters, two missionary brothers, and the other two student priests, Brothers Clément and Lievin. Twenty-nine hours later the travel-weary group arrived in Bremerhaven and proceeded directly to the port, where they boarded the *R. W. Wood*, a three-masted merchantman flying the flag of the Kingdom of Hawai'i. In command of the vessel was Captain Geerken, who welcomed the Catholic contingent with a hearty greeting and the assurance that the upcoming voyage was little more than a routine crossing of the Atlantic and Pacific Oceans—a navigation feat he had successfully accomplished on fourteen previous occasions.

Captain Geerken, his wife, his cousin, and the sixteen-member crew were all German Protestants. From the first meal on board ship to the last, the Catholics were invited to eat at Captain Geerken's table, where before each meal he bowed his head and said grace. This was Damien's first protracted contact with Protestants, whom he had been taught embraced a heretic form of Christianity. The gracious hospitality and religious tolerance shown the Catholics during the long voyage so impressed Damien that he in turn resolved to extend the same degree of religious tolerance to those of other Christian denominations.

Brother Damien's account of the 139-day voyage is detailed in three surviving letters.[9] In the first of these letters, posted in Bremerhaven after the ship's departure had been delayed several days due to unfavorable winds, Damien confided what he believed would be the personal sacrifices and the dangers required to bring the Word of God to a pagan land: "The sacrifice is great for a heart which tenderly loves his parents, family, religious brothers, and the land where he was born. But the voice which invites us, which has called us to make the offering of everything we have, is the voice of God Himself. It is our Divine Savior Who says to us as to His first apostles: 'Go, teach all nations, instructing them to observe all my commandments, and behold I am with you always, even to the end of the world.' (Matt. 28: 19–20)."[10]

Finally, on November 9, after nine frustrating days of contrary winds that confined the *R. W. Wood* to port, the weather improved sufficiently to allow the ship to weigh anchor and commence what was to be a voyage of four and a half months. It had been anticipated that the lengthy ocean voyage would provide an opportunity for the three student priests to commence an accelerated study of religion, philosophy, and elementary English, the language of the Americans who dominated the business and the financial markets in the Islands. But during the first month, seasickness was a constant and disruptive presence whose nausea and vertigo silenced prayer and ruffled serenity. To exacerbate the situation, rain squalls limited the time spent on deck, where one could take a deep breath and appreciate the stimulating fragrance of the fresh ocean breeze. Below deck the air was fetid with the mixed odor of vomit and unwashed bodies deprived of sufficient water with which to bathe. Father Christian was so incapacitated that he was forced to relegate many of his duties to the young Belgian who seemed better able to tolerate the giddy rolling of the ship. When the white-capped waves swelled to heights of eight feet, Damien found himself in the role of the self-appointed physician and nurse to his retching shipmates. In his diary, Father Christian wrote of Damien, "He's really been the man of the hour."[11]

By January 19 the *R. W. Wood* reached the infamous Cape Horn. An anxious Father Christian assembled the missionaries on deck, where they recited the Office of the Dead in memory of the twenty-five

Catholic missionaries bound for Hawai'i in 1843 who had drowned when their ship—the *Marie Joseph*—broke up in a tumultuous gale lashing the waters of Cape Horn.[12] The following day the *R. W. Wood* began the treacherous passage only to be driven "by a strong wind about 200 leagues farther south than we wished. There we were becalmed for ten days without being able to move a foot forward. . . . February 5, we experienced a frightening tempest. . . . The strong wind pushing mountains of water exerted an unbelievable force so that our ship seemed like a small fisherman's boat which seemed about to be swallowed up. . . . Wave after wave followed, striking blow after blow, making the ship suffer a continual buffeting."[13]

The *R. W. Wood* withstood the rigors of the potentially mast-toppling wind and the savage waves, and—for the fifteenth time in his career—Captain Geerken successfully navigated Cape Horn. Once in the Pacific Ocean, the captain assured the travel-weary missionaries that in two months or less they would reach the island paradise of the South Seas.

On March 17, 1864, after 139 long, arduous days at sea, the journey-weary Sacred Hearts missionaries were summoned topside by a crewman who enthusiastically pointed out the distant silhouette of snowcapped Mauna Kea soaring 13,796 feet above the tropical vegetation of the island of Hawai'i, the "Big Island," the largest of the eight inhabited islands in the Hawaiian archipelago.[14] Then an equally impressive mountain came into view—Mauna Loa, the companion mountain, lower in elevation than Mauna Kea by only 116 feet, but just as majestic, with its steep green sides rising to meet the snow that crowned its single peak. Damien was jubilant. The cramped quarters, the seasickness, and the monotonous diet of hard biscuits, salt pork, and beans were soon to be a memory.

At dawn on the morning of March 19, the *R. W. Wood* dropped anchor off Honolulu and waited for a tugboat to guide her into port. Damien stood on the steady, unrolling deck, savoring the sunrise and the cooling northeast breeze. He was pleased, for as he had predicted halfway through the voyage, the missionaries had arrived on the Feast of St. Joseph.[15]

The reception as the missionaries disembarked was tumultuous. Hundreds of Native Hawaiians proudly displaying their rosaries and chanting the traditional "aloha" greeting crowded the wharf behind the official welcoming committee. When the ten arriving sisters, resplendent in their immaculate white habits, walked down the gangplank, a hush fell over the crowd. The Christian God was indeed powerful. The sheer number of the newcomers was impressive, increasing the number of Catholic missionaries in the Islands from forty to fifty-six.

At the head of the reception line stood the elderly but ramrod-straight Bishop Louis Desire Maigret, affectionately known as *Lui, Ka Epikopo* ("Louis, the Bishop") by the Hawaiians. Standing at the bishop's side was Father Modeste Favens, the provincial. After a prayer of thanksgiving for the safe voyage, Bishop Maigret led the way to the Cathedral of Our Lady of Peace, a magnificent French-style structure. The Belgian was surprised "to find so beautiful a church in the Sandwich Islands."[16] The accompanying crowd of people surged into the church after the missionaries to attend a Mass celebrated by Father Christian, jubilant and articulate now that he was no longer handicapped by seasickness. Mass was followed by a Te Deum superbly sung by a native choir under the direction of Father Hermann Koeckemann, the priest who would one day succeed Bishop Maigret. The remainder of Saturday and most of Sunday was devoted to being introduced to members of the Catholic community, each of whom insisted on adhering to the introduced custom of hand shaking. "I believe I have done so one thousand times in the two days," Damien wrote to Father Pamphile. "It is the principal sign of welcome here, as much by women and children as by men."[17]

Bishop Maigret announced that the three student priests would be ordained subdeacons on Holy Saturday of the coming week, and following ordination they would attend the special classes and seminars at the nearby 'Āhuimanu College to prepare them for ordination as priests. To give the three the chance to acclimate, he was granting them a five-day hiatus before their formal classes began.

Damien appreciated that he was a guest in the island kingdom, so it was essential that he understand the political, social, and economic problems now besetting the population he had come to serve. In the first week he learned that many changes had occurred in Hawai'i during his lengthy ocean voyage. Alexander Liholiho, King Kamehameha IV, Hawai'i's twenty-nine year old monarch who was in the eighth year of his reign, had died unexpectedly after a brief illness, having failed to sire a living heir or to designate a successor to the Hawaiian throne.[18] He had been the most anti-American of all the Hawaiian monarchs, and the man who had induced the British to bring the competing Church of England to the Islands. The deceased king's older brother, Lot Kamehameha, the last direct male descendant of Hawai'i's first king, Kamehameha the Great, promptly began his reign as King Kamehameha V. Aggressively opposing any further erosion of his royal power by the Americans, he had moved immediately to draft a new constitution designed to strengthen the monarchy so he might better address the two major problems confronting the kingdom. The weak economic base had forced his deceased brother to sell the entire island of Ni'ihau, one of the eight inhabited islands, for $10,000 to Mrs. Elizabeth Sinclair, a wealthy widow and emigree Scotswoman.[19] More alarming was the decrease in the disease-susceptible Native Hawaiian population, which by the latest count had dropped to a new low of only 62,000.

ON HIS FIRST STROLL through Honolulu, Damien discovered that the capital, with its dirt streets, was more of a village than a city. While there were a few magnificent houses that belonged to the ali'i—the Hawaiian chiefs and nobility—the majority of the native homes were small thatched hovels. In the center of Honolulu, three buildings dominated the landscape: the king's residence; Kawaiaha'o, the main Protestant church; and the Cathedral of Our Lady of Peace. Interspersed between these imposing structures were the elegant New England-style, two-story, gable-front houses of the sons of the first Congregational missionaries who had elected to remain in the Islands and establish businesses. In contrast to the spartan homesteads their parents had occupied, these "rich young rulers" seemed obsessed with material possessions. Equally luxurious were the homes of the senior ministers of the Protestant clergy. From Damien's perspective, this was dangerously wrong. Unless a clergyman pledged himself to a life of poverty and celibacy, family demands and material possessions would be major distractions that would deter him from serving God with all of his soul, heart, and mind. Of this Damien was convinced.[20]

Damien paused before the 'Iolani Palace of the Kingdom of Hawai'i, built in 1844.[21] It was an extraordinary two-story home, and by far the most impressive dwelling in central Honolulu. Thirty 12-foot high Greek Revival columns supported a low-pitch hipped roof whose overhang shaded the deep porch that surrounded the living quarters. As a Belgian, Damien was accustomed to seeing the palaces and luxurious country homes of members of the royal family. But the disparity between the palatial home of the king and queen and the flimsy-appearing thatched huts of the Native Hawaiians was startling. In stark contrast to Belgium, only the wealthy in Hawai'i appeared to enjoy what he considered to be suitable housing. It was the same with clothing. There were the well-dressed and the poorly attired; between the two extremes of the clothing spectrum there was a wide void. The Hawaiians appeared to be second- or even third-class citizens in their own country.

At the close of the first week in Hawai'i the three student priests, Brothers Damien, Clément, and Lievin, enrolled in the Sacred Hearts' college at 'Āhuimanu, located in Windward O'ahu. The campus was situated on a gorgeous 216-acre site that had been ceded to the Church for use as a private secondary school in 1845 by King Kamehameha III. Because the three brothers were to be ordained in but two months, the emphasis was on the hands-on, practical aspects of the priesthood rather than the academic. The seminarians were shown how to assemble and use a lightweight, collapsible altar that could be transported on a packhorse when it would be necessary to celebrate Mass in a remote location that had neither a church nor a chapel. Instruction for hearing confessions in an open-air setting was offered, along with practical pointers on how to offer the sacraments in the wild. Practice church services were conducted in both the Hawaiian and English languages. The French that Damien had struggled to master would now be used only for written communications within the Sacred Hearts Order, while his Flemish would be reserved for the letters to his parents.

In addition to theological instruction and the study of the English and Hawaiian languages, the three brothers' education was broadened by lectures on Hawaiian history and culture. These supplementary sessions covered the discovery of the Islands by Captain Cook in 1778, which resulted in the introduction of syphilis, gonorrhea, and tuberculosis.[22] Once Hawai'i's mid-Pacific Ocean location had been disclosed to the world, ships from the seafaring nations began to use the Islands as a convenient mid-Pacific port of call. Sea captains, whalers, and fur traders bartered for food and supplies—and nights with the native women. These Caucasian foreigners were called *haole*—a somewhat disparaging reference to the white-skinned newcomers who considered themselves superior to the Native Hawaiians.

The haole came ashore from their ships with more than money. Some of them were ill with one of the common communicable diseases present in their homelands—influenza, measles, smallpox, tuberculosis, syphilis, and typhoid fever. In the spring or summer of 1804 a major typhoid epidemic, believed introduced by American sailors, followed by numerous "minor" epidemics, rapidly reduced Hawai'i's native population, which had perhaps been as high as 400,000 in 1778, to a phenomenally low 84,000 by 1853.[23] Later that year smallpox came ashore and killed another 10,000. It was evident to the few resident American and European physicians that the Hawaiian race, isolated from the common infectious diseases for over one thousand years, lacked the natural immunity that protected the majority of the world's population. From the perspective of the Hawaiians, the Christian God seemed to protect the haole preferentially. When the haole became sick, their illnesses were mild by comparison to those experienced by the Native Hawaiians. The haole seldom died.

Belatedly, in 1825, Pope Leo XII assigned the Roman Catholic missions in the Hawaiian Islands to the Congregation of the Sacred Hearts. Two years later the first Catholic missionaries arrived, only to be exiled by the Protestant-influenced government of King Kamehameha III. Catholic converts were persecuted and imprisoned. Outraged, the French, who viewed themselves as protectors of the Catholic Church, sailed the frigate *L'Artemise* into Honolulu harbor in 1839 and threatened to bombard the royal palace unless all Catholic prisoners were immediately released and all Hawaiians given the right to choose the Catholic religion. The French ultimatum was heeded, and King Kamehameha III reluctantly granted freedom of religion to all of his subjects in the Edict of Toleration, issued on June 17, 1839.

In 1840, the year of Damien's birth, the cornerstone of the Cathedral of Our Lady of Peace was laid in Honolulu, and the rivalry between the Protestants and Catholics for the souls of the Hawaiians reached a very unchristian intensity as they exchanged demeaning remarks from the pulpit and in the press. Then in 1850, the Mormons from the California gold diggings entered the fray. The late King Kamehameha IV had further heightened the competition for church membership by inviting the Church of England to the Islands in 1863.

That same year the New England Congregationalists, who had sent out the original missionaries in 1820, announced that they had successfully completed their mission, declared the Hawaiian Congregational Church autonomous, and transferred all authority to the fledgling Hawaiian Board. This left the majority of the Congregational pulpits filled by Hawaiian pastors, and these less well trained ministers proved to be poor evangelists. Following the withdrawal of the Americans, the determined Catholic missionary effort, spearheaded by well-trained priests, prospered.

When Damien arrived in Honolulu the Catholics were well on their way to becoming the largest of the Christian denominations in the Hawaiian Islands. Because the Native Hawaiians found the vibrant rituals of the Catholic Church not too dissimilar from some of the rituals of their outlawed native religion—and much more to their liking than the harsh, moralistic approach to Christianity demanded by the Protestants from New England—the Sacred Hearts Hawaiian mission was judged to be a meritorious success.

SEVEN WEEKS BEFORE the ordination of Damien as a Sacred Hearts priest, a Mormon delegation from Salt Lake City, Utah, arrived at Pālāwai, Lāna'i, to investigate the questionable activities of one Walter Murray Gibson, an American entrepreneur who had deceitfully represented himself as the appointed head of the Mormon Church in Hawai'i.[24] To their disgust, the delegation discovered that Gibson had used Mormon contributions to purchase large tracts of land in his name on Lāna'i. When confronted, Gibson resolutely refused to make restitution. In making the transactions he had been careful not to violate any Hawaiian law, so the Mormon's only recourse was to excommunicate him, which they did. An unrepentant Gibson remained in Hawai'i and developed the ill-gotten land into a highly profitable plantation. Using the accruing profits he later purchased the bilingual newspaper, *Ka Nupepa Nuhou [Nūhou]*, which he used to catapult himself into the national spotlight. It was this same Walter Murray Gibson writing in *Ka Nupepa Nuhou* who first focused the world's attention on the "courageous" priest who at the risk of his life had gone to minister to the Hawaiian lepers isolated on Moloka'i. The resulting notoriety elevated Father Damien, an obscure Belgian priest, to "the Hero of Moloka'i" status. Had Gibson not used the profits from his plantation, ill-gotten or legitimate, to purchase a bilingual newspaper, the world might never have heard about a Sacred Hearts' priest named Father Damien De Veuster.

ON SUNDAY, APRIL 17, 1864, the feast of the Patronage of St. Joseph, Brothers Damien, Clément, and Lievin took the next step toward ordination and were ordained deacons. The following four weeks for the three new deacons were hectic. Their ordination as priests was scheduled for May 21, so every moment was devoted to learning details that under normal circumstances in Europe would have taken months.

Finally, the day of ordination arrived. With Bishop Maigret officiating, Deacons Damien, Clément, and Lievin, wearing spotless black cassocks, entered the Cathedral of Our Lady of Peace to be ordained priests of the Congregation of the Sacred Hearts of Jesus and Mary. The temperature in Honolulu that day was in the high eighties, and it was humid. It was a day that prompted a person to walk slowly and seek the shelter of the shade, thankful for the ever-present, prevailing ocean breeze that made life in the Islands tolerable. Inside the vaulted cathedral, sunlight streamed through the tall stained glass windows, further warming the uncomfortable interior.

As the solemn ordination ceremony began, Damien remembered the intense emotional and spiritual impact he had experienced in Paris when taking his vows. Lying prostrate in the darkness beneath the black mortuary pall with his cheek pressed against the cold stone floor that whispered of death, he had willingly renounced his earthly life. Instead of the deep voice from the dark shadows asking whether he was worthy of becoming a brother of the Sacred Hearts, he now heard the soft, prayerful voice of Bishop Maigret ask God to guide the footsteps of his priests in the ministry of the mission and protect them from all evil.[25]

Father Damien had begun his trek as a priest. He had placed his feet in the footprints of Saint Damien and taken his first step.

5

Puna: Father Damien's First Parish

Then Jesus told his disciples, "If any man would come after me,
let him deny himself and take up his cross and follow me.
For whoever would save his life will lose it, and whoever
loses his life for my sake will find it."
—Matthew 17:24–25

BISHOP MAIGRET'S FACE was a mask of solemn reverence as he observed each of the newly ordained priests celebrate his first Mass, but behind the mask his spirit was jubilant, almost ecstatic. The fact that the three young priests had mastered the basic essentials in only a few months and could pray, administer the sacraments, and celebrate Mass in either the Hawaiian language or passable English was impressive. The superior general had sent him talented young men. Time would tell whether the drastically shortened preparatory program for the priesthood would prove adequate to meet the trials that lay ahead in the mission field.

Because Father Lievin was the most accomplished in written and spoken English, the business, professional, and educational language of the Islands, the bishop appointed him to the faculty of the Sacred Hearts College at 'Āhuimanu. Fathers Clément Évrard and Damien De Veuster, whose English was serviceable but less polished, were assigned to districts on the Big Island of Hawai'i, the largest of the islands in the Hawaiian Archipelago.

Father Clément was to serve the Kohala-Hāmākua District, a huge 1,000-square-mile area nearly twice the size of the island of O'ahu, which had been without a resident priest for four years. Scattered across its valleys, rain forests, hills, and mountains were two thousand natives, fewer than half of whom were Catholic. To minister to these parishioners required a priest to spend much of his time on horseback, traveling from one small collection of Christians to the next. The Kohala-Hāmākua District was a physically taxing assignment.

Father Damien was assigned the Puna District, located on the eastern side of the diamond-shaped island. In area, Puna was half the size of Father Clément's district and had been without a resident priest for seven years. Predictably, the number of parishioners had decreased to fewer than 350. Damien had been forewarned that all of the chapels in Puna were in deplorable condition, with collapsed roofs and missing walls. The chapels had been constructed like the native huts—a light wooden framework held together by stout twine, the roof and walls covered with a thick grass thatch. When buffeted by high winds they disintegrated, so prompt restoration following storm damage was essential. Since no one had assumed the responsibility to maintain these chapels, the dwindling number of Catholics in Puna had resorted to holding religious services in parishioners' homes. The challenge of reinvigorating the Puna parish was Damien's to wrestle with, and he was eager to begin.

Bishop Maigret elected to take his two charges to their respective districts, and on June 7, 1864, the three boarded an interisland steamer bound for the Big Island with a scheduled intermediate stopover at Maui. When the steamer docked at Lahaina, Fathers Aubert, Grégoire, and Léonor, the resident priests, were on hand to extend a welcome. After the customary alohas, the group went directly to a newly constructed church where Father Damien accepted the invitation to celebrate Mass. He appreciated the offer because each time he spoke Hawaiian there were fewer disruptive pauses as his fluency improved.

No sooner had the Mass concluded than the steamer's whistle announced it was about to depart for the Big Island. The abrupt departure precluded the opportunity to visit with the veteran priests and glean the practical pointers they could offer neophytes. "I naively complained to almighty God, and asked Him to let us stay at least several more days to profit from their experience in the ministry," Damien later wrote to the superior general. "As you may know, our benevolent God heard my prayer. Hardly had we left the bay when . . . a fire broke out in the engine room and for three weeks there was no boat service."[1]

On the first Sunday of the extended stay, Father Aubert gave Damien the opportunity to journey to one of the more distant Christian villages to celebrate Mass. Upon his return the following Monday, Damien learned that during his absence a schooner had arrived, and that the bishop and Father Clément had departed for the Big Island without him. Resigned to wait until the arrival of another ship, Father Damien commenced an unscheduled, mini-apprenticeship with Father Aubert that subsequently proved immensely useful. He had learned in Paris that fully a third of the Native Hawaiians still embraced the ancient native religion that had been desecrated and abandoned in 1819 by the young King Kamehameha II at the insistence of the powerful high chiefess, Ka'ahumanu, the favorite wife of his recently deceased father. The spiritual void created by this act had opened the door for the successful entrance of the Congregational missionaries the following year. Without a rudimentary knowledge of the now outlawed native religion to which many Hawaiians still clung, Father Aubert felt a young priest would be greatly disadvantaged when attempting to replace it with Christianity. Thus the older priest took the time to tell the neophyte what he knew about the clandestine ancient religion: its gods and goddesses, and the network of *kahuna*—the mysterious but elite core of highly educated natives who were trained professionals in each of the major fields of human endeavor, including religion and medicine, who continued to practice their art covertly.

As in the other Polynesian religions, the Hawaiian version featured a multitude of gods, goddesses, and family spirits that reportedly governed the destinies of man. One could solicit supernatural assistance by reciting an appropriate prayer and laying an offering before the altar or wooden image of the chosen deity. Chiefs, warriors, craftsmen, and commoners had their own exclusive deities. These gods—"false deities" as Father Aubert insisted on calling them—were figments of an ancient imagination kept alive by the *kahuna pule*—the priests.

The hierarchy of gods was headed by four whose powers were far superior to those possessed by a host of lesser gods. *Kāne*, the creator of the entire universe, was the most powerful. He was also the god of sunlight, fresh water, and forests, a god to whom no human sacrifices were made. Kāne ruled in concert with *Lono*, the god of the clouds, the winds, the sea, agriculture, and fertility. *Kanaloa* was the god of the sea, the squids, and the *'ala'alapūloa* weed. *Kū* was the god of war. Father Aubert contended that it was obvious to even the most ignorant Hawaiian that someone had created the earth, so the *kahuna pule*, who knew nothing about the true God, had fantasized an unbelievable story of creation. They taught that before the memory of man, Kāne, the god of creation, had picked up a huge calabash floating in the sea and tossed it high into the air. The top of the calabash had fallen off and become the curved bowl of the sky. Two other pieces of the calabash which had broken away became the sun and the moon. The seeds of the calabash scattered across the heavens to become the stars. The remainder of the calabash fell back into the sea and formed the earth.

Father Aubert found it intriguing that this ancient culture in its groping for God had actually invented priests, the *kahuna pule*, who in turn had invented a primitive form of prayer and sacrificial offerings to please the imaginary gods. Aubert counseled that the most powerful adversarial deity Damien would have to contend with on the Big Island wasn't Kāne or Lono, but *Pele*—the volcano goddess whom the Hawaiians believed had created their island home by spewing lava from the tips of her underwater volcanoes. While Pele was ranked with the lesser deities, the natives paid more attention to her than any other god. The reason for this was obvious. Each time Kīlauea, the most active of the island's volcanoes, belched a plume of dirty gray smoke and lit up the night sky with a new outpouring of hissing, yellowish orange lava, the Hawaiians knew instinctively that Pele was in her underground temple busily exercising her mystical powers.

To anger this powerful goddess in any way was to invite disaster. For even minor infractions, Pele was known to explode in fury and ride the leading edge of her molten lava in pursuit of the offending party. Pele could appear in many guises to retaliate for wrongful conduct—a wrinkled hag, a child, a beautiful girl, or most horribly as a consuming flame. Consequently, each time a native walked near one of her volcanoes, it was with reverence and with an offering in hand.

As he listened to Father Aubert, Damien resolved to climb Pele's volcano at the earliest opportunity and confront his imaginary rival in full view of the natives. Elijah, the Israelite prophet in the ninth century B.C., had confronted the imaginary Baal and challenged him to a contest to demonstrate whether Baal or the Israelites' Yahweh was the true god.[2] Elijah had won, and Yahweh, the true and almighty God, had been revealed. The Native Hawaiians, like the ancient Israelis, would witness him openly defy the fictitious Pele on her volcano and return unscathed. Like Baal, Pele would lose, and Damien would lead the people to the true God.

Father Damien was fascinated by what Aubert told him about the outlawed *kahuna*, especially the two factions who served as religious priests or physicians.[3] Aubert explained that the *kahuna* who were the healers or physicians were a particularly interesting group because they had divided the field of medicine into multiple specialties. *Kahuna lapa'au* identified the general physicians who employed prayer and herbs to heal; the *kahuna pa'ao'ao* and the *kahuna 'ea* diagnosed and treated childhood illnesses; the *kahuna ho'ohanau keiki* delivered babies; the *kahuna haha* were the diagnosticians; and the *kahuna 'o'o* lanced boils and superficial abscesses. But regardless of their area of specialization, these native physicians always invoked the aid of *'aumakua*, the spirit-guardians of the ill person, and often the *akua*, one of the ancient gods.

When a Hawaiian became ill, he prayed to either Kāne or Lono for forgiveness and made an offering of a pig or a fowl. If the illness persisted, he turned to a *kahuna lapa'au*.[4] In addition to more prayer, animal sacrifices, and herbal medicines, the *kahuna* physicians commonly employed a physical treatment such as steaming, induced sweating, immersion in fresh or salt water, or sunning.

Father Aubert warned Damien that each time he entered a native village to hear confessions, attend to the sick, and celebrate Mass, he would be infringing upon the authority of the underground *kahuna* priests and doctors and to be cautious and diligent regarding the food and drink offered. There were *kahuna 'ana'ana*, the sorcerers who used magic and allegedly could pray a person to death, usually accomplished by the simultaneous, clandestine administration of a poisonous plant. Know your hosts before you sit down to a meal, Aubert advised; and never insult the *kahuna* physicians. Surprisingly, the *kahuna* probably did more good than harm. As he listened, Damien recognized that he indeed was a stranger in a strange new land.

THREE WEEKS ELAPSED before the fire-damaged steamer was again seaworthy and able to transport Father Damien to Hilo on the eastern coast of the Big Island. There he found Bishop Maigret in the church baptizing the latest group of converts and their children. Following a brief meeting, for the bishop was anxious to return to Honolulu, Damien was placed in the custody of Father Nicaise, the priest serving the Ka'ū District, located immediately southwest of Puna. For seven years Nicaise had functioned as the designated itinerant priest for Puna and was best able to introduce Damien to his scattered parishioners.[5]

Father Damien's first solo tour of the Puna District required six weeks of traveling, mainly on horseback trailing a pack mule, but on foot when the rough volcanic terrain with its ankle-twisting crevices was too treacherous for an animal with a rider. As he moved from community to community becoming acquainted with the small groups of Christians who had remained faithful, he was pleasantly surprised to discover that the Native Hawaiians were universally hospitable to the itinerant priest who arrived unannounced and toting a collapsible altar and church supplies on a pack mule. When he swung down from his saddle after a day of riding and greeted a Hawaiian family, he found he could count on an invitation to the evening meal and the loan of a sleeping mat upon which to spend the night in the family's thatched hut. The natives marveled that Damien would do what was unheard of for one of the Western-educated Congregational minis-ters—sit on a straw mat in a thatched hut and enjoy sharing the fam-ily meal. This meant joining the family circle seated around the com-munal calabash filled with poi, the Hawaiian staff of life made from cooked taro and served as a thick gray paste. During the meal each person would repeatedly dip his fingers into the poi, then lick them clean with his tongue. No one used spoons, and the fingers dipping in and out of the poi calabash were seldom clean.

In a letter to Father Pamphile, Damien commented, "You could not find a better people. They are gentle, having extremely tender hearts, not desirous of enriching themselves or living luxuriously or dressing stylishly; they are very hospitable, depriving themselves even of necessities in order to supply your every need if you are obliged to spend a night with them. Even heretics will treat a priest well if he comes to their house."[6]

One evening after sunset, Father Damien was ushered into a small thatched hut where an elderly woman lay dying. She was Catholic, and as he stooped to enter he said in Hawaiian, "Peace to this house, and to all who dwell herein." The woman looked up from the mat on which she lay, and smiled weakly. Father Damien returned the smile and, kneeling next to the woman, heard her private confession. *"Aloha ʻoe, ē Maria, ua piha ʻoe i ka maikaʻi"*—"Hail Mary, full of grace." *"Ē Maria hemolele, e aloha mai ʻoe iā mākou"*—"Holy Mary, have mercy on us." Then he set up the collapsible, three-legged stand near the head of her mat, covered it with a white cloth, and on it placed two lighted candles and a crucifix.

The woman, sensing this would be her last Holy Communion, held out her hands. Father Damien took the woman's thin, cold hands in his and said, "May almighty God have mercy on you, forgive you your sins, and lead you to everlasting life. Amen." Then he lifted the Sacred Host, a tiny piece of bread, from the stand and placing it in her mouth, said, "Receive, my sister, this food for your journey, the Body of our Lord Jesus Christ, that he may guard you from the wicked enemy and lead you into everlasting life. Amen." Extending his right hand over the woman, he anointed her face, hands, and feet with the holy oil previously blessed by the bishop. "I implore you, O Lord, look with kindness on your servant, who is growing weak as her body fails. Cherish the soul which you created, so that, purified and made whole by her suffering, she may find herself restored by your healing. Through Christ our Lord. Amen." And as he turned to leave he said in a low voice, "May the blessing of almighty God, the Father, and the Son, and the Holy Spirit, descend upon you and remain forever. Amen."

Father Damien stooped and stepped outside. Overhead the first scattering of evening stars was visible. Soon the woman's soul would be swept into the beauty of the universe, the loving arms of Almighty God. For a brief moment Father Damien knew pure joy.

IN TIME FATHER DAMIEN was able to devise a more efficient visitation schedule, one that reduced the time to make a complete circuit of his district from six to three weeks. After completing a circuit it became his habit to journey either north or south so he could meet with Father Charles in Hilo or Father Nicaise in Kaʻū for confession and communion. This arrangement, however, was far from ideal. For a priest, weekly confession was highly desirable, but the great distances between the priests on the Big Island precluded weekly contacts.

Fathers Charles and Nicaise monitored the ministry of Father Damien with keen interest. The accelerated two-and-a-half month whirlwind finishing school in Honolulu following the abbreviated instruction aboard ship had taught the Belgian the proper motions, like an actor on a stage, but had done little to nurture his spiritual development. Whether a young, partially trained priest could consistently function satisfactorily in a primitive environment when isolated from brother priests was a concern.[7]

As Father Damien traversed his district, riding horseback through its fertile sunlit valleys, trudging over its mountainous terrain, crossing the massive expanses of hardened, coal-black lava that surrounded the towering but silent Mauna Loa and the smaller Kīlauea to the southeast, he was constantly aware of the latter's restless nature—billowing smoke by day, and by night lighting the overhanging clouds a dull red. Each time he journeyed near Kīlauea the people watched expectantly to see what Pele, the goddess of the volcanoes, would do to punish the arrogant haole who wore a black robe and a broad-brimmed black hat, and who had the audacity to claim that she didn't exist.

Damien was aware of the contest and decided that the time had come to imitate the Old Testament prophet Elijah and openly challenge Pele. To accomplish this feat he decided to climb Kīlauea, view firsthand the fiery summit, and—for the benefit of the Native Hawaiians—defy Pele and return unscathed. In full view of the locals, on a day when the sun was warm on his back, the black-robed priest the Hawaiians now called *Makua Kamiano*[8] rode his horse 12 miles from a coastal village to a spot some distance from the summit of Kīlauea. He tethered his horse and began his trek, following the footpath that meandered its way up the gradual slope of the mountain. Initially, the scene was tranquil. From the dense vegetation the melodious songs of several *'oma'o* birds were carried on the ever-present prevailing breeze. As he climbed higher he began to perspire and breathe more heavily.

Nearing 4,000 feet in elevation, the panorama abruptly changed as he entered the gray haze of the cloud bank that cloaked the top of Kīlauea and hung over the bubbling lava in the gigantic volcanic crater that crowns the mountain. Somewhere ahead of him, shrouded in the gray murk, lay the crater's open mouth, and in the subdued light he had to step carefully over the rough lava outcroppings to keep from tripping or stepping into an ankle-twisting crevice. The air was no longer fresh, and the burning sulfur irritated his eyes and burned his throat. In the gray of the low-lying cloud that partially obscured the dreary terrain, the only color contrasting the coal-black deposits of hardened lava was an occasional outcropping of rust red lava. There were no songbirds in this drab world. The hissing and bubbling sounds emanating from deep within Kīlauea's several-mile-wide volcanic crater were interrupted only once when a lone white-tailed *koaʻe kea* soared overhead on its outstretched gull-shaped wings and voiced its displeasure with a harsh, rasping scream. Visually, the scene before him resembled the entrance to the hell he had visualized in his imagination—a pox-marked landscape, shrouded in gray, devoid of beauty and song.

As Damien cautiously crept forward, he came upon a Hawaiian with outstretched arms, reciting a prayer to Pele. Drawing closer, he noted that in the man's hands were several dozen red and yellow berries from the *ʻōhelo* bush, a small native shrub whose berries were an acceptable offering. Not to pay homage to Pele, not to show respect, the *kahuna* priests had warned, was to guarantee catastrophic bad luck, if not death. Father Damien interrupted the ceremony by seizing the man's right arm and yanking it down, scattering the berries. Against the backdrop of billowing smoke and bubbling lava, he admonished the man and sent him scurrying back down the mountain. Damien later commented in a letter, "One poor Hawaiian was just on his way to offer sacrifice to the goddess. I took the opportunity to give him a short sermon on hell."[9]

Father Damien then proceeded to the crater's edge and looked down several hundred feet into the heaving sea of bubbling lava. The glare from the surging surface was nearly as blinding as gazing at the sun, and the tremendous heat being generated painted the hot, writhing lava all the shades of red and yellow to a brilliant white.[10] The awe-inspiring spectacle underscored the extraordinary, creative power of his God, and scoffed at the notion that a goddess lived in the depths of the sea of molten lava.

Damien remained at the crater's edge for nearly an hour, mesmerized by the display of colors and the showers of sparks that followed the burst of a lava bubble. Then he turned and made his way out of the gray mist back into the world of blue skies and sunlight.

The local people observed him return unharmed from his mountain climbing encounter with Pele and her fire-breathing crater. They were impressed by both the priest's bravery and the apparent superior strength of the haole god. That evening they discussed in whispers Father Damien's audacious climb as they dipped their fingers into the communal poi calabash and licked their fingers clean. One older and presumably wiser member reminded them that on occasion, Pele didn't strike immediately, but later meted out a more severe punishment to the infidel—a horrible death might be in the offing for the priest who wore black. When Damien later developed leprosy, the *kahuna* may have nodded knowingly.

HAVING DONE WHAT he could to demonstrate that Pele was a figment of the imagination of the *kahuna*, Father Damien focused his attention on two pressing challenges: the rebuilding of the chapels in Puna and securing an adequate supply of Bibles and religious literature for the growing number of parishioners. In an August 15 letter to Father Modeste, his provincial, he wrote: "A parent's first duty is to provide for the children. I have the obligation of giving my children, newly born of water and the Holy Spirit, the things that are necessary for spiritual life. This is the reason, Reverend Father, that I humbly beg you to send me as soon as possible some Catholic manuals, a large quantity of the little Red Catechisms, copies of *Mysteries of the Rosary*, and any other books you deem useful. Because the people of Puna are very poor I will be obliged to give these things away free. I'll make up the expense by living as frugally as I can, spending no money for food or shelter."[11]

Fortunately, the Church was able to respond to his request for educational materials because Bishop Maigret had had the foresight to have a small printing press shipped to Honolulu in 1841. Once operational the press not only printed Bibles, prayer books, devotional brochures, and catechisms, but a monthly devotional newspaper.[12]

The dilapidated chapels in Puna were a frustration that gnawed at Damien's inner serenity. During his first months in his new district, he waited patiently for the arrival of one or two of the brothers to undertake the rebuilding of the chapels.[13] His ministry needed beautiful sanctuaries that would inspire his Catholics to worship God in earnest. In the minds of the Hawaiians, the goddess Pele had a sanctuary—an awe-inspiring, fiery throne deep within the volcanoes. A Native Hawaiian could feel the presence of Pele each time he set his foot on the rough black lava and saw huge pillars of smoke billowing upward into the sky. If the mighty Christian God was the one true

God, and Pele was only a myth as the priest dressed in black robes insisted, where was the Christian God's sanctuary, and where could one go to worship him?

No brothers came to his aid, and Father Damien came to believe that were he to succeed in "harvesting" the souls he had come to save, the initiative, the ingenuity of the approach—even the financial means to build the requisite churches and refurbish the dilapidated chapels—rested entirely with him. So he undertook the project, beginning with an earnest request for chapels and churches in a prayer to God. Confident that the prayer would be answered, he turned to God's hands on earth for the response—Bishop Maigret, Father Modeste, and the members of his scattered native congregations.

When his prayers and requests were honored with monies and building supplies from both his superiors and his parishioners, Damien undertook the construction of two chapels, employing the simple techniques the locals used to build their thatched huts. The basic problem was that the newly completed chapels would still be relatively flimsy structures—cool in the heat of the day, but drafty in high winds; large enough to seat forty persons, but poorly illuminated through the small open windows; durable in fair weather, but collapsible in foul.

With the help of his Native Hawaiian parishioners, the two new chapels were constructed in record time. However, Father Damien began to question the wisdom of utilizing the age-old Hawaiian methods. Instead of the light wooden frame bound together with twine, he pictured a chapel boasting stout wooden beams held solidly in place by steel nails, and he resolved to build a third chapel, this time employing European construction techniques.

The enthusiasm and vigor with which Damien pursued his ministry elicited favorable comments from his missionary colleagues. Fathers Charles and Nicaise each wrote to Father Modeste expressing their admiration for what he had accomplished in so short a time. Nicaise was especially complementary, and in an October 5 letter stated: "I have just taken Father Damien to Puna and Hilo where he is serving after spending three weeks with us here. The natives have been delighted with his zeal and with his rapid progress with their language."[14]

Father Damien's nearest fellow priest was Father Charles Pouzot, the veteran in the Hilo District. As Damien became better acquainted with the older priest, he found much to admire and imitate. Most intriguing was the priest's pragmatic approach to the religious life of the missionary. Whatever brought one of the lost sheep of Hawai'i into the Catholic fold was a justifiable tool to be used for the greater glory of God; and to Damien's surprise and delight, one of these tools was the treatment of illnesses amenable to medicines. Father Charles was living proof that by serving as a part-time doctor, a priest could offset the influence of the outlawed *kahuna* physicians and attract the Native Hawaiians to Christianity.

During one of the early visits, Father Charles had startled Damien when he informed him that several of his closest friends were Protestants, an almost unheard of admission by a Sacred Hearts' priest. There were among these Protestants, the older priest revealed, several men of outstanding virtue whose heretic beliefs could be forgiven and over-looked because of the good they accomplished. One of these Protestants whose friendship he valued was Charles Hinkley Wetmore, M.D., the solitary Congregational missionary doctor in Hilo. Father Charles considered Dr. Wetmore not only a good friend, but a valued tutor of clinical medicine. When requested to do so, this physician had taught Father Charles the basics of diagnosis and therapeutics in the treatment of diarrhea, dermatitis, and the upper respiratory illnesses that had become more virulent with the coming of the haole. Father Charles reminded his younger colleague that Christ's ministry had been greatly enhanced by his ability to heal the sick; and in like manner, by practic-ing medicine he had gained many Hawaiian souls for their Lord and God. Then in a quiet voice Father Charles confessed that he had learned enough about the proper treatment of open wounds and skin ulcera-tions to permit him to care for the several lepers in his district. Father Damien was stunned. No one had mentioned that there were lepers in Hawai'i. He had never seen a leper, and he admitted that he knew noth-ing about the disease. Father Charles assured him that an encounter with a leper was inevitable and promised to introduce him to the dis-ease of the Old Testament that had begun to plague Hawai'i.

In exchange for the ongoing instruction in medical practice, Father Charles was tutoring Dr. Wetmore's son and daughter in Latin and French as both aspired to become physicians and serve in the Protestant mission field.[15] While certain members of the Catholic clergy frowned upon tutoring Protestants who planned to become missionaries, Bishop Maigret had given his tacit approval. Teaching Protestant children foreign languages was not an official sin.

Father Charles explained that while it was true that Dr. Wetmore was a heretic in a strict religious sense, he was without question one of the most capable physicians in the Islands. An example of his competence was his astute recognition of an islandwide outbreak of smallpox in 1853 and his prompt administration of the vaccine to Catholics and Protestants alike. This initiative prevented the smallpox epidemic from annihilating the Native Hawaiian population in the Hilo area, as it had elsewhere in the Islands. Then in a whisper he confided that when a member of the Catholic clergy became seriously ill on the Big Island, it was Dr. Wetmore who was summoned to bedside.

Dr. Wetmore was a 6-foot tall, blue-eyed, 45-year-old Congregationalist with an athletic build. After graduating from medical school he had practiced for two years in Lowell, Massachusetts, before receiving his appointment as a physician and surgeon for the Congregational mission in Hawai'i.[16] To comply with the Mission Board's strict policy that a missionary had to have a wife, young Dr. Wetmore commenced a whirlwind courtship that culminated in his marriage to Lucy Sheldon Taylor, the vivacious 5-foot tall daughter of the farm couple in whose home he had resided during his medical school days. Three weeks after the wedding, the newlyweds boarded the 349-ton *Leland* for the tedious 146-day journey from Boston to Honolulu.

Following his arrival Dr. Wetmore was given the primary responsibility for providing the medical care for the handful of Congregational missionaries and their families on the Big Island. This duty seldom required more than a few hours a week, which allowed him to devote most of his professional effort to treating the Native Hawaiian population. For six years he did this, making frequent field trips to distant native villages, often accompanied and assisted by his wife.

In 1853, when the Congregational Mission Board discontinued its financial support to the American mission in Hawai'i, Dr. Wetmore was one of four Protestant missionary doctors who elected to remain in the Islands and continue the practice of medicine; only now, by necessity, it was on a fee-for-service basis. Still, when a penniless Hawaiian sought his medical assistance, that person was never turned away.[17]

Noting Father Damien's fascination with the prospect of adding medical therapeutics to his armamentarium, Father Charles winked, and with a broad smile commented that a priest named Damien was obliged to learn a little medicine; and would he like to commence his medical education? Father Damien nodded affirmatively, and the instruction began.

Medical therapeutics was not difficult, Father Charles explained. With a dozen remedies properly employed, one could ameliorate the majority of symptoms stemming from an illness. For example, he had learned that the most common serious disease a priest would encounter in a native village was a case of fulminating or protracted diarrhea, a potentially lethal illness in an infant or an elderly adult. The therapeutic steps were simple. In such cases, Dr. Wetmore administered opium in sufficient quantity to calm the irritable gastrointestinal tract, plus calomel and dilute fruit juices to produce formed stools and prevent dehydration. High fevers could be lowered with the appropriate dose of quinine. When he encountered an older adult who was short of breath, Father Charles examined the person's ankles. If they were puffy and you could indent the swelling with your finger, the elderly person probably was in congestive heart failure, although kidney failure was a possibility. In either instance the proper therapeutic approach was to give a diuretic agent, and the best available was digitalis, a cardiac glycoside obtained from the common foxglove plant. Digitalis would strengthen a weakened heart and the excess fluid in the ankles and lungs would be eliminated through the kidneys. Another commonly encountered illness was acute cystitis, which generally responded to doses of tincture of turpentine, but one could anticipate frequent treatment failures necessitating the administration of another course of turpentine. Curing an illness with one of the medicines he carried with him in a small black bag often resulted in gaining a soul for the Lord God when the treatment proved successful.

The problem illnesses were the diseases of Western culture to which the Native Hawaiians were highly vulnerable. In Puna, Father Damien was warned, the common childhood diseases were devastating. Within two weeks of an outbreak of measles, 30 per cent of the inhabitants of a village, adults as well as children, would be seriously ill with high fevers, seizures, and encephalitis. Then pneumonia would strike. While the epidemic would run its course within a month, it would leave in its wake an unbelievable mortality rate approaching 40 per cent. In Father Charles' experience, the only medicines that had proven effective in the treatment of measles in the Native Hawaiians were quinine and the herbal concoctions that lowered the high fevers, reducing the number of febrile convulsions. Measles was brutal, but typhoid fever and smallpox were even more lethal, with mortality rates soaring into the 50 percent range.

Promiscuity and polygamy, esteemed cultural traits of the Hawaiians, were devastating because of the spread of the haole's venereal diseases, a calamity the isolated islands had been spared until the arrival of Captain Cook and his sailors in 1778. The Hawaiian viewed sexual intercourse with a member of the opposite sex as a natural act without serious consequences, except for pregnancy. By 1864, syphilis and gonorrhea were rampant in the adult population, and the resulting misery was immense.

Father Damien was fascinated by the art of medicine and the available remedies with which one could treat almost any illness. Each month when he journeyed to Hilo for confession he made it a point to learn more medicine, and when he departed he carried in his saddlebags the pills, herbs, and ointments with which to treat the latest acquisitions to his knowledge base. How much he learned from Father Charles and whether Dr. Wetmore played a major role in his instruction is not known. It is not surprising that nowhere in the surviving Damien correspondence is Dr. C. H. Wetmore mentioned by name. Dr. Wetmore was viewed by the Catholic hierarchy as a misguided heretic, and to have openly lauded the doctor's charitable acts would not have been politically prudent.

Initially, Father Damien made errors in diagnosis and treatment, but like a new medical intern he learned from his mistakes, and within a few months Father Charles judged he was doing more good than injury. Timidly at first, then with increasing confidence, Damien was continuing in the footsteps of his patron saint.

FREQUENTLY, THE ROUGH volcanic terrain in Puna necessitated walking long distances over the huge expanses of hardened lava to search out the remote home of a parishioner, an especially urgent matter when Father Damien learned that the person was seriously ill. While the physical exertion of trekking over the fields of lava was not a problem, Damien began to experience a peculiar burning and aching sensation in his feet. By late summer he noted that the foot discomfort was constantly present regardless of whether he walked or rode. He tried various ointments and salves but discovered empirically that the burning and aching was best relieved by soaking both feet in a basin of warm water before retiring. By late afternoon on most days, he found he was looking forward to the relief that followed wiggling his toes in warm water at day's end. This has caused some to speculate that the foot discomfort Damien first experienced in Puna may in fact have been the first symptom of leprosy.

While the foot irritation was a nagging nuisance, the isolation from his peers and superiors loomed as the major personal problem with which Damien had to cope. No longer was there immediate access to a higher ranking prelate, a father figure to whom he could take his troubles and failures and in return receive solace and absolution. There was no brother priest with whom he could share his triumphs and defeats. He was isolated and lonely. In his mind he pictured the ideal solution—the arrival of his brother, Father Pamphile, to fill the void and reintroduce camaraderie and laughter. On August 23, 1864, he wrote a long letter to his older brother, urging him to expedite the process by which he could be assigned to Hawai'i as a missionary priest.[18] He hoped the bond of fraternal loyalty would be strong enough to induce Pamphile to leave his books. For months he waited patiently for a positive reply, but no promising response was forthcoming.

In late October, Damien reflected on the accomplishments of his first eight months as a missionary priest in a letter to his provincial.[19] Thanks to the incorporation of the practice of medicine into his ministry, he had converted and baptized more Native Hawaiians per capita than had his peers in adjacent, more populous districts on the Big Island. While he was realizing his dream and experiencing moments of exhilaration, the oppressive spiritual isolation he was experiencing became the bars on a cage labeled "depression."[20] The key to unlocking and escaping from this cage for brief periods of time was using his hands to build something. No sooner was the work on one chapel nearing completion than he began planning the construction of another. In but eight months he had managed to build two new chapels and to rebuild the roofs and walls of four others.

In Puna the stresses of a missionary life were indeed formidable—the rigors of daily travel, the task of speaking in English or Hawaiian while thinking in Flemish or French, and worst of all, the mental anguish of accumulating his daily sins for three to four weeks before he could meet with a fellow priest and kneel in confession. He was a healthy male with the normal feelings of a male who found himself enmeshed in the noisy bustle of a Polynesian culture where seeing a half-naked Hawaiian female was a common, sexually arousing occurrence. He found this temptation especially disturbing.[21] The weekly confessional that could erase the guilt of worldly thoughts and sinful imagination was a necessity denied him.

IN KOHALA-HĀMĀKUA, a physically and emotionally exhausted Father Clément began 1865 with the recognition that he was functioning poorly as a priest. The hours he was forced to spend on horseback coupled with the stress of isolation and loneliness were taking their toll. He simply had lost the will to minister effectively. Plagued by the knowledge of his lackluster performance, he had become deeply depressed, which further degraded his efforts. In an effort to salvage his career he devised a survival plan—one that might enable him to succeed, but one that would completely disrupt Father Damien's ministry in Puna.

Father Charles Pouzot empathized with Father Clément's plight, and in the hope of rectifying the situation he invited both Clément and Damien to join him for a brief retreat at St. Joseph's Church in Hilo during the second week of January. A fatigued and despondent Father Clément arrived on schedule, and after the vesper service he broached the problem of his failing ministry with his fellow priests. To him the solution was simple. The one essential attribute he lacked, physical stamina, Father Damien possessed in abundance. Because Puna was only half the size of Kohala-Hāmākua, Father Clément felt confident that he could successfully manage the smaller parish. All that was required to remedy the situation was a swap of districts.

The eyes of Fathers Clément and Charles searched the face of Father Damien for his response to the proposed exchange. Damien in turn had little choice but to acquiesce, and reluctantly he agreed. He had become very fond of his small band of Christians in Puna and to leave them on such short notice would be grievous. Worst of all, doubling the area of his old parish would magnify the disparaging negative influence of his nemesis—*loneliness*.

With Father Charles' endorsement, the exchange plan was submitted to Bishop Maigret who promptly approved it, and Damien returned to Puna to make his final tour of the district and bid his parishioners aloha and good-bye. As he looked into the large brown eyes of his Christians and gripped their hands in friendship for the last time, he knew the heartache a parent experiences when forcibly separated from a beloved child.[22]

On March 19, 1865, Father Damien mounted his horse and, leading a second horse and two pack mules, left Puna and headed for the challenge of Kohala-Hāmākua.

6

Kohala-Hāmākua:
The Second Parish

And he said,"With what can we compare the kingdom of God,
or what parable shall we use for it? It is like a grain of mustard
seed, which, when sown upon the ground, is the smallest of
all the seeds on earth; yet when it is sown it grows up and
becomes the greatest of all shrubs, and puts forth large branches,
so that the birds of the air can make nests in its shade."
—Mark 4:30

FATHER DAMIEN SOON discovered that it was a physical impossibil-
ity to accomplish all that needed to be done in his new parish in a
timely fashion because of the huge distances to be covered between
the small groups of parishioners scattered across the huge Kohala-
Hāmākua District. His first circuit ride to introduce himself to the few
hundred Catholics required a full six weeks, and he calculated that he
had spent more time as a horseman extraordinary than functioning as
a father of the Sacred Hearts. During the circuit he mentally cataloged
the district's assets and liabilities. On the negative side there were fifteen
chapels in deplorable disrepair, which Father Clément had simply
ignored during his short tenure. Broken support beams, collapsed roofs,
and missing thatch were stark testimony to the years of neglect. As he
analyzed the situation, he believed that he had little choice but to launch
another chapel-building program, this time employing the European
construction techniques that had proved so successful in Puna. Not only
would his chapels withstand the destructive force of windstorms, but
they would be beautiful. The major deterrent, however, was time. There

simply wasn't enough time to do all that needed to be attended to—
yet he welcomed the latest of God's challenges, for it was the next test
of true discipleship.

On the positive side he discovered a small wooden church in the
middle of his new district, a beautiful structure that had been well
maintained and that would accommodate a congregation of sixty to
eighty persons. Adjacent to the church was a five-room, thatched-roof
rectory. Damien was jubilant. Not only did he have a fine wooden
church, but a house he could call home.[1]

Within four months of his arrival in Kohala-Hāmākua, Father
Damien managed to restore three of the previously abandoned
chapels, build a new one, and secure approval and funding from his
superiors to build a new chapel at Waipi'o in Hāmākua and another
at Kawaihae in Kohala, towns on the eastern and western sides of the
Kohala Mountains. Father Modeste, the provincial, while pleased that
Damien possessed the requisite skills for chapel construction, was
troubled by the substantial drain on the mission treasury to purchase
the lumber and building supplies. No sooner had he funded one chapel
than the energetic Belgian was requesting financial assistance to build
another. In an August letter to the superior general, Father Modeste
wrote, "In a letter which I sent him today, I told him that he must cultivate patience. It is easy to conceive good projects, but it is not so easy
to execute them, above all, when they call for money."[2]

The hectic pace of Father Damien's ministry continued unabated.
The trademarks of his ministry became the exuberant enthusiasm with
which he launched each new project, the seldom absent smile, and the
deep compassion he showed the sick. The haole in the black cassock was
revered by the natives for the black bag he toted and from which he gave
medicines to relieve the troublesome symptoms of an illness. This additional service he offered freely to all persons, and never did he accept
compensation. A quiet *"Mahalo"*—"Thank you"—was sufficient.

As his reputation as a successful healer of illnesses grew, he
became acutely aware of his competition—the *kahuna lapa'au*, those
kahuna who were the physicians and healers. In 1865 Damien viewed
all *kahuna lapa'au* with suspicion, believing that they were nothing
more than inept Polynesian witch doctors. He therefore continued to
devote considerable effort to his part-time practice of medicine, especially in the remoter areas of his district where there was no access to

Western-trained medical doctors.[3] In time he would acknowledge that the *kahuna lapaʻau* were reasonably competent in treating the majority of the common native illnesses, employing a holistic approach that included ancient prayer rituals, animal sacrifices, water baths and steaming, and the astute use of medicinal plants. But he also observed that the *kahuna* were as powerless as the best-trained American and European doctors of medicine to treat successfully the common infectious diseases of Western culture to which the natives had little natural resistance.

While practicing medicine in Kohala-Hāmākua, Father Damien began to encounter natives with small whitish spots on their skin that were insensitive to pain and in time broke down to become ugly ulcerations. These skin lesions fit the descriptions of the early manifestations of leprosy. The Hawaiians called the lesions *maʻi Pākē*, the "Chinese disease," blaming the Chinese immigrant workers for introducing leprosy into Hawaiʻi. As Father Charles had correctly predicted, leprosy was a growing problem throughout the Islands.

Bishop Maigret, cognizant of the threat of the dread disease of the Old Testament, was adamant in his warning that his priests abstain from any physical contact with a suspected leper if they wished to escape contagion. Prayer for divine protection was fine, but when dealing with leprosy, prudence was the watchword. This was not an easy mandate for Father Damien to obey. In his flock there were several suspected lepers, persons whom he believed were precious in the eyes of God, persons whom he did not wish to offend or shame by administering the sacraments in an awkward manner that precluded touching them. Christ had touched lepers. St. Damien and St. Comas had undoubtedly touched lepers when dressing their sores and ulcers. He, Damien De Veuster, would not flinch from doing the same. If it were God's will that he be protected from all harm, he would be safe. Should God choose otherwise, it would be a sign that he was worthy of joining the select group of his Lord's apostles who were judged virtuous enough to be martyred for the sake of the Kingdom of God.[4]

To gain a more comprehensive knowledge of leprosy, Damien turned to his mentor, the erudite Father Charles. The older priest obligingly detailed what he knew about leprosy, the loathsome disease of antiquity that had ravished Europe between A.D. 1000 and 1400. The first cases in Hawaiʻi were recognized in the 1830s, but no public health measures had been instituted to control the spread of the disease that was ravaging the bodies of an estimated 1,000 Native Hawaiians.[5]

No one, Father Charles counseled, knew for certain what caused leprosy, but in order to contract the disease one had to make physical contact with a leper. Actually, touching a leper with one's bare hands was extremely dangerous. Each time he did so, he washed his hands as soon as he could. Father Charles explained that leprosy wasn't a simple disease like epidemic typhus with its high fever and a characteristic rash followed by survival or death in two weeks. Leprosy was a chronic, mutilating disease that took months to years to kill its victims. Because there were no medicines to cure or arrest it, there were no survivors.

Leprosy first attacked the skin and the nerves to the face, arms, and legs. This made diagnosis difficult because in the early stages of the disease, it mimicked many other skin disorders such as psoriasis, warts, or carbuncles.[6] The sudden appearance on the skin of a small whitish spot that was insensitive to pain was generally the earliest recognizable skin lesion. Over time this spot enlarged and was joined by similar anesthetic lesions. With the loss of normal skin sensation, trauma from burns and splinters led to infections, followed by the unsightly ulcerations that emitted the sickening odor of rotting flesh so repulsive to most people. When the facial nerves were involved, the loss of protective eye sensation could lead to blindness. Nerves closest to the skin's surface were attacked early and became swollen and enlarged. This caused severe neuritic pain followed by atrophy and weakness of the muscles with which the nerve communicated. When the nerves to the muscles of the lower arm and hand were involved, the fingers lost strength and contracted into an unsightly, unusable claw.

Individuals more susceptible to the disease developed what the doctors called *lepromatous leprosy*. In this highly malignant form of leprosy, the skin eruptions were widespread. Instead of a single small lesion, multiple nodules, plaques, and papules covered the skin's surface. The face, especially the forehead, became swollen and took on a thickened, corrugated appearance (*leonine facies*). Eyebrows disappeared and the earlobes became pendulous, occasionally drooping to touch the shoulders. The nasal septum disintegrated and the nose collapsed. In adult males the testes were destroyed, which led to breast enlargement. Death within two years was common.

The practicing physicians in Hawai'i recognized that leprosy was contagious, and to protect themselves they assiduously avoided any direct physical contact with lepers by wearing gloves and using a cane to lift clothing to view the skin lesions. From the beginning of his ministry to lepers, Father Damien elected not to take these precautions because it was impossible to offer Holy Communion without coming in contact with a leper's tongue. To cleanse a leper's wounds as Father Charles had instructed him did require direct physical contact. Another major problem was the food a leper may have prepared or touched. When the hospitality of a meal and a night's shelter was extended by a family, one of whose members had early leprosy, he would seat himself in the family circle on a grass mat, offer grace, and with a grateful smile dip his fingers deeply into the same communal calabash containing the poi as did the leper beside him. For the first nine years of his missionary ministry in Hawai'i and prior to his becoming a resident priest at the remote leper settlement, Father Damien repeatedly had direct physical contact with lepers and ate food possibly contaminated by lepers. He did not adhere to Bishop Maigret's directive. The *kahuna lapa'au* and the *kahuna pule* waited patiently to see if Pele might use leprosy to punish the infidel who wore the black robes.

DESPITE THE PRESS of his many duties, 1865 proved to be a year of personal and spiritual loneliness for Father Damien. The Sacred Hearts mission in Hawai'i was guilty of violating Article 392 of the Holy Rule, which dictated that no priest serve in a district where he was isolated from a confrere, yet each priest on the Big Island was forced to tolerate this breach of policy. To remedy this disheartening situation, Damien made an appeal in his annual report to the superior general for a priest to share the duties of the huge Kohala-Hāmākua District as he was unable to attend to all of the essential needs of his scattered Christian communities.[7] He was in a vast wilderness where several days could elapse before he could reach the bedside of a seriously ill parishioner and administer the sacraments. Without question, the presence of a second priest was absolutely essential to meet the needs of his parishioners and ease the stress of the spiritual isolation he was experiencing.

As an inducement for a speedier response by the superior general,

Father Damien built a second rectory in Hāmākua for the priest he prayed would soon arrive. Regrettably, the new rectory stood vacant for four years, forcing Damien to push himself to the limit to perform the duties that would have taxed the endurance of two priests.

LOT KAMEHAMEHA, King Kamehameha V, began the third year of his reign in 1866 with the sobering knowledge that the survival of the Kingdom of Hawai'i depended upon the segregation of the lepers from the healthy. Not only was the dread disease further decreasing the dwindling native population, but the presence of lepers in the port cities was frightening foreign traders. The king's advisors were adamant: Enforce the 1865 Segregation Act to Prevent the Spread of Leprosy or the consequences to the Kingdom would be catastrophic—too few people to rule, less tax money for the royal coffers, and no foreign trade.

There was no viable alternative, so on January 6, 1866, the segregation of lepers began. The first contingent of nine men and three women was transported on the deck of the sailing schooner *Warwick* to the newly designated leper settlement on Moloka'i's Kalaupapa Peninsula.[8] All had advanced disease, for the goal was to remove the most hideously deformed first. Accompanying the lepers was a small group of helpers or *kōkua*—the spouses, family members, or paid employees—whose task it would be to care for the exiles, the majority of whom were unable to fend for themselves.

The lepers were a pitiful sight with their misshapen faces, claw-shaped hands, and ulcerated arms and legs as they stepped ashore from the *Warwick*'s longboats and trudged the 2.5 miles from the landing site on the western side of the Kalaupapa Peninsula to Kalawao, the designated leper village on the eastern side. There they took up residence in one of the abandoned dwellings purchased by the Board of Health from a previous owner or accepted the hospitality of one the remaining *kama'āina*—native residents—who had stubbornly refused to relinquish their property to the Hawaiian government. The resident *kama'āina* had little knowledge about leprosy and, hence, little fear of contagion.

Two weeks later, a second group of twelve with advanced leprosy was put ashore, and every few weeks thereafter a new group of lepers arrived. Soon all available housing in Kalawao was occupied, and new arrivals were forced to construct the traditional thatched huts, a difficult task for those with missing fingers, a missing foot, or those coping with a high fever. By October 1, 1866, 101 men and 41 women lepers had been exiled to Kalawao, where they faced a nightmarish existence.[9] Not only were there no doctors, nurses, hospitals, clergy, chapels, or churches, but in that village of death there was insufficient food for the disabled, a shortage of water for drinking and bathing, and no law. *"'A'ole kanawai ma keia wahi!"* the incarcerated cried out. "In this place there is no law!" The collection of lepers and their kōkua degenerated into a savage society where the stronger, desperate for food, shelter, and clothing, preyed on the weaker.

The Kingdom of Hawai'i was not an affluent realm and so had limited funds with which to establish and operate the leprosy settlement. It was the Board of Health's contention that the lepers could fend for themselves at the leper settlement. They could farm and fish. They could make clothing and build houses; they could help one another. The problem was that the majority of the lepers were too incapacitated to care for themselves.

DURING THE TIME Father Damien was serving as a missionary priest on the Big Island, a time when leprosy was placing a hangman's noose around the neck of the tiny kingdom, one of the subplots to the Damien story was unfolding in distant Norway. For some inexplicable reason, leprosy had become epidemic in Norway, infecting a staggering 2 per cent of the population—a prevalence similar to that being experienced in the Hawaiian Islands. A young physician, Dr. Gerhard Armauer Hansen of Bergen, Norway, began his practice of medicine in Lofoten, Norway, where the nation's heaviest concentration of lepers resided. As he cared for these unfortunate victims, he became convinced that the prevailing understanding of leprosy as a hereditary disorder was wrong. His observations led him to conclude that he was witnessing the manifestations of a disease whose cause was obviously an infectious agent. Colleagues scoffed at his schoolboy theory, but Dr. Hansen doggedly set about to prove that leprosy was an infectious disease.

FOR THE MAJORITY of persons in the Islands, the Christmas holiday season ended on a joyous note. In his 1867 New Year's greeting to his parents, Father Damien summed up his activities for the year.

As for me, thanks be to God, I am still well and in good health, and very, very happy . . . I have no time to become bored in my large parish which the Savior has confided to my care. . . .

I have an enormous number of sick whom I must visit, and to whom I must administer the Sacraments when they are in danger of death. I have four Catholic schools which I try to oversee, and where I teach catechism. I have three wooden churches and several chapels which are thatched. I try to be in each church at least once a month on Sunday in order to offer my dear Christians the holy sacrifice of the Mass and to instruct them in their religion. Thus you can understand, my dear parents, that I don't have much time for other things. As a priest I am usually on the road, and at my rectory very little. I am, perhaps, traveling three or four out of every six weeks to visit my dear children in Christ.[10]

Father Damien's pastoral routine continued at a punishing pace throughout 1867. While his ministry was progressing satisfactorily, he was increasingly aware of the public's growing dissatisfaction with the treatment of the lepers. In the quiet of the chapels, parishioners whispered shocking stories about the plight of family members, friends, and neighbors from the Kohala-Hāmākua District who had been sent to the leper settlement on Moloka'i. These tales were confirmed when reports highly critical of the settlement began appearing in the local newspapers.[11]

To expedite compliance with the Segregation Law, all Hawaiian residents—Native Hawaiians and foreigners alike—who had skin diseases suspected to be leprosy were transported to Honolulu for examination by government physicians at Kalihi Hospital, the temporary holding facility for lepers. The observation period at Kalihi was short. Mistaken diagnoses resulted, and persons with skin lesions resembling leprosy, the great imitator of skin diseases, were branded lepers and shipped to Moloka'i. On one occasion while in Honolulu, Father Damien witnessed the departure of a group of lepers from Kalihi destined for Moloka'i. At dusk a group of fifty lepers—men, women, and children under police guard—trudged sullenly down the dirt streets to the waterfront where longboats waited to ferry them to the interisland steamer used exclusively for transporting lepers and supplies to the Kalaupapa Peninsula. Family members and friends shadowed the group, wailing and chanting a *kanikau*—a haunting farewell. Damien witnessed mothers waving to sobbing children whom they would never see again and the heart-wrenching separation of husbands and wives who kept their eyes fixed on the other's face, trying to memorize the features of the lover they were losing. While it troubled Bishop Maigret that there was no priest at the leper settlement to minister to the Catholics, he was powerless to correct the situation. He was a man of God, not an executioner of young priests.

Initially, the Board of Health pointed with pride to what it believed was a model leper settlement, so it was with reluctance that it was forced to abandon the notion that the settlement was capable of self-sufficiency. Over 50 percent of the incoming lepers had advanced disease and were absolutely unable to care for themselves, so the board continued to encourage *kōkua* to accompany the afflicted exiles to live with and provide for the material needs of the victims. The board had originally purchased two-thirds of the tiny but fertile Kalaupapa Peninsula along with a few wooden houses, the majority of the thatched huts, the fields of taro and sweet potatoes, and the fruit trees of the previous owners. All of this was made available to the arriving lepers and their *kōkua*, but it was insufficient to meet the basic needs of the sick and the dying. As the number of lepers increased, hunger gave way to starvation, and the board was forced to supply a weekly food supplement.

To oversee the on-site day-to-day operation of the leper settlement the board hired a resident superintendent, Louis Lepart, a non-leper, a Frenchman and former Sacred Hearts brother who spoke no Hawaiian. Lepart's main responsibility was food distribution. Each week after the arrival of the food shipment, he gave each leper the authorized 4 pounds of beef or salmon plus 4 pounds of *'ai pa'a*—cooked taro that had been pounded into a hard mass for shipping and from which to make poi, the staple of the Hawaiian diet. Those lepers judged too weak to farm or fish were given an additional pound of each commodity. Rough seas, especially during the winter months, frequently prevented the weekly shipments, adding hunger to the torments of the disease. The disgruntled *kōkua*, who were not eligible for the free food rations, habitually stole or confiscated food from those lepers unable to fend for themselves. Hunger became a way of life.

The overall responsibility for the settlement was assigned to Rudolph W. Meyer, a German immigrant, a trusted friend of the king who lived atop the *pali* in a village named Kala'e. Meyer, a highly successful rancher and sugar planter, was the settlement's true "superintendent," for he was given full responsibility for ordering all supplies and dispersing all the government funds. Lepart, the acting "resident" superintendent, was Meyer's subordinate. Once a month the rancher rode a mule down the narrow, saw-toothed trail he had hacked into the face of the *pali* to check on the status of the settlement. Inevitably, he was appalled by what he witnessed. Lepers with advanced, debilitating disease who were unable to care for themselves were often abandoned and left unattended to die in an open field. Those with a *kōkua* fared better, but in the absence of a medical facility staffed by a resident doctor and nurses, the majority of the lepers died prematurely and without the benefit of clergy. There were no churches, no ministers, no priests. There was no school for the children. Resident superintendent Lepart spoke no Hawaiian, so there was no effective communication or administrative leadership. There was no law—no police, no court, no judge. The physically strong and ruthless victimized the weak. Those few that cultivated the land had their crops stolen by those too lazy to work. Drunken midnight orgies were commonplace. Rape and child molestation occurred. "Each leper felt himself a Pariah, ready to turn his hand against every other one in the village."[12] Kalawao was no community; it was little more than a collection of dying, misshapen creatures forced to prey on their neighbors for survival.

After each inspection, Meyer forwarded his observations and recommendations to the Board of Health. He urged that Resident Superintendent Lepart be replaced by someone who spoke Hawaiian and who would be responsible for maintaining law and order. To prevent hunger and starvation, the weekly food ration needed to be increased and a food storage facility to provide emergency rations needed to be built and stocked. The absence of medical care was a travesty; equally upsetting was the absence of a resident clergyman.

The board grimaced, for it had limited resources. To address the critical need for medical care, the board voted to hire a physician to make periodic visits to the settlement to treat those ailments that were amenable to therapy. To house the seriously ill, it allocated funds for the construction of two hospital buildings, one for men and the other for women. *Kōkua* were to be hired to serve as orderlies in the hospitals. The board next appealed to both the Protestants and the Catholics to send clergymen to attend to the spiritual needs of the lepers.

The Protestants in Honolulu responded by announcing that they were raising money to build a church at the settlement; however, they could not comply with the request for a resident minister since all Protestant ministers were married and had the responsibility for providing for their families. Should a pastor contract leprosy and be permanently interned at the leper settlement, his family would be left desolate. A frustrated Bishop Maigret made an ambiguous reply for the Catholics while he pondered the risk of his current policy of allowing a priest to slip ashore at the settlement for a few days each year. If he increased the length or frequency of the unauthorized visitation period, he believed he would be placing the lives of one or more of his priests in grave jeopardy.

IN FEBRUARY 1867, Father Damien received a letter from his brother, Father Pamphile, dated September 1866, announcing that he had accepted the post of director of novices at Issy. The words had the impact of a betrayal. To his dismay, his older brother had opted to pursue an academic career instead of joining him in the Hawaiian mission field. Dejected by the news, Damien came to the realization that his cherished dream of serving with his brother had been relegated to the level of a boyhood fantasy. So disappointed and upset was he that he let eight months elapse before sending a brief reply, in which he wrote: "As for your assignment to the novitiate—well, I do not know if I should congratulate you or not. How impenetrable are the designs of God. Far from being a poor missionary among savages, you are raised to a position of dignity. It is best to say, 'Let Thy Will be done,' without ceasing and with resignation. The Will of God before all else. One can do no better. I do wish to congratulate you."[13]

BY THE CLOSE OF 1867, Damien had become highly proficient as a practitioner of medicine and had acquired the skills to function as a master builder of churches and chapels. Like his patron saint, his fervor in leading an exemplary Christian life while serving his fellow man in multiple capacities was attracting many to Christianity. He reported to his provincial, "During the last year I had 40 baptisms and 8 marriages. I count 14 deaths that I know about; of course, there may be others of which I am uninformed or which I have forgotten."[14]

His name was Damien, but unlike his patron saint, he had no brother with whom to share his aspirations and his sorrows, his triumphs and his defeats.

7

The Calm before
the Storm of Moloka‘i

*Wait on the Lord and He will renew your strength; You
will mount up with wings like eagles. You will run and
not be weary. You will walk and not faint.*
—Isaiah 40:31

IN JANUARY 1868, Bishop Maigret announced that his recruiting
efforts had been blessed, and that a new group of Sacred Hearts' missionaries was soon to arrive in Honolulu. Encouraged by the news,
Father Damien promptly wrote to Father Modeste soliciting the support of his provincial to have one of the new fathers assigned to the
Kohala-Hāmākua District.[1]

The encouraging news reinvigorated Damien, and he devoted the
next two weeks to completing the chapel at the mouth of the beautiful Waipi‘o Valley. After he applied the final coat of paint he wrote to
Father Modeste to inform him that the new chapel possessed a serene
beauty as it faced the sea. In the letter he detailed how he had managed to finance the undertaking with money earned from the sale of
his homegrown tobacco, supplemented by the rent of church land to
local farmers. After explaining how minimally the construction costs
had impacted the mission's operating budget, he politely asked permission to build a chapel of similar size at Waimea, a town located
about 10 miles inland from Waipi‘o, closing his letter with a startling
statement, "If I can build it (this is between the two of us) the good
God has made it known to me that He wishes it dedicated to St. John,
the evangelist."[2]

A few weeks later, Father Damien thanked Father Modeste for sanctioning the Waimea chapel, and in the letter expanded on his John the Baptist revelation: "However, the principal reason why I am eager to build there is that I believe I have seen John the Baptist showing me the park which the King has just ceded to us, and the Saint said, 'Here is the place where the chapel is to be built.'"[3] While he had occasionally experienced premonitions of future events, Father Damien had never before had a vision or a dream that he interpreted to be a divine revelation.

As he worked out the logistics for building the chapel at Waimea, Damien was aware of an occasional mild earth tremor lasting from thirty to sixty seconds. Initially, these tremors were of no concern because earth tremors of low intensity and short duration occurred sporadically throughout the year on the Big Island. Within a few weeks, however, the tremors were occurring hourly and with increasing severity. From parishioners Father Damien learned that the *kahuna* interpreted this phenomenon as a prelude to an impending catastrophe, a reminder from Pele, who was watching from below in her fiery palace, that she, not the haole god, was the creator of the Big Island. During February the periodic tremors rattled dishes on shelves, occasionally causing them to tumble. By mid-March the tremors increased to a magnitude that forced the people to remove all dishes from the shelves for safekeeping. The apprehensive population looked toward the slumbering volcanoes and exclaimed to all who would listen, "It is the work of Pele! Pele is angry with us!"

A highly respected Hawaiian, a former member of the House of Representatives and a district judge, increased the tension when he stepped forward and prophesied that the end of the world was at hand. Joseph Ka'ona was his name.[4] He was a devout Protestant, a graduate of Lahainaluna School, and a lay preacher in the Congregational Church. From the pulpit he shouted that "divine voices" had told him the Big Island was about to be obliterated. When Father Damien learned of Ka'ona's pronouncement, he shrugged his shoulders in irritated disbelief. Fortunately the ground tremors were less severe in the Kohala-Hāmākua District than were felt over the rest of the Big Island, so the dire predictions of the self-proclaimed prophet were easier to refute. On the western side of the Island in Kona, however, where the tremors were the worst in living memory, the nervous Hawaiians gave Ka'ona their undivided attention. Ka'ona gathered his followers about him in South Kona and established a commune, a cult modeled after those of the early apostles. Believers were instructed to sell all that they possessed and to pool their resources for the common good. Gowned in white robes, they knelt in prayer awaiting the end of the world.

The more traditional Protestants judged Ka'ona's prophetic claims not only to be ridiculous, but dangerous, so they pressured the local constabulary to arrest the perpetrator. Ka'ona was seized and under armed guard taken to Honolulu where he was examined by government-appointed physicians, judged to be suffering from psychotic delusions, and confined to an asylum for observation. From the barred window of his cell Ka'ona continued to shout, "The wrath of Jehovah is about to descend and destroy the wicked!"

As if in response to Ka'ona's dire warning, Nature's wrath did "descend." At 4:05 P.M. on Thursday afternoon, April 2, the tropical tranquility of life on the Big Island was shattered by a colossal earthquake, the most violent in the history of the island. With tremendous force, the earthquake shook the island for several minutes. Palm trees toppled into long cracks in the volcanic soil. The cracks widened and swallowed thatched huts and their screaming occupants. The force generated by the collision of the massive plates of rock beneath the earth's surface unleased a tsunami, a gigantic seismic wave, which smashed into the western coast of the Big Island.[5] To the Hawaiians, this was proof that Pele was furious with them and that Ka'ona had correctly predicted the dire consequences of her displeasure.

When the smoky haze lifted, a vindicated Ka'ona was released from the asylum and allowed to return to South Kona where he reassembled his followers, warning them of the latest pronouncement of the "divine voices"—the Big Island's volcanoes would spew forth lava and engulf the entire island, except for the small coastal area where he and his two hundred followers were encamped. Damien's parishioners were in a near panic. To calm them he made a whirlwind circuit ride of his district to reassure his flock that it was Almighty God who had created the islands and the sea, the mountains and the volcanoes, the awe-inspiring sunrise as well as the violent storms and earthquakes. It was the Almighty to whom they should listen, not the mentally deranged Ka'ona. Even the Protestants, he argued, recognized how absurd Ka'ona's claims were.

The owner of the coastal land upon which Ka'ona's commune

was encamped summoned the local sheriff to force the cult to vacate. In the ensuing fracas, the sheriff and one of his constables were killed. When Sheriff J. H. Coney of Hawai'i learned of the murders, he assembled a large armed force and surrounded Ka'ona's camp. This time there was no violence and the two hundred Ka'onaites, resplendent in their white robes and turbans, were arrested. Following the burning of the cult's church and houses, the handcuffed cult members were led to prison. Ka'ona was convicted of manslaughter and sentenced to ten years at hard labor.[6]

By June the aftershocks ceased and island life returned to normal. That month a young, superbly trained French priest, Father Gulstan Ropert, arrived in Honolulu prepared to go where Bishop Maigret would assign him. Father Gulstan was the long-awaited and often prayed for priest who would assume responsibility for half of Father Damien's huge district.[7] From the time the two priests first met and greeted each other, they got along famously. In the surviving correspondence only warm compliments about each other are to be found. Father Gulstan's initial impression of his new assignment was that Father Damien was a tireless taskmaster and that the Protestants were a formidable religious adversary with whom he must learn to cope.[8]

Mark Twain, who had visited the Islands two years earlier as an investigative reporter, reflected on the merits and the weaknesses of the rival Christian factions in his letters from Hawai'i. Of the Protestant missionary movement, he reported:

> The wonderful benefit conferred upon this people by the missionaries is so prominent, so palpable, and so unquestionable, that the frankest compliment I can pay them, and the best, is simply to point to the condition of the Sandwich Islanders of Captain Cook's time and their condition today. Their work speaks for itself . . . .[9]

> The Sandwich Island missionaries are pious; hard-working; hard-praying; self-sacrificing; hospitable; devoted to the well-being of this people and the interests of Protestantism; bigoted; puritanical; slow; ignorant of all white human nature and natural ways of men, except the remnants of these things that are left in their own class or profession; old fogy—fifty years behind the age; uncharitable toward the weaknesses of the flesh; considering all shortcomings, faults, and failings in the light of crimes, and having no mercy and no forgiveness for such.[10]

Twain's observations about the Catholic mission are surprisingly affirmative in light of his Protestant upbringing.

> The French Roman Catholic Mission here, under the Right Reverend Lord Bishop Maigret, goes along quietly and unostentatiously; and its affairs are conducted with a wisdom which betrays the presence of a leader of distinguished ability. The Catholic clergy are honest, straight forward, frank, and open; they are industrious and devoted to their religion and their work; they never meddle; whatever they do can be relied on as being prompted by a good and worthy motive.[11]

IN THE QUIET OF the chapels, Father Damien continued to commiserate with the dissatisfaction his parishioners expressed regarding the treatment of family members and friends at the two-year-old leper facility, referred to by many as the "Kalaupapa prison." To add rancor to dissatisfaction, it was common knowledge that there were several hundred lepers scattered throughout the archipelago who were either in hiding or using their wealth to shield themselves from incarceration. The Segregation Law of 1865 appeared to many to be a flawed, hypocritical policy.

To quell the public outcry, the Board of Health dispatched several of its members, accompanied by a newspaper reporter, on a hurried visit to the leper settlement to assess the situation. Upon the group's return, its findings were published in the *Hawaiian Gazette*. The article, intended to assuage the public's concern, had quite the opposite effect. Statements in the article incensed many readers, such as: "They [the lepers] were well clad, had the appearance of well-fed, independent owners of the land. . . . We found about twenty of the worst cases lodged in the hospital, a plain building, rather narrow for its purpose, but comfortable. . . . The lepers in and about Honolulu, with those at Kalihi (leper receiving station), will find on their removal to this settlement ample accommodations in their new home. . . . We left the settlement deeply impressed with the real benevolence of the Hawaiian Government as manifest in the provisions and surrounds of this institution."[12]

When the newspaper article was read by the lepers, a sense of betrayal was superimposed upon their feeling of abandonment. The alleged "comfortable" hospital was a putrid-smelling, elongated hut with a dirt floor. No doctors walked its narrow central aisle to ameliorate pain. No nurses were there to comfort the mind and cleanse the body. The only therapies available were the native remedies supplied by one of the leprous *kahuna lapa'au*, who treated illnesses with medicinal plants. Water, food, and clothing were in short supply. Crime was rampant. The Board of Health had built a two-occupant jailhouse, but it stood empty as no one had been appointed to act as sheriff or judge. And death generally came in the absence of a clergyman! So much for the "benevolence of the Hawaiian Government."

In response to the complaints solicited during the investigative visit and the deluge of letters following the visit, the Board of Health hired Mr. and Mrs. Donald Walsh, both nonlepers, to staff the settlement's facilities. Both were English and skilled in their professions, but neither was fluent in the Hawaiian language. Mr. Walsh, a former officer in the British Army, was named the resident superintendent and schoolmaster with the additional responsibility for maintaining law and order. Mrs. Walsh was the settlement's first nurse. With a competent couple at Kalawao, the board authorized the construction of a schoolhouse for the leper children and two new hospital buildings for the terminally ill, one for men and the other for women.

In an attempt to introduce some semblance of law and order, Walsh appointed several of the male *kōkua*, husbands of lepers, to serve as paid constables. But the well-intentioned effort was only partially successful. Because there was no legal or recognized code of behavior for lepers and no judge or court system to adjudicate complaints, the stronger continued to do as they wished and to prey upon the weak.

FOR THE REMAINDER OF 1868, Father Gulstan and Father Damien managed their shared ministry of the two new districts, Kohala and Hāmākua, awaiting the decision of Bishop Maigret as to which district each would be assigned. Free to devote more time to the refurbishment and construction of chapels, churches, and rectories, Damien surveyed the needs of the new districts. In the Waipi'o parish in Hāmākua, he razed the rectory that had been built by the Hawaiians and replaced it with an all-wood structure.[13] He celebrated the winter months by constructing a new all-wooden church at Kapulena, the village where he surmised Father Gulstan would be permanently quartered.

DECEMBER 1868 BECAME a month of horror and death as the island kingdom reeled under the impact of Hawai'i's second major smallpox epidemic.[14] Several sailors suffering from smallpox had been carried ashore at the ports of Honolulu and Lahaina, where Native Hawaiians hired to care for them became infected and spawned the epidemic. The kingdom's "first smallpox epidemic" had occurred in 1853, and among the unvaccinated natives the mortality rate soared to 80 per cent. Because Dr. Wetmore predicted that this "second smallpox epidemic" had the potential to be equally lethal, Father Damien urged everyone in his district, Catholics and Protestants alike, to be vaccinated. Men, women, and children patiently waited in long lines outside the doctor's office for the tall, lean physician to place a drop of milky fluid on the skin of their upper arm and then scratch the area with a small knife. The Hawaiians trusted this man and did as he recommended. Additionally, on the recommendation of Dr. Wetmore, Damien advised his parishioners not to visit the ports of Hilo or Kona until the epidemic was over, nor were they to make contact with anyone coming from one of the ports. From the pulpit he warned of the folly of relying on the prayers of the *kahuna pule* or the remedies of the *kahuna lapa'au*, for he correctly believed that their incantations and herbal concoctions were powerless against the smallpox.

Smallpox ran its appalling course in eight to ten months, diverting everyone's attention from the steadily increasing number of Hawaiians contracting the dreaded leprosy. Thousands of Native Hawaiians succumbed to smallpox and were buried in the volcanic soil. Thanks to Dr. Wetmore's vaccination program, the mortality rate in the districts of Hilo and Kohala was less than 10 percent.

DURING THE MONTHS that smallpox was ravaging Hawai'i, Dr. Armauer Hansen in Norway was awarded a gold medal by the University of Christiania for a scientific paper in which he described tiny granular masses, yellowish brown in color, found in the lymph nodes of Norwegian lepers.[15] He was convinced that the granular masses held a key to unlocking the mystery of the cause of the disease. The following spring he went to Germany to learn new technologies with which to search for the elusive microbial agent he believed was lurking in the tiny bits of granular tissue found in lepers. Upon his return, the Norwegian Medical Society in Christiania elected to sponsor his research into the cause of leprosy.

BISHOP MAIGRET LAUNCHED the New Year, 1870, by assigning Father Damien the sole responsibility for Kohala and Father Gulstan the responsibility for Hāmākua. The 29-year-old Belgian was elated. With a confrere close at hand, loneliness and depression would vanish, replaced by camaraderie, the weekly confessional, and laughter. Finally, he would have the time to attend to all of the essential duties of a priest. His three largest congregations in Kohala were each clustered around one of the all-wood chapels he had built and were within five to seven hours of one another by horseback. Visiting each on a regularly scheduled basis was now feasible, and now there would be sufficient time to devote to the practice of medicine without compromising the more important spiritual components of his ministry.

Oblivious to the leprosy epidemic in Norway and Dr. Hansen's research endeavors, Father Damien noted with alarm the increase in the number of Hawaiians in Kohala with the early manifestations of leprosy. The children of several of his parishioners who were now confined at the leper settlement had contracted the disease. The tiny whitish spots on the cheek of a twelve-year-old girl had enlarged rapidly, then ulcerated, forming an ugly, foul-smelling crater 3 inches in diameter. The fingers on the right hand of a nine-year-old boy were contracting into the shape of a claw, rendering the hand useless. Two young lives were in ruin and would terminate on Moloka'i in the absence of a priest.

Thanks to his previous teaching sessions with Dr. Wetmore, he had learned how to recognize the early signs of leprosy. When a parishioner with tear-filled eyes stood before him and pointed to a small whitish spot, a freckle of depigmented skin on the face, arms, or leg, they both knew the potential consequences should the blemish prove to be the initial manifestation of leprosy. Damien would calmly pick up a pin and gently prick the center of the suspicious lesion. If the pinprick elicited pain, he would smile and reassure the person that leprosy was not the problem. Then both would kneel and offer a prayer of thanksgiving.

When there was no sensation of pain following the prick of the pin, Damien would run his fingers over the skin surrounding the lesion, searching for a confirmatory sign—a telltale swollen nerve. The presence of an enlarged palpable nerve in combination with a depigmented anesthetic spot on the skin spelled *ma'i Pākē*—leprosy! Then both would kneel and offer a prayer for intersession. Father Damien then had no alternative but to urge the unfortunate person to comply with the law and journey to the Kalihi Hospital in Honolulu to have the skin lesion evaluated by a licensed government physician.

The initial reaction of most Hawaiians who discovered that they had leprosy was to hide the suspicious skin lesion from everyone, especially the authorities, for as long as possible. Predictably, when the lesions could no longer be hidden, some elected to flee and spend the remainder of their lives hiding in remote areas, concealing themselves in caves or in the dense foliage of rain forests near villages where relatives could surreptitiously supply them with food and clothing. In the Hawaiian Islands the Segregation Law of 1865 seemed unenforceable—and the growing epidemic unstoppable.

ONLY EIGHTEEN OF Father Damien's letters written between 1870 and the day he departed for the leper settlement, May 10, 1873, have survived. They are terse and factual, yet cheerful and enthusiastic. In the three and a half years that they span, Damien tells of his first serious illness in Hawai'i. The details of the illness are sketchy. In early 1870 he was incapacitated by a dysentery-like disease that reduced him to "skin and bones." The resulting weight loss from the fever and diarrhea that plagued him for weeks probably was in the 40- to 50-pound range, rendering him too weak to attend to his normal duties. Fathers Charles and Gulstan would have attended to the critical needs of his parishioners, and if Father Charles had his way, Damien's attending physician would have been none other than Dr. Wetmore from Hilo.

The most probable cause of a dysentery-like illness was an infection of the bowel caused by one of the invasive intestinal bacteria such as Salmonella, Shigella, or Campylobacter, or perhaps the intestinal parasite that causes amebiasis. These infections would have featured fever, abdominal pain, and a profuse diarrhea, bloody at times. Without treatment with one of our modern-day antibiotics, the diarrhea could have persisted for weeks until the body was finally able to muster sufficient antibodies and defensive blood cells to neutralize, then eliminate the invaders.

During his protracted recuperation, Father Damien was kept

informed as to the key happenings in the Hawaiian mission effort. He learned of the sudden death of Donald Walsh, the second resident superintendent of the leper settlement. In the short time Walsh had been in charge of the Kalaupapa operation, he and his wife had been responsible for several major improvements. First, Walsh had overseen the construction of an all-wooden house for himself and his wife and a small school building for the children with leprosy. Mrs. Walsh, the "nurse of the lazaretto," had improved the care provided the hospitalized lepers by emphasizing better nutrition and insisting upon cleanliness. Together the couple had successfully negotiated with the Board of Health for a herd of milk cows to supply milk for the children and the most seriously ill adults.

When no one applied for the position of resident superintendent to replace Mr. Walsh, the Board of Health prevailed upon Mrs. Walsh to remain until a qualified replacement for her husband could be found. In the absence of a male authority, the impotent constabulary made little effort to maintain law and order, and two rival factions of lepers revolted, throwing the settlement into chaos. In an effort to restore order the board replaced Mrs. Walsh with a Hawaiian by the name of Kaho'ohuli, a leper who had been a captain in the king's guard. He was able to crush the revolt and reestablish a semblance of order, but during his brief sojourn in office nothing further was done to improve the lot of the lepers.

AFTER A LENGTHY convalescence, Father Damien resumed his duties, which included his part-time practice of medicine and his favorite pastime, the construction of all-wood chapels and rectories. In his July 9, 1870, letter to Father Modeste he wrote: "We are thinking of building a small rectory in Kua [Ka'ū] for the priest and his helper. Perhaps you can spare a Brother to come to help with the chapel; if not, I shall be patient and build it myself assisted by a Christian native who is skilled."[16]

No brother was free to assist with the project, so Damien—with the help of a native carpenter—built the rectory in Ka'ū, the district southwest of Puna. The task was a way of saying thank you to Father Nicaise, the priest who had graciously spent weeks with him in 1864, introducing him to his parishioners in Puna.

As the year ended, Damien closed his annual letter to his brother,

Father Pamphile, with a plaintive request: "Is there no more hope of seeing you in our ranks in the Sandwich Islands? . . . Remember, in entering the Novitiate you were especially drawn to the missions, and you once criticized me for not having the same zeal as you did to become a missionary. I was deeply pained when I learned that you remained silent in 1867 when our Very Reverend Father invited you to join us, and instead allowed another to take your place as you had in 1863."[17]

Father Pamphile's response to his younger brother's criticism was a protracted silence.

ONE SUNDAY IN mid-July, 1872, Damien wrote long letters to his parents, to his sister Pauline, the Ursuline Sister, and to Pamphile. In each he mentioned that he had had no news from any family member in over three years. He suspected, and probably correctly, that the poor mail service to the Islands was responsible for the protracted delay.

In his letter to Pauline he confided that he was heavily engaged in the practice of medicine: "Visiting the sick is one of my chief duties each day. One must above all fight off their native doctors, most of whom are sorcerers. In cases of sickness they still use idolatrous sacrifices. Almost every illness is attributed to a mysterious cause. One must use every possible means to disabuse these poor people of these superstitions. By preaching and watching over them at all times when they are sick, I hope that a good number of my Christians will die properly, not prematurely."[18]

Resigned to never seeing his older brother again, Damien began his letter to Pamphile with an apology, surmising that his sharp criticism in 1870 had deeply offended his older brother: "It seems to me that you are angry with me; for the last three years you have not condescended to write me a letter. Perhaps you were offended by the criticisms I made in my letter of October, 1870. Pardon me, dear brother, for my discourteousness."[19]

THE SITUATION AT THE leper settlement deteriorated further in 1872 as a huge number of new inmates taxed the crowded facility's resources. Two to three percent of the Native Hawaiian population was infected, and the number was steadily increasing. Complaints decrying the absence of medical care at the leper settlement rose to a crescendo, forcing the Board of Health to hire a physician who would make periodic, one-day visits to Kalawao. Dr. Hutchison, a practicing physician in Honolulu, accepted the challenging task. In 1872 he made several visits to Moloka'i, spending a day at a time examining the lepers and dispensing medicines for the complicating secondary illnesses. As was the practice of the day, Dr. Hutchison diligently avoided direct physical contact with the lepers. Following each visit he repeatedly warned the board that the epidemic was clearly out of control.

On January 8, 1873, less than a month following the death of King Kamehameha V, the thirty-seven-year-old Prince William Charles Lunalilo, called *"ke ali'i lokomaika'i"*—"the kind chief"—by his countrymen, was elected king of the Hawaiian Kingdom.[20] Although King Lunalilo was handicapped by alcoholism and pulmonary tuberculosis, he promptly addressed the kingdom's major health problem—leprosy—which continued to threaten to annihilate his subjects. Since in his opinion the Board of Health had failed in its mission to enforce the mandatory segregation policy, he appointed a new Board of Health.[21] To add executive authority to the board, King Lunalilo appointed E. O. Hall, a successful American businessman and his minister of the Interior, to be its president. This new board, and each one thereafter, was chaired by a member of the king's cabinet. The president was assisted by a recording secretary, knowledgeable physicians, and prominent citizens, including lawyers and clergymen—all Protestants.

Prompted by his advisors, the king choose Dr. George Trousseau, a French physician with impeccable credentials, to study the leprosy epidemic and make recommendations to contain it. Dr. Trousseau stunned the monarch by predicting that within three years, 5 to 6 per cent of the native population would be infected if there were not an immediate all-out implementation of the Leprosy Segregation Act of 1865. He was appalled, he claimed, to observe that there were more lepers residing outside of the leper settlement than were confined within it. The French physician warned that a continuation of the failed public health policy would inflict catastrophic suffering on the Hawaiian population, and that the current laissez-faire attitude toward leprosy could result in the extermination of the Hawaiian race. Confronted by so frightening a prospect, the king gave the board full authority to rectify the situation and save his kingdom.

As a first step to meet the crisis, Samuel Wilder of the Board of

Health was authorized to seek out and segregate all lepers, by force if necessary. Accompanied by Chief Marshal Park and a band of armed marshals, Wilder systematically scoured the Islands and identified all persons with a skin condition that could possibly be leprosy. Natives with eczema, psoriasis, and syphilis were forced to board the *Kilauea* for transport to the Kalihi Hospital in Honolulu for examination by government physicians who would determine whether or not their dermatitis was true leprosy. The program proved effective, and during the first months of 1873 nearly 1,200 persons with suspected leprosy were examined by government physicians; 560 with confirmed leprosy were sent to the Moloka'i settlement.[22] No one with leprosy was exempted and, much to everyone's surprise, it was announced that Peter Kaeo, Queen Emma's cousin and a distinguished member of the House of Nobles, would be deported to the settlement along with an American and five other foreigners.

To limit the burdensome expansion of the population at the settlement, family members and the hired *kōkua* were no longer granted residency. Spouses were prohibited from accompanying wives or husbands; a parent was no longer allowed to accompany and care for a child with leprosy. This was an unwelcomed reversal of the earlier policy and it provoked a storm of bitter complaints.

Another new ruling that met with even greater resentment was the curtailment of all visitation rights. In a letter to the editor of the *Pacific Commercial Advertiser*, Dr. Trousseau, the Board's medical consultant, stated, "Isolation, and *thorough* isolation, as the Board understands it, and is carrying it out, will be one of the most efficient means of arresting the progress of the disease. . . . I never in my life had to witness more painful scenes of physical and mental suffering."[23]

The settlement's major problems, however, remained unaddressed: inadequate housing; a limited water supply; insufficient food stuffs for the majority; poor clothing; no staffed children's home; no resident clergymen; and most lamentable, no on-site professional medical care.

While Father Damien knew of the problems plaguing the leper settlement, he prudently remained aloof from any direct involvement in the political dialogue regarding the operation of the settlement. This was the official stance of the Catholic Church in the islands—no direct involvement in the internal affairs of the host nation. Damien commiserated with distraught family members denied visitation and prayed for the Lord God to comfort and console the victims of leprosy, but he never publicly criticized the Hawaiian government's administrative policies.

In May 1873, Father Damien took what was to be a short leave of absence from the Kohala District and boarded an interisland steamer for Maui where he was to join Bishop Maigret and his fellow priests at Wailuku to celebrate the dedication of the recently completed St. Anthony's Church, a magnificent structure that had taken the brothers six years to build. He enjoyed these excursions because it gave him the opportunity to escape from the intellectual isolation of the Big Island and enjoy a stimulating reunion with his peers. But as he departed Kohala his peace of mind was jolted by an "inner voice" that told him that he would never again minister to his congregations in Kohala.[24] Damien was bewildered by this revelation, but upon arrival in Maui he said nothing to his superiors about his startling premonition.

Following the dedication of St. Anthony's Church, Bishop Maigret assembled the dozen attending priests for a roundtable discussion regarding the problems facing the Catholic mission in the Kingdom of Hawai'i. He opened the session by confessing that one of his major frustrations was the Church's inability to minister effectively to the several hundred Catholics on the island of Moloka'i and to the two hundred Catholic lepers confined to the leper settlement. Looking directly into the faces of Fathers Raymond, McGinnis, Léonor, Rupert, Boniface, Gulstan, Grégoire, Aubert, and Damien, he told of his receipt of a petition signed by the two hundred incarcerated Catholic lepers begging for a resident parish priest. "They ask me for a priest who can remain permanently with them; but where to find one?" he had written in his diary.[25] The absence of a resident doctor and ready access to medicines condemned the disease-weakened lepers to a premature death. Facing death alone without the spiritual comfort of the sacraments and a clergyman's prayers was a nightmarish conclusion to life which no person should be forced to experience.

Since the establishment of the leper settlement, Bishop Maigret had allowed one of his priests to journey to the settlement each year, but he had adamantly refused to permit anyone to remain longer than a few weeks. Father Raymond, one of the veteran missionary priests who was stationed on Maui, had been the first to volunteer for the hazardous duty. His initial sojourn had been judged successful despite its brevity. To avoid close contact with the lepers he had begun each day by celebrating Mass outdoors by the sea, and at day's end he conducted an outdoor vesper service against the backdrop of a tropical sunset. Confessions, baptisms, marriages, and burial services crowded the intervening hours. Following his departure the lepers knew the depression of abandonment and steeled themselves for a year in which the presence of God would fade. They contended that this once-a-year visit by a priest was intolerable. To have confession and communion so seldom while attempting to cope with a lethal disease was unacceptable.

Father Aubert Bouillon of Maui, the priest whom Bishop Maigret had turned to the most often to visit the leper settlement, had written in December, 1872, "Since you lack the courage to put a priest there [leper settlement], I am going there without orders, if you do not forbid me." There was no equivocation in the bishop's reply, "Stay where you are!" Bishop Maigret believed that leprosy was far too contagious to risk the life of one of his priests. To have sanctioned such a request would have made him an accomplice to suicide.

In the course of the ensuing discussion, four of the younger priests—Father Damien from Belgium, Father Gulstan Ropert from France, and Fathers Boniface Schaeffer and Rupert Lauter from Germany—proposed a workable rotation schedule in which each of them in turn would spend two or three months at the settlement on Moloka'i before returning to their home districts. During the sojourn at the leper settlement the other three priests would care for the absentee's district.[26] The four convincingly argued that such a rotation scheme wouldn't be detrimental to their district's ministries.

To everyone's surprise, Bishop Maigret approved a trial of the rotation scheme—but with the clear understanding that there was to be no physical contact with a leper, that his priests would never eat food prepared by a leper, nor would a priest ever sleep in a leper's house. The bishop was resolute: *Never touch or allow yourself to be touched by a leper!* The government physicians who examined all suspected lepers at Honolulu's Kalihi Hospital adhered to this dictum, and these physicians remained healthy. His priests must do likewise.

The bishop looked the group over and excluded Father Boniface since he had just concluded the annual Easter visitation. After a moment's reflection the bishop chose Fr. Damien. Not only was the

Belgian priest the youngest and physically the strongest of the four, but he possessed the requisite survival skills—a knowledge of construction, farming, and husbandry. The bishop announced that he would accompany Father Damien to the leper settlement at the end of the week when the next interisland steamer departed for Moloka'i. There was no need to return to Kohala. He would see to it that Father Damien's belongings were packed and shipped to Moloka'i along with the required food and church supplies.

Damien quietly pondered the message of the "inner voice." Could he have misinterpreted the words? While he was to become the first resident priest at the leper settlement, it was only for a term of three months, after which he would be expected to return to Kohala. Time would tell whether he had correctly understood the inner voice.

The bishop was a prudent planner, and he proceeded to list the conditions for serving as a priest to the lepers. Clean, uncontaminated living quarters were essential. None existed at the settlement, so the first order of business would be the construction of a rectory for the priest in residence, and until a suitable rectory was erected his priests would do what Fathers Raymond and Boniface had done—sleep in the open under the stars—and not infrequently in the rain.

Another concern was safe food. Uncontaminated food would be shipped in each week and supplemented by food grown and harvested in a garden tended only by the priest or a nonleper. Each priest would either prepare his own food or have it prepared by a nonleper.

Father Damien had the requisite experience to handle both the construction of the rectory and the farming. During his nine-year tenure on the island of Hawai'i, he had built or refurbished four all-wood churches plus a dozen chapels. The Belgian had been raised on a farm, so planting and tending a large garden in his spare time would be an easy task, pleasant enough to be considered recreational. Damien was the man most likely to succeed in the settlement's wretched environment.

Bishop Maigret's intention was to limit Father Damien's first sojourn to a maximum of three months. Then he would relieve the Belgian by rotating a second priest for a briefer stint. Under ideal conditions—good weather for the prompt delivery of materials and supplies—he believed that Damien could build the rectory and plant the food crops within a three month span while performing the most essential duties of a priest. Given decent housing and an uncontaminated food supply, Damien's replacement would, for the first time in the settlement's history, be able to carry out the full quota of priestly duties. Bishop Maigret knew these four young men. Were one of them allowed to serve the lepers for a period longer than a few months, expediency and complacency would inevitably replace vigilance, and the Sacred Hearts' community would witness its first leper priest.

8

Exile: The First Weeks

*...for I was hungry and you gave Me food; I was thirsty and you
gave Me drink; I was a stranger and you took Me in; I was naked
and you clothed Me; I was sick and you visited Me; I was in prison
and you came to Me....Truly, I say to you , as you did it to one of
the least of these my brethren, you did it to Me.*
—Matthew 25:35–36, 40

IT WAS SUNDAY, May 11, 1873. Dawn of his second day at the leper
settlement found Father Damien sheltered beneath the branches of the
lone *pū hala* adjacent to the St. Philomena Chapel. He opened his eyes
and looked up. The sun's invisible brush was tinting the edges of the
cumulus clouds a pale orange and priming the dull gray dome of the
sky a soft pink. A piercing, loud bark from high overhead shattered
the reverie as the jet-black silhouette of a large bird glided effortlessly
across the morning sky. The bark was followed by a piercing scream,
identifying the bird as the *koaʻeʻula*, the red-tailed tropicbird, a species
frequently seen off the windward coasts of the main islands. The bird's
scream was reminiscent of a human cry of anguish and focused
Damien's thoughts on the plight of the lepers and the labors of the day
before him.

He eased himself from under the branches of the *pū hala*, stood
up, and stretched. This would be his first full day as the resident priest.
As was his customary routine, he began it with God by holding his
morning devotions alone, choosing to do so on the shore behind the
tiny St. Philomena's Chapel where the rhythmic caress of the waves on
the rocks was conducive to prayer and meditation.

His morning devotions concluded, Father Damien built a small fire adjacent to the *pū hala* and boiled water for his coffee. Breakfast was simple and quick—strong, black coffee and two of the hard biscuits he had brought with him from Maui. As he munched on his biscuits he surveyed St. Philomena Chapel. Not only was the box-shaped structure too small, but it lacked the esthetics in which to worship so mighty a God, the Creator of mountains, the moon, and the stars. The chapel had no steeple, no bell, and no cross pointing heavenward. At the first opportunity, Damien resolved to remodel and enlarge the box, converting it to an attractive chapel replete with a bell tower. The worship of God was meant to be a joyful and meaningful experience. Only the jubilant ringing of a deep-throated metal bell could provide the proper ambience. Summoning lepers to Mass with the melancholy wail of the conch shell as he was currently forced to do was unacceptable. The disfigured and slowly dying deserved better.

Father Damien blew three times on the conch shell, and within ten minutes St. Philomena Chapel was packed. The overflow congregation surrounded the building, pushing and shoving each other for a chance to peer through one of the open windows and witness what was happening inside. Father Damien stood before the altar and surveyed the congregation of dirty, deformed, poorly dressed lepers that filled the sanctuary and looked up at him expectantly. With a broad smile he repeated his promise to celebrate Mass each morning and hold a vesper service each evening. Following the morning Mass he assured everyone that he would visit the nonambulatory sick and dying. That mission accomplished, he would systematically visit each leper and extend an invitation to each to attend church services.

His announcements completed, Father Damien closed his eyes for a moment of silent prayer. As he prayed his smile vanished, and when his eyes opened his face was solemn. Slowly he turned his head, making eye contact with everyone in the assembled congregation. Then he opened the service with "*We lepers* come into your presence, Almighty God. . . ."[1] The pronouncement "We lepers" stunned the congregation. All eyes were riveted on the priest. Was Father Damien a leper? Was this why he had come to Moloka'i, or was he simply resigned to becoming one of the "unclean"?

In a letter to his brother, Damien described that first morning and his use of the words "We lepers."[2] It was his way of establishing a strong rapport with the lepers—a way of saying he was one of them, a way of assuring them that although he was a haole, he would not shy away from them for fear of contracting the dreaded *maʻi Pākē*.

As the morning Mass proceeded, the putrid odor from the open, festering wounds of the lepers grew stronger and more objectionable. Father Damien did his best to ignore the stench until it became so noxious that he had difficulty concentrating on his homily. The saliva in his mouth took on a salty taste, and he feared he was about to vomit. He swallowed hard and repeatedly. It required all of the self-discipline he could marshal to suppress the urge to excuse himself and rush outside.[3] Such a display of weakness would have been an unforgivable transgression, an indelible memory that his new parishioners would never forget even though they might one day forgive. The benediction lowered the curtain on the agony before the altar. Father Damien walked swiftly down the center aisle to the entrance door, flung it open, and stepped outside into the uncontaminated air. His broad smile returned, and one by one he greeted his parishioners as they left the chapel.

The hours following Mass were as trying as the Belgian had ever known. From the serenity of St. Philomena he walked briskly the 100 yards to the center of Kalawao, where a low picket fence enclosed a cluster of dingy-appearing thatch-roofed buildings, two of which were the designated hospitals that sheltered those lepers unable to care for themselves.[4] It was his intention to minister first to these dying and seriously ill, comforting each victim regardless of religious affiliation. Christ had compassion on the Samaritans. He could do no less for the Protestants and the misguided worshipers of the ancient native gods. For the Catholics he would administer the Sacrament of Extreme Unction to the dying, hear the confessions of the seriously ill, and where appropriate, baptize those who professed belief in the Catholic faith and life eternal.

Resolutely he opened the gate in the picket fence and entered the compound. Anticipating the horror and the stench he was about to encounter, he paused at the entrance to the hospital for the male patients and took a deep breath of untainted air. Then he stooped and stepped through the low entrance into the main room, which was shrouded in shadows. The only light gaining access peeked in through the squares of several small windows. As his eyes accommodated to the dimness, he could make out a long row of patients on either side of a central aisle that ran the length of the room. The lepers lay side by side on the dirt floor. Most lay on thin, woven mats; a few lay directly on the earth. The rank odor from the unwashed bodies and infected skin ulcerations was staggering. His senses of sight and smell were assaulted by the view before him and the nearly overpowering odor of human decay.[5]

From a pocket Damien withdrew a new, long-stemmed clay pipe whose bowl he had already packed with tobacco.[6] He had been counseled that there were only two ways to combat the foul odor of leprosy. One was to mask the odor by inhaling a potent counterodorant like strong tobacco smoke; the other was to wear a neck band soaked with camphor and work in an atmosphere of the vapor. He chose tobacco smoke as the less intrusive alternative. Without apology he struck a wooden match and lit his pipe. As he drew the tobacco smoke into his nose and then exhaled a bluish white cloud, heads turned to stare at the intruder.

After several deep puffs, Father Damien stepped into the room and systematically went from one anguished face to the next. Kneeling at each mat, he removed the pipe from his mouth and introduced himself. He was there to comfort and console, to cheer and encourage, and to pray for forgiveness and eternal life. There was no privacy, no confessional booth, so he bent low to place his ear close to the mouths of the Catholic lepers so he could hear their whispered confessions. In a crouched position, the malodor from the leprosy lesions was so strong he could taste it deep in his throat. The tobacco smoke helped, but it was not enough. To keep from retching he swallowed frequently and fast. His mind screamed: *Dear God in Heaven, am I able to do this?*

As he proceeded from one leper to another, the horror of leprosy—the disease of mankind with the greatest propensity to maim, mangle, and deform the human body—was unveiled: large, open wounds filled with blood-stained cellular debris; hands with fingers contracted into the shape of a claw that could no longer pick up a cup; and bodies that had lost fingers, eyes, noses, ears, toes, and feet. The faces of the patients with lepromatous leprosy were so swollen and grotesquely puffy as to make their owners unrecognizable. Father Damien puffed hard on his pipe. It was repulsive to witness the plight of the adult lepers; but the children—to witness the suffering of God's youngest who were isolated from parental love and support was agonizing.

Conspicuously absent in this so-called hospital were doctors, nurses, and a supply of medicines with which to treat the more common diseases that plagued the lepers and often precipitated their demise. Diarrheal diseases, the full spectrum of skin infections, pneumonia, and tuberculosis stalked the weak and dying. Water for cleaning the open sores and bathing was in disturbingly short supply. The Board of Health had authorized the resident superintendent to hire the *kōkua* or those lepers with the less debilitating tuberculoid form of the disease who were still ambulatory to serve as hospital orderlies. These persons portaged the drinking water, prepared foodstuffs for the patients, and emptied the slop buckets. Little else was done to make the lepers' last days more bearable.

Each time Father Damien knelt down to hear a confession and placed his ear close to a leper with a disfigured face, he experienced "a peculiar sensation in the face, a sort of burning or itching."[7] The same eerie sensation then crept over his lower legs. This was the same discomfort that he had occasionally noted on the Big Island when hearing the confession of a parishioner who had leprosy, and he wondered if this peculiar skin discomfort was merely an overly emotional response to the leprosy victim's plight or whether he might already have contracted the disease. Yet each time he distanced himself from a leper, the itching and the burning vanished. He concluded that the peculiar sensations were a sympathetic, emotional reaction to a horror to which he would never become accustomed.

In the women's hospital he encountered a problem for which he had received no instruction. Before him lay a teenage girl who was being devoured by leprosy. She had never heard of the Christ. Now she was delirious with a high fever from pneumonia, and as she turned her head from side to side in agony, she could not comprehend what he was attempting to tell her about salvation and eternal life. To follow the rules and let this unfortunate girl slip into oblivion seemed unjust. Surely an all-merciful God would understand and forgive what he was about to do. He baptized the girl in the name of God the Father, the Son, and the Holy Ghost. Then he puffed hard on his pipe and proceeded to the side of the next victim.

Before leaving the women's hospital he turned and surveyed the two rows of victims. This wasn't a hospital—it was a morgue! Sprawled on the earthen floor before him was a collection of helpless, dying lepers. In the absence of doctors and nurses, these women were being killed by diarrhea, malnutrition, and fevers of many causes. As a result of this mismanagement, these women were experiencing a prelude to hell, and many precious souls were being lost. What he was witnessing was an affront to the Almighty. Father Damien was convinced that it was his duty to once again assume the role of a part-time physician. Respite from pain and delirium produced an inner peace that allowed a more meaningful worship of Almighty God.

IN HONOLULU, Walter Murray Gibson, the editor and owner of *Ka Nupepa Nuhou*, was ecstatic when he was informed that a relatively unknown Catholic priest had voluntarily gone to Moloka'i to become the leper settlement's first resident clergyman. He credited the priest's prompt response to his persuasive April 15 editorial.

On May 13, the following appeared in *Ka Nupepa Nuhou*:

> *A Christian Hero.* We have often said, that the poor outcast lepers of Molokai, without pastor or physician, afforded an opportunity for the exercise of a noble Christian heroism, and we are happy to say that the hero has been found. When the *Kilauea* touched at Kalawao last Saturday, Bishop Maigret and Father Damien, a Belgian priest, went ashore. The venerable Bishop addressed the lepers with many comforting words, and introduced to them the good father, who had volunteered to live with them and for them. Father Damien formed this resolution at the time and was left ashore among the lepers without a home or a change of clothing except such as the lepers offer. We care not what this man's theology may be, he is surely a Christian hero.[8]

The story struck Honolulu with the force of a tropical storm. Within a few hours everyone was discussing the pros and cons of Father Damien's act. A Catholic priest was sacrificing his life to do what no Protestant minister had had the courage or the brotherly love to do—live among and serve the lowly, outcast lepers. This Catholic priest was condemned to a miserable death, but while he lived he would be revered by all. Gibson's announcement that Father Damien had gone to the leper settlement "without a home or change of clothing except such as the lepers offer" sparked a spontaneous fund drive. People from all walks of life and religious convictions donated money—Catholics, Protestants (including Episcopalians and Mormons), and agnostics.

The first day, $130 was raised—an amount equivalent to the annual income of a day laborer.

An outwardly smiling but inwardly apprehensive Bishop Maigret continued to receive unsolicited public donations for Father Damien, and in less than a week the Belgian priest was referred to throughout the Islands as "the Hero of Moloka'i." The bishop attempted to explain that the Church hadn't abandoned one of its priests on the shore of the leper settlement, that lumber for a house had been ordered, that the young Belgian priest wasn't being martyred—but few chose to listen. Within a month, newspapers in Europe and the United States carried the story of the "priest to the lepers," and "Damien" became a household word.

While pleased by the public's intense interest in Father Damien and the Catholic outreach to the lepers, both Bishop Maigret and Father Modeste were worried about the Board of Health's response. Should the board, whose members were all churchgoing Protestants, become resentful of the laudatory publicity being heaped on a Catholic priest, it could retaliate and permanently confine Damien to the settlement as it had the recalcitrant kama'āina who refused to leave their homesteads.

Totally oblivious to the fact that he had become a celebrity, Father Damien began the task of seeking out and introducing himself to each leper confined to the Kalaupapa Peninsula. As he did so he made a mental list of his nonspiritual priorities. Heading the list was the urgent need for a supply of basic medicines with which to alleviate much of the misery and pain. He believed that it was difficult if not impossible for most persons to contemplate God and his goodness while in the throes of a painful, debilitating illness.[9] St. Damien had led many to Christianity by compassionately treating them when sick. He could do no less, but in so doing there was a risk, especially when he cleaned and bandaged the dirty, pus-filled wounds. He pondered the consequences should he violate his bishop's directive and knowingly make physical contact with lepers in order to administer the sacraments or cleanse a wound.[10]

Second on his list was how to solve the problem of the inadequate supply of clean water.[11] Because of the serious shortage, hands and bodies were washed infrequently; consequently food was frequently contaminated, and weekly bouts of diarrhea had become a way of life. Worse yet was the lack of water for proper wound cleansing. Open skin ulcerations crusted with pus needed to be cleaned and dressed on a daily basis. Dr. Wetmore in Hilo had been emphatic in his instructions regarding the necessity of wound cleanliness to prevent infection and premature death. Father Damien was appalled to see open skin ulcers exposed to dirt, lice, and flies. It wasn't that the lepers were too lazy to wash, the problem was the great distance they had to go to obtain water. To reach the nearest stream in the distant Wai'ale'ia Valley required a trek of over a mile, a feat lepers on foot found difficult, especially when they had to carry the water in large tins or calabashes. Only the affluent who owned horses were able to portage an adequate supply of water.

The solution was obvious. When it rained, tiny streams cascaded down the face of the *pali* to form larger streams that merged before making their way to the ocean. If dammed at the base of the *pali*, these streams could provide the water not only for drinking and personal hygiene, but for irrigating fields in which to grow both the wet and the dry taro, sugarcane, and the nineteen varieties of sweet potatoes for which the Kalaupapa Peninsula had once been renowned. Father Damien envisioned a large reservoir in the Wai'ale'ia Valley that would supply water to Kalawao by gravity feed through a pipeline.[12] He discussed the feasibility of such an undertaking with the resident superintendent who concurred with his idea and offered to help implement the plan by recruiting some of the healthier lepers to supply the labor. The two men agreed that when next Father Damien went to Honolulu for confession he would introduce himself to the current Board of Health members and offer to supply the labor to construct a proper water system, provided the board supplied the water pipes. The offer of free labor would have great appeal to the board, which was doing its best to operate within its limited budget.

Another pressing problem was adequate nutrition so essential to the health of the lepers.[13] What he observed troubled him. Not only was the food of questionable quality, but it was unfairly distributed. To obtain the recently increased weekly food ration of 5 pounds of mutton or beef, plus 21 pounds of *pa'i 'ai*,[14] a leper had to be physically able to make the 2.5-mile trek to the Kalaupapa wharf or rely upon another person to pick up his food. All too often the designated porter demanded payment in food for his services. *Kōkua*, who were ineligible for the food rations, usually shared the rations of the person for whom they were caring, and often their share was disproportionately large. Milk, so essential for the health of the children with leprosy, was in short supply because there were too few milk cows. Only those lepers housed in one of the two "hospitals" received milk on a regular basis. Worse yet, when stormy weather prevented the longboats from landing at the wharf in Kalaupapa, an all too common occurrence in the winter months, a food shortage resulted. Then the stronger, when hungry, stole from the weaker and the helpless.

Providing an adequate food supply seemed a simple matter. First, incentives could be offered to those lepers physically capable of cultivating large vegetable gardens. Second, a storehouse could be built in which to stockpile emergency food rations to be issued when rough seas prevented the weekly shipment of food. Third, the Board of Health could be petitioned to increase the weekly food allotment and to supply enough dairy and meat cattle to establish self-sufficient herds on Molokaʻi.

Warm clothing was needed. Only the affluent had suitable wardrobes. Because the *pali* blocked the warmth of the sun both morning and late afternoon, those lepers with infected skin lesions shivered when the frequent rain squalls chilled the prevailing wind.[15] Then the poorly clad cursed Kalawao, calling it "Ka Lua Kupapaʻu"—"the corpse tomb." In response to this need the Board of Health annually issued some clothing and blankets.[16] Men received two blankets, a denim shirt, a pair of pants, a hat, and in some years a pair of shoes. Women were given one blanket, a shirt of blue or brown cotton, and a calico dress. These items were expected to last an entire year; however, within two to three months of issue the clothing and blankets were thin, worn, and shabby from the lack of water with which to wash them regularly. For lepers awaiting death, to lie shivering on tiny mats was cruel, and Father Damien resolved to write to the sisters in Honolulu to ask their aid in supplying the necessary clothing and blankets for his lepers.[17]

Much to Father Damien's relief, his concern over the negative reaction of the Protestant lepers to his presence vanished when Deacon Heulu, the leper who was serving as the acting pastor of the Siloama Church, warmly greeted him on that first full day. After introducing himself, Deacon Heulu assured Father Damien that any medical assistance the priest might render to a member of the Protestant congregation would be deeply appreciated, and with Damien's permission he would like to announce from his pulpit the priest's availability and willingness to assist the sick. It was Deacon Heulu's hope that Catholics and Protestants could put aside their theological differences and live in harmony.

During his second full day on Moloka'i, Father Damien took time to write a brief note to update his provincial, Father Modeste:

> I am sending this letter by way of the schooner *Waniki* to let you know that from now on there ought to be a permanent priest in this place. Boat loads of the sick are arriving, and many are dying. I sleep under a pu hala while I wait for the lumber to build a rectory such as you would judge appropriate. Please send me a cask of wine, some spiritual books for reading and study, some shirts, trousers, shoes, a bell, some rosaries, some catechisms, some altar breads both big and small, a sack of wheat and a chest which can be locked. Please ask Father Gulstan to take charge of Kohala while I wait to see if I am to return. At least you should be able to find one of the fathers of Kona to take charge of my district.
>
> You know my conviction; I wish to give myself unconditionally to the poor lepers. The harvest appears to be ripe here. Pray, and ask others to pray both for me and for all here.[18]

It required a full week for Father Damien to search out and minister to each seriously ill leper. When he discovered that a leper had a medical complication such as an upper respiratory tract infection or an improperly cared for skin ulceration, he assumed the role of physician and prescribed a remedial course of treatment. This practice of medicine seriously compromised the time required for a meaningful pastoral visit. He next discovered that lepers who had the assistance of a *kōkua* preferred to live and eventually die in one of the traditional grass huts as far removed from the village center as possible. These Hawaiians were adamant. To be admitted to one of the hospitals was a guarantee of an early death in a setting devoid of family and friends, an ignominious fate that those who could do so opted to avoid. To accommodate this segment of the population, Damien again became a horseman.

Father Damien soon observed that the complaints about premature deaths in the hospitals were valid. To be placed on a mat in those buildings was akin to suicide. Pneumonia and diarrhea were rampant among the debilitated, a guarantee of cross-infection. When death closed the eyes of a hospitalized leper, the body was unceremoniously wrapped in a blanket and dropped like a bag of garbage at a designated pickup site just outside the hospital entrance. Within a few hours a burial detail would arrive, shoo away the flies, and transport the body to a shallow grave they had dug. With no clergyman in attendance, there was no funeral service to assuage the grief of a loved one or friend. Each dead body, an outcast even in death, was simply placed in an open grave as quietly and expeditiously as possible and covered with volcanic earth. This was obscene, and Father Damien promised God that he would reintroduce dignified burials with wooden coffins, constructed by himself if necessary.

As he made his ministerial rounds, Father Damien was appalled by the rampant immorality and lawlessness. Because the resident superintendent was not inclined to confront the perpetrators, robbery, child abuse, and rape went unpunished. In this nightmarish environment, Damien heard repeatedly from the victims of abuse, *"'A'ole kanawai ma keia wahi!"*—"In this place there is no law!" When forced to leave their harmonious family life, the foundation of their security and happiness, many of the lepers engaged in drunken orgies as a means to escape from the segregation nightmare. Damien observed, "The people, mostly all unmarried or separated on account of the disease, were living promiscuously . . . and many an unfortunate woman had to become a prostitute to obtain friends who would take care of her; and her children, when well and strong, were used as servants. Once the disease prostrated them, such women and children were often cast out."[19]

To halt the drunkenness that was responsible for much of the social misbehavior, Father Damien appointed himself the confiscator of home-brewed alcohol and the destroyer of alcohol stills, an action applauded by Deacon Heulu. Armed only with his stout walking stick, Damien dramatically shattered each still he discovered. Because he was recognized to be a holy man, a white man's *kahuna pule*, none of the protesting natives dared to engage in a fight with the short, muscular priest who swung his walking stick with such determination and accuracy.

BACK IN HONOLULU, Father Modeste, the provincial, was flabbergasted by the continuing attention and admiration focused on Father Damien. Because of the Walter Murray Gibson editorials, all Honolulu

was watching the selfless efforts of the lone priest, which in an awkward way placed the entire Catholic mission on trial. To support fully
the efforts of the young priest was essential. Failure was not an option,
so Father Modeste responded promptly to each of Damien's requests
for supplies—food, clothing, and medicines. Even a bell for the St.
Philomena Chapel was shipped before the priest had received the lumber with which to construct the bell tower.

Father Modeste discussed Father Damien's offer to remain permanently at the leper settlement with Bishop Maigret, and the two
were in agreement that once the public's interest in the priest to the
lepers waned, they would commence the agreed-upon rotation of the
four young priests as originally planned. Father Modeste wrote to
Damien: "As to your request regarding your new assignment, nothing
has yet been decided as to whether or not you may remain at Moloka'i.
The white citizens of Honolulu are filled with admiration for your
devotion, and soon will send you some help. You represent something
to them. Be prudent not to expose yourself unnecessarily to contracting this disease. I hope the good God will protect you."[20]

On May 20, Father Damien wrote a hurried note to his provincial updating him and outlining a plan to minister to the healthy
Catholics residing outside the settlement. He knew that leaving and
then returning to the settlement could be viewed as a deliberate violation of the Board of Health's segregation rules, which insisted that
those confined to Kalaupapa remain there in strict isolation. He rationalized that his ministry to all the Christians on Moloka'i would be
pleasing to God who was his lord and master, not the Board of Health.
Since he had no concept of how leprosy was transmitted from one person to another, he believed that as long as he himself was disease free,
he posed no danger to another person.

> There is enough to do here to keep a priest busy from morning to night. I
> already have a list of 210 sick Christians, 20 catechumens, and about 20
> Christians not seriously ill at present. The Chapel will soon be too small, I
> hope. Yesterday at High Mass the singing was magnificent, and there were
> many communions. Since my arrival confessions have been numerous.
>
> After Mass I was told that there are a great number of Christians in
> a valley some miles from here reachable by sea. The place is called
> Pelekunu. It is well populated, about 300 Hawaiians, I would estimate.
> Wednesday after Ascension I plan to spend Sunday there. . . .

I would appreciate a sack of rice, a supply of coffee, and a mule as soon as they can be sent; also a horse with saddle and bridle. This will help me avoid having to use those of the Hawaiians with leprosy. So many dying! So much misery! . . . All of my repugnance for the lepers has disappeared. I do, however, take great precautions.[21]

Father Damien soon discovered that sleeping in the open as he had been instructed was far from ideal. He could cope with the rock-hard mattress of volcanic soil, and he could slip into the bush to relieve himself, but he would never develop a tolerance for the centipedes, scorpions, and ants with whom he shared the shelter of the *pū hala*.[22] Then there were the nights when a chilling rain squall swept out of the blackness and soaked him. On those all too frequent occasions, he grabbed his wet blankets and ran for the shelter of the chapel.[23] Once inside, he draped the wet blankets over a pew in the rear of the dark sanctuary, then groped his way to the altar for a few minutes of prayer. From beneath the altar he would retrieve a native mat he had stored there for such emergencies, make his way back to the chapel entrance, roll out the mat near the open door, and, sheltered from the rain, ease himself down and sleep. He vowed that as soon as the lumber for the rectory arrived he would immediately commence construction.

BECAUSE OF THE acclaim that was being heaped on one of the mission priests by the Hawaiian press and the knowledge that news of the "hero of Molokaʻi" would eventually appear in the European newspapers, Father Modeste wrote to Superior General Bousquet to prepare him for the unanticipated revelation. With the letter he enclosed the newspaper clippings from the various Hawaiian papers and copies of Father Damien's first two letters from Molokaʻi.

As soon as the steamship *Kilauea* arrived at Honolulu the news of this action spread everywhere. One could only hear of the devotion of Father Damien, of the danger he ran of contracting this incurable disease. They admire him, they exalt his sacrifice in staying in the midst of the lepers without lodging and without the necessities of life. Twelve people gathered, among them the Governor, to contribute 50 francs each to be sent to Father Damien for his use. These same twelve, ten of whom were Protestants, came to Mass the following Sunday in the spirit of gratitude.[24]

In the concluding sentences of the letter, Father Modeste revealed that while it had never been the intention of the mission to station Father Damien permanently at the leper settlement, circumstances now dictated that the rotation schedule was being temporarily abandoned.[25]

When Father Damien belatedly received the newspaper stories regarding his "hero of Moloka'i" status, he was aghast. "They are talking about me in the papers. It would be better if they kept quiet. Things here are much more serious than any esteem they might give me."[26]

Within two weeks of his arrival at Kalawao the lumber with which to build the rectory arrived, but there was nothing with which to roof it. In a letter dated May 27, Damien gratefully acknowledged the effort of his provincial to accomplish so swift a delivery and requested "10 packages of shingles with 100 feet of lath and some 2 x 3 rafters" with which to roof the rectory.[27]

By the end of the third week, Father Damien had completed a census of the leper population. Several hundred lepers professed to be Catholic. Double that number were non-Catholics but would benefit from his medical assistance, so he established a visitation schedule that included the option of treating any seriously ill leper regardless of his religious affiliation. He would adhere to the modus operandi of St. Damien; he could do no less.

When he expanded his visitation to include the village of Kalaupapa on the western side of the peninsula, he discovered a colony of more than fifty healthy kama'āina and their families, obstinately clinging to their homesteads in order to carry on farming and fishing as their ancestors had for generations. The kama'āina candidly admitted that the disgrace of abandoning one's ancestral home evoked a far stronger negative emotion than the fear of contracting a chronic—albeit fatal—disease. Half of the kama'āina professed to be Catholics, but they had never had a chapel or a church in which to worship. The only priest they had seen in the past year was Father Boniface from Maui during his Easter visit. The Catholics in Kalaupapa indicated that they would greatly appreciate regular pastoral visits by Father Damien and would be delighted to assist him in constructing their own chapel. He nodded his thanks as he visualized the Kalaupapa chapel. Its beauty would surpass anything he had achieved before.

By the close of his first month, Father Damien found that he was officiating at two to three burials a week, and funerals at the leper settlement were an ordeal. He detested the established routine of burial in a shallow grave without a clergyman. For all Catholics he insisted on burial in a pit 6 feet in depth. True, the soil was volcanic and difficult to dig, but he would have it no other way. At the 6-foot depth the body was protected from being unearthed by the rooting of wild pigs or heavy rains. In addition to insisting on a proper depth for each grave, he introduced the practice of burial in a wooden coffin, a sturdily constructed rectangular box he himself built. Protestants observing the Catholic funeral services politely asked if they might purchase wooden coffins from the priest. Damien answered with a tentative "yes," provided the Protestants join with the Catholic journeymen he was training to become builders of the wooden coffins. To finance the operation he suggested the establishment of an association to raise the money to buy the necessary wood and nails.[28] Catholics and Protestants ignored their religious differences and enthusiastically joined in this venture.

By rising at dawn and laboring until dark, Father Damien was able to find the "free" hours between his duties as a priest and part-time physician to complete the construction of a two-room wooden rectory measuring 10 x 14 feet. The larger room was to serve as a storeroom for the medicines, food, and clothing he planned to obtain and distribute to the impoverished lepers. The smaller room was to serve as his study and bedroom. It was furnished with a table that doubled as a desk, a straight-back chair, and some shelves for the storage of books, utensils, and food. A native mat in a corner of the room, when unrolled on the wooden floor, was his mattress and bed.

As Father Damien went about his daily duties, he planned his next outreach venture. The visit to the thirty isolated Christians in Pelekunu had been successful.[29] He believed that were he to leave the settlement for a few days he could explore the remainder of the island and visit each of the Catholic communities. To reach Moloka'i's main land mass, however, would be a difficult and demanding task. He would first have to scale the nearly vertical 2,000-foot *pali* that isolated both Pelekunu and Kalaupapa from the rest of Moloka'i. After reaching the top, he must then rent a horse from a rancher to explore the main island.

Learning of Damien's need to scale the *pali*, the lepers pointed out the crude zigzag trail that had been carved into its face by Rudolph

W. Meyer, the Board of Health's appointed overseer and the official superintendent of the leper settlement. It was Meyer who controlled the money allocated by the legislature for the leper settlement. They told how Meyer, who lived in the village of Kala'e just over the top of the *pali*, would periodically ride a mule down the treacherous trail to inspect the leper settlement. Once the hour or two inspection tour was completed, Meyer would carefully make his way back up the steep incline and report his findings to the Board of Health. It was possible, however, for a healthy person with two good legs to traverse the trail on foot. Several of the lepers whose legs as yet were unaffected by their disease had used the trail to escape. Father Damien resolved to scale the *pali* and introduce himself to Rudolph Meyer. If the meeting went well, he would rent a horse from Meyer and the exploration of the rest of the island of Moloka'i could begin.

9

A Prisoner Forever!

*The leper who has the disease shall wear torn clothes
and let the hair of his head hang loose, and he shall cover
his upper lip and cry, "Unclean, unclean." He shall remain
unclean as long as he has the disease; he is unclean; he
shall dwell alone in a habitation outside the camp.*
—Leviticus 13:45

BY EARLY JUNE, Father Damien had managed to establish an uneasy balance between his spiritual ministry and his practice of medicine, the latter activity consuming over half of his time. He had asked for and promptly received a large supply of medicinals, which he stored in the new rectory with the temporary thatched roof. The locals watched as the priest dressed in black moved from leper to leper, opening his black bag of medicines to take out and offer a remedy to relieve diarrhea, suppress a bad cough, alleviate a pain, treat indigestion, or combat insomnia. A leper's outlook on his remaining days on earth was brighter in the absence of a nagging, distracting health problem, be it a complication of leprosy or an unrelated illness.

In mid-June, longboats from the leper steamer *Kīlauea* offloaded the shingles and planking for the roof of the rectory. Using a borrowed horse and cart, Father Damien toted the shipment across the peninsula to Kalawao and began. As he labored, he smiled broadly. An unanticipated bonus of his newly acquired notoriety was the promptness with which his superiors were responding to his requests for supplies.

From his rooftop, Father Damien paused to survey the thatched huts that housed the majority of the lepers. Housing for these unfortunates needed to be substantial, with wooden floors and shingled roofs—

109

clean, dry, airy structures that boasted whitewashed exteriors.[1] The homes of his lepers shouldn't mimic the deformities of the occupants.

Were he to establish an all-wood house-building program, he could in time replace all of the thatched huts. To accomplish this he could train a team of carpenters to provide the manual labor. The only problem—and a major one—was the financing of the building materials not available on the peninsula. He was hopeful that the Church would provide start-up funds for such a project and that the Board of Health could be persuaded to help. He resolved to begin his carpenter training program once St. Philomena had been enlarged.

There was another pressing concern. A month had passed since his arrival at the leper settlement and Superintendent Rudolph Meyer had not come down the *pali* trail to make his periodic inspection and meet the new priest. Meyer was a Protestant, and he hoped that religious differences weren't responsible for the slight. So Father Damien decided to scale the 2,000-foot *pali* and meet the man.

As Damien began the ascent he elected to follow the crude, zigzagging path that Meyer had cut into the face of the steep *pali* rather than take a more direct route that would require climbing the steeper, more dangerous portions. Step after careful step he made his way upward, never deviating from the narrow, twisting mule trail. The ascent proved to be physically taxing, even for a young man in peak physical condition. As he climbed, his foot occasionally dislodged a rock that clattered and bounced a hundred feet down the face of the *pali*. There were short stretches where the trail narrowed to a 2-foot wide ledge, from which a person could pause and look straight down several hundred feet. A misstep could be fatal. Concentration on the task at hand and physical fitness were the essential requirements for ascending the *pali*. It would be foolhardy for a leper with a crippled arm or foot to attempt the climb. The *pali* was a formidable prison door, so steep and treacherous that no lock was needed.

Upon reaching the top of the *pali*, Father Damien paused to mop the perspiration from his face and neck. Then he brushed the dust and bits of small leaves and grass from the front of his cassock, straightened his broad-brimmed hat, and trudged along the narrow trail that he had been told led to Superintendent Rudolph Meyer's home. A mile inland he found it: a large, single-story wooden structure. At his knock a balding, well-muscled man opened the door and extended his right hand to welcome the priest. Rudolph Wilhelm Meyer, a well-to-do Protestant landowner, had read about the young Belgian priest in the newspapers, and as they shook hands he inquired whether they should converse in French, German, English, or the Hawaiian language, as he was fluent in all four. The two decided upon English because all of the leper settlement's business matters were conducted in English. Meyer expressed surprise that his guest had had the audacity to leave the leper settlement without the express written permission of the Board of Health. Damien simply stated that he was healthy and so posed no threat to anyone. As a Catholic priest it was his responsibility to minister to all of the Catholics on Moloka'i, not just those at the settlement. Meyer frowned. In his opinion the Board of Health would judge the priest's action as a willful violation of the segregation law.

To lessen the tension, Meyer cordially invited Father Damien into his home and introduced him to his wife, the High Chiefess Kalama Waha. Then, over a cup of freshly brewed coffee, the two learned about each other. Rudolph Meyer, age 47, was a successful rancher and farmer who had immigrated from Germany as a young man with a degree in civil engineering in the hope of participating in the California gold rush.[2] To reach the West Coast of the United States he had sailed first to Australia, then on to Tahiti. By the time he had reached Maui in 1850 the prospect of hunting for gold had lost its appeal, eclipsed by the opportunity to become a rancher on one of the islands in this semitropical paradise. He decided upon Moloka'i, where he met and married the eighteen-year-old high chiefess who owned the land at Kala'e overlooking the Kalaupapa Peninsula. At Kala'e, Meyer built his home and established his ranch. In time the couple had eleven children. Because of his professional background and his marriage to a high chiefess, Meyer was appointed manager of the 150,000-acre cattle and sheep ranch on Moloka'i owned by Princess Ruth Ke'elikolani, the half-sister of King Kamehameha IV and Kamehameha V. He managed well, using his earnings to purchase additional large parcels of land, systematically enlarging his ranch and farm. By age forty he had become the wealthiest and most influential private citizen on Moloka'i.

When queried about his role as the superintendent of the leper settlement, Meyer informed Damien that his success as a manager of the royal lands had prompted the appointment. Living within a mile of the *pali* made it possible for him to visit the settlement on muleback via the *pali* trail every four to six weeks. A sure-footed mule could manage the trek, but cattle found it too steep, and his first attempts to herd beef cattle down the trail to the settlement had been disastrous. The lumbering animals had lost their footing and plunged hundreds of feet to their deaths.

Meyer looked squarely into the eyes of the priest and confided that he feared leprosy more than any other malady. Consequently, during his inspection trips he remained seated on his mule and insisted that no leper approach within 6 feet. Nevertheless, he felt pity for the afflicted and did his best to serve as liaison between the lepers and the Board of Health. In his opinion many of the difficulties experienced in the early years were directly attributable to poor communication, a situation arising from the inability of the resident superintendents appointed by the Board of Health to speak Hawaiian.

Meyer was pleased that Father Damien spoke reasonably good Hawaiian, and he pledged to help implement any reasonable venture the priest might wish to undertake to improve the quality of life in the settlement. After a second cup of coffee the priest stood up to leave and the two men shook hands again. Meyer's grip was firm and his smile sincere. He admired a man who could work with his hands and build things. This Catholic priest was indeed an asset, and when Father Damien rode off to explore the rest of Moloka'i he did so on one of Meyer's fine horses. Meyer watched the priest in black leave and wondered how long the Board of Health would tolerate such a flagrant violation of the segregation law.

Father Damien spent two days traversing the 37-mile-long and 10-mile-wide slipper-shaped island. In sharp contrast to the world's highest sea cliffs that form Moloka'i's northern coast, he found the southern portion of Moloka'i to be a rolling plain of parched grasses, for the annual rainfall is light. The southern coast was lined with *loko i'a*—large fishponds built by the ancient Hawaiians—that supplied the populace with choice fish. It was here in the southern portion of Moloka'i that the majority of the island's two thousand inhabitants lived, including the two hundred who embraced the Catholic faith. Using the homes of the more affluent Catholics as substitute chapels, Father Damien heard confessions and celebrated Mass. In time, he promised himself, he would build beautiful chapels in which these faithful parishioners could worship. His first tour completed, Damien returned the horse to Rudolph Meyer and, after enjoying another cup of coffee, he carefully picked his way back down the *pali* trail.

Two weeks later, Father Damien scaled the *pali* a second time, had coffee with Rudolph Meyer, borrowed a horse, rode to the main port of Kaunakakai, and boarded an interisland steamer for Honolulu. Seven weeks had elapsed since he had knelt in confession and received absolution, a spiritual hiatus that weighed heavily on his conscience. In Honolulu he was warmly received by both the bishop and his provincial. He was invited to devote the first few days of his visit for prayer and meditation in the hushed resplendence of Our Lady of Peace Cathedral.

His spiritual well-being restored, and with the permission of Bishop Maigret, Father Damien introduced himself to Edwin O. Hall, minister of the Interior and president of the Board of Health. In the early course of the discussion that followed, he enthusiastically outlined his plan to dam the river in the Wai'ale'ai Valley and run a pipeline from the resulting reservoir to the leper village using volunteer labor. Hall listened patiently, apparently approved of the idea, and agreed to supply the materials with which to construct the pipeline.

The tenor of the meeting then changed as the expression on Hall's face assumed the demeanor of a judge about to pronounce a sentence of life imprisonment. Had anyone other than this popular priest done what Father Damien was doing, the official response would have been prompt arrest followed by a lengthy jail sentence. In unequivocal terms, Hall reminded the priest that the Board of Health had recently published a revised set of regulations for the better control of leprosy, and that these regulations were intended to insure that *all lepers* resident in the Hawaiian Islands, irrespective of social position or affluence, were to be promptly and permanently segregated at the leper settlement on Moloka'i. Once confined, there was to be *no contact* with visitors except with persons bearing written authorization from the Board of Health, persons deemed critical to the proper operation of the settlement such as Superintendent Rudolph Meyer, or members of a Board of Health inspection team. Leprosy, the Board of Health decreed, was a contagious disease transmitted by person-to-person contact. The new regulations forbade all contact between the infected and the noninfected. All visitation privileges had been suspended. The revised regulations also denied permission for either a family member or a *kōkua* to accompany a leper to the settlement. The noninfected *kōkua* currently in residence at the settlement had been given the option of departing at once or remaining as permanent residents. Any healthy person in residence was indefinitely confined. There would be no exceptions made for members of the clergy—Catholic or Protestant.

Hall paused, noting the concern in Damien's face. Then he continued. Should Father Damien choose to continue as a permanent resident at the leper settlement, the board would not stand in his way, but it could not, would not, ignore his repeated comings and goings. His presence in Honolulu was an affront to the nation's segregation policy. The board was committed to enforcing this policy and most assuredly would do so. The choice was Damien's. To remain a free man he must never return to the leper settlement. If he chose to return, it meant incarceration for the remainder of his life.

A worried Damien hurried to inform his superiors of these disturbing changes in the segregation policy, but was told to ignore the warning because the board would probably continue, as it had done in the past, to disregard the comings and goings of the clergy.

ON THE MORNING OF June 29, while Father Damien was still in Honolulu, the schooner *Kīna'u* dropped anchor 75 yards from the Kalaupapa wharf and began to disembark the latest group of lepers. Among the somber-faced exiles were three celebrities: Peter Kaeo, William Ragsdale, and Jonathan Napela.[3] Peter Young Kaeo, one of the *ali'i*, was the dowager queen's cousin and a lifetime member of the prestigious House of Nobles, whose royal rank had shielded him from incarceration until William Lunalilo became king. Kaeo is important in the Damien story because he was an obsessive letter writer, and the letters he wrote to Queen Emma give his impressions of Father Damien and tell of the conditions at the leper settlement during the period of his brief residence.[4]

The second celebrity, William P. Ragsdale, was less affluent but far better educated than Peter Kaeo. Ragsdale, a *hapa haole*, a part-Hawaiian whose father was an American immigrant, was a prominent lawyer who was best known for his service as the principal bilingual translator for the Hawaiian legislature. Overnight he had become a celebrity when he voluntarily committed himself to the leper settlement before a visible lesion of leprosy was apparent.

Jonathan H. Napela, the third celebrity, was another of the *ali'i*, a nonleper of chiefly rank, a former Maui magistrate, and one of the first three Hawaiians to join the Mormon Church, which he now served as an elder. His primary concern was for his wife, Chiefess Kiti Richardson Napela, who had advanced leprosy. Since nonleper spouses were no longer permitted to reside at the leper settlement, Napela had requested and been granted special permission by the Board of Health to serve as her *kōkua* provided he would accept the position as the new resident superintendent of the leper settlement and remain there indefinitely.

The lepers, including Ragsdale and Napela but not Kaeo, left the *Kīna'u* in groups of twelve, each clutching a bag of possessions and taking a seat in one of the longboats for transport to the landing wharf. An exception was made to accommodate royalty. Two longboats transported Peter Kaeo and his possessions to the wharf—the trunks that contained his wardrobe, his boxed library, a desk, several chairs, two caged birds, a horse, and a week's supply of food.[5]

Despite the preferential treatment, Kaeo was despondent. He had been humiliated when he had been escorted aboard the *Kīna'u* under armed guard along with the other lepers. The offense was an unforgivable breach of royal etiquette. He was, after all, a prominent member of the royal family, a descendant of the ancient kings of Kaua'i and a great-grandson of Keli'imaika'i, a younger half-brother of King Kamehameha I, the founder of the united Hawaiian Kingdom. Because of his royal lineage he was not only affluent but one of the twenty lifetime members of the House of Nobles.[6] True, he had leprosy, but in his opinion he wasn't one of the common lepers, one of the "unclean" *maka'āinana* that people of his social status had to fear.

Although Peter Kaeo had had leprosy for several years, he had not only continued to attend the House of Nobles sessions in Honolulu, but every social event sponsored by Lot Kamehameha, King Kamehameha V. In 1868, the concerned king, Queen Emma's brother-in-law and ardent admirer, had written to her expressing his concern: "Peter Kaeo ought to be put in Kalihi Hospital.[7]. . . It would be an act of humanity to have him removed there because he would get the proper restraint on his appetite and person. Shall I see that he is put in?"[8] How Queen Emma replied is unknown, but Peter remained a free man until 1873 when King William Lunalilo complied with the advice given him by Dr. Trousseau on behalf of the newly appointed Board of Health: *All lepers must be isolated! No exceptions! No one is above the law!*[9]

From the landing wharf, Peter, assisted by an entourage of well-paid *kama'āina*, moved directly into his own private residence, the best frame house on the peninsula, which had been purchased for his exclusive use. The house stood on the lower reaches of a treeless slope between the *pali* and Kauhakō Crater and was well separated from the clusters of thatched huts that housed the majority of the "unclean" *maka'āinana*. Four disease-free kama'āina were hired as permanent servants—two men to do the manual labor, a girl to cook, and a boy to care for his horse. Fearful of further contamination, Peter avoided all contact with the resident lepers.

Peter was thirty-seven, a single male who like so many of the *ali'i* during those days abused alcohol, ate to excess, and avoided physical exercise. His goal in life was to revel in the activities of the royal court with its convivial social agenda of parties, carousing, and gambling. His major social impediment was his poor command of the English language, which was reflected in his halting speech, faulty grammar, and atrocious spelling.[10]

During his confinement Peter wrote three or four letters each week to his friends and acquaintances in the Islands. Queen Emma was a frequent recipient because she was the one person with the authority and resources to respond promptly to his needs while commiserating with his isolation-induced melancholia. In a letter written to Queen Emma two weeks after his arrival, Peter mentioned that he had met the resident Catholic priest, Father Damien. "I have had a call from the Catholic Priest. He has been Converting some Natives and a Woman by the name of Hila, Mrs. Tallant once, has become a member of that Church. He has not spoken a word about Religion to me. I think that Bill Ragsdale told him that I belong to the Reformed Church. He is a very nice man and he has told Napela (Mormon elder) for all the different Religions to set aside a day for Fasting."[11]

Peter's second encounter with Father Damien occurred four days later, and religion was one of the topics of discussion. To Queen Emma he wrote:

The Catholic Priest called on me last Friday the 18th. He had been calling on the sick. We got to talking on different matters till we got to Religion. He asked me whether I was ever Baptized. I told him I was. He asked me whether I had any Catholic Papers. I told him I had not but pointed to my Prayer Books. He then opened one and asked me whether I belonged to the Church of England. I told him I did. Then he said their was very little difference between the English and Catholic Church, that they the Catholics acknowledge the Pope as their head and the Queen as the head of the Church of England. I told I believed and was satisfied in the Church I am now in and that alone. So we dropet [sic] the subject but I do really believe he wanted to get me in theirs.[12]

As was his custom, Father Damien introduced himself to each new arrival. He found William Ragsdale an engrossing personality. The man had a reputation for being a shrewd politician who relished power and loved women, yet he had voluntarily committed himself to the leper settlement.[13] What Damien did not know at the time of their meeting was that Ragsdale was maneuvering to become the next resident superintendent. In that post he hoped to regain some of his lost power and be in a far stronger position to command female companionship.

Shortly following his arrival at the leper settlement, Ragsdale wrote to the Board of Health to reaffirm his secret pledge to keep them informed about the living conditions and the morale of the lepers. "I will carefully report upon everything that occurs here, either to yourself or through Mr. Meyer."[14] The Board of Health was pleased. For the first time it had a trusted and knowledgeable informant inside the leper settlement. The board had already made the commitment to replace the present resident superintendent with Jonathan Napela, but should Napela not work out, Ragsdale would be the logical successor.

Later in the week Father Damien greeted Jonathan Napela, the Mormon elder, and his ill wife, Kiti. The reception was frigid for the Mormon considered Damien a misdirected heretic who was leading the lepers away from the true God. Napela informed Damien that in addition to serving as the new resident superintendent, he would now minister to the Mormons. If Father Damien chose to continue to aid the Mormon lepers in his capacity as a physician, Napela would sanction the act, but he would not tolerate proselytizing.

The first Sunday Napela was in residence he held an open-air church service for the Mormon lepers, a practice he continued throughout his sojourn at the settlement. Since he had been educated at the Lahainaluna Seminary by Congregationalist teachers, the board judged he would be a definite asset, and within a week of his arrival the board confirmed his appointment as the new resident superintendent.[15] Ragsdale would keep them fully informed as to how well the Mormon governed.

AT THE HAWAIIAN Evangelical Association's annual meeting in June, forty-eight Protestant ministers, Caucasians and Hawaiians, wrestled with the dilemma the leprosy epidemic had thrust upon them.[16] Because of the Gibson editorial, a lone Catholic priest was being eulogized for his courage in ministering to the lepers confined on Moloka'i. This was an embarrassment to the Congregational Church because there was no way they could match the fearless act. This relatively unknown Catholic was risking his life in a venture of which they were mortally afraid. He was doing what Christ would have done, but Christ was the Son of God and immune from leprosy. They were mortal and not immune. Were a Protestant to take up residency in Moloka'i, he would not only be placing his life in jeopardy, but he would be forced to leave his wife and children behind in a safe environment—or take them with him and risk their lives. To add to the association's humiliation, the Protestant lepers at the settlement were employing the same strategy that apparently had proved successful for the Catholics. They had petitioned for a resident pastor, a call no Protestant minister in the Islands was willing to answer.

The association's ministers concluded that their duty was to "teach and persuade all the people to obey the law of God and segregate the lepers from among us. . . . teach every leper who cleaves to his people and refuses to go away, that he is sinning against the lives of men and against the law of God."[17] The biblical support they cited for this stance was the Mosaic law in the thirteenth chapter of Leviticus that mandated that all lepers were unclean and therefore were to be isolated from the healthy populace.

During Father Damien's sixteen-year residency at Kalawao, no white Protestant clergyman had the courage or the faith to answer the call to become the first resident Protestant minister.

IN JULY THE BOARD of Health made good on King Lunalilo's April promise to do everything within his power to make the leper settlement more livable. Building materials arrived at the Kalaupapa wharf and were transported by oxcart to Kalawao for the construction of a community store in the Kalawao village. *Kōkua* were hired to staff the store, which "sold every variety of staple goods" and clothing at cost. The board announced that it was abandoning the failed policy of an annual clothing distribution and instead would issue each leper a voucher in the amount of "six dollars" on the first of October for the purchase of winter clothing.[18]

During July and August there was an acute shortage throughout the Hawaiian Islands of poi, the main staple in the native diet. On several occasions the leper settlement did not receive its weekly supply. In his letters to Queen Emma, Peter Kaeo commented on the distress the food shortage caused the common leper, and he always remembered in closing to thank her for shipping his uninterrupted supply of quality foodstuffs, which always included poi.[19]

As the food shortage became more acute, the disgruntled lepers looked for a scapegoat and focused their anger on Jonathan Napela, the recently appointed resident superintendent. When Napela distributed the rice and salted salmon that had been stockpiled to meet such emergencies, he was accused of gross incompetence. In the midst of the altercation, William Ragsdale suggested to the Board of Health that there was no reason why the leper settlement couldn't supply most of its own poi by simply cultivating taro in the three valleys of the Kalaupapa Peninsula, provided there was an incentive to do so. The Catholic priest was setting an example by cultivating a large garden. The lepers could be induced to do the same. The board seized the offer and on August 15 Ragsdale was commissioned "to carry out a contract . . . with 42 residents of Kalawao, *kōkua*, and others, to cultivate taro."[20] The board recognized that in Ragsdale they had a problem solver who would be an excellent replacement for Napela. The Mormon elder seemed incapable of maintaining order and quelling the rising discontentment at the settlement. The expedient solution was obvious. A motion was made and passed to discharge the ineffective Napela and replace him with the dynamic Ragsdale by the end of the year.

In August the anticipated water pipes were delivered to the settlement. Father Damien joined forces with William Ragsdale, who had assumed the unofficial role of settlement leader, to recruit the able-bodied lepers and *kōkua* to supply the labor to construct a reservoir and lay the water pipes from the spring in Wai'ale'ia Valley to the hospital grounds. To ensure that a good water supply was within easy reach of the Kalawao lepers, intermediate taps along the course of pipeline were installed.[21]

Finally the lepers had the water they needed, but the continuing food shortage was resulting in widespread hunger and malnutrition. In a valiant effort to offset the poi shortage with meat and milk, Rudolph Meyer tried repeatedly to herd cattle down the treacherous *pali* trail, losing a third of the animals with each attempt. In early August the Board of Health dispatched a small delegation that included Samuel G. Wilder and Dr. Trousseau to assess the situation. Peter Kaeo wrote to Queen Emma to tell of his invitation as a member of the House of Nobles to a luncheon hosted by Father Damien for the visiting members of the Board of Health: "I forgot to tell you that when Wilder and his party were here Father Damien asked us to his House to partake of his Luncheon which he had served out on the table for the Party. We all sat to the table and a Bottle of Clarate was opened and served, some in glasses and the rest in bowls, as Damien had only three glasses."[22]

WHEN FATHER DAMIEN assumed the duties and responsibilities of a part-time physician, he did so at the expense of his spiritual ministry. To care for the forty lepers in the hospital required the services of a full-time doctor, time Damien simply did not have. As if in answer to his prayer for assistance, a man who had earned his living as a physician's aide at the Kalihi Hospital stepped ashore with the latest group of lepers. His name was William Williamson, a haole with a genuine desire to continue in his chosen vocation. Father Damien immediately invited Williamson to join him in his hospital rounds and was impressed with the man's knowledge of medicine and his skill in caring for the most desperately ill lepers. Williamson was about as close to a true physician as the leper settlement was apt to have, and Ragsdale, the new resident superintendent, was persuaded to hire him to work exclusively in the two hospitals. Relieved of this arduous task, which was consuming five to six hours a day, Father Damien was able to focus his attention on spiritual matters and confine his medical practice to the care of the less seriously ill lepers residing outside the hospital.[23]

Father Damien continued to challenge both the resolve and the tolerance of the board by climbing the *pali* each month to minister to the small Catholic congregations on Moloka'i. The board viewed Damien's actions as a flagrant violation of its segregation policy, and in September it took a definitive step to curtail the unauthorized wanderings of the itinerant "hero of Moloka'i." In an official letter, Damien was ordered to obey the segregation laws and to immediately desist from leaving and then returning to the leper settlement.[24]

A distraught Father Damien immediately wrote to Bishop Maigret and Father Modeste, enclosing the Board of Health's letter. Were he to choose to remain at the leper settlement, he would be incarcerated for the rest of his life, and no priest would be allowed to visit and confess him.

Bishop Maigret had anticipated this action by the board, so he assumed an indignant pose and lodged a strong protest with both the Board of Health and French Consul Theodore Ballieu. The French were viewed as protectors of the Catholic Church in the Pacific, and the bishop gambled that the Hawaiian government wouldn't risk another visit from French gunboats.

The Board of Health refused to be intimidated and, in a lengthy letter to Bishop Maigret, reiterated the reasons why the prohibition was nonnegotiable.[25] Bishop Maigret passed the letter to the French consul, who in turn intensified the diplomatic pressure on the Hawaiian government. The king and his Board of Health refused to be coerced. There was a strong American naval presence in the Islands, and a French show of force would undoubtedly invite American countermeasures. Weeks passed. Father Modeste, the provincial, found the delay intolerable so he boarded an interisland steamer for Moloka'i to meet with and confess Father Damien. No priest for whom he was responsible would be denied confession for a protracted period. But when Father Modeste attempted to leave the steamer when it anchored off the Kalaupapa wharf to offload some cattle and sheep, the ship's captain threatened to arrest him should he violate the Board of Health's prohibitions by going ashore.

In a letter to the superior general, Father Modeste recounted the incident:

> The dear Father who wished to go to confession tried to come on board, but as soon as his canoe approached the steamer they shouted to him to come no nearer. What to do?

"I am going to make a general confession," he [Father Damien] said, "and can you give me absolution? The letter from the ministry prohibits me from going beyond the limits set for the lepers. If I go outside these boundaries I will not be allowed to return to administer the last sacraments to the dying Christians."[26]

Kneeling in the bobbing canoe, Father Damien shouted his confession in French to his provincial who stood at the ship's railing encircled by a few curious bystanders.[27] The provincial sensed the humiliation the bareheaded priest in the wave-tossed craft was forced to endure and vowed never again to permit such an indignity.

When Father Aubert Bouillon, the resident priest on Maui and a colleague who had become a good friend of Father Damien, learned from Father Modeste of the open boat incident, he decided that his brother priest deserved a proper, private confession, so he carried out a clandestine plan to accomplish it. A year later he wrote of this misadventure:

In November, 1873, I was asked by a sick, old Frenchman who resided on Moloka'i to come. . . . I saw a chance to strike two blows with one stone.

So I rented a horse for ten sous under the pretext that I wanted to go to visit some Christians on another part of the island. This was in part true; I left my biretta behind and put on the straw hat. When I got near the village on the road to the leper settlement I took off my cassock and dressed like a haole with a red necktie. In the village I kept myself at a distance from the houses, lest anyone recognize me. I proceeded without difficulty until I passed the last house on the trail to the pali. Then I became aware of suspicious glances and elected not to proceed, but to spend the evening hours in the house of a Christian until it was dark. . . . I descended the 2000 foot pali in the dark using only a pickaxe. It was filled with precipices and its length was doubled by the continual zigzagging of the trail. I groped my way down, dragging myself along for three long hours. At the bottom of the pali I lost my way. . . . Finally, after 3½ hours I knocked on Fr. Damien's door. He was waiting for me. I stayed with him a day and a night, and at dawn of the second day I began my ascent of the pali on foot. I climbed up in half the time it took me to go down.[28]

Fifteen years later, Father Aubert related the outcome in another letter: "In spite of the secrecy, I had been seen. The police came to arrest me on my return to Maui with a formal complaint from the government. I in my turn denounced them to the Bishop. Fortunately, public opinion was on our side, and the government was forced to relent."[29]

In a letter to Queen Emma dated October 27, 1873, Peter Kaeo described a distraught Father Damien who had apparently lost or misplaced the food vouchers he had offered to redeem for some of the bedridden lepers. Without a voucher, regardless of whether it had been lost, stolen, or sold, food could not be obtained at the store in Kalawao.

> I learned that Father Damien had lost some checks which belong to the Natives, and which he Damien had taken the responsibility to take from Mr. Rose and give it to the poor Natives that belongs to his church, and are too weak to appear personally to Mr. Rose. The poor Man was so confused that he was picking [up] strips of Paper that was scattered on the floor, asking the Natives whether they had seen any checks, and whether he had given checks to the natives by mistake, and all sorts of questions, and actually Crying.[30]

How the matter of the missing vouchers was resolved is unknown. An appeal to either William Ragsdale or Rudolph Meyer may have resulted in the prompt issuance of replacement vouchers.

Confined to the Kalaupapa Peninsula, Father Damien vented some of his frustration by turning to his favorite pastime—church building. After doubling the size of St. Philomena Chapel, he constructed Our Lady Health of the Sick Church at Kalaupapa for the healthy but incarcerated kama'āina. The church was an all-wood structure replete with a cross and, of course, a bell tower. It measured 30 feet in length, 16 feet in width, and had a vaulted ceiling 23 feet high at its peak. From a structural and aesthetic standpoint this church was superior to the St. Philomena Chapel. Damien's craftsmanship was steadily improving.

DR. G. ARMAUER HANSEN, the Norwegian physician in the subplot to the Damien story, was experiencing a period of intense frustration in his continuing quest to document that leprosy was a disease caused by an infectious agent. For hours he scrutinized the "rod-shaped organisms" under his microscope, absolutely convinced that they were directly responsible for leprosy. The problem he faced was how to prove the causal relationship. Try as he might, each of his many attempts to isolate and culture the rod-shaped microbes failed. The microbe simply would not grow on artificial media, and when he deliberately inoculated laboratory animals with leprous material teeming with the rod-shaped microbes, the animals thrived.

In the fall of 1873, Hansen invited Dr. H. V. Carter, the surgeon-major of the British Army in Bombay, India, where leprosy was rampant, to view the rod-shaped microbes. Dr. Carter, who was in the process of touring both the Hawaiian and the Norwegian leprosy hospitals, recorded his observations in an official report, thus documenting that Dr. Hansen was the first scientist to discover the bacteria responsible for leprosy.[31]

THROUGHOUT HIS ADULT LIFE it was Father Damien's prayerful wish that he be permitted to walk in the footsteps of St. Damien. That wish had been more than granted, but he was walking alone, without the support of a confrere or a brother figure, a St. Cosmas. While he was experiencing the satisfaction that came from helping the world's most despised outcasts, his inner joy was dampened by a profound loneliness. When the loneliness spawned melancholy, Damien found that one sentence quietly repeated could restore a sense of purpose, and with renewed purpose, soul-saving serenity: *"Come on, Jef, my boy, this is your life's work!"* With repetition, the words would bring a smile to his lips. *"Come on, Jef, my boy, this is your life's work!"*[32]

10

Free at Last!

*Because you have made the Lord your refuge, the Most High
your habitation, no evil shall befall you, no scourge come
near your tent. For he will give his angels charge of
you to guard you in all your ways.*
—Psalm 91:9–11

ESCALATING DIPLOMATIC PRESSURE from the French finally coerced
the Kingdom of Hawai'i to reverse its policy regarding Father Damien's
confinement, and on November 13, 1873, the Board of Health "unanimously" adopted the resolution that "the visits of doctors and ministers of religion in the exercise of their duties and their professions"
at the leper settlement were permitted, "on condition that a written
permission be obtained previously from the Board of Health."[1] On
November 25, Father Damien learned of the decision and in the margin of his year-end letter to his parents, which he was in the act of dis-
patching, he hastily scribbled, "I have just this moment received my
liberty!"[2] In a letter from the Department of the Interior dated December 18, 1873, he received written confirmation that the prohibition
against his leaving and returning to the leper settlement had been
rescinded.[3] Enclosed with the letter was a copy of the public announcement by Dr. George Trousseau, the board's chief medical advisor, stating that Father Damien did not pose an "immediate threat to the public health." Damien was euphoric. He was free!

In the year-end letter to his parents, Father Damien tactfully
informed them for the first time of his "change of residence" and that
he was now the "chaplain to 800 lepers." Completely absent was the

self-righteous, sermonizing tone that had characterized his earlier letters. In his greeting he told of his deep love for the two of them, unaware that his father had died in May when he was sleeping under the *pū hala*.

A second letter he dispatched that November day was to Father Pamphile. In it he disclosed the gruesome details of his six long months at the leper settlement.[4]

> In the confessional when I hear the confessions of the sick whose wounds are filled with maggots like corpses in the tomb, I must hold my nose. There are times, too, when I don't know where to put the ointment for Extreme Unction, when feet and hands are only open wounds, announcing approaching death. . . . Imagine yourself a chaplain in a hospital with eight hundred sick, all of whom are lepers. There is no doctor. . . . After my Mass I usually go to visit my sick, about half of whom are Catholic. I go from one hut to another, above all trying to administer the medicines for the soul, each according to their need. Those who do not wish to take the spiritual medicine of the Catholic priest, nevertheless receive the temporal medicine.[5]

"Temporal medicine" continued to consume much of his time. His willingness to practice medicine without charging a fee slowly overcame the suspicion that the priest who wore the broad-brimmed black hat might be one of the avaricious haoles. His efficiency in prescribing effective medicines for the fever, pain, respiratory infections, and diarrhea—combined with his skill in cleaning and dressing the sores and skin ulcerations—was the key to the Hawaiians' acceptance of him as a trusted father figure and friend.

IN LATE FALL Father Damien received a letter from Father Bousquet, the superior general, which had been dispatched from Paris in August, notifying him of the pending arrival of Father André Burgermann, a veteran missionary from the Tahitian mission. "This worthy priest is very desirous of joining you and furthering your noble apostolate. I have granted him permission to do so provided that the Bishop and Father Modeste have no objection."[6] The initial surge of relief that a brother priest would soon be in residence on Moloka'i erased any lingering hope that one day the superior general might send Father Pamphile to join him in the Hawaiian mission.

TWO DAYS BEFORE FatherAndré Burgermann's scheduled arrival at the leper settlement, the ailing King Lunalilo died coughing up or vomiting blood.[7] He left no heir to the throne. His massive hemorrhage came from either his tuberculous lungs or his esophageal varices caused by alcohol-induced liver damage. During his short reign of only one year and twenty-five days, this popular monarch had been warned repeatedly by the highly respected Dr. Trousseau that if he did not abstain from all alcohol, he would "not live very much longer." The warning had gone unheeded.[8]

Nine days following Lunalilo's death, David Kalākaua was elected king of the Kingdom of Hawai'i, defeating the Dowager Queen Emma by a vote in the legislature of 39 to 6. Kalākaua's campaign had been aided immensely by Walter Murray Gibson's editorial support in the bilingual newspaper *Ka Nupepa Nuhou*. Gibson craved political power and by promoting Kalākaua he believed he could bring his aspirations to fruition.

The accession of King Kalākaua dramatically boosted the morale at the leper settlement because the majority of the 415 lepers admitted to the settlement during 1873 believed they had been incarcerated by the order of a misguided king.[9] The new monarch was a known opponent of segregation, so freedom was seemingly at hand.

THE DAY THE INTERISLAND steamer carrying Father André Burgermann arrived on Moloka'i, Father Damien was waiting to greet him. The tall, lanky priest who strode down the gangplank to shake his hand was a man in his mid-forties, a missionary who had the reputation of having genuine competence in the practice of medicine.[10] Father Damien pumped the Hollander's hand and enthusiastically helped unload the large supply of bulk medicines the priest had brought with him. It was obvious, however, that the new arrival had a medical problem of his own, an infirmity believed to be elephantiasis.

Elephantiasis is a disease transmitted by mosquitoes in which the larvae of the nematode *Wuchereria bancrofti* enter the body through the bite of the mosquito. The larvae circulate in the bloodstream and grow into threadlike worms that reach a length of several inches. These worms take up residence in the lymph channels, blocking lymph drainage and causing ugly swelling of the legs and external genitalia. Elephantiasis can be as disfiguring to the body below the waist as is leprosy.

Nowhere is there a description of Father André's disease, but in the Sacred Hearts correspondence the question was raised as to whether his suspected elephantiasis might in actuality be leprosy, for in the early stages the two diseases can be mistaken for each other. Father André's disease, whatever its origin, may have borne a close enough resemblance to leprosy to have been instrumental in his transfer to Moloka'i, the island of misshapen people.

After Father André's few personal belongings and his boxes of medical supplies were safely stored in his temporary residence at Kalua'aha on the southern coast of Moloka'i, the two priests rode overland to Kala'e where Father Damien introduced the new priest to Rudolph Meyer. Then the two priests proceeded to the *pali* trail for the treacherous descent, which they accomplished without incident. The fact that Father André did manage the physically demanding trek is an indication that his elephantiasis had not progressed to the advanced stage, which is characterized by grotesque swelling of the legs, restricting physical activity.

During Father André's first tour of the settlement, his chief interest was in the hospitalized lepers. He disclosed that he had encountered a few cases of leprosy in Tahiti and confided that because of his deep interest in the practice of medicine he was intrigued by the various manifestations of the disease and the numerous treatment options. His insistence on interrupting the tour to examine the skin ulcers and deformities of some of the lepers astonished Father Damien, for such behavior was in sharp contrast to the revulsion generally evidenced by first-time visitors, a revulsion that he himself had experienced during his first weeks at the settlement.

After the tour of the hospital, Father Damien escorted Father André through the enlarged St. Philomena Chapel and then to the Our Lady Health of the Sick Chapel in Kalaupapa, which he had recently constructed for the healthy *kama'āina*. While the veteran priest nodded approvingly and commented that the two structures were functional enough, he startled Father Damien by stating unequivocally that he would never permit a church of similar design and crude craftsmanship to be built at Kalua'aha where he was to be stationed. His church, the church in which he would minister, would be larger, feature a much higher vaulted ceiling, and be lighted through Gothic-style windows in place of the plain glass employed by the Belgian. Most importantly, the bell tower of his church would look down on Kaluaʻaha from a height of at least 50 feet. He diplomatically conceded that what Father Damien had accomplished was quite good considering the time constraints, the available tools, and the fact that the carpentry had been done by an amateur. However, the Dutch priest was insistent that the proposed church for Kaluaʻaha promised him by Bishop Maigret would be built by the same brothers who had constructed the magnificent Our Lady of Peace Cathedral in Honolulu.

Father Damien shrugged off Father André's half-hearted compliments about his achievements as a builder of chapels and churches. Throughout his tenure in the Islands, he had never enjoyed the luxury of the guidance or the assistance of one of the skillful brothers in his construction projects. He had learned his carpenter's trade in much the same way he had learned about the practice of medicine—observation, questions, trial and error. If Father André had Bishop Maigret's word that he would have a finer church than the Belgian could provide, so be it. For the first time he would have the opportunity to observe the master builders in action.

The following day, Father Damien sustained a soul-numbing, emotional blow that dwarfed the hurt of Father André's remarks. In a letter from Father Pamphile, written eight months earlier, he learned that their father, Frans De Veuster, had died the previous May.[11] Since his arrival at the leper settlement, Father Damien had included his father in his daily prayers. Now the man whom he revered, the man who had taught him so many useful skills, was dead. Father Damien went directly to St. Philomena and with bowed head walked slowly down the central aisle to the altar, where he prayed.

WITH FATHER ANDRÉ SETTLED at Kaluaʻaha, Father Damien was finally able to focus his full attention on the needed physical improvements at the leper settlement, the next of which was a community project to replace the thatched huts—home to the majority of the lepers—with substantial wooden houses.[12] He announced he would begin construction of the first wooden house, using it as a model for instructing the more able bodied lepers in basic carpentry. In return for the training, these apprentices could graduate from his course in carpentry by building a second house and instructing a new group in the craft of house construction.

While he was building the first of the all-wooden replacement houses, Father Damien received a letter from Father André bemoaning the fact that the master carpenters, the brothers whom he had wished to build the Kalua'aha church, had not been assigned to do so. In an accusatory tone, he admonished Father Damien for not having done his part to persuade the hierarchy to free the brothers to build the new church: "Regarding the church, you have not pressed the point with Monsignor that he should assign a Brother to the task. I choose not to deal with second hand carpenters. And as you have told me, we could build it now with the materials at hand, and embellish it later. However, if a Brother came they would give him everything he needed to do it properly the first time."[13]

In early March, Father André returned to the leper settlement, ostensibly to hear Father Damien's confession, but in his backpack he carried Father Modeste's revised plans for a much smaller church, plus a letter from the provincial explaining that in the absence of the two master builders who were currently at work on another church, Father Damien was to be assigned the task since he possessed the requisite skills for the smaller project. Father André was adamantly opposed to this compromise. Bishop Maigret had promised him a quality church. Under no circumstances would he accept a sanctuary in which to worship Almighty God that was built by anyone less than a master craftsman.

Determined not to let Father Damien build his church, Father André began his descent of the treacherous *pali*. As he neared the bottom of the trail, he lost his footing and fell, striking his head. He lay unconscious at the base of the *pali* until the next morning. When he opened his eyes and attempted to stand, waves of vertigo dropped him to his knees, and he vomited. Recognizing that he had a concussion, he hailed some passing lepers and asked to be taken to Father Damien. The surprised lepers obliged, and half carried, half dragged the priest to the nearest corral where they propped him on a horse and took him to the rectory. Father Damien promptly cleaned and dressed his colleague's head wound and gave him medication to control the pain and the nausea. For the next three days the groggy priest remained at near bed rest, able only to stand and take a few wobbly steps. His persistent headache was incapacitating, and twelve days elapsed before he could function normally.[14]

During Father André's convalescence the two priests became

friends, and Father André gratefully acknowledged that Father Damien was an accomplished physician. Damien in turn wrote to his provincial stressing the Hollander's wish that the new church at Kalua'aha not only be larger than was currently approved, but that skilled craftsmen construct it.[15] Father Modeste's reply was not entirely to Father André's liking. In a compromise proposal, the provincial agreed to supply the building materials for the larger 44 x 22-foot church, but insisted that the only carpenter available to build it at this time was Father Damien. The opportunity to build a larger church than any he had previously attempted was a challenge Damien wished to accept. Reluctantly, Father André consented.

Father Damien packed his tools and was preparing to trade parishes with Father André when he learned from Rudolph Meyer and an excited William Ragsdale that the king and the queen were planning to inspect the leper settlement in two days. Both Meyer and Ragsdale insisted it was essential that Damien be present to greet the royal couple. The priest obligingly agreed to delay his departure until after the royal visit.

The lepers were excited because of the persistent rumor that King Kalākaua was of the opinion that leprosy wasn't contagious and that segregation could be abolished, so on April 14 they gleefully trooped into Kalaupapa and crowded around the wharf, expectantly awaiting the arrival of their king and queen. The daylight hours passed, but no interisland steamer came within sight of Kalaupapa. Bitterly disappointed, the lepers returned to their homes, hopeful that the royal visit would take place the following day.[16]

Four days of expectant waiting passed without further word of the royal visit, so on the morning of the fifth day of his delayed departure for Kalua'aha, Father Damien climbed the *pali*, toting his favorite hand tools. That afternoon the king and the queen arrived unexpectedly by interisland steamer and were welcomed tumultuously by the ambulatory lepers who had quickly assembled at the Kalaupapa wharf. The royal visit, possibly the shortest ever made by a dignitary, lasted only a few minutes, and was reported in the *Pacific Commercial Advertiser* under the headline, "The Leper Asylum of Molokai." "Their Majesties the King and Queen landed at Kalaupapa at half-past 12 o'clock, and were received by the assembled lepers at the beach with hearty cheers. . . . After a few words of kindly recognition to personal acquaintances and a general 'aloha oukou,' 'aloha to you all,' their Majesties returned to the steamer, painfully affected by the sights of human affliction that they had witnessed."[17]

Peter Kaeo was indignant that the visit had been so brief, which to him demonstrated quite clearly the king's fear of contracting the disease. In a letter to Queen Emma he told how very disappointed the expectant natives were not to have been liberated. So certain were several of the more affluent lepers that the king would keep his campaign promise and free them that they had disposed of essential pieces of furniture in anticipation of a speedy return to their home islands.[18]

BY MID-APRIL the construction of the Church of Our Lady Of Sorrows was underway, but conditions were far from ideal.[19] In his letters to Father Modeste, Father Damien told of the difficulties he was encountering, which included being forced to begin construction with tools he considered unsuitable and having to substitute less than ideal materials while awaiting the tardy shipments of building supplies. Father André was not pleased, but during the four months of the construction of the Church of Our Lady of Sorrows, he faithfully served the leper community. Like Father Damien he found himself spending most of his day as a treating physician. William Williamson, the American medical assistant assigned to the two hospitals, astutely recognized Father André's medical skills and welcomed his help with the more seriously ill and dying in the two hospitals. The lepers soon came to adore Father André, the priest whose chief occupation was the practice of medicine, the priest with a gentle bedside manner, an understanding priest who didn't emphasize Western morality with the intensity of a Father Damien. He was a compassionate man with a gentleness toward the ill that dispelled leprosy's twin shadows, depression and dread. In a report to the superior general, Father André wrote:

> The day after my arrival I visited the sick, the hospital, I spoke to them, I preached, I heard confessions, I buried the dead, I gave out medicine, I was the pharmacist; my drugs were successful, and they inspired confidence, and the number of deaths diminished.
>
> I gained the confidence of everyone, and that gave me strength and courage. In the daytime I took care of the sick: in the evening and night I made about 4 or 5 thousand pills a week, and gave three each day to every sick person. During the four months I also performed 48 bap-

tisms, married some among the lepers, and heard the confessions of a great number.[20]

Periodically during the four-month construction of the new church at Kalua'aha, Father André climbed the *pali* and journeyed overland to inspect the structure, resigned to the fact that he wasn't living in an ideal world, but hopeful that his new church would at least be serviceable.

IN KOHALA, Father Damien's former parishioners, wishing to support his mission to the lepers, collected money to be used solely at his discretion. Father Gulstan, his former confrere and confessor in Hāmākua, encouraged the giving and notified Father Damien of the growing aid chest. When Bishop Maigret and Father Modeste learned of the pending infusion of additional funds, Father Gulstan was informed that a cap of 40 to 50 piasters had been placed on the amount of money he was authorized to send on to Father Damien.[21] Donated moneys exceeding the cap were to be placed in the mission's general operating budget. The Catholic outreach program was intended to reach and benefit all of the thousands of Hawaiians, not just the eight hundred lepers.

Pleased with the continuing public acclaim for Father Damien and the favorable light this cast on the entire Catholic mission, Bishop Maigret and Father Modeste were reticent to commence the rotation of the other three priests to the settlement as originally planned. To do so would tarnish the celebrity veneer with which Gibson had painted Father Damien, revealing that the solitary hero of Moloka'i was an ordinary priest who had done no more than other visiting priests. Bishop Maigret, who for many years rejected the offers of any priest to become a permanent resident at the leper settlement, now found it expedient to regard Father Damien as expendable.

Then an event occurred that damaged Father Damien's rapport not only with his superiors, but with his peers. Without his prior knowledge or approval, Father Damien's 1873 year-end letter to Father Pamphile was published in the *Annals of the Sacred Hearts*.[22] The person most responsible for this act was the original recipient of the letter, Father Pamphile, who wished the world to know about the Christian heroics of his younger brother. Following the letter's publication, hundreds of sympathetic readers wanted to help the gallant priest and charitable collections were taken to assist in his work. In Europe the donations were sent directly to the Congregation of the Sacred Hearts in Louvain—funds which Father Gabriel Germain, the treasurer, forwarded to the Hawaiian mission for the discretionary use of Father Damien.

However pleased the European Catholics may have been with the published letter, Father Damien's peers—the Hawaiian missionaries—were not. Fourteen missionary fathers and brothers who gathered for a retreat in Honolulu denounced the letter and its author. Bishop Maigret reportedly was displeased with its contents, and Father Modeste dutifully admonished the young priest for the multiple "improprieties" it contained.[23]

The published letter was an unedited, truthful account of Damien's experiences at the leper settlement from the time of his arrival on May 10 through November 26, 1873. But in the judgment of the Hawaiian missionaries, the lament of the hardships endured by a solitary priest who was ministering to lepers was little more than a ploy to solicit more praise and adoration as the "hero of Moloka'i." In the opinion of his superiors, the letter lacked even a whisper of humility, and nowhere did it mention the substantial financial aid provided by the Sacred Hearts mission nor the chief funding agency for the leper settlement, the Hawaiian Board of Health. The Sacred Hearts Fathers in Hawai'i condemned the letter as an open invitation for charitable contributions from the misinformed.[24]

Father Léonor Fouesnel, the veteran priest stationed on Maui, who was being groomed to become the mission's next provincial, summed up the general consensus of the missionaries regarding the letter: "I know that Monsignor has been very displeased with it, and in addition, Father Damien has received from Father Modeste what he told me was a lecture which ought to make him desist from a desire to write all that passes through that 'brainless little head.'" In the surviving Sacred Hearts correspondence, this is the first evidence of Father Léonor's displeasure with the ministry of Father Damien.

In a June 21 reply to Father Modeste, Father Damien expressed his regret that his personal letter to Father Pamphile had been published without his knowledge or approval. "As to my published letter, I was surprised. It was not written with that intention. Would you rather that I not write any more? Should I keep silent about the leprosarium, so they do not catch me thus again?"[25]

All of the charitable donations from Europe and the United

States designated for the lepers were placed at Father Damien's disposal. No funds were diverted. When the monies from the Congregation of Sacred Hearts in Belgium reached him, he expressed his gratitude by inviting additional contributions, an invitation he knew would be displeasing to his immediate superiors. He wrote to his former mentors in Belgium, "I hope that Catholic charity will continue to furnish me with alms from time to time such as you sent."[26]

In late summer, Father Damien informed Father André and Father Modeste that with the exception of some minor interior work, Our Lady of Sorrows Church at Kalua'aha was finished.[27] Upon receipt of the news, Father André climbed the *pali* and journeyed to view the completed structure. The Church of Our Lady Of Sorrows was nestled on the southern coast of Moloka'i about 7 miles east of the village of Kamalo in a lush valley that opened onto the sea. To André's amazement and delight, the completed church had a 53-foot-high bell tower topped with a cross, and it was a stunning, white silhouette against the vibrant green semitropical foliage that cloaked the steep mountainous outcroppings behind it. Father André entered through the double doors and slowly walked down the central aisle to the altar, awestruck by the beauty surrounding him. He later wrote of his impressions of what he found: "When I arrived I was astonished to find there a beautiful church that had been built in so little time. As soon as I arrived I wrote a letter to his Excellency telling him that the Church of Our Lady of Sorrows is beautiful, truly beautiful. There are many parishes in Europe which do not have the like; the architect has surpassed his masters."[28]

The 120-year-old Church of Our Lady Of Sorrows stands today where Father Damien built it. The church is a survivor of time, wind and rain, and the occasional Pacific hurricane. It has been well maintained, and electric lights have been added to the sanctuary. The handiwork of the original builder is still clearly visible and invites the visitor to inspect the quality of the craftsmanship. In the silence of the empty sanctuary, with daylight streaming through the Gothic windows, a person may determine for himself whether the stocky Belgian priest who took off his cassock to build the lovely structure was a secondhand carpenter or the master craftsman who "surpassed his masters."

IN THE LATTER MONTHS of 1874, Father Damien's feet became "hot and feverish" in the evening hours, the troublesome sensations so uncomfortable that they began to interfere with his sleep.[29] Empirically, he discovered that he had two options. Either he slept with his feet uncovered, or took the time to soak his feet in cold water before retiring. His previous habit of soaking both feet in hot water before retiring definitely exacerbated the discomfort. Suspicious that he was being attacked by leprosy, he carefully inspected his skin each day, searching for the telltale skin lesions of the disease. He found none, but each evening as he eased his feet into the cold water to relieve the burning discomfort, he wondered if he had become a leper.

WINDS OF NEAR HURRICANE force struck the Kalaupapa Peninsula on November 24, 1874, destroying "at least half of the huts" in the leper settlement, forcing the occupants to sleep "in the rain and wind."[30]

The devastation afforded Father Damien the opportunity to turn his attention once again to the housing problem. He was convinced that the small, flimsy huts furnished only with skimpy sleeping mats that were placed on dirt floors did little to protect the lepers from the chill wind, rain, and insects, which were major factors in shortening their lives. With a request to Father Modeste for square laths, rough boards, and shingles, Father Damien resumed the construction program to replace the thatched huts that had been destroyed with sturdy wooden houses. William Ragsdale supported the venture and solicited additional building materials from the Board of Health, materials which were promptly delivered.

To further the all-wood house project, Father Damien established a program that encouraged church members to build their own homes under his supervision and using church funds. At his insistence these houses were larger and more substantial than those constructed with materials supplied by the government; hence they were in greater demand. To be eligible to live in one of these more elegant Catholic dwellings required that the resident attend church regularly and behave as a good Christian. Failure to do so resulted in immediate eviction.[31]

In his annual year-end letter to his family, Father Damien summarized the key events of 1874, and included an outline of his daily schedule.

During the summer I worked for four months in another part of the island as a carpenter building a new church. . . . I am not ashamed to transform myself into a mason or a carpenter, since it is all for the glory of God. For the ten years I have been at the mission I have built a church or chapel every year. . . . Now for a few words concerning my way of life. I live all alone in my little house; the sick never enter it. In the morning after Mass a woman who is not tainted with the illness comes to prepare my meals. Breakfast consists of rice, meat, coffee, and a few biscuits. For supper I eat what was left over from the earlier meal, adding a cup of tea, the water for which I boil over a lamp. My poultry yard furnishes me amply with the eggs needed in my kitchen. I generally take only two meals a day, one in the morning, and the other in the evening; rarely do I eat at midday. During the day I am seldom at home. My biggest occupation consists of going to visit the sick. In the evening, seated near my lamp, I pray my Breviary, I study a little, or I write a letter. So don't wonder at getting only one letter a year.[32]

The year 1874 had been a pivotal one in the ministry of Father Damien, a year of small triumphs and little tragedies. On the positive side, he could point to a successful ministry with over a hundred baptisms, capped by the construction of Our Lady of Sorrows Church in Kalua'aha, a superbly crafted and beautiful sanctuary. On the negative side, Gibson's "hero of Moloka'i" label had focused the attention of his better-educated peers on his ministry, and the unauthorized publication of his letter to Father Pamphile had been condemned as an act of attention seeking by a priest lacking a modicum of humility. His biggest flaw as a priest in the opinion of his peers was the time spent in the practice of medicine, time better allocated to saving souls. A true Sacred Hearts priest devoted his every waking hour to the service of his Lord as a spiritual leader—not as an inconsequential physician dispensing medicines to relieve such earthly complaints as diarrhea, fever, and pain.

11

Like the Christ:
Priest, Physician, Carpenter

"Teacher, which is the great commandment in the law?"
And he said to him, "You shall love the Lord your God with
all your heart, and with all your soul, and with all your mind.
This is the great and first commandment. And a second is
like it, You shall love your neighbor as yourself."
—Matthew 22:36–39

BISHOP MAIGRET AND Father Modeste were braced for the negative comments they anticipated Father André would hurl at them once he had inspected the completed Church of Our Lady of Sorrows at Kalua'aha, so it was with some trepidation that they opened André's late-August letter. To their astonishment the communication overflowed with laudatory remarks. It was Father André's conviction that Father Damien was not only a master craftsman, but he had built the church at Kalua'aha in record time using tools that would have handicapped the finest builders in Europe. The bishop and the provincial were relieved. The energetic Belgian might not possess all of the attributes of the ideal priest, but he certainly had emerged as a master builder of churches—quality construction and always at a very low cost to the mission. Father Damien was an asset to utilize to the fullest. Additional churches and chapels were needed on Moloka'i, and Damien was the man on site who could build them.

The most pressing need for a new church, Bishop Maigret decided, was at Pelekunu, the village to the east and adjacent to the Kalaupapa Peninsula from which much of the food for the leper settlement was purchased. Father Damien was acquainted with Pelekunu, for he had been visiting the village on a regular basis to minister to the small but growing number of Catholics. Since mission funds were limited, the bishop proposed that the charitable donations for the lepers that had been collected by the Sacred Hearts Congregation in Louvain now be diverted to cover most of the cost of the building materials. Confident that Father Damien would not only obey the order to build another church, but would be delighted to do so, he had Father Modeste notify Damien that the lumber and other essential building materials for Pelekunu had been purchased and were being shipped directly to Kalaupapa for later transport to Pelekunu on a day when the seas were calm.

Father Modeste dutifully informed the superior general of the proposed church-building program for Moloka‘i, purposely neglecting to trouble his superior with the financial details: "Father Damien is waiting for materials to build a church at Pelekunu, Molokai, and that finished, two others await him topside on the island of Molokai."[1]

What transpired next wasn't exactly what Damien's superiors had anticipated. Father Damien knew that the funds sent from Louvain were designated to be used at his discretion for the benefit of the lepers, and he was determined to honor that trust. But the funds from Louvain were controlled by his bishop and his provincial who had already purchased the building materials for the church at Pelekunu where there were no lepers. Still, there was a compromise solution, Father Damien reasoned, that would please everyone. Increasing numbers of lepers were relocating to the village of Kalaupapa on the western side of the peninsula where the climate was milder. To meet their needs, he had built a small church in Kalaupapa the previous year, but it was now apparent that the structure was too small to accommodate the steadily increasing number of parishioners. Were he to obey his bishop and build the proposed church in Pelekunu, a church the size of Our Lady of Sorrows, the structure would be disproportionately large for the number of parishioners. So the solution was obvious. He would raze the tiny Kalaupapa Church and use the incoming construction materials designated for Pelekunu to build a more suitably sized church at Kalaupapa. This strategy would not trouble his conscience because the alms from Louvain would have been spent for the benefit of lepers. Then he would transport the used lumber from the razed church to Pelekunu and build a smaller church than his superiors had originally instructed him to erect. Two churches for the price of one—a fantastic bargain—but to achieve this economy he would be guilty of disobeying his bishop's directive, a major transgression.

Without notifying his superiors of his innovative plan, Father Damien demolished the church at Kalaupapa, erected a new one in its place with the new building supplies, and transported the used lumber to Pelekunu where he erected the second, smaller church.

During the construction at Pelekunu, Father André again took up temporary residence in Kalawao and attended to the needs of the lepers. For the first time since joining the Hawaiian mission he witnessed a priest defy a direct order from his bishop, and he anticipated that Father Damien's devious actions would have dire consequences. While he waited to learn the outcome of the unfolding drama, he again devoted the majority of his time in the practice of medicine.

Following the completion of the Pelekunu Church, Father Damien wrote to Father Gabriel Germain, the treasurer of the Sacred Hearts Congregation in Louvain, to inform him of the good use to which the alms had been put: "The gifts received last year for the leprosarium were, for the most part, used to cover the costs of a beautiful church which I built to replace a small one which had become inadequate for the second parish in the leprosarium."[2]

When the bishop and the provincial learned of Father Damien's independent action they were shocked. Father Modeste complained of the blatant disobedience in a letter to the superior general:

> Father Damien has "followed his head," he has disposed of a cargo of materials according to his own will. The materials were destined by the Bishop for the building of a church at Pelekunu. He had the audacity to have it all unloaded at Kalaupapa, demolished an almost new church at that place, and built a new one with the materials destined for Pelekunu, and with the debris of the destroyed church along with some additional expenditures, he made a little chapel at Pelekunu. The Bishop is far from satisfied with what transpired, so contrary to his wishes. I don't know what excuse Father Damien will offer.[3]

What excuse Father Damien gave his superiors for initiating his innovative but unauthorized building program is not known, nor is his penance for this act of deliberate disobedience.

THE TWO NARROW buildings designated as "hospitals" that had been built in the center of Kalawao shortly after the arrival of the first lepers were acknowledged to be hospitals in name only. Their thatched roofs leaked, ventilation came through the drafty walls when the wind was strong, light peeked in through a few tiny windows, and the dirt floors on which the patients slept on tiny mats were damp and crawling with insects. Both William Williamson, the American leper serving as a physician's assistant, and Father André joined Father Damien in pointing out the glaring deficiencies to Rudolph Meyer and William Ragsdale, who in turn conveyed the matter to the Board of Health.

The medical consultants to the Board of Health concurred with the negative assessment of the hospitals, so the Board commissioned Rudolph Meyer to oversee the construction of two new, state-of-the-art hospital buildings at Kalawao.[4] Meyer responded by employing William Mutch, an experienced building contractor, to build the two hospitals. Mutch hired immigrant Chinese laborers for the project and completed the first hospital in 1875. It was a praiseworthy, all-wood, two-story structure with an eighty-bed capacity. In appearance and functionality it rivaled similarly sized hospitals in the United States. The following year Mutch built the second hospital, a mirror image of the first, again employing Chinese laborers. But the hospital project failed to correct the major flaw in the medical care provided the lepers, for these hospitals continued to operate without doctors or nurses.

AT FATHER ANDRÉ's request and with the approval of his two superiors, Father Damien left the leper settlement in 1876 to construct St. Joseph's Catholic Church at Kamalō on the southern coast of Moloka'i. It was an all-wood church, smaller than the Church of Our Lady of Sorrows at Kalua'aha, but it exhibited the same stellar craftsmanship. St. Joseph's measured 18 by 24 feet and featured a slender cross atop a tall steeple with a deep-throated bronze bell. During the daylight hours the sanctuary was lighted through six rectangular windows, each comprised of twelve panes of plain glass. However, the delicately carved woodwork surrounding each window, inside and out, gave the impression that the viewer was looking at a Gothic-style window. On either side of the central aisle Father Damien constructed five pews, each about 6 feet in length, which limited the seating capacity to about fifty adults. At night two large oil lamps suspended from the vaulted ceiling filled the sanctuary with a soft, amber light. Father André was pleased with the church even though it lacked authentic Gothic windows. He judged the craftsmanship to be superb. St. Joseph's Church has been preserved, and to enter its sanctuary is to step back in time and admire Father Damien's handiwork.

While Father André and Father Damien continued to disagree about the priorities of a priest, the priest who viewed his mission through the eyes of a would-be physician never openly criticized Damien in writing.[5] Yet each time the two met to hear the other's confession, Father Damien felt uneasy. Father André's philosophy of life, the drumbeat by which he marched, was not focused on the spiritual well-being and salvation of the soul. His was a worldly, pragmatic approach: Relieve suffering; combat illness and disease; let God watch over the soul.

AFTER THREE INTERMINABLY long years of incarceration, a restless Peter Kaeo resolved to escape. He could no longer endure the boredom and the intolerable social isolation of the leper settlement, and was desperate to experience once more the joy of a riotous party in Honolulu where he could drink alcohol and lose himself in a crowd of laughing, high-spirited people. After all, he was a Hawaiian chief and a member of the prestigious House of Nobles, and as such he believed that he posed no threat to the kingdom's public health. The leprosy segregation laws were meant for the common man, not the ali'i. Royalty was above the common law. The only rational solution to his incarceration was escape.

The Dowager Queen Emma, his childhood companion and life-long friend, concurred. With the assistance of Edward Preston, one of the more talented attorneys in the Islands, she arranged for an outrigger canoe manned by two accomplices, Robert Charlton and Jack Smith, to cross the Moloka'i Channel after sunset, rendezvous with Peter on the beach opposite his cottage, and then transport him to O'ahu's windward shore before daybreak. Preston was of the opinion that to secure his freedom, Peter needed only to appear boldly in Honolulu among his own people. "Once you landed here everyone would be in defense of your rights and this would bring things to a climax . . . a stir is now wanted to check the present unscrupulous management of the Government."[6] Unfortunately for Peter, Charlton and Smith "leaked" the details of the planned escape, and the scheme had to be abandoned once King Kalākaua learned of it.

A month later Queen Emma masterminded a second escape plan. On June 20, 1876, a group of thirteen leading members of the legislature landed at the Kalaupapa wharf, charged with the task of investigating "the present condition of the lepers." They were accompanied by several members of the Board of Health, a reporter, and Dr. G. W. Woods, the visiting medical inspector of the U.S. Navy. William Ragsdale, the resident superintendent, welcomed the blue-ribbon committee and escorted them on horseback to Kalawao.[7] In the course of the visit, thirty to forty lepers who claimed to be free of the disease were examined by the Board of Health delegation, assisted by Dr. Woods. Two cases were judged to be "cured," and were referred to Honolulu for confirmation by government physicians. Peter was not one of the two.[8] The two "cured" cases probably had one of the many dermatitides, such as psoriasis, that for a while mimicked the skin manifestations of leprosy.

At the conclusion of the inspection tour, the thirteen legislators excused themselves from Dr. Woods and the Board of Health members so they might present themselves to Peter Kaeo to offer the customary courtesies to a member of the royal family before departing. Inexplicably, the committee of thirteen then announced that they were of the unanimous opinion that Peter was "not a leper," and invited him to accompany them on their return to Honolulu. Peter quickly gathered a few key possessions and hurried to the wharf. When he attempted to board the *Kīlauea*, he found the gangplank blocked by a stern-faced Samuel Wilder of the Board of Health. Wilder informed Peter that absolutely *no one*—leper, nonleper, or royal personage—could leave the settlement without the express permission of the Board of Health; and that he, Wilder, refused to give it. A crestfallen and indignant Peter Kaeo made his way back to his house. Once again his escape had been thwarted.

One week later the same Samuel Wilder who had staunchly refused to allow Peter to board the *Kīlauea* meekly acquiesced and agreed to the recommendation of Dr. McKibbin, a medical consultant to the Board of Health, that Peter be granted his release and be allowed to take up residence in Honolulu. Following his return to the capital,

Peter reoccupied his old seat in the House of Nobles and attended the majority of its sessions despite the public outcry.[9] Long live the resourceful Queen Emma!

BY 1876 THE MAJORITY of Hawai'i's lepers were confined at the leper settlement. A census listed 872 lepers living at the settlement—569 men and 303 women and children.[10] Included in the group were eighteen foreigners: two Americans, two Germans, one Englishman, a native of Mauritius, and twelve Chinese. The Germans, the Englishman, four of the Chinese, and one American died before year's end. When the leper settlement opened in 1866, the life expectancy of a leper was only two to four years. Following Father Damien's arrival in 1873 and the Board of Health's renewed efforts to improve the living conditions at the settlement, life expectancy increased three- to fourfold. By 1876, 129 substantial wood frame houses stood in juxtaposition to the remaining 171 traditional thatched huts. Alcohol abuse and immorality were under control. The Board of Health reported that "during the two years past there has not arisen any trouble at Kalawao; there has been at all times sufficient food. The Board have not on file a single complaint made by any of the sick."[11]

IN JULY 1876, Dr. Woods, the navy medical inspector, was ordered by the U.S. Bureau of Medicine and Surgery to return to the leper settlement and investigate the "dread disease" in depth, following which he was to submit "a report on the subject of Leprosy." To many U.S. congressmen the eventual annexation of Hawai'i by the United States was a distinct possibility, but in acquiring the "garden of the Pacific" with its strategic Pearl Harbor, one also took possession of the garden's deadliest serpent—leprosy. An assessment of the situation by a knowledgeable physician was deemed essential.

Dr. Woods, who was stationed aboard the USS *Lackawanna*, one of the warships patrolling Pearl Harbor, requested permission from the Hawaiian Board of Health to make a weeklong stay at the leper settlement for the purpose of conducting a study on leprosy. Permission was granted, and both William Ragsdale, the resident superintendent, and Rudolph Meyer were notified of the doctor's scheduled arrival date, a Friday in mid-July.

On that particular Friday the surf was so rough that a landing by a U.S. Navy longboat at the Kalaupapa wharf was judged to be impossible. To assist the Navy, a "large whale boat, manned by eight lepers, put off from the shore" as the USS *Lackawanna* neared the Kalaupapa side of the peninsula—but found that the sea was too rough to permit "the heavy boat to be brought to the [ship's] ladder."[12] After several unsuccessful attempts, a rope was tied around the doctor's waist and he was lowered from the extended arm of a small derrick until he was dangling over the whaleboat. Then he was dropped "into the arms of the leper crew, whose mutilated hands were extended upwards" to catch him, "their disfigured faces looking a welcome, while their lips gave an Aloha in chorus."[13]

With Dr. Woods safely aboard, the whaleboat rode the long heavy swells of the sea to an outcropping of tall volcanic rocks jutting out into the ocean. Crouched on the outcropping was a single line of male lepers, drenched from the spray of the pounding surf, waiting to pluck the doctor from the bobbing craft. In Dr. Woods' words,

> as we slipped abreast of them, as if by magic, I was seized gently by those at the head of the long line and passed from hand to hand, over the slippery rocks and up the bluff, where I found myself confronted by at least a hundred men and women on horseback, and three times as many on foot. They formed a unique sight in their gaily colored attire, heightened by bright flowers in pendant wreaths on neck and hat. . . . As I confronted these people, two horsemen advanced and dismounted. The first came forward and announced himself as Governor Ragsdale, presenting to me his contracted claw-like gloved hand, and introduced to me the second as Father Damien, the priest to the lepers of Molokai. . . . He presented Father Damien to me as the true "Father" of the settlement and his "right-hand coadjutor."[14]

Dr. Woods scrutinized the priest as though he were a patient, as most doctors unconsciously do. Later he recorded his impressions:

> The priest was at this time—July, 1876—in the prime of life, being about thirty-three years of age, and the perfection of youthful health and vigor. His face was smooth and rather thin, but not emaciated; his features irradiated by an earnest expression intensified by a fixed gaze of calm dark eyes. The chin slightly projected, with a deep sulcus below thick widely parted lips, and the head, poised upon rather a long neck, was covered with black curly hair carelessly brushed or unbrushed. He wore a

soutane which had seen much wear and not been too well cared for, and carried in his hand a broad brimmed straw hat of native manufacture.[15]

The remainder of the day was devoted to a thorough inspection of the leper settlement. Dr. Woods recorded in his journal, "I was entertained by the Governor [Ragsdale] with a little history of the settlement, and of the great improvements since Father Damien's advent but three years before; and, as we approached Kalawao, he called my attention to the churches, the hospital, the store, the numerous comfortable whitewashed houses surrounded by gardens,—all the work of the people themselves under the supervision of my two companions."

That evening, Dr. Woods was served a dinner of "broiled chicken with a tomato salad" in the isolation of the guest house, following which Ragsdale joined him. "Taking a chair some distance," Ragsdale stated that he was proud of the fact that he had voluntarily surrendered to the authorities after he had accidentally discovered that he had lost the sensation in his now-clawed hand when he lifted an oil lamp that had exploded and covered his hand with burning oil. After extinguishing the flames he had watched the skin redden and blister, but he had felt no pain. Slowly, the realization that he was a leper overwhelmed him, and he recalled sitting down in his favorite chair and weeping.[16] The doctor noted that in addition to the badly contracted claw hand, Ragsdale's nose was flattened due to the destruction of his nasal septum.

The two men adjourned to the veranda where they lighted cigars and relaxed. Dr. Woods wrote:

> The tranquility was suddenly disturbed by distant music, strange and shrill, with beating drums. "What is that?" said I, after listening for some time to the increasing sounds. "Oh," replied the Governor, "that is Father Damien and his band coming to serenade you," and almost simultaneously a dozen boys playing upon flutes, another dozen or more swinging lanterns, and two standard bearers carrying Hawaiian and American flags, with Father Damien in the lead, marched into the enclosure, the musicians playing the Hawaiian national air. This was followed by the "Star Spangled Banner," after which the good Father came on to the veranda and greeted us. "Permit me, monsieur le docteur, to present my boys, who have come to welcome you and to thank you for coming so far to inquire after them, and to see if anything can be done to cure them." . . . Then Father Damien, taking one of the instruments, showed me how this and all the others, were a sort of clar-

inet or flute made of old oil cans, fashioned by himself, on which he had patiently taught the boys to play by ear.[17]

The youth band then continued their concert, playing several national airs, some American war songs including "Marching through Georgia," and concluded the concert with an original composition by Princess Liliuʻokalani. Following three cheers for the United States, the band left playing a military march. At this juncture Ragsdale excused himself to join a lady whom Dr. Woods presumed was Mrs. Ragsdale, leaving Father Damien and the American doctor to become better acquainted. Damien knew but did not disclose to Dr. Woods that William Ragsdale was a bachelor who enjoyed the company of multiple mistresses.[18]

> Father Damien filled his large German pipe, and we settled down to a chat, which continued late into the night. The Father told me the story of his life in Hawaii. . . . His first duty was to transform the rude chapel into a worthy place of worship, and then, with the materials abundantly supplied by the Government and generous Hawaiians, an improved hospital was completed, and neat houses began to take the place of the ancient huts, framed of rough native woods and thatched with grass and leaves. In this work Father Damien was architect, constructor, carpenter and painter, instructing and working, and yet finding time to attend the sick and dying, dress the hundreds of mutilated beings who came to him for salve and bandage, besides conscientiously administering every holy office of the church. He also inculcated temperance, sexual morals, family life, the avoidance of gambling, cleanliness of person and attire, and instructed the people in gardening, cooking, and many little household arts, adding greatly to their comfort. It was a wonderful recital of the work of an energetic man performing the work of fifty, by example and precept, and the inspiring of others with his own marvelous energy, so that all who came under his influence became "helping hands."
>
> On the completion of breakfast the following morning, Father Damien again presented himself, and with him I made a round of visits to the hospital and to the sick in their own houses. . . . and in this sociability . . . we find the explanation of how leprosy has spread with such rapidity throughout this kingdom, and the means by which the good father, in later years, acquired it.
>
> The pipe was filled and passed to him, although but it was removed from a leper's mouth; he ate poi out of the family calabash; he fondled the children, and dressed the wounds of all who needed his attention,

all of which would have been offensive but that it was done with intention, and evidently to secure the confidence and love of these people,
whom he had adopted in his heart, that he might bring them to Christ,
though he "died for them" of a loathsome disease. . . . Thus, we made
the rounds of twenty houses, squatting on the mats with the family. . . .
On Sunday morning at 10 o'clock I was in attendance at the Church, and
a more extraordinary sight never greeted a worshipper than the celebration of the Holy Mass in this diminutive church of Kalawao before
a congregation of lepers which fairly packed the little building.

All were in their best garb; bright holokus and straw hats trimmed
with gay ribbons for the women, decent calico shirts and white trousers
for the men, and all wearing garlands of flowers (leis).

But oh, what a pitiable army of decorated deformity: scowling, leonine, hairless faces wrinkled and tubercular, the tubercles often in a state
of ulceration; rigid foreheads, beetling brows, averted red eyelids, drip-
ping purulent matter, red congested eye balls with various cicatricial dis-
tortions, sightless or nearly so, with corneal opacities and cataracts; flattened noses and other facial changes from disappearance of supporting
bones; open running sores, hands with claw-like contracted fingers and
missing portions, spontaneously amputated, often to the extent of an
entire disappearance of the hand, leaving an unsightly mutilation, or
perhaps, only a wrist stump; and finally the cripples, unable to walk
from the loss of feet or contraction of limbs, carried tenderly, seated and
cared for by those who still possessed strength, and arms capable of
bearing burdens.[19]

After the church service Father Damien and Dr. Woods visited
with members of the congregation, following which the two retired to
Father Damien's rectory.

"My days are all too short," said he, "and I carry my works into my
dreams. I am subject to call day and night to attend the sick and dying,
administer the last sacraments or bury the dead, and the lesser work of
religious instruction, with the superintendence of house building now
constantly in progress, including the enlargement of my church with a
bit of help at agriculture and horticulture, make such demands that I
begrudge the time spent at my meals. But it is all happiness to me, and
I am blessed in thus having an opportunity to do the Lord's Work." . . .
He said further, "This is my work in this world. Sooner or later I shall
become a leper, but may it not be until I have exhausted my capabilities
for good to these my unfortunate afflicted children. I have endeavored

to help them verbally, materially, and as a healer of physical wounds, and in all my work have received abundant encouragement and help, both from the Government and from private sources; in which I am seconded and aided by that best of men, Mr. R. W. Meyer, the agent of the Board of Health, with the support of Governor Ragsdale."[20]

When Father Damien uttered the words, "Sooner or later I shall become a leper," he was expressing his deep concern that quite possibly he had several of the early skin and peripheral nerve manifestations of leprosy. For some unfathomable reason his Lord and the Virgin Mary were treating him differently than he had been led to believe they would. He had repeatedly expressed in his letters to his family that "Jesus Christ treats missionaries in a very special manner, for it is He who guides their footsteps and preserves them from all dangers."[21] At this juncture, Father Damien saw no purpose in disclosing his disturbing thoughts to Dr. Woods.

For the remainder of the week Dr. Woods availed himself of the opportunity to study the multifaceted disease. Each evening Father Damien, William Ragsdale, and he would gather to smoke their pipes and discuss the events of the day. Dr. Woods reported that their conversations invariably "strayed into literature under the lead of the Governor, who would repeat pages of Scott and Byron, and Tennyson, often manifesting great dramatic emotion."[22]

At the end of the week Dr. Woods shook the strong hand of the priest and the gloved hand of the resident supervisor and bid them good-bye after obtaining from both of his new friends a promise to correspond. In Dr. Woods' words, the visit "ended with a sorrowful parting, as under the guidance of Mr. Meyer" he ascended the *pali* for a quick horseback tour of Moloka'i before departing from one of the ports that opened into a calm sea.

12

"We Lepers . . ."

But Jesus answered and said, "Ye know not what ye ask.
Are ye able to drink of the cup that I shall drink of, and to
be baptized with the baptism that I am baptized with?"
They said unto him, "We are able."
—Matthew 20:22

ON NEW YEAR'S DAY, 1877, Father Damien studied the suspicious spots on his face and arms that he had been treating with "corrosive sublimate lotion" for several months. With each application the lotion burned away the upper layers of the skin, temporarily removing a spot, but when the treated areas healed the suspect spots returned and now had assumed a yellowish color.[1] Each time the spots reappeared after an application of the lotion, Damien used the clinical test taught him by Father Charles on the Big Island to determine whether or not the spots were an early skin lesion of leprosy. With the point of a small pin he gently pricked the center of each spot on his face and arms to determine whether it had normal pain sensation. The majority did not, and anxiety gripped his being. The corrosive sublimate lotion hadn't destroyed the invaders of his skin. A few days later he repeated the pinprick test on each of the suspicious spots, and again he failed to feel the hoped-for pain. Blood oozed from several of the spots where the pin had painlessly penetrated more deeply. This left little doubt as to the diagnosis. He—Joseph De Veuster—had joined the ranks of the lepers.

The anxiety intensified as he connected the presence of the abnormal spots with the problems he was having with his feet. In addition to the uncomfortable hot flush that he alleviated with the cold water soaks each evening, he had begun to experience a peculiar tingling feeling in both feet as if they were falling asleep. Damien knew that when leprosy attacked a person, it seized the nerves in the body. The damaged nerves beneath the skin were responsible for the anesthetic spots on his face, and now the nerves in his feet were under siege.

As he pondered this ominous development, he recalled the countless times he had touched the open sores and ulcers of the lepers when administering the sacraments or cleansing their wounds. He had eaten food prepared by lepers, he had dipped his fingers into the communal poi calabash of lepers, and worst of all, he had even smoked a common pipe after it had been in the mouths of lepers. His justification for these actions, which Bishop Maigret had prohibited, was that he had done so to enhance his rapport with the lepers so that he might lead them to God. He was, after all, a haole—and by acting as he did, showing no fear of contagion, he was able to bridge the barrier that separated the haole from the Native Hawaiian. If it were now God's will that he become one of the "unclean," so be it. He would kneel in prayer and plead with the Almighty to heal him, as St. Paul had done with his affliction; but he was prepared for the worst should his plea, like St. Paul's, be rejected. Then he would rejoice that he had been judged worthy to join the select group of apostles who had forfeited their earthly lives in the service of mankind. In the meantime he would continue to apply the corrosive sublimate lotion to the hateful spots and take sarsaparilla as a blood purifier.[2] Hopefully, the sarsaparilla would help the nerves in his feet.

On that first day of January there were 744 lepers at the Kalaupapa leper settlement—465 men and 279 women and children—not counting Father Damien.[3] During the previous year there had been 178 admissions and 149 deaths. To further reduce the mortality rate, the Board of Health continued in its effort to recruit a resident physician for the settlement but lamented in its minutes that "up to this time no medical man has been found willing to go and reside there."[4] This continued to place the major burden for any medical care provided the lepers on Father Damien and the American, William Williamson. Once a month the two welcomed the assistance of Father André for a day or two when he came down the *pali* to confess Father Damien. The medical care of the lepers was further compromised by the lack of bathing facilities so essential for wound hygiene. In 1877 there were only three washtubs available for bathing the lepers in the new hospitals.

The budget for the leper settlement for the biennial period ending March 31, 1878, was $59,675.[5] This was a most generous outlay of funds by a government with a growing national debt, supported by a tax base of fewer than seventy thousand people whose average daily income was in the 50- to 75-cent range. To fund the government programs, the Kingdom of Hawai'i was increasingly dependent upon the taxation of the aggressive haole businessmen who owned the shipping firms, cattle ranches, farms, and sugar plantations.[6]

In March there was a general consensus that four additional chapels were needed on Moloka'i to accommodate Father André's rapidly growing parishes. In years past, this task would have been assigned to the two brothers who were the master builders in Hawai'i, but their advanced age now limited their service to the maintenance of the Cathedral of Our Lady of Peace in Honolulu. The solution to the shortage of chapels on Moloka'i was obvious to Father André. Father Damien had demonstrated that he could not only build as fine a chapel or church as the brothers, but in less time and for less money—so let the Belgian do what he seemed to enjoy most in life. And while Father Damien was so engaged, Father André would reside at the leper settlement and do what he enjoyed most—practice medicine. The bishop and the provincial concurred with Father André's assessment. On March 20, an obliging Father Damien wrote to Rudolph Meyer to request his help in surveying the proposed building sites at Kaunakakai and Hālawa for the first two of the proposed chapels.[7]

Jealous that the growth of the Protestant congregations had been stunted by the more colorful and aggressive ministry of Father Damien, the Siloama elders and deacons launched a two-phase plan to rescue their lagging church program. First, they planned to build a chapel in Kalaupapa to rival the new church Father Damien had built; and second, they intensified their efforts to belittle the labors of the Belgian priest by publishing a flood of derogatory comments about the Catholic mission in the weekly Protestant newspaper. Damien found the unsubstantiated attacks on his character and actions slanderous and hurtful, but he declined to defend himself or respond in kind. There was no doubt in his mind that the primary instigator, if not the author for the majority of the demeaning articles, was the acting pastor, Mr. Pogue.

WHEN RUDOLPH MEYER descended the *pali* in June 1877 to make his monthly inspection tour of the settlement, he was alarmed by the gaunt appearance of William Ragsdale, the resident superintendent. He found Ragsdale confined to his bed with a debilitating high fever, too weak to venture outside. Ragsdale's claw hand had become ulcerated, swollen, and badly infected. While the resident superintendent was as articulate as ever, he was totally incapable of attending to his duties. Upon his return home, Meyer alerted the Board of Health that Ragsdale was a dying man. "The disease has made progress on him, his right hand was a mass of ulceration and writing is of considerable effort to him."[8]

Believing that Ragsdale's death was imminent, Father André seized the opportunity to correspond with the Board of Health and offer his services in a dual capacity—as the resident superintendent and as the resident physician. The all-Protestant Board of Health debated the pros and cons of allowing a Catholic priest to assume these two posts, at least until a bonafide physician could be found. Rudolph Meyer believed that Father André's proposal had merit and urged the board to accept it, believing that Father André would not have made the offer without the consent and approval of Father Damien and his superiors. Father André, however, had chosen not to mention this gambit to either his superiors or to the absent Father Damien, who was busily engaged in chapel construction at Hālawa.

William Ragsdale died on November 29, 1877, of the complications of leprosy.[9] On that day, Father André disclosed to Father Damien for the first time that the Board of Health had accepted his offer, and he solicited his confessor's endorsement to secure ecclesiastical approval. He wrote, "If they do not give permission, which would give me much pain, I will ignore them and reenter the lay state. . . . I have no other end in view than to live and die with the poor sick, and to help them bear their illness with resignation.[10]

The revelation stunned Father Damien. He viewed such clandestine deception as inexcusable. More importantly, he was Father André's confessor, and something he had learned about the man, some colossal flaw that could not be overlooked, convinced him that as the resident superintendent Father André would be a liability to the operation of the settlement. Father Damien felt so strongly that the appointment of Father André would be detrimental to the settlement, he believed that he had no recourse but to threaten to resign were the appointment made. But before he could voice his objections, he received a startling letter from Rudolph Meyer enthusiastically endorsing Father André.[11]

Damien replied immediately, listing his reasons for opposing the appointment of Father André and stating unequivocally that should the Board of Health proceed with the appointment, he would leave the settlement. Meyer was flabbergasted. From his perspective, Father André was a perfect choice for the position: a well-educated Sacred Hearts priest who had no fear of contracting leprosy, a capable physician who enjoyed practicing his art, and most importantly, a companion and confrere for Father Damien. On occasion he had witnessed the differences of opinion between the two priests over procedural matters related to the operation of the settlement, but he had never sensed the bitter rivalry that now surfaced.

Meyer destroyed Father Damien's letter and quickly dispatched a second letter to the priest, beseeching him not to resign: "If Father André did wrong in offering his services to the Board, all the members of the committee were ignorant at the moment when they accepted him. If the Father did this without the permission of his Bishop, he alone must be blamed. . . . I assure you that I acted with the best of intentions in this affair, and I really thought you would be happy to have your confrere living near you."[12]

Father Damien adamantly refused to retract his promise to resign. This left Rudolph Meyer in the unenviable position of having to choose between the two priests. Without hesitation Meyer alerted the Board of Health to Father Damien's firm resolve to leave the settlement were Father André named resident superintendent, and that the loss of Father Damien would have serious consequences. The leper settlement would lose not only its moral conscience, but its most dedicated part-time physician, house builder, coffin maker, and most importantly, guardian of the orphans.

Upon Meyer's recommendation, the Board of Health rescinded its acceptance of Father André's offer and named Father Damien as the provisional resident superintendent, a salaried position. Father Damien accepted the post and its responsibilities, but refused to take the salary. He had taken a vow of poverty, and stated that if he took the money neither the Church nor his own mother would recognize him as her child. Surprisingly, Father André voiced no objection to the Damien appointment and meekly continued his ministerial duties and the practice of medicine.

From the beginning of his tenure as the provisional resident superintendent, Father Damien was criticized by Protestant and Catholic alike. The Belgian was stern and uncompromising in administering his version of justice. When people complained about his decisions, they were curtly dismissed and told to present their complaints in writing to Rudolph Meyer for adjudication. After several weeks of unrest and a mounting stack of letters of complaint, Meyer wrote to his friend: "Please do not tell these people to write to me about every little thing. . . . I urge you to make as few changes as possible for the present, and to accept some irregularities. Unless you take care to do this you will find that there will be no one on whom you can count."[13]

One of the duties of the resident superintendent was to maintain law and order. In his new position Father Damien had the authority to arrest an individual for minor infractions such as drunken and disorderly conduct and to punish the person by imprisonment for a day or so in the small jail in the Kalawao village compound. For misdemeanors and the more serious crimes, a rare occurrence at the settlement, the presumed guilty person was sent to Honolulu for trial and sentencing. In January 1878, Father Damien used his new authority to arrest and send to Honolulu the person whom he considered to be one of the chief sources of discord in the settlement, none other than Mr. Pogue, the acting Protestant minister. Father Damien claimed that the clergyman was a "great rebel and disturber of the peace," who used "infamous and rebellious" language to undermine the efforts of the Board of Health.[14] He had the Protestant minister arrested, forcibly removed from his home, and deported to Honolulu for imprisonment. Armed with clubs and rocks, members of the Protestant congregation rebelled and threatened an uprising. What transpired in Honolulu after the arrival of Pogue is only partly known. Since the city had no facility in which to jail a leper, Mr. Pogue's stay was short. The clergyman was admonished and promptly returned to the leper settlement on probation. Following his return to the settlement, Mr. Pogue never again challenged the authority of the Belgian priest or uttered another disparaging remark. In the eyes of the Board of Health, however, the Catholic priest who had been so helpful in the past was becoming a nuisance in his new administrative role.

The deluge of written complaints to Rudolph Meyer about Father Damien's misuse of his authority continued to mount. Meyer tried but found that he could not reason with his friend. His patience exhausted, Meyer had no alternative but to inform the Board of Health that Father Damien's administrative talents as the resident superintendent were woefully inadequate. He pleaded for permission to dismiss Damien and appoint a new resident superintendent so that tranquility might be restored. This prompted Samuel Wilder from the Board of Health to visit the settlement and assess the validity of the complaints. After listening for several hours to a long list of perceived injustices, Wilder prudently granted Meyer permission to make the necessary change in personnel.

William Sumner, a part-Hawaiian who was in an advanced stage of leprosy and who had been selected to serve as Father Damien's *kāko'o* (assistant), was promoted to the post of resident superintendent. A relieved Father Damien wrote to his provincial, "For the last three months I patiently bore the duties of *luna* [superintendent], until Wilder finally got here. I asked him to put Sumner in charge, freeing both Keolaloa and me."[15] A haole, Clayton Strawn, was named Sumner's *kāko'o*. No one was happier with the Sumner appointment than Father Damien, except perchance Rudolph Meyer, who for three months had been inundated with complaints.

The appointment of William Sumner failed to have the stabilizing effect Rudolph Meyer had hoped for. While the number of complaints carried up the *pali* to Meyer decreased dramatically, he was disturbed to find that Sumner's poor health prevented him from dealing expeditiously with the problems arising each day. Sumner's assistant Mr. Strawn, eager to become the head *luna*, undermined his superior's position with a poorly written letter to the Board of Health in which he stated that "the Govenor is failing fast."[16] He called Sumner "old and forgetful," a man too weak to ride any distance. He also complained that Father Damien was still viewed as the acting resident superintendent. "It hurts the Govnors feeling to think that the natives go to Father Damien before comeing to him he says it makes him look small." Strawn urged that Sumner be dismissed, and that he be named to the post. At the time, Strawn was living with two female lepers, a married lady and a young girl. Father Damien viewed this behavior as immoral, and it cost Strawn the priest's endorsement. Meyer relayed Father Damien's concern to the board, and it was the consensus of the conservative membership to endorse the status quo and let the Belgian priest continue in his role as the unofficial mediator of complaints and guardian of civil morality.

In late February 1878, Father André, convinced that Father Damien unquestionably had the early signs and symptoms of leprosy, informed both the bishop and the provincial of his concern. A disturbed Father Modeste in turn wrote to the superior general detailing the mounting stresses the leprosy epidemic had placed on the Hawaiian mission and confirmed what many had predicted—that Father Damien had become a leper.[17] This unsettling news upset other priests in the mission who had had physical contact with lepers. Father Boniface, who was stationed on Maui, reported that he feared the eruption on his face and hands was leprosy. He had spent several weeks at the leper settlement during the Easter season of 1873, a few weeks before Father Damien's arrival, and so had experienced a heavy exposure to the disease. This prompted several government physicians to examine Father Boniface, and while the consensus was that his dermatitis wasn't true leprosy, the doctors cautioned that it would be prudent to keep the priest under medical surveillance until the dermatitis cleared. This prompted questions about the health status of two other priests. Father André had a skin condition initially diagnosed as elephantiasis that certainly resembled leprosy; and Father Charles had developed a neuritis in one arm that would place him in the ranks of the lepers should a skin ulceration develop. The provincial expressed his concern that the mission to Hawai'i would collapse if its priests did not immediately desist from ministering to lepers.

Father Damien, tormented by the realization that he had become a leper, waited expectantly for the development of the hideous skin sores and ulcerations that Father André argued convincingly would soon appear. The anesthetic skin spots on his face and arms had not responded to treatment and had increased both in size and number. Most ominous was the progressive loss of normal feeling in his left foot. Walking became increasingly difficult because he couldn't feel the contour of the ground beneath his foot. He began tripping when stepping on small stones, which made climbing the *pali* more hazardous.

Instinctively he knew that whatever he wished to accomplish at the leper settlement should not be postponed. The question about the danger he posed to the nonlepers on the island he placed in the hands of God. Salvaging a soul for eternal life was infinitely more important than safeguarding a physical body for a few years. As best he could, he resolved to avoid all unnecessary physical contact with nonlepers.

Upon review of the evidence that Father Damien had leprosy as early as 1878, Dr. A. A. St. M. Mouritz, resident physician at the leper settlement from 1884 to 1887, concluded that Father André's diagnosis probably was correct. He learned that during the summer of 1878 the "true prodromal symptoms of leprosy manifested themselves, to wit, chills, osteal pains, slight swelling and tenderness of the joints, slight irregular fever, tingling, numbness of the extremities, supersensitive and painful sensation in patches along the extensor surface of the upper and lower extremities; all of which signs, even in the absence of skin lesion, clearly indicated primary infection of Damien's system with leprosy. After about five years of intimate contact with lepers (from the year 1873 to year 1878), he suffered the before mentioned symptoms."[18]

By 1878, Walter Murray Gibson, the man whose editorials in the bilingual newspaper *Ka Nupepa Nuhou* in 1873 had focused the world's attention on the plight of the Hawaiian lepers and the "hero of Moloka'i," the same man whose newspaper articles in 1874 had been the dominant factor in electing King Kalākaua, decided to enter the political arena by declaring himself a candidate for the national legislature representing the island of Maui. Gibson's campaign platform was simple and direct: "Hawaii for the Hawaiians!" Not surprisingly, the Native Hawaiians on Maui enthusiastically voted for him. Those who did so disregarded the fact that this was also the man who had been excommunicated by the Mormon Church for filching the Church's money and land. The Caucasians, on the other hand, hadn't forgotten the chicanery, and most viewed the English-born Gibson not only as a renegade, but as a traitor to the United States. To the Native Hawaiians, however, Gibson was a white man who could confront the growing number of haole and champion their rights. Gibson won the election in a landslide.

No sooner had Gibson taken office than he electrified the nation with his activity. The *Hawaiian Gazette* reported, "He got up more special committees, made more reports, and by his officiousness and vanity kept the legislature in a continual ferment of excitement, merely to enable him to air his inordinate ambition to shine as a leader of the Assembly; and par excellence, the special friend and protector-general of the remnant of the Hawaiian race."[19]

Gibson adroitly maneuvered himself to the chairmanship of the Special Sanitary Committee of the Legislative Assembly, a group with the oversight responsibility for the leper settlement. Then, accompanied by the six members of the committee and a government physician, he boarded an interisland steamer bound for the Kalaupapa Peninsula and a two-day inspection tour of the leper settlement. Gibson was eager to meet the man whom his editorials had elevated to the status of national hero. When he stepped ashore at Kalaupapa and shook hands with the "hero of Moloka'i," he was unaware that he was making physical contact with a leper. With a broad smile he presented Father Damien a gift of $100 from Queen Emma that she wished distributed to the most needy of the lepers—an assignment Damien speedily carried out.[20]

Following his return to Honolulu, Gibson submitted a detailed report of the group's findings and recommendations to G. Rhodes, the president of the Legislative Assembly.[21] While wordy, the lengthy report does relate the findings of the visiting committee and voices the high esteem in which Father Damien was held. While the committee was pleased "that plenty of good water is supplied by pipes, and that there are many hydrants or taps at convenient places for the distribution of water throughout the settlement and at the hospital buildings," they were shocked to find "a notable deficiency in respect to bathing vessels, as only three medium sized bathing tubs were provided for the use of about sixty patients, usually in a filthy and excoriated condition." The suboptimal food supply and the lack of warm clothing were critical issues to be addressed. His report continued:

In the hospital dispensary there was no adequate supply of medicines for such an assemblage of sick people, and no suitable liniments or disinfectants; nor a strip of lint to help cleanse or bandage the sores of the sufferers. . . . At the present time, the Reverend Father has a large burial ground adjoining his church well enclosed, in which deceased lepers, whether of his communion or not, are decently buried. . . . Assistant Superintendent Damien is a devoted and heroic priest, who has voluntarily sacrificed his young life for the welfare of lepers. But his spiritual duties necessarily engross the larger portion of his attention; and it would seem to be a pity to impose the details of secular work upon such a man, and interrupt his holy work of mercy in consoling his wretched parish.[22]

Gibson's report accurately reflected the committee's concern for the welfare of the lepers and reawakened the public's interest in the priest to the lepers. To thank Father Damien, a charity subscription raised the funds to build a two-story rectory to replace the tiny one that had housed the priest for five years.[23] Damien promptly constructed the new rectory just west of St. Philomena, in close proximity to the cemetery. His new home had eight times the square footage as the original rectory and featured an exterior stairway leading to the upper veranda.[24] The first level served as a dispensary/storeroom and consultation room; a workroom/office and bedroom occupied the second floor.

The legislature responded to the Gibson report by increasing the weekly meat ration from 5 to 7 pounds, reducing the 10-pound rice allowance to 9 pounds of rice plus 1 pound of sugar, supplying lumber to build more wooden houses, and, for the first time, it supplied the 692 lepers with soap and kerosene oil.[25]

By April, resident superintendent Sumner was too ill to function effectively. Father Damien, in his role as the chief communicator between the settlement and Rudolph Meyer, informed his friend: "Our old man is very forgetful, and his clerk although a good writer, had no head. . . . My concern for the people and the Board of Health makes it my painful duty to inform you that everything in the administration" is impaired by the "incapability of the captain." He closed with an offer to Meyer: "I would be happy to assist them in any way possible" if such help didn't evoke "any religious jealousy."[26] Meyer accepted the priest's offer to help and continued to rely heavily upon his assistance in the management of the settlement. This expanded Father Damien's role as the unofficial assistant superintendent, and he assumed full responsibility for such critical matters as overseeing the proper distribution of the incoming food.

IT WAS COMMON KNOWLEDGE that the board had budgeted $10,000 for a full-time resident physician, but had found no one willing to take the position. Tired of waiting any longer for the promised physician, several hundred lepers submitted a petition to the Board of Health in May, requesting that Father André be appointed to the post. The medical consultants to the board, however, were unanimous in their insistence that only a properly trained and licensed physician be hired.

An indignant and ailing Father André took matters into his own hands, and in June 1878, he inched his way down the *pali* to take up temporary residence in the house that Peter Kaeo had occupied during his short stay. The priest offered no apologies for his unauthorized move, simply stating that his elephantiasis was too incapacitating to permit him to continue ministering to Moloka'i's healthy residents. He had, he insisted, sufficient stamina to continue his practice of medicine, which he viewed as a major contribution to the leper settlement. Since he and Father Damien had frequently disagreed on Church policy in the past, he felt it would be prudent for the two to live as far apart as possible, so he announced his intention to reside in the village of Kalaupapa where he would practice medicine during the week and celebrate Mass on Sundays. The four parishes topside that his illness was forcing him to abandon he relinquished once again to the care of Father Damien, even though he knew the Belgian priest was a leper. Most of the resident lepers, Protestants and Catholics alike, were overjoyed with the return of Father André to the settlement, and daily a parade of patients rode or hiked to his residence to seek help.

In a brief letter written on June 24, 1878, Father Modeste informed the superior general that Father André's poor health had forced him to abandon his parishes and take up residence in the leper settlement. Since Father Damien's skin lesions were barely visible, Father Modeste saw no reason for the Belgian not to resume ministering to Father André's former parishioners.

FROM FATHER ETIENNE, a Dominican priest in Trinidad, Father Damien learned of a new medicine called *Noang nan* being promoted as a possible cure of leprosy. *Noang nan* had been discovered in the Tonkin region of Southeast Asia and reportedly was extremely effective. Father Damien wrote for and received a supply of *Noang nan* from Father Lesserteur, the director of the Dominican Seminary for Foreign Missions, stationed in Paris.[27] Later he confided to Meyer that he had given the new remedy to a good Christian with early leprosy and achieved excellent results. Based on the encouraging results of this single trial, Bishop Maigret authorized Father Damien to purchase a large enough supply with which to treat all of the lepers at the settlement. The "good Christian whose illness is just beginning" to whom he had administered the pills with "salutary effects" may well have been Father Damien himself, taking the medication to judge its efficacy before recommending it for use by other lepers.

TO DISTANCE HIMSELF as far as possible from Father Damien, Father André moved from Peter Kaeo's former residence to Kalaupapa, where he rented a small room in a house near the church. In the cramped quarters he managed to formulate the multiple medicinals he prescribed each day for his patients. His illness progressed and large, weeping sores appeared on both legs. When the odor emanating from the pus and the ulcerations became obnoxious, Father André became an undesirable tenant and was asked to vacate his room. None of the kama'āina were willing to house a person who had skin lesions every bit as ugly as those seen in leprosy. In desperation, Father André sought help from Father Damien, requesting that the original rectory in Kalawao, now vacant, be relocated in Kalaupapa for his use.[28]

Father Damien responded immediately to Father André's plea for help. Within a few days he dismantled the original rectory in Kalawao and, with added lumber, constructed a house with nearly twice the square footage in Kalaupapa.

As requested, Rudolph Meyer kept the Board of Health apprised of Father André's activities and of his continuing practice of medicine. The medical consultants to the board were displeased. Unlike Father Damien, who treated the common illnesses with recognized medicines supplied by the board, Father André was guilty of formulating his own medicines and employing unorthodox methods of diagnosis and treatment. The board's medical consultants viewed his impudent practice as little better than the type of medicine practiced by the outlawed kahuna lapa'au, and they resolved to find a way to bar the Dutch priest from treating the lepers whom they themselves were fearful to touch.

Father Damien's main concern was not Father André's somewhat unorthodox practice of medicine, but his continuing withdrawal from the Church. In a letter to the provincial, he wrote:

I am witnessing my only companion, Father André, isolating himself more and more from the Congregation, from the mission, from his superiors, and from his companion. . . . I understand that he wishes to establish himself independent from the mission, in which case he will find himself without a church. My advice has enraged him. He replied with a letter filled with insults, showing his determination to separate himself entirely from the Congregation. I went to see him last night, and after an animated conversation, he was persuaded not to do it.[29]

Each morning when Father Damien looked into his mirror to assess the progress of the invader, he saw the lines of concern in the face of a priest confronting an overwhelming task. There were far too many ill lepers for a solitary priest to minister and care for, especially a priest whose pace was now slowed by leprosy. He desperately needed assistance. Father André's presence in Kalaupapa as a physician, while valuable, left a huge void in Moloka'i's spiritual realm. Three parishes topside on the island had been precipitously abandoned, parishes Damien simply lacked both the time and the physical endurance to service; and the quality of Father André's religious ministry in Kalaupapa was questionable. His immediate superiors seemed hesitant to offer a solution, so what recourse did he have but to appeal to the superior general for help? "A new missionary is greatly needed for the post that Father André has left empty; three churches without a priest. Do not count him your child any longer; he wishes to be independent. This distresses me greatly, especially when there is no other confrere on this island. Please send me a good child of the Congregation, and not a stubborn gentleman."[30]

Pressured by the superior general, Father Damien's immediate superiors agonized over what to do. Under no circumstance would they permit a healthy priest to come into direct physical contact with Father Damien or one of his lepers. The only near-term solution was to assign the abandoned Moloka'i parishes to an expendable priest—and there was in Honolulu at the time an obnoxious, overly self-righteous priest from Tuamotu who was recuperating from a weird dermatitis. This priest they could sacrifice.

13

Hutchison, the Survivor; Emerson, the Courageous Physician

And there were many lepers in Israel in the time of the prophet Elisha; and none of them was cleansed, but only Naaman the Syrian.
—Luke 4:27

ON THE EVENING OF January 4, 1879, the clouds above Oʻahu were streaked with crimson and gold as the majority of Honolulu's inhabitants prepared to rest. At the Leper Detention Station on King Street, there was to be no rest as the chief jailor lined up twelve despondent adults who, after a month's detention, had been certified as lepers by the government physician. The jailor curtly instructed the group to take only those belongings that they could carry and proceed two by two to the pier at the foot of Fort Street where the *Mokoliʻi* was waiting to transport them to the leper settlement.

Outside, the newly diagnosed lepers were escorted by a squad of police who denied any contact with the small group of spouses, sobbing children, and friends who shadowed the procession and filled the silence of the night with the mournful chanting of the ancient songs reserved for the dying and the dead. The only comfort the outcasts experienced was the cool breeze that caressed their faces as they plodded their way along the dirt streets that led to the pier.

The twelve lepers were herded up the gangplank of the *Mokoliʻi*, where a crew member pointed to the corral on the open deck generally used for the shipment of live cattle to the leper settlement, where they were to be quartered for the overnight voyage to Molokaʻi. Once inside this enclosure each leper dutifully spread out a blanket on which to sit and sleep. There the twelve sat huddled under police guard until Samuel G. Wilder, the president of the Board of Health, and Dr. Nathaniel B. Emerson came aboard.

Dr. Emerson, the son of one of the original Congregational missionaries and a graduate of Harvard Medical School, had returned to Hawai'i as the general inspector of lepers and leper stations. After several months of unsuccessful efforts to recruit a full-time resident physician for the leper settlement, he had volunteered to serve in that capacity for one year—and one year only. With everyone on board, the *Mokoli'i* headed out to sea.

One of the twelve unfortunates crouched on the main deck was a half-Hawaiian teenager, Ambrose Hutchison by name, who later recorded the events of his first day at the leper settlement.[1]

The next morning at 7 a.m. the steamer anchored. We entered a rowboat in the company of the two officials and rowed to the Kalaupapa landing, and were put ashore and received by the local officials of the Leper Settlement.

After our names, ages and places we hailed from were taken down, we were left on the rocky shore without food and shelter. No houses were provided for the likes of us outcasts.

I was taken in by a kinsman of my mother's [a leper with advanced disease] who sent a man with a saddled horse to bring me to him. On the way in tow of my guide, as we reached the village [Kalaupapa], a priest [Father Andre] came out of a house that stood near the road partly surrounded by a stone wall on one side and a picket fence in front. He walked briskly, passed through the gate on to the road and came on as I approached to pass on my way.

Seeing me a stranger he stopped short and in Hawaiian greeted, "Aloha maika'i 'oe." [A fine greeting to you.] I checked the horse and reciprocated, "Aloha maika'i 'oe e ka Makua." [A fine greeting to you, Father.] He asked if I had eaten. "Not since leaving Honolulu," said I. "All right and follow me to the house and have a cup of coffee." He turned around and walked back to the house. I followed him and dismounted and walked to the house and stood on the veranda. The Father was busy. In a few moments coffee was made. He put food on the table with steaming coffee. . . . From the bottom of my heart I asked God's blessing for the food which my good, unexpected, kind friend had placed before me. Never has food tasted so sweet as that I ate on that day.[2]

Ambrose Hutchison wrote this commentary in 1927, thirty-eight years after the death of Father Damien. Not only was he a survivor, but a keen observer who later became the resident superintendent of the leper settlement, which placed him in an excellent position to chronicle the events that occurred during Father Damien's tenure.

The day following my arrival in the Settlement for "shut in outcasts," I strolled to Kalawao taking in the sights. . . . I leisurely went along till I reached . . . a picket fence surrounding a group of houses (about 12 in number). . . . This was the hospital that sheltered the sick outcasts, men and women. . . . My eyes caught sight of another object that attracted my attention. . . . A man, his face partly covered below the eyes with a white rag or handkerchief tied behind his head, came out from the house . . . pushing a wheelbarrow loaded with a bundle, which at first I mistook for soiled rags. He wheeled it across the yard to a small windowless shack . . . and stopped before the doorway. The man half turned over the wheelbarrow and shook it. The bundle (instead of rags, it was a human being) rolled out on the ground with an agonized groan. The fellow turned the wheelbarrow around and wheeled it away, leaving the sick man lying there helpless. After a while, the dying man raised and pushed himself in the doorway; with his body in and his leg stretched out, he lay there face down.

This spectacle of inhumanity which I witnessed that day filled me with intense horror. . . . Later I was told by old timers that this shack had the reputation and name of Ho'opau Keaho [the "End of Life"] where all dying patients are removed from the hospital to die unattended.[3]

Shortly after witnessing the "End of Life" episode, Hutchison met Father Damien.

Before me there appeared on the scene a priest who had made his round of visits to the inmates of this institution. A well knit stocky man of medium height, dark hair, prominent straight line nose, plump round smooth face and wearing gold rimmed spectacles, garbed in a black cassock with a rope girdle of the same color around his waist, on his head a black stiff brimmed hat held by four bands on the crown. His right hand held the curved end of a stout cane and the other hand held his folded stole. He walked jauntily across the yard and through the gate on to the road and up to where I stood. . . . He asked my name, where I came from and with whom I lived. Answering his queries we stood talking familiarly like old friends for a while, and before going [he] invited me to call on him at his residence which I did later. . . . This was the famed Father Damien, Joseph De Veuster, the Christian hero. There began an acquaintance which grew into an intimacy that lasted ten years and up to the day of his death.

Father Damien was a man of deep faith. He believed in the goodness and the love of Almighty God. He preached faith and hope with all the ardor of his soul in order to uplift the people out of the depravity into which they had fallen and to turn them into good and sincere followers of Jesus Christ.[4]

Nathaniel B. Emerson, M.D., the forty-year-old physician who stepped ashore to become the leper settlement's first resident physician, was the son of the Reverend John S. and Ursula Sophia Newell Emerson, Congregational missionaries. He had been born at Waialua, Oʻahu, where his father was serving as pastor of the native church. Educated at Punahou School in Honolulu, he attended Williams College in the United States until enlisting in the First Regiment of Massachusetts Volunteer Infantry. In Civil War battles, he was wounded twice at Fredericksburg and again at Chancellorsville. He recovered in time to fight at Gettysburg, where the back of his cap was shredded by an exploding shell. The carnage and human misery he witnessed during the war focused his attention on the merits of medical practice. After the Civil War he returned to Williams College where he earned his bachelor's and master's degrees, then studied medicine at Harvard University Medical School and the College of Physicians and Surgeons in New York. For eight years following graduation he practiced medicine in New York before accepting the position as the general inspector of lepers and leper stations in 1878.[5]

At the time he volunteered to serve as the resident physician, Dr. Emerson was actively courting a young lady in Honolulu whom he planned to marry at the conclusion of his one-year commitment. He fully understood that he was exposing himself to a contagious and usually fatal disease, but he believed he could protect himself by assiduously avoiding all physical contact with the lepers.

Dr. Emerson, a devout Congregationalist, was intrigued by the spiritual and medical ministry of Father Damien, a priest who had no formal medical training but who had the audacity to be called "Damien"—the name of the most famous third-century physician. He was intent on discovering what motivated the priest to risk contracting leprosy by cleansing and dressing the skin lesions of the sickest and dying lepers with his bare hands. No knowledgeable physician would be guilty of so suicidal an act.

When he toured the settlement for the first time, Dr. Emerson noted "a large number of people suffering with syphilis in an early stage."[6] The doctor was not surprised by this observation because syphilis was epidemic in the disease-susceptible Native Hawaiian population. He recorded this to emphasize the fact that many of the lepers with advanced leprosy had an *early* stage of the venereal disease. The majority of physicians practicing in Hawai'i in 1879 believed leprosy to be a *late* or *fourth stage* of syphilis. Dr. Emerson never ascribed to this popular theory for two reasons. First, nearly 20 per cent of the lepers at the settlement were children who never had shown signs of the early stages of syphilis; and second, patients with advanced leprosy contracted syphilis for the first time long after they had become lepers.

As an additional safeguard, Dr. Emerson resided in a newly constructed, all-wood bungalow strategically located on the main trail connecting the village of Kalawao with the village of Kalaupapa, over half a mile from the nearest dwelling occupied by lepers. For even greater security, Dr. Emerson had a fence erected around the "clean" house in which he lived, and no leper was ever allowed to enter this enclosure. A nonleper resident was hired as a *kōkua* to prepare his meals and attend to the household chores.

Each time Dr. Emerson made his hospital rounds, he diligently avoided any direct physical contact with a leper, and when he wished to inspect an area of the body he used the traditional approach—a wooden cane to lift the clothing. Even the medicines he prescribed were handed to his patients by one of the hired *kōkua*. When an ill leper needed a doctor after Emerson had retired for the night, he could go to the doctor's bungalow, stand just outside the picket fence, and be examined by questions and the wooden cane. The medicines dispensed on such occasions were first placed in a glass bowl perched on a fence post next to the gate, and once the doctor had backed away from the fence post, the leper was free to reach into the bowl and retrieve the medicine.

Father Damien didn't judge Dr. Emerson's method of practicing medicine to be objectionable or cowardly. All physicians knew how contagious leprosy was and couldn't be faulted for protecting themselves. Even Dr. Wetmore, the physician whom he held in the highest esteem, never touched a leper's open skin lesion with his bare hands. As a priest, Father Damien found this an impossible precaution to follow. The proper administration of the sacraments and the dressing of skin lesions required limited physical contact.

As Dr. Emerson made his initial hospital rounds and home visits, he took a census and counted 782 lepers, 477 of whom were men. Over half of the lepers were seriously ill and ideally needed to be seen on a daily basis, an impossible task for a lone doctor without a supporting staff. Toiling from dawn until dusk, he could care properly for approximately fifty lepers. If he skimped on his evaluations and treatments, he could raise the number to one hundred. Serving as the resident physician was akin to what he had witnessed in the Union Army during the grisly four-day battle at Gettysburg in 1863—but his current tour of duty was scheduled to last not four days, but a year. He was surrounded by death, and death at Kalawao did not come with the merciful quickness of a bullet or an exploding shell on the battlefield. During an average week, he witnessed four deaths, the culmination of days of agonizingly slow deterioration he was powerless to impede. It was a ghastly experience, even for a seasoned physician.

Dr. Emerson was disturbed to observe that the ambulatory lepers preferred the medical services of Father André to his own. Each day, ill lepers made a pilgrimage to the Dutch priest's house where they waited patiently in line to be seen. The majority of the bedridden lepers, Catholic, Protestant, or Mormon, chose to have daily visits from Father Damien in addition to his own. At all hours of the day and night he witnessed Father Damien kneeling at bedside to comfort the dying. The prayers that soothed the patients' mounting anxieties, and the declaration that they would soon be with their Heavenly Father for an eternity of happiness and joy, made the terminal struggle less frightful. Dr. Emerson's medicines could ameliorate the pain and induce sleep, but they were not nearly as effective as the priest's words in buoying the human spirit.

Dr. Emerson scrutinized Father Damien's practice of medicine, and judged the priest's diagnostic acumen for non-life-threatening illnesses to be sound and his treatment of these disorders to be reasonably acceptable. Similarly, William Williamson's able assistance with the sicker lepers in the hospitals was a blessing. Without the help of

Father Damien and Williamson, he estimated that the mortality rate in Kalawao would double. Still, he shuddered when he observed Father Damien clean and dress a leper's skin lesions, a task he viewed as suicidal and personally refused to chance. He was convinced that this Good Samaritan activity would cost the Catholic priest his life; but still, he had to admire the raw courage of any man who would voluntarily sacrifice his life to lessen the suffering of another human being.

The new resident physician found Father Damien to be friendly, universally cheerful, and amenable to using only those medications of which he approved. About the only criticism he had of the priest's practice of medicine was the program Damien had initiated that encouraged the use of *Noang nan* therapy for the treatment and alleged cure of leprosy. After a lengthy debate, the two reached a compromise. Father Damien could continue to prescribe the *Noang nan* medication until such time as Dr. Emerson could objectively determine its effectiveness.

Father André's medical practice in Kalaupapa was another matter. The Dutch priest was as friendly and cheerful as Father Damien, but stubborn and resistant to any suggestions for the improvement of his medical practice. Dr. Emerson observed that Father André not only diagnosed diseases using outmoded methods, but he spent hours each evening compounding a variety of pills from locally gathered herbs or drugs he had obtained in bulk from Europe for use in the treatment of the various illnesses he encountered. His small rectory was a veritable pharmaceutical factory. When Dr. Emerson politely asked him to modify his medical practice and prescribe only those medicines of which he, Dr. Emerson, approved, Father André shook his head and announced that he not only considered himself to be a far more experienced practitioner in treating semitropical illnesses than the doctor from Harvard, but that he was perhaps a superior physician as well. He pointed to the hundreds of lepers who sought his help as proof of his skill.

After three weeks of nonstop doctoring, interrupted only by the bickering with Father André, Dr. Emerson found that he was physically exhausted and emotionally drained. To recuperate, he left the settlement for Honolulu and a one-week respite in the carefree environment of the healthy, where the food was clean and the air one breathed odor free. During the week of rest he packed a sufficient supply of food and medicines for his next three-week sojourn in the horrors of

Moloka'i, then boarded the interisland leper steamer and returned to help the lepers.

It became Dr. Emerson's practice to spend a recuperative week in Honolulu each month, and with each respite he became more intolerant of the numerous people with the obvious skin lesions of leprosy who were allowed to roam the Islands at will, totally disregarding the segregation ordinance. The government, instead of curtailing the spread of leprosy, was selfishly profiting through the sale of indulgences to exempt affluent lepers from incarceration. This behavior was, in Dr. Emerson's mind, unconscionable, and he voiced his strong disapproval in a report to the Board of Health.

> I cannot refrain from remarking with great regret the comparatively small number of lepers that have been brought to this settlement from without during the past year, when one considers . . . the lepers now outside of the leper settlement cannot number less that five or six hundred. . . . Of all the causes, therefore, now operating to sap the vitality of the Hawaiian race, and to bring about its extermination, none is so fraught with danger, and so calculated to alarm the mind of the wellwisher of this race as this disease of diseases.[7]

Dr. Emerson's denunciation did little to change the status quo. During his one-year tour of duty, there were only ninety-two admissions to the leper settlement because of the apathetic enforcement of the segregation policy.

FOR AMBROSE HUTCHISON all went well until his relative, Richard Una, became too ill to care for himself. Hutchison compassionately nursed the dying man during his terminal struggle with leprosy so that hospitalization with its inherent indignities and risks could be avoided. Then one day he witnessed a blatant injustice that he found not only despicable, but a practice that was widespread throughout the settlement.

> I was yet to witness four months later [May] another act of ill treatment of sick lepers, in this case a person living . . . in his own home. . . . An officer with a high sounding name "Ilamuku" [marshal], . . . [came] to the house of my makua kane [kinsman] . . . the week before his death. . . . This officer seized every movable belonging of the sick man. Trunks of clothes, dishes, pots and hogs, etc. and loaded them on an ox cart and carried them away, taking the horse, saddle and bridle along with

him and against the owner's protest which the brute paid no attention
to, leaving only what the sick man had on his person. A few days after
this incident happened my makua kane died. I had the disagreeable task
with the help of friends to place the remains of my relative in his coffin
with nothing on but a calico print muu muu. He was carried by friends
and buried at the Kalaupapa burial ground near the sea shore. This
unpleasant, sad experience moved me to call on Dr. N. B. Emerson, resident physician of the Leper Settlement at his residence. To him I stated
the high handed unjust act of the officer sent by the administration.

The doctor acted promptly and had the deceased's personal property
sold at public auction and the money sent to Honolulu to be given to
the deceased's daughter who is still living in Honolulu, and the forcible
taking of personal property of unfortunate sick lepers before the owner
is dead stopped.[8]

DURING THE SEVENTH month of Dr. Emerson's tenure, measles, the
highly infectious childhood disease caused by a paramyxovirus, struck
the leper settlement with an attack rate approaching 90 percent in
those who had no previous exposure to the virus.[9] The death rate for
this usually benign disease of childhood exceeded 25 percent among
the Native Hawaiians.[10] In the minds of many, the haole who had
brought God and the alphabet to Hawai'i continued to plague the land
with his contagion and death.

EARLIER IN THE YEAR, Father Damien had appealed to Bishop Maigret for building materials with which to construct domiciliaries to
house the growing number of orphan children. Mid-year the materials arrived for the first boys' home and Damien, with the assistance of
a leper, undertook the construction of an orphanage designed to
accommodate twelve orphan boys.[11] So that he could efficiently supervise the operation of the orphanage, he located the structure about 40
feet to the west of his rectory. A small cookhouse and a dining vestibule
located 10 feet to the rear of the dormitory completed the first home
for orphaned boys. The orphan boys thrived in this compassionate yet
disciplined environment. Schooling, which included religious instruction and band practice, made the orphanage the envy of the settlement.
Other orphans, girls as well as boys, asked to join the twelve "lucky"
boys. Each child Father Damien had to turn away seemed a personal

betrayal to the Christ who never turned a child away, and he began to plan how best he might house more of the orphans.

ACCORDING TO AMBROSE HUTCHISON, Father Damien confided that after he had placed himself on *Noang nan* therapy, he had noted a temporary regression of his skin lesions. This was the stimulus to order a supply of the medicine sufficient to treat all of the lepers. For nearly a year, Father Damien remained optimistically hopeful about the efficacy of the *Hoang nan* pills. He attributed the dramatic reduction in the number and the size of the spots on his arms and trunk to the pills, which contained the powdered bark of the *Hoang nan* tree mixed with alum and realga. But there was a problem. Dr. Emerson remained dubious and discouraged the Native Hawaiians from taking the remedy. Jonathan Napela, the Mormon elder, seconded the doctor's concern. He was skeptical that any drug promoted by a Catholic would prove beneficial. He advised the Mormons not to use it, stating that he had learned of a medicine used in India that was curative. He urged patience as he had written to the minister of the Interior requesting that the government procure the lifesaving medicine from India for the lepers.[12] Finally, Father Damien found that it was frustratingly difficult to get the Hawaiians to take the *Hoang nan* pills three times a day in the prescribed manner.[13]

One by one the Hawaiians withdrew from the *Hoang nan* treatment program despite the fact that it was credited with clearing the skin lesions of two Caucasian lepers.[14] Dr. Emerson was of the opinion that neither individual had actually been a true leper, that the skin lesions had merely mimicked those of the dread disease and then cleared spontaneously. Father Damien was not deterred and continued swallowing the pills three times a day and following the strict dietary restrictions, hopeful that he was benefiting from the regime. The skin spots on Father Damien's face and arms that had initially regressed reappeared, this time larger and in greater numbers. The area of numbness in his left foot increased, and it became difficult for him to walk without a limp. When the telltale nodules of leprosy appeared on his face, he consulted Dr. Emerson, who insisted that he discontinue *Hoang nan*. A disappointed Father Damien resolved to continue with his ministry as long as God gave him the physical

strength to do so. Forcing a smile, he dispelled depression by repeat-
ing, "Come on, Jef, my boy! This is your life."

When Dr. Emerson became ill toward the end of 1879 and was
forced to leave the settlement for a few weeks, he asked for and was
given the entire *Hoang nan* inventory, which he carried aboard the
interisland steamer. A few miles from Honolulu he tossed the failed
medicine over the side into the sea.[15]

After completing his year as the leper settlement's first resident
physician, Dr. Nathaniel Emerson married Dr. Sarah E. Pierce, whom
he had continued to court during his free weeks in Honolulu. The couple took up residence in Honolulu, where Dr. Emerson established a
private practice of medicine while continuing to serve as an active
member of the Board of Health. In time the couple had a son, Arthur
W. Emerson.

IN NORWAY, the indefatigable Dr. Armauer Hansen doggedly continued his quest to prove that a bacterium caused leprosy. During the
summer months of 1879, he cordially received Albert Neisser, a 24-
year-old student of Dr. Robert Koch, the world-famous German bac-
teriologist, and graciously demonstrated his rod-shaped microbes in
the hope that Neisser could devise a means to stain the bacterium,
which would facilitate the microscopic study of the organism. Neisser
failed in his initial attempts, but when he left Bergen a few weeks later
he took with him a large suitcase packed with leprous tissue samples
given him by Dr. Hansen. As soon as the young man returned to Bres-
lau, he proceeded to apply recently devised staining methods—and to
his "intense surprise," he succeeded! In October 1879, he gave a lecture detailing "his discovery" to a local association of scientists and
promptly published a dissertation of his findings.[16]

Not once did Neisser acknowledge that Dr. Hansen had demonstrated the microscopic rods to him during his visit to Bergen. He contended that the discovery of the rods was his and his alone. Neisser's
piracy, however, did achieve one thing of value. The resulting controversy as to the true identity of the discoverer of the leprosy bacillus
focused the scientific world's attention on the tiny *Bacillus leprae*, now
known as *Mycobacterium leprae*, and established without question
that leprosy was a unique, contagious disease unrelated to syphilis.

Father Damien at the age of thirty-three in 1873, the year he went to Moloka‘i.
Courtesy of the Sacred Hearts Archives, Louvain, Belgium.

The birthplace of Father Damien in Tremeloo, Belgium. The attached building on the left is the Father Damien Museum. Courtesy of the Sacred Hearts Archives, Louvain, Belgium.

Father Damien at age twenty-three, taken before sailing to Hawai'i, 1863. Courtesy of the Sacred Hearts Archives, Louvain, Belgium.

Father Damien at age thirty-five, with members of the St. Philomena Girls' Choir. Courtesy of the Sacred Hearts Archives, Louvain, Belgium.

St. Philomena Church, Kalawao, Moloka'i. Photograph by R. D. Stewart, M.D.

Interior of St. Philomena Church, Kalawao, Moloka'i. Courtesy of the Sacred Hearts Archives, Louvain, Belgium.

Father Damien's Hawaiian grave, adjacent to St. Philomena's Church. Photograph by R. D. Stewart, M.D.

Mother Marianne in 1878, after her election to the post of second mother provincial of the Sisters of St. Francis of Syracuse. Courtesy of the Cause of Mother Marianne of Moloka'i, Sisters of St. Francis, Syracuse, NY.

Brother Joseph Dutton at the age of twenty in 1863, as a lieutenant in the 13th Wisconsin Volunteers, where he was known as Ira B. Dutton. Courtesy of the Sacred Hearts Archives, Louvain, Belgium.

Brother Joseph Dutton, age 85, stayed on Moloka'i from 1886 to 1931. Courtesy of the Sacred Hearts Archives, Louvain, Belgium.

Kalawao, post-1873, looking west. Hospital compound to the right of the road, store to the left. Courtesy of the Hawai'i State Archives, Honolulu.

The sea cliffs of Moloka'i's north shore rise above the Baldwin Home at Kalawao, ca. 1900. Courtesy of the Hawai'i State Archives, Honolulu.

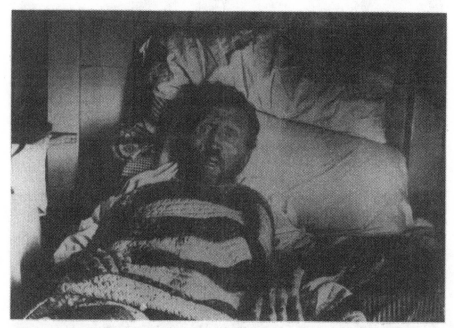

Father Damien on his deathbed, photographed by Dr. Sidney Swift shortly before he died on April 15, 1889, at age 49. Courtesy of the Sacred Hearts Archives, Louvain, Belgium.

St. Joseph's Chapel, Louvain, Belgium. Courtesy of the Sacred Hearts Archives, Louvain, Belgium.

Father Damien's tomb in the crypt of St. Joseph's Chapel, Louvain, Belgium. Courtesy of the Sacred Hearts Archives, Louvain, Belgium.

14

His Finest Works

*Then the children were brought to him that he might lay his
hands on them and pray. The disciples rebuked the people;
but Jesus said, "Let the children come to me, and do not hinder
them; for to such belongs the kingdom of heaven."*
—Matthew 19:13–14

THE CHILDREN WITH leprosy were of special concern to Father
Damien. Each year ten to twenty unattended children, ranging in age
from eight to fifteen years, disembarked at the Kalaupapa wharf. Those
few who were fortunate enough to have resident relatives physically
capable of caring for them found shelter. Those who did not were
placed in foster homes by the resident superintendent. The foster home
setting invited exploitation, and all too often the child was relegated to
the status of a slave. Most abhorrent to Father Damien was the knowledge that sexual molestation of the orphan children was commonplace.
All too frequently, when the orphan's disease progressed to the point
where he or she no longer was able to serve the adults, children were
cast out of the home and left to fend for themselves.

Father Damien had addressed the problem of the orphans in mid-
1879 by building a domiciliary for twelve orphan boys. To supervise
the orphans and oversee the food preparation, he hired a male *kōkua*,
a nonleper, who was paid a small salary by the Board of Health. The
facility proved to be so popular that other boys unhappy in their foster home situations begged to be allowed to live there. The priest
responded to the demand by building a second and larger dormitory,
20 x 40 feet, just north of the original structure.

So successful were the two boys' orphanages that Father Damien persuaded the Board of Health to supply the building materials for a dormitory for the orphan girls. When the lumber, nails, and paint arrived he donned his carpenter's shirt and trousers, and for a short time he enjoyed the euphoria of creating a structure over which he was in control of the outcome. Manual labor continued to be a welcome escape from the gut-twisting agony of coping with death and dying. When the orphanage was completed, with funds supplied by the Board of Health he hired a female *kōkua* to be the supervising matron and cook.

In a letter to his older brother in Louvain, he described the undertaking: "I have a small orphanage for young leper girls. An aged widow, who is not sick, is their cook and mother. Although the orphanages are separated from my house, we have meals in common and share our rations. We each get seven pounds of beef and twenty-one pounds of taro weekly; with that we think we're pretty well fed. We have also planted a big field of potatoes as a reserve when the rations don't get here on time. Some charitable souls send me bundles of clothes for the children which come to me via the Mother Superior in Honolulu."[1]

In the words of Dr. Arthur Mouritz, the settlement's fourth resident physician, the building and supervision of the orphanages was "one of the finest works that this priest undertook and carried out."[2]

The Board of Health budgeted for schools for the children, one for the boys and a second for the girls. Qualified lepers were given a small stipend to teach. By 1880 the boys' school building was so overcrowded that Father Damien requested—and promptly received—the materials with which to build a larger building.[3] No sooner had the construction been completed and the building occupied than Father Damien enthusiastically added a course in religious instruction to the curriculum. This elicited a strong objection from the Protestants, who lodged a formal complaint with the resident superintendent, who in turn relayed the matter to the Board of Health for adjudication. While the all-Protestant Board of Health genuinely appreciated Father Damien's efforts to improve the quality of life for the leper children, they were unanimous in their decision to ban the teaching of Catholicism in the public schools on the grounds that the Hawaiian constitution mandated that church and state remain separated. The Board insisted that the Kingdom's policy of neutrality toward all religions must be preserved.[4] Father Damien silently complied.

In contrast to the relatively short, infrequent letters Father Damien wrote to Father Pamphile following the publication of several of his narrative letters in the *Annales des Sacres Coeurs*, letters which had elicited such bitter criticism from both his peers and his superiors, a lengthy letter written in late January 1880 indicates that a reconciliation had taken place. Father Pamphile had promised never again to submit one of his younger brother's letters for publication without first securing permission to do so.

My dear brother,

Your kind letter of the 12th of November from Louvain reached me on the 2nd of January. It is difficult to believe that I have been here nearly seven years among the lepers. During that long period I have had the opportunity of closely observing, as it were, touching with my fingers human misery in its most frightening aspect. Half of our people are like living corpses whom the worms have already begun to devour, at first interiorly, and soon exteriorly, forming the most hideous wounds which are rarely cured. As to the odor, imagine what the stench of Lazarus' tomb must have been.

The Hawaiian government still continues to collect and send new lepers here as soon as they find them, and as their means permit. The 65,000 piasters appropriated for the maintenance of the lepers for two years are not sufficient to defray the cost of gathering all those whom they find in the different islands. The exiles sent to Molokai maintain the leper population at seven to eight hundred; we cannot take more for lack of resources.

Since I have been here we have buried from 150 to 200 lepers a year, and the number of living is always greater than 700. Last year death carried off an unusually large number of Christians. There are many empty places in the pews in the church, but in the cemetery there is hardly room left to dig the graves. I was annoyed the other day because they had begun to dig a grave near the large cross to the right of which I had planned for a long time to be buried. I insisted that they leave that place empty.

The cemetery, the church, and the rectory form a park where I am the lone gardener. During the night I tend this beautiful garden of the dead where my spiritual children sleep. I delight to go there to say my rosary, and to meditate on the eternal joy which most of them are already enjoying.[5]

THE NATIONAL ELECTION of legislators held February 4, 1880, focused on the nation's economy, and the majority of the candidates adroitly sidestepped the politically sensitive issue of the control of leprosy. In Honolulu alone, an estimated one hundred lepers were being hidden by their families, and for the proper contribution to the king's personal money chest, the affluent and the well connected were exempted from the segregation ordinances. For a politician to be either "for" or "against" the stiffer enforcement of the segregation program could cost votes.

Candidates favored by King Kalākaua campaigned on a platform promising to borrow sufficient foreign money to enhance the prestige of the monarchy and to develop a military force strong enough to discourage future foreign intervention. Queen Emma's candidates were conservative and supported the status quo. The third collection of candidates, those voicing the concerns of the haoles who controlled most of the wealth in the islands, were unhappy with the king's extravagance, the growing national debt, and the excessive taxation. Of the haole candidates, only three were elected. Those who had clamored for fiscal reform and lower taxes garnered only those few votes cast by the haole minority. Of the three successful haole, the man who won by the largest margin was none other than newspaper editor Walter Murray Gibson.[6] His campaign slogan, "Hawaii for the Hawaiians," had great popular appeal; and his bold promise to improve conditions at the leper settlement was applauded. With over 2 percent of the native population infected, nearly everyone had a family member or a friend who was incarcerated on Moloka'i's hostile peninsula.

Samuel Wilder, the minister of the Interior and president of the Board of Health, in a banquet speech presented ten days after the election, permanently alienated himself from his monarch by openly repudiating the king's desire to obtain a large foreign loan.[7] An irate King Kalākaua promptly began the search for a replacement for his disloyal minister. On August 14, 1880, he assembled his cabinet to inform them that since they no longer reflected his interests nor supported of his goals, they were all dismissed. In Samuel Wilder, the lepers lost the support of the Protestant who had done the most to provide for them. Later that day the king appointed a new cabinet, one that guaranteed compliance with his wishes—but a cabinet devoid of the expertise to govern a country. Such irresponsibility stunned the tax-paying business community.

All was not peace and contentment at the leper settlement. Father

Damien's ecumenical tolerance of the Mormons exasperated his bishop. The priest was repeatedly guilty of being hospitable to Mormon elders who were permitted by the Board of Health to visit the settlement and minister to the lepers embracing the Mormon beliefs. This seemingly harsh judgment on the part of his superiors was in large measure a retaliation for the overt hostility to the Catholic Church exhibited by the Mormons elsewhere in the Pacific in the several locales where the Mormons were in the majority.[8] Catholic priests had been attacked and beaten; Catholic churches had been burned. In Bishop Maigret's opinion, the Mormons were guilty of despicable behavior, so their elders were not to be befriended. Following a reprimand for his misguided hospitality, Father Damien was forced to write to the Mormons.

> Please have the kindness to inform your headman at Laie that I have received from my bishop a positive prohibition to receive as I am used to do any of your people who in the future may visit the Leper Settlement.
>
> This, my bishop's order pains my heart very much. Please excuse me—I want to obey orders.[9]

A more vexatious situation for Father Damien arose in the early months of 1880. Father André began a deliberate withdrawal from the Church. While the older priest condescended to hear Father Damien's weekly confession, he steadfastly refused to have his confession heard. At the same time his practice of medicine intensified to the point that his spiritual ministry was seriously neglected. When queried as to why, Father André talked of his dissatisfaction with the priesthood and of his intent to abandon his post. During one of these altercations Father André volunteered that in addition to leaving the priesthood he was also considering marriage. The shocked look on Father Damien's face afforded him a modicum of amusement. When Father Damien tried to reason with him, the discussion erupted into a loud and unpleasant shouting match.

Bishop Maigret was cognizant of the increasing discord at the leper settlement, but he was fearful of a public scandal should he order the Dutch priest to comply with Dr. Emerson's rules for the medical care of the lepers. Father André might actually renounce the priesthood and—heaven forbid—even marry if forced to limit his practice of medicine.[10] Because Father André's skin disease so closely mimicked the lesions of leprosy, the priest could legitimately request permanent asylum at the settlement and further complicate the matter.[11] For help with the delicate affair, Father Regis, the vice-provincial, appealed to the superior general to remove Father André from the Hawaiian mission before the situation worsened.[12]

While Father André clashed with Father Damien, his bishop, his provincial, and Dr. Emerson, to most people he appeared to be a model priest—calm, even-tempered, a gentle person who loved books and his garden. Ambrose Hutchison, the young leper who would become the resident superintendent in 1884, was a frequent afternoon visitor, and Rudolph Meyer held the priest in high esteem. The Native Hawaiians trusted his diagnostic acumen and preferred his treatment regimes to those offered by American doctors.

The superior general responded to the request to transfer Father André, and in a compromise move directed the priest to leave Moloka'i and take a parish assignment at Lahaina on Maui. Prior to the date of Father André's scheduled departure, Father Damien called on him for a last "friendly conversation." The Dutch priest "became very violent towards him and without provocation threatened to take his [Damien's] life, at the same time hastily going into an adjoining room as if to procure the means of carrying out his threat."[13] An alarmed Damien fled and appealed to Dr. Emerson, who was visiting the settlement at the time, for protection.

Young Ambrose Hutchison happened to be on his way for an afternoon visit with Father André when the fracas began and witnessed Father Damien's hasty departure. Hutchison reported that as Damien leaped into his saddle and rode off, he shouted a warning not to go in because "there is a devil in there."[14] Hutchison, who had always enjoyed Father André's company and considered the priest a friend, ignored the warning and entered the rectory. There he found the Dutch priest seated in a chair with a book in his lap, calmly smoking his long-stemmed meerschaum pipe. When Hutchison asked what had caused Father Damien to flee, Father André puffed on his pipe for a few moments while contemplating a reply. Then he pointed the pipe at him and holding it by the bowl, calmly remarked, "Nothing, it's only in the blood."[15]

Following his one-day visit to the leper settlement, Dr. Emerson reported to the board that measures had to be taken to correct what he judged to be a schizoid practice of medicine. Father Damien was conscientiously prescribing the medicines supplied by the board for the treatment of the common maladies plaguing the lepers. The Belgian's diagnostic acumen was surprisingly good considering his lack of formal training. Father André, on the other hand, was practicing a *kahuna* type of medicine, prescribing herbal remedies about which little was known, remedies he compounded himself. The Dutch priest stubbornly refused to use those medicines recommended and supplied by Dr. Emerson. Someone had to put a halt to this poor practice and since Bishop Maigret was unable to control his priest, the board would have to act.

One week later, Father André received a summons to appear before the French government commissioner in Honolulu to answer a charge lodged against him by the Board of Health for practicing medicine without a license. In a brief meeting the ailing priest was told to cease and desist in his practice of medicine or face imprisonment. An embittered Father André returned to the leper settlement just long enough to collect his few belongings, and then—to demonstrate to everyone that he was in reasonably sound health—he left the Kalaupapa Peninsula via the strenuous climb up the *pali* trail, toting his few possessions in a pack slung over his shoulder. On a borrowed horse, he rode to the coast and boarded a steamer for Lahaina, Maui, where he meekly assumed his assigned post. Never again did Father André set foot in the leper settlement, nor did he again practice medicine in the Hawaiian Islands.[16]

Contrary to the Rule of the Sacred Hearts, Father Damien was once again the lone priest for the entire island of Moloka'i. His peers sympathized with the soul-numbing isolation with which the young Belgian once again had to contend. On August 23, Father Gulstan wrote to him from the Big Island: "I know that you have made your retreat at Honolulu; I know also that you find yourself alone on your island, and that Father André arrived at Lahaina Saturday, the 14th of the month. As I believe you are happier now than in the past, I wish you the best with all my heart."[17] An October note from Father Charles confided, "I beg you to pray very much for him who is sincerely yours in the Sacred Hearts, and who will be happy if it be the will of Almighty God, to finish his days with you."[18] When Father Charles wrote this letter, he probably suspected that he too had contracted the foul *ma'i Pākē*.

ON THE MORNING of September 18, 1880, Dr. Charles Neilson, an American-trained doctor who had been recruited by Dr. Emerson to become the settlement's second resident physician, stepped onto the wharf at Kalaupapa and handed Father Damien a letter addressed to him from none other than Walter Murray Gibson, the legislator. Damien opened the envelope and read the short note:

> My dear Father Damien,
>
> I recommend to your kindness Doctor Neilson who will present these lines to you. I hope that this worthy doctor will be for the poor lepers a true friend. I have great hope that he will prove to be the man that I hoped to find in 1878 when I so earnestly proposed the appointment of a doctor for the lepers. Be a friend to him, and I will be very grateful to you.
>
> Your friend,
> Walter M. Gibson[19]

In the company of the resident superintendent, Clayton Strawn, Dr. Neilson proceeded to inspect the leper settlement. As he did so, he took detailed notes on what he observed and later reported his assessment of the complex in a lengthy report to the Board of Health.[20] Most disturbing to the new doctor was the fact that there had been only 51 admissions to the settlement in 1880, dropping the census to 568, an all-time low. It was apparent that the Segregation Law was being circumvented, and Dr. Neilson seconded Dr. Emerson's dire prediction that unless the situation were rectified the public health consequences would be devastating.

Dr. Neilson's report contains information about the settlement found nowhere else in the surviving documents. He inventoried the medical supplies, the emergency food rations, the available clothing, the number of blankets in the hospitals, and the salaries of everyone who was providing a contract service, including the resident superintendent. He stated that the "hospital complex" in 1880 consisted of four "hospital barracks," seven smaller houses for seriously ill patients, a small cookhouse, and a dispensary, the largest building in the group.

A few excerpts from Dr. Neilson's report follow.

> There were in the hospital forty-seven patients, male and female, in separate wards. . . . I revisited the hospital to examine into the clothing supply. I found (30) blankets which had been in former use by leprous

patients now deceased, also collections of their clothing. They had been washed and dried in the sun and were placed away for safe keeping. . . . This constituted the entire stock of clothing on hand. . . . I found the hospital accommodations insufficient for the reception of the more aggravated cases. As they are naturally inclined to help each other, those who are scarcely able to help themselves should receive assistance in hospital and not be allowed to increase the general debility of others. . . . I wish to remark here that there were no disinfectants remaining on hand among the medical supplies and that the hospital nor buildings pertaining thereto, nor the houses on any portion of the settlement . . . have been disinfected for the past two years. . . . I will add that the medical supplies now on hand are insufficient to meet the present demand; they are in need of many articles (pharmaceutical) that have been expended, and many remedies are wanting that they constantly require. A requisition should be made out immediately for their benefit in order that they be not deprived of regular and continuous treatment. . . .

The hygienic condition of patients would be much improved if additional hospital accommodations could be procured. I would suggest that an additional hospital be constructed for the accommodation of at least one hundred patients, that it be constructed in a proper manner to insure more perfect ventilation.[21]

Dr. Neilson's report was the stimulus for a renewed effort on the part of the Board of Health to segregate Hawai'i's lepers and resulted in quadrupling the number of new admissions to the leper settlement. This forced the new resident physician into the same awkward predicament that had frustrated Dr. Emerson. Without the support of a professionally trained staff, he was powerless to care for all of the ill lepers in a timely manner. Father Damien became a welcomed ally, a man he could trust to treat the less seriously ill lepers with conventional medicines.

READERS WHO SCANNED the obituaries listed in the *Hawaiian Gazette* on December 1, 1880, learned of the death of Peter Young Kaeo, the notorious escapee from the leper settlement, the leper who had managed through his royal connections to escape lifelong incarceration. Reportedly, Peter had died after a five-day illness. The direct cause of death was never disclosed.[22]

PRIMARILY TO ASSUAGE the concerns of the business community whose taxes were essential to his continuing reign, King Kalākaua dismissed every member of his most recently appointed cabinet in September 1880 and appointed an all-haole cabinet, one exceptionally well qualified for the tasks at hand.[23] The absence of a single Native Hawaiian in the king's cabinet elicited a howl of anguish from the native population, which the king ignored. When it appeared that the newly appointed cabinet could quite adequately govern the nation in his absence, Kalākaua turned his attention to fulfilling a dream he had coveted for years—to be the first monarch in history to circumnavigate the globe, visiting each of the countries important to the Hawaiian economy.

The stated purpose of the global trip was to explore ways by which peoples from other countries could be induced to come to Hawai'i to help reverse the population decline. But King Kalākaua had a secret agenda—the dream of becoming the master ruler of the Pacific Basin. Surreptitiously, he planned to use the tour of the world to promote the concept of a Polynesian federation of nations headed by himself.[24] The king commenced the journey that would last nine months but achieve little of substance.

In the king's absence, his sister Princess Lili'uokalani was named regent because Queen Kapi'olani did not wish to assume any of her absentee husband's responsibilities. During the months that Kalākaua was away, the multitalented Princess Lili'uokalani instituted measures that resulted in many improvements in the administration of government.[25] Cognizant of the financial drain that the leper settlement was placing upon the treasury, the princess decided to inspect the settlement later in the year and meet the Catholic priest who had achieved the economies touted by both Rudolph Meyer and the Board of Health. A staunch Protestant, Lili'uokalani was curious to learn what motivated a Catholic to risk his life to help lepers, a sacrifice none of the clergy of her church was willing to make.

FATHER DAMIEN'S STAUNCHEST supporter during his sojourn in the Hawaiian mission field was Bishop Maigret. The elderly priest had been a tolerant, forgiving father figure who patiently guided and occasionally chided the young Belgian priest whose eagerness to please God sometimes resulted in minor indiscretions. Now, however, the seventy-seven-year-old prelate found himself no longer able to maintain the vigorous pace that had characterized his earlier years. Since the late 1870s he had become more and more a recluse, and it was apparent to all that the aging bishop needed an assistant if the Catholic missionary movement in Hawai'i were to maintain its momentum. Consequently, on May 17, 1881, Father Hermann Koeckemann was named titular Bishop of Olba and coadjutor to Bishop Maigret with the right of succession. In contrast to Bishop Maigret, Father Hermann was a strict disciplinarian with little tolerance for even a minor infraction. Bishop Maigret had quietly admired the vigor and enthusiasm with which Father Damien served God by ministering to the Native Hawaiians and later to the lepers. The priest's occasional faux pas, attributable to his abbreviated formal training, could be readily forgiven. Bishop Hermann, however, viewed Damien's ministry quite differently. He was highly critical of the acclaim that had been heaped repeatedly on a priest who, in his opinion, lacked a modicum of humility and clamored for notoriety by allowing his personal letters to be published. Still, he had little choice but to accept the Belgian for what he was—flawed but irreplaceable. He recognized that Father Damien's tenure at the leper settlement was a death warrant, and he prayed that Damien would be able to continue in his role as priest to the lepers for years to come for he doubted that he could justify permanently assigning another priest to a post that guaranteed death from leprosy.

IN HIS SECOND biannual report to the Board of Health, submitted in July 1881, Dr. Neilson was "pleased to acknowledge" that during his tenure substantial improvement in the hygiene of the leper settlement had occurred, due in large measure to the addition of sturdy wooden houses. These houses were the product of the ongoing house-building project championed by the Catholic priest. One by one the thatched huts were being replaced. The most flagrant failure, in Dr. Neilson's opinion, was the Board of Health's visitation policy. "Leprosy being a contagious disease, may I ask why are people allowed permits to visit this settlement, to eat, and dwell among the lepers during their sojourn, returning to their respective homes to mingle among the healthy. I will say I am powerless to prevent it. . . . This pernicious practice of permits being granted to a people entirely ignorant of the dangers attendant upon visiting this settlement is known to every medical mind in this Kingdom."[26]

The resident physician concluded his report with a summary of the latest treatment modality, which he judged to have been benefi-cial—*gargon oil*: "Of the twenty-five cases in hospital who began the use of this oil as divided by myself, many of whom were in an advanced stage of the disease, three only have died; the remainder still continue its use expressing themselves as feeling well when asked the state of their health. . . . I will say that in every instance both in hospital and outside (where it has been used extensively), I know of no case in which it has failed to improve the general health of the patient."

In late summer 1881, Father Damien consulted with Dr. Neilson regarding a nearly incapacitating pain that gripped his feet in the evening hours. Initially the pain had been a dull ache confined to the left foot, but within a few weeks he had begun to experience frank, unadulterated pain in both feet, always more pronounced in the left.[27] Neilson's presumptive diagnosis was bilateral sciatic nerve pain prob-ably secondary to arthritis of the spine caused by all of the heavy lift-ing Damien had been doing when building churches, chapels, and houses. Despite additional rest, the disturbing pain in his feet grew worse, and under Dr. Neilson's supervision he was placed on a trial of the highly touted gargon oil. Dr. Neilson recognized that the sciatic pain of which Father Damien complained could well be a manifesta-tion of the leprosy that would ultimately claim the priest's life. Regret-tably, during Dr. Neilson's tenure it became evident that the efficacy of gargon oil was minimal at best.

IN AUGUST, Princess Lili'uokalani announced that she and her en-tourage would make the promised visit to inspect the leper settlement on September 15. This provoked intense activity in the villages of Kalawao and Kalaupapa as Father Damien and his parishioners cleaned and whitewashed every structure in sight. So that the princess and her chosen guests would have an uncontaminated place in which to eat and rest, a special pavilion with triumphal, flower-covered arches was constructed. Large, colorful banners of greeting were hung, and the children's choir rehearsed their program daily. Father Damien wished the princess to see that it was possible to not only enjoy beauty while being ravaged by leprosy, but to sing and laugh if one had faith in the ultimate goodness of God.

One week before the princess' scheduled arrival, a fifty-six-year-old priest with a disfiguring dermatitis stepped onto the wharf at

Kalaupapa accompanied by the incoming group of newly deported lepers. It was claimed that his malady was not leprosy, but it evidenced some of the features of the disease. He walked straight up to Father Damien and introduced himself as Father Albert Montiton, Father André's replacement. He stated that he was a veteran missionary priest who, because of a dreadful dermatitis, had been transferred from the 3,000-mile-distant Tuamotu Archipelago to Hawai'i to recuperate. Seven years had passed without a visible improvement. Since he was capable of limited service, Bishop Maigret was stationing him in the village of Kalaupapa so Father Damien would have a confrere close at hand.

A review of the Sacred Hearts correspondence between Father Modeste, Father Regis, and the superior general, however, suggests an additional, more compelling motive. On May 10, 1875, Father Modeste had written to the superior general: "I have acted on your advice regarding Father Albert. May he profit by it in order to live in peace, and to let others be. We have much trouble in satisfying him; his illness, the special food he needs, the means he uses to obtain what he judges useful for his mission are difficult obstacles to surmount. His system of evangelism, used at Tuamotu is not applicable in the Sandwich Islands."[28]

In 1879, Father Regis complained to the superior general: "As to Father Albert, he is satisfied with nothing; everything must be done over, everyone is at fault, and also almost everyone complains of him, I among the first. His district is too large, he says, and he has done almost nothing, other than to embellish in his fashion some room or chapel. Under various pretenses he is often absent for a long time, running far and wide, even to other islands in order to go to confession . . . others must bow to his caprice, exposing themselves to catching his illness. . . . Furthermore, he treats all those who do not agree with him rudely, as well as those who do not do as he wishes, above all the Kanaks whom he wants to treat like the savages of Tuamotu."[29]

And in April 1880, Regis wrote: "When one hears anything about Father Albert, it is that peace with him is impossible. He is said to have, from your Reverend, a commission to tell you all that is happening, and to do all he wishes relative to reform, laws, usages, men and buildings. With all that, he empties chapels and churches. Everyone complains of him."[30]

Father Albert Montiton, Father Damien learned later that day, was a Norman from Sourdeval, France, with a reputation for achievement. Following the completion of a superb formal education for the priesthood, he had volunteered to be a missionary in the Tuamotu Archipelago, a group of the most hostile islands in the South Pacific. Another veteran missionary who had closely followed Father Albert's career stated: "You would have to have seen those islands in their savage state, as I did, and as they are now to appreciate the extent of his work. Churches, schools, people as civilized as our own. He was in the midst of disease and dangers that overcame others."[31] When Father Albert's dermatitis dramatically impeded his ministry, he had been transferred to the Hawaiian mission to recuperate. Once well, the plan was to return him to the Tuamotus.

During his protracted stay in Honolulu, the superiors for the Hawaiian mission found Father Albert to be a vociferous, opinionated individual who repeatedly disturbed the ecclesiastical tranquility. Without question they believed that their lives would be far less harried were Father Albert removed to the isolated Kalaupapa Peninsula. He had a repulsive skin disease that looked like leprosy, so were he confined at the leper settlement as a suspected leper in compliance with Hawaiian law, such action would be deemed appropriate by both the superior general and the Hawaiian Board of Health. Then too, Father Damien was hopelessly overburdened and needed assistance. Father Albert was well enough to manage the parish at Kalaupapa and could serve as Father Damien's confessor. What could be better? The irritating priest from Tuamotu could be useful while he was out of sight. For the present, Father Albert was Damien's problem.

Father Damien had been forewarned that Father Albert was a most difficult person to deal with and that for seven years he had bedeviled the Honolulu Catholic hierarchy with his criticisms and demands. Damien took the warning with a grain of salt. After his experience with Father André, he believed he could get along with any priest. Thus he took pity on the new arrival, who appeared utterly exhausted after the choppy sea voyage from Honolulu. He insisted on personally helping the older man move his possessions into the small rectory at Kalaupapa, Father André's former residence.

A day or so later when Father Damien knelt before Father Albert in confession, he realized that the relationship was going to prove stressful. The older priest assumed an all-righteous, all-knowing pose and patiently encouraged Father Damien to confess his covert sins—especially the illicit sexual relationships he must have enjoyed with the native women. Damien was stunned by the accusation and vehemently denied any violation of his priestly vows. He told his confessor that the rumors of his womanizing were whispered by those persons who despised him for destroying the alcohol stills, stopping the abuse of children and women, and prohibiting the hula. Those few persons, he stressed, wanted to see him discredited and removed from the settlement so that they could resume their sinful ways. Father Albert nodded knowingly, but he persisted in his efforts to elicit a confession regarding Father Damien's alleged mistresses. When pressed for specifics, Father Albert demurely claimed to have been informed about Damien's scandalous behavior with women by authoritative sources, sources whom he refused to identify. Father Damien tried to reason with Father Albert, but the older priest would not desist in his accusations. Indignant and hurt, Damien rose to his feet and departed.

Ambrose Hutchison, the resident superintendent during the last five years of the priest's life, was later asked whether or not the rumors about Father Damien's illicit affairs with the native women were fact or ugly fiction. Hutchison had been a longtime observer of the Catholic priest, and in his capacity as the resident superintendent he knew more about the goings on in the settlement than anyone else. Hutchison responded:

> The origin and basis of the scandalous story which darkened the reputation of Father Damien in his conduct with women rested on three well known non-leper, devoted Catholic, native Hawaiian women named Maria Hoolanakani, Pilomela Kulia, and Elikapeka Punana. They had followed their leper husbands into exile, and were scandalized by evil minded men and women of the Leper Settlement as the mistresses of Father Damien. These women from the time that Father Damien arrived in the Leper Settlement at Kalawao and for years thereafter, voluntarily worked to help their spiritual father, alternately taking turns to take care of and clean his house, cooking for him, and doing his laundry. The conduct of these persons was above reproach, and the helpful services of these good women meant much to Father Damien in his active missionary work in the Leper Settlement. Even in the presence of strangers he affectionately called these noble women "makuahine"[mother, aunt, or a caring relative of one's parent's generation]. Without the help of

these good women father Damien would have been handicapped and compelled to do his own housekeeping and domestic work. This steadfast devotion of the three women to help their spiritual father in spite of the idle, scandalous tales of gossipers heaped on them by enemies saved the Father much inconvenience in the earlier years of his mission among the leper outcasts, as well as the other Fathers who later joined Father Damien. . . . I can witness that I am personally convinced that Father Damien never committed any evil of this nature.[32]

At Father Damien's next encounter with Father Albert, he was informed that Father Regis, the vice-provincial, had given the older priest precise instructions as to the role he was to assume at the leper settlement. He was to be the senior priest sent to reacquaint the junior priest with the proper demeanor and conduct of a Sacred Hearts' father. Father Regis firmly believed that Father Damien had been too long by himself, that he was not a priest in the "mold of Louvain," and that the ugly rumors regarding his improper relationships with the native women were possibly true. Father Damien was viewed as a well-meaning but inadequately trained priest who needed a senior counselor for a spiritual guide.[33]

Father Albert pontifically announced that he was to be that senior counselor and guide.

15

A Medal of Honor
and a Crown of Thorns

And behold, a leper came to him and knelt before him, saying,
"Lord, if you will, you can make me clean."
—Matthew 8:2

ON A DAY IN mid-September, 1881, when the sea's assault on the leper settlement's landing wharf was minimal, Princess Regent Liliʻuokalani—the future queen of Hawaiʻi—and her retinue were carefully helped into the longboats of the interisland steamer that had ferried them from Honolulu.[1] To have taken the overland route to the settlement and have the princess, who was an overweight and quite sedentary lady, attempt to descend the steep and treacherous *pali* trail was unthinkable.

Once seated in the bobbing boats, the royal party was rowed over the long, heavy swells to the wooden landing wharf where some eight hundred cheering lepers, dressed in their vibrant best and wearing flower leis around their necks, waved banners of welcome. Rudolph Meyer, stiffly erect, and a smiling Father Damien stepped forward to greet the princess and lead the way though the crowd to the horses for the ride across the peninsula to Kalawao. Father Albert, standing unobtrusively among the lepers, nodded and smiled when the princess glanced his way, but throughout the visit he remained quietly in the background.

With Rudolph Meyer and Father Damien serving as guides, Princess Liliʻuokalani was escorted along the narrow dirt road to Kalawao where the royal party began a systematic tour of the leper settlement. With a smile and the traditional "Aloha," the princess entered several of the newer, freshly whitewashed wooden houses that had replaced the thatched huts. She noted the wooden floors and the substantial construction, and she expressed her approval. As she left each house, she smiled a second time and repeated a heartfelt "Aloha."[2]

Next on the agenda was a walk-through visit of the dormitories for the orphan boys and girls. The princess was impressed by the happiness that she saw reflected in the eyes and the smiles of the children, most of whom were suffering from advanced leprosy. A tour of the Protestant and the Catholic churches and an inspection of the settlement store concluded the planned inspection. Rudolph Meyer, acting on the advice of Dr. Neilson, judiciously bypassed the hospital complex for fear that the sights and odors of the most seriously ill and dying might sicken the princess, but she insisted on visiting the hospitalized lepers. Although Princess Lili'uokalani was whisked through the infirmaries, she was nearly overcome by the horror she witnessed. Women with faces distorted by ugly tumor masses and collapsed noses looked up at her from their mats on the wooden floor. Children with missing feet and claw hands stirred and reached out to her. Men, emaciated and sullen faced, attempted to sit and bow their heads. In the newspaper accounts of the visit, the reporters accompanying the princess detailed every move she made.[3] They noted how she winced and then courageously forced a pleasant smile when looking into a leper's face with an empty eye socket or swollen earlobes that reached to the shoulder. Her eyes filled with tears when she paused to speak with a disfigured, crippled child.

The tour of the settlement completed, Princess Lili'uokalani was led to the flower-decorated pavilion. There she was seated comfortably in the shade and serenaded by the girls' choir, which had been practicing for weeks. When the choir concluded its program, all eyes focused on the princess for her response and comments. Slowly the gallant lady rose from her seat and stood silently looking into the misshapen faces of her outcast subjects. Her cheeks were tear-streaked as she told the lepers how very proud she was of their courage to deal with the unmerciful disease responsible for separating them from their loved ones. Before she completed her speech, she was overcome by emotion and for several minutes she wept openly. When she was able to resume speaking, she promised that the Kingdom would do even more to enhance the quality of life at the leper settlement.[4]

Upon her return to 'Iolani Palace, the princess called a meeting of the king's cabinet and told them what she had observed during her visit to the leper settlement. She enumerated the many projects the energetic Catholic priest had completed in his efforts to improve the lot of the outcasts, irrespective of their religious creeds. Rudolph Meyer, the members of the Board of Health who had accompanied her, and even the resident physician—all devout Protestants—were unanimous in their praise of the priest. She herself was impressed with the housing and especially the orphanages. Makua Kamiano[5] had indeed become the benevolent father of all the lepers, and for his selfless service she decided that this humble priest merited more than the customary verbal "Thank you very much."

Finding the cabinet in agreement with her assessment, she announced that in acknowledgment of Father Damien's courageous sacrifice to better the life of the lepers she was knighting him, along with the aging Bishop Maigret, the man who had supported Father Damien in his endeavors. Hereafter the two Catholic priests would be knight commanders of the Royal Order of Kalākaua, the highest honor the Kingdom could bestow.

The princess informed Father Damien of his knighthood via a letter:

Reverend Sir:

It is my desire to express to you my great appreciation of your heroic and self-denying labors, among the most unfortunate of the subjects of this Realm, and in some public manner to testify to the fidelity and patient, loving care with which you labor for the physical and spiritual good of those who are necessarily shut off from the tender ministrations of relatives and friends. I am aware that your labors and sacrifices are dictated solely by a desire to benefit your unfortunate fellow-men, and that you look for your reward and inspiration to the divine Father and Ruler of us all,—nevertheless, in furtherance of my desire, I ask you, Reverend Father, to accept the Order of Knight Commander of the Royal Order of Kalakaua in testimony of my sincere appreciation of your efforts in alleviating the distresses and mitigating in many ways the sorrows of the unfortunate lepers of Kalawao, as I had occasion to observe during my recent visit to that place.

I am your friend,
Liliuokalani, Regent[6]

The same day that Princess Lili'uokalani dispatched this letter, she received Bishop Hermann Koeckemann, Bishop Maigret's successor, and six of the local Catholic priests who were presented to her by the French consul. The purpose of the meeting was to inform the new bishop of her intention to confer knighthood on both Father Damien and Bishop Maigret. She requested that the French consul present the official citation and the medal of knighthood to the elderly Bishop Maigret and that Bishop Hermann journey to the leper settlement to do the same for Father Damien.

The press had a field day with this human-interest story, especially those newspapers owned by Walter Murray Gibson. A Protestant princess had acknowledged the selfless humanity of two Catholic priests by bestowing upon them the Kingdom's highest honor. The *Hawaiian Gazette* reported: "We felt great pleasure when we heard yesterday of the graceful act of her Royal Highness, the Princess Regent. . . . Father Damien receives a mark of distinction for self-devoted services which few men would undertake. We have ever regarded this gentleman's work as one of the noblest that man can do. A man without any desire for earthly reward, who willingly takes up his abode among the unhappy sufferers at Kalawao, devotes himself to the good of the poor lepers, and runs the risk of taking a loathsome disease that will eat his body piecemeal."[7]

Bishop Hermann immediately made plans for his first visit to the leper settlement. He would have preferred to have Father Damien come to Honolulu for the honor, but were he to hesitate to go where the princess had gone, the damage to the public's perception of the Catholic mission would be irreparable. He would beseech God to watch over and protect him from all harm.

At 2 A.M. on Monday, October 3, 1881, a weary and seasick Bishop Hermann disembarked at Kaunakakai, Moloka'i, where Father Damien was waiting to welcome him. Thoughtfully, Damien had made arrangements to take his bishop to the nearby former home of King Kamehameha V where the two offered their morning prayers and rested. At dawn the two mounted their horses for the 12-mile overland ride to the home of Rudolph Meyer. After lunch the descent of the treacherous *pali* trail began with Father Damien leading the way. Both priests carried a backpack, although the bishop's was far heavier than Damien's as it contained the vestments he deemed desirable for the knighthood ceremony to be held later that afternoon. Understandably, the good bishop lacked both the nimbleness of foot and the physical stamina required for the *pali* trail. During the first minutes of the descent he repeatedly lost his footing, slipping and sliding over the rough rocks while determinedly hanging onto his heavy pack. Fearful that he was about to witness his bishop plummet over the edge of the *pali* trail and topple a hundred feet to his death, Father Damien slowed the pace and insisted that Bishop Hermann let him carry both packs. Lighter by 30 pounds and with both hands free, the bishop was better able to manage the descent.[8]

By the time the two reached the bottom of the *pali*, the dust-covered bishop was battered, bruised, and breathing heavily. Hobbled by muscle cramps in both legs, he slowly made his way to the waiting horses for the ride to Kalawao. When the exhausted bishop reached the rectory, he collapsed into a chair and rested until porters arrived with the rest of his baggage. Then he dressed in the proper vestments for the civil ceremony, which was conducted under the same garlanded arch that had sheltered Princess Lili'uokalani. Everyone in the leper settlement—lepers and *kōkua*, Protestants and Catholics—attended the ceremony. To commence the proceedings, Bishop Hermann raised his arm to quiet the gathering and in a solemn cadence read the notice proclaiming Father Damien a knight commander of the Royal Order of Kalākaua. As the crowd cheered, Bishop Hermann removed the silver medal from its case and ceremoniously pinned it on Father Damien's cassock over his heart. As soon as the official ceremony concluded, the exuberant crowd sat on the ground to enjoy the feast of roast pig, fresh fruit, and poi. Before he sat down to eat, Father Damien unpinned the medal—only to have the smiling bishop rise and once again pin it on his chest with the stern admonition not to remove it again. Dutifully, Father Damien did as ordered, but when he retired that evening, he removed the medal and never again wore it, even on the few occasions when members of the royal family visited the leper settlement.[9]

The ceremony at Kalawao concluded, Bishop Hermann and Father Damien mounted their horses and rode to Kalaupapa so that parishioners in that village might meet and be blessed by the bishop. This afforded Father Damien the opportunity to point out the overcrowding problem in the tiny Our Lady Health of the Sick Church.

Sensing the bishop was receptive, Father Albert voiced his support for enlarging the church and handed Bishop Hermann a petition to this effect that was signed by everyone in his congregation. Without hesitation, Bishop Hermann turned to Father Damien and asked if he were willing to undertake the task if the mission supplied the building materials. Father Damien nodded affirmatively, a twinkle in his eyes and a hint of a smile on his lips.[10]

The next morning the Catholics crowded into the Kalawao church to celebrate Mass. Bishop Hermann was eloquent, but every movement, every gesture he made was painful as the muscles in his arms and legs were stiff and sore from the *pali* descent. Following the benediction the bishop slowly made his way to the church entrance. There he was pleasantly surprised to find a delegation of banner-waving Protestants waiting to accompany him to the *pali* trail. Father Damien wrote that "while there is no unity of faith, at least there is a genuine tolerance of one sect for the other."[11]

Bishop Hermann did manage to scale the *pali*—but never again during his long tenure as bishop did he repeat the strenuous feat.

The story of Princess Lili'uokalani's visit to the leper settlement and her knighting of two Catholic priests dominated the news in Honolulu for several weeks. Island residents of all faiths, wishing to express their admiration for the princess, responded sympathetically by contributing money and clothing for their outcast brothers. The royal visit became front page news throughout the world, prompting churches and philanthropic organizations in many countries to send charitable donations. Father Damien's superiors, while pleased, were astonished by the amount of money contributed—not only by the Protestants in Hawai'i but by Protestants in the United States and far-distant England. Initially, they didn't know whether to rejoice or reject the unsolicited aid. Without question the moneys received were primarily a result of the world's admiration of their Father Damien. Bishop Hermann contemplated the irony of the situation. One of the priests with the least formal education and hence one of the least likely to excel had been elevated to Christian martyr status by a poignant Gibson editorial, and now a royal princess had honored that priest with knighthood.

Princess Lili'uokalani, pleased with the public's response to her fact-finding visit, next focused her efforts on the most disturbing complaint that she had heard during her questioning of the lepers—the practice of "cruel seizure." On all of the islands except O'ahu, suspected lepers were given a cursory medical examination by a government physician. Those judged to be true lepers were immediately deported to Kalawao, without recourse to a second medical opinion or a period of careful observation in equivocal cases. In its early stages leprosy was, and still is, acknowledged to be the great imitator of skin disorders, so errors in diagnosis were not a rarity when the period of diagnostic observation was short. A receiving hospital in which to observe suspected lepers for a month or more was required. For this purpose, the princess leased a tract of land at Kaka'ako, a site near Honolulu Harbor, and the receiving hospital was promptly erected.[12]

The choice of Kaka'ako as the site for the hospital proved far from ideal. There were physical and administrative problems. The hospital buildings were constructed on low-lying land close to the ocean shore and surrounded by a salt marsh. When winds lashed the islands, the hospital grounds were submerged beneath a foot or so of water. Added to this inconvenience was patient overcrowding, which made reasonable hygiene difficult. No effort was made to police the grounds, which were surrounded by a high fence over which inmates climbed at night to join their spouses, or over which nonleprous spouses climbed to spend a few hours with a loved one. During the daylight hours visitors' permits were issued on a "very liberal scale." Strict segregation was unenforceable.[13]

When Dr. Charles Nielson learned that the Board of Health was in the process of recruiting Dr. George L. Fitch, an American physician knowledgeable about leprosy, to serve as the medical director of the new Kaka'ako Branch Hospital—a post he viewed as more prestigious than his at the leper settlement—he abruptly announced that he would not extend his contract and departed. This thrust the burden for the medical care of the abandoned patients squarely on Father Damien, and once again the Belgian found himself standing in the shoes of St. Damien.[14]

With the departure of Dr. Nielson, Dr. George L. Fitch's duties were expanded to include a monthly visit to Moloka'i to treat the lepers until such time as a replacement resident physician could be recruited. Dr. Fitch was adamant in his belief that leprosy was the fourth stage of syphilis: "A person with syphilis presents a most favorable field for leprosy . . . . I defy anyone to produce a single case of leprosy in which syphilis inherited or acquired has not been antecedent."[15]

Once persons with suspected leprosy began arriving at the new branch hospital for evaluation, Bishop Hermann assigned priests stationed in Honolulu to minister to the spiritual needs of Catholics during the time they were under observation. Mass was celebrated, confessions were heard, and the wafers celebrating the Lord's Supper were carefully positioned above the outstretched tongues of the suspected lepers, then dropped. Direct physical contact with any part of a person believed to be a leper was prohibited by Bishop Hermann; all priests unwaveringly adhered to this directive.

Not to be outdone by the Catholics, a senior pastor from the Congregational Church, the Rev. Dr. Charles McEwen Hyde, began regularly scheduled pastoral visits to Kaka'ako to minister to the Protestants at the branch hospital. Rev. Hyde, a man who would later play a key role in the Father Damien story, had arrived in Honolulu in 1877 to become director of the theological institute for the training of Hawaiians in the Protestant ministry. Because he had been assured by Dr. Fitch that sexual intercourse resulting in syphilis was the essential and predisposing factor to contracting leprosy, the good reverend believed he was safe from contagion. In their dual ministries to the lepers, the pastor and the physician became friends.

IN LATE NOVEMBER 1881, the building supplies to enlarge Our Lady Health of the Sick arrived. As agreed, the two priests exchanged parishes for the duration of the construction. The day Father Albert took up residence in the Kalawao rectory, he was shocked to have two Hawaiian women announce their arrival and then enter the small rectory. When challenged, the women claimed they were the volunteers who regularly cleaned the rectory, did the laundry, and helped with the food preparation. Outraged, Father Albert pointed to the front door and ordered the women to leave and never return. In Father Albert's experience, native women in the rectory were a curse, a needless temptation that gave credence to the rumors besmirching Father Damien's reputation. Later that day Father Albert stamped out another perceived evil. He denied entrance to the boys' orphanage to the wife of the man Father Damien had hired as the cook for the orphan boys. She had come, as she had been doing for several months, to assist her husband in the preparation of the boys' evening meal. Father Albert insisted that women were a sexual temptation to boys and hence they should not be underfoot in a boys' domiciliary.

Two weeks later when Father Damien briefly returned to Kalawao while awaiting the shipment of more building supplies, he was distressed to learn that Father Albert had dismissed the women volunteers as though they were harlots. These ladies saved him hours by caring for his quarters, doing his laundry, and preparing his two meals each day. When confronted, the older priest was adamant about the correctness of his actions. Women in the rectory or in the boys' quarters were instruments of Satan, and under no circumstances would he tolerate their presence. Sensing that Father Damien might reinstate the women, Father Albert reminded him of their promise to their superiors that the two of them would do whatever it took to work in harmony. If women were allowed access to the rectory and boys' dormitory, there would be no harmony. The one exception would be the women's choir practice which he himself would conduct in the rectory one afternoon each week. He informed the disgruntled Belgian that he was older and wiser and above the temptation of a woman.

A frustrated Father Damien immediately dispatched a letter to Bishop Hermann, reflecting his displeasure with Father Albert's dismissal of the women volunteers.

> Your Excellency,
>
> For the past two weeks I have worked at Kalaupapa while Father Albert lived at Kalawao. He has lived there by himself for over a week with the people who for five years have been true Sisters of Charity to the numerous Catholic children whom I have had the good fortune to shelter under my guardianship. One woman, who with the permission of Father Regis, has worked in the kitchen for five years (she is more than fifty years old) is not now permitted to enter the house, but must stay outside. . . . All would be well if he were not so "on his high horse with his demands." Excuse these complaints; I am a little upset because the man in charge of all of the material needs of the 34 leper children and the kitchen as well is quitting because of this incident.[16]

Bishop Hermann made an ambiguous reply:

> I thank God for the good spirit which inspires you, and I presume the same holds for Father Albert, although he did not write to me. Continue

to pray for each other, and for the good of the mission in general. . . . Regarding your question on the extent of your responsibility, I do not like to determine the question in too precise a manner. As the ecclesiastical superior, I view you as a kind of prelate for the entire leper colony. However, since Father Albert is at Kalaupapa it seems to me that you should consider him as an equal and the pastor in his village. I intend to make known to Father Albert that in your absence he ought not make any decisions even when he believes himself obliged to do so for his conscience sake. You have all the responsibility for Kalawao."[17]

When the second shipment of church building supplies for Our Lady Health of the Sick arrived later in the month, the two priests once again traded parishes. In the remodeling Father Damien retained the original six Gothic windows Father André had insisted upon and added four more Gothic windows, two in each of the wings. While the exterior of the enlarged church was modest in design, photographs taken of its interior reveal it to be a masterpiece of craftsmanship, featuring Gothic arches and a vaulted ceiling decorated in the European style of the time.[18] The efficiency with which Father Damien accomplished this feat in but two months—assisted only by a single helper and using the limited hand tools available—many judge to be an extraordinary achievement.

IN 1882 WALTER MURRAY GIBSON, the political opportunist, now white haired and white bearded, announced his intention to seek reelection to the legislature. The *Saturday Press*, the most conservative of the haole newspapers and the most supportive of the white business community, launched a campaign to defeat Gibson by publishing a pamphlet entitled *The Shepherd Saint of Lanai*, which detailed Gibson's dishonorable Mormon past and his purchase of land with money filched from the Mormon Church. Because the pamphlet was printed only in English, it had little influence on the outcome of the election.[19]

Gibson's emotional speeches delivered in impeccable Hawaiian fanned the flames of nationalism and racism, elevating him to the status of national hero. He reminded the electorate that it was through his efforts that the lepers, who now comprised 2 to 3 percent of the Native Hawaiian population, were so well cared for. He was the one who had first recognized the many contributions of Father Damien, and he was the one most responsible for obtaining the funding for the leper settlement and the new branch hospital at Kaka'ako. His campaign slogan, "Hawaii for Hawaiians," became a national chant and on election day Gibson garnered 1,153 of the 1,451 votes cast.[20]

In May 1882, charges of corruption and embezzlement precipitated a crisis of confidence in the government. King Kalākaua, in a move to appease the populace, appointed Walter Murray Gibson to the two most prestigious cabinet positions: prime minister and minister of Foreign Affairs. Overnight the fifty-eight-year-old Gibson became the most powerful man in the Hawaiian Kingdom.[21] Finally he was positioned so that he could breathe life into the many grand schemes his imagination had concocted. While the majority of the programs Gibson proposed to benefit the Kingdom and that the king subsequently endorsed were well intentioned, there was the underlying suspicion that both Gibson and King Kalākaua were dishonestly profiting from the ventures. Still, ample funding for the various leper projects was never interrupted. In 1882, the sum of $200,000 was appropriated for the various components of the leprosy program, an amount exceeding 10 percent of the tax revenue of the Hawaiian Kingdom. Of this amount, $85,000 was designated for the leprosy settlement. This was a staggering outlay considering the diminutive size of the shrinking tax base.

IN EUROPE, the dispute as to who had discovered the leprosy bacillus erupted into an angry debate. Dr. Hansen initially tried to counter Dr. Neisser's false claim by publishing his research in a series of scientific articles that he submitted to journals in England and Germany, in addition to Norway.[22] Then he circulated copies of Dr. Carter's 1873 report, which documented his claim of first discovery. This was the coup de grace, and Dr. Gerhard Armauer Hansen was acknowledged as the discoverer of *Mycobacterium leprae*. Finally scientists could focus their undivided attention on the responsible bacterium.

DR. NATHANIEL B. EMERSON continued to make periodic inspection tours of Kalawao in his capacity as a physician member of the Board of Health. In March 1882, he was pleased to observe that the number of new wooden houses had increased substantially since his visit the previous year. There was no question in his mind that the leper settlement on Moloka'i was the proper environment in which to enforce the segregation law. With the limitation that it lacked a professional medical staff, Kalawao had become a village as fine as any in the Islands.

In a lengthy report to the board, Dr. Emerson refuted the notion that the Kaka'ako Branch Hospital should become the new permanent residence for lepers as advocated by its new director, Dr. Fitch. First of all, Dr. Emerson reasoned, it was impossible to enforce segregation in a location so easily accessible to Honolulu; and second, the physical location of a hospital in a salt marsh so close to the ocean was not conducive to good health. He acknowledged that while Father Damien was performing a useful service as a part-time doctor, what the lepers desperately needed and frankly wished to have was the dedicated care of a full-time physician assisted by a competent nursing staff. In his opinion, the brief monthly visits to the settlement by Dr. Fitch were simply inadequate to cope with either the acute or the chronic medical problems.[23]

During those periods when there was no visiting physician, Father Damien continued to devote more than half of his time to the practice of medicine.[24] Father Albert sharply disagreed with this practice, arguing that it was a priest's first duty to salvage souls, not attempt to repair physical bodies. This sharp difference of opinion as to the proper conduct and activity of a priest continued to strain the working relationship between the two.

In April the two priests clashed over the matter of a marriage that Father Albert insisted Father Damien had mismanaged, a marriage ceremony that in his opinion should never have been performed. So irate did Father Albert become that he wrote to Bishop Hermann detailing why the marriage in question was invalid and demanding that Father Damien be reprimanded. Father Damien had married a dying leper and his mistress three days before the man's demise. Father Albert contended that in the eyes of the Church, the dying man was still married to his Hawaiian wife, even though Hawaiian law automatically divorced any couple when one of them was segregated from his mate. Since Church law superseded Hawaiian law, Father Damien was guilty of a violation.

Bishop Hermann concurred with Father Albert. In a sternly worded letter, he informed Father Damien that he had indeed celebrated an improper marriage. Father Damien was deeply offended by the tone of the Bishop's letter and the implication that he was a disobedient and incompetent priest. In a carefully worded letter of his own, he offered to resign as the leper settlement's resident priest:

> Your Excellency,
>
> I wish to tell you my motives, concealed in my priestly heart, which have caused me to act in a way which has shocked and provoked Father Albert, action which religious authority now forbids.
>
> Shortly after your visit here, the Mormons sanctioned concubinage, which resulted in illegitimate unions. Administrative officers, directors, the superintendent, and even the head of the hospital not only permitted the practice, but encouraged it, so much so that the voice of the priest is ignored. In my temporary capacity as the assistant doctor I am in a position to intervene and prevent many of these unions which are a scandal. I begged Mr. Gibson to send me official authorization so that with the document in my hand I might begin to sweep the hospital yard clean, for it is there that the disgraceful action is most offensive. Thus, little by little I might stop this wickedness. While serving as the assistant doctor takes much of my time, it does place me in direct contact with those who are sick and miserable of soul. My nine years of doctoring experience, using simple and effective medicines, affords me the unique opportunity to intervene. I am not guilty of the imprudence and rashness of which I have been accused.
>
> Furthermore, I have asked Gibson for official authorization to be the guardian of a large number of orphans for the obvious reasons which you know well. I decided to act quickly in this matter so I have already taken guardianship of some of the children, but not without opposition because of the jealous administration. If my conduct displeases you, and you share the Father Albert's negative opinion of me, I will gladly leave Molokai.
>
> Your very humble servant,
> Father Damien of the SS.CC.
>
> Please share my two letters with Father Regis. If you are unable to soften the unbearable temperament of my companion, you will soon see me there, even without orders to do so. I do not wish to live at war with the priests which the Congregation has given me at Molokai.[25]

Bishop Hermann had not anticipated that his reprimand might prompt Father Damien to abandon the leper settlement. Good priests never threatened their bishops in this manner. To make the situation absolutely untenable, there was no ready replacement for the "hero of

Moloka'i." Father Albert could barely handle the ministry at Kalau-papa, so there was no way the priest who was perpetually complaining about Father Damien could minister to Kalawao and the rest of Moloka'i in addition to his duties at Kalaupapa. Thus the bishop quickly assumed the role of mediator. In separate letters to both priests he stressed that each had the best interests of the Church at heart even though they all too frequently disagreed with each other. He urged both to continue to serve their respective parishes while remaining as isolated and independent of each other as possible. A fragile reconciliation was achieved. Father Damien remained at his post.

In November Father Damien was delighted to learn from Rudolph Meyer that the Board of Health was presenting him with a new horse-drawn buggy. "Mill Morris will probably come tomorrow and will bring you bread, wheat, and also a carriage. That which you sent to Honolulu to be repaired was not in a condition to be repaired any longer, and the Committee decided to send you a new carriage in its place."[26]

Father Damien wrote to Walter Murray Gibson to thank him for the new buggy, as all government funding for the leper settlement was now authorized or approved by Gibson.[27]

During the latter months of 1882, Father Damien noted a new and worrisome sign of his leprosy—numbness along the outside of the left foot.[28] The sciatic pain in his left leg and foot was as intense as before, but now there was no feeling along the side of his foot when he pulled on a sock. By early spring he could draw a line across his left foot where the pain stopped and the surface anesthesia began. What had been a testimony to his physical fitness when he climbed the *pali* in the past now became a test of patient endurance because his partially numb foot could no longer feel the rough ground beneath it. To avoid stumbling and falls he was forced to climb with greater care, which lengthened the time of the ascent and the descent.

Father Damien's growing apprehension about his leg problems cast a pall over his cheerful outlook on life and at times quenched his smile. He wondered whether his symptoms were due primarily to leprosy or to a combination of leprosy and arthritic pressure on his sciatic nerve. The combination of the pain and the numbness was a chilling reminder of the uncertainty of man's brief sojourn on earth. Now his fate was in God's hands. When he had knelt beside his mother and bowed his head in prayer at Our Lady of Montaigu Shrine shortly before his departure for Hawai'i, he had asked his Lord God that he might be allowed to serve in the mission field for twelve years. His supplication had been more than answered, for he had already been granted eighteen years. He thanked God for the eighteen years, but humbly beseeched his Lord to grant him sufficient time to complete his mission to the lepers. There was a great deal yet to be accomplished, and his time on earth to do so was now severely compromised.

As he agonized over his failing health, Father Damien recalled St. Ignatius Loyola's cryptic response to a question asked him about impending death. Ignatius had been engaged in a game of ball with his fellow students when someone interrupted the game to demand with absolute sincerity what each of them would do if he knew that he were to die in twenty minutes. All, with the exception of Ignatius, stated that they would rush frantically to church and pray. Ignatius answered, "I should finish my game."[29] Father Damien had always admired that answer, and in imitation of the saint he decided to "finish his game." He resolved to continue doing exactly what he had been doing until leprosy would end his earthly life. He would not abandon his lepers and "rush frantically to church and pray."

FROM THE QUIET of his study in Honolulu, Bishop Hermann commiserated with Father Damien, for he knew from firsthand experience just how exasperating Father Albert could be.[30] In an effort to add a modicum of serenity to the priest's holiday season, he invited Father Damien to Honolulu for the celebration of Christmas. Father Damien's momentary jubilation over the invitation was short lived, however, for when he conferred with Father Albert regarding the latter's care of the Kalawao lepers during his absence, the older priest insisted that he felt too poorly to minister to both Kalaupapa and Kalawao for even a single day during the Christmas season. Father Damien implored Father Albert to reconsider, but the older priest was unyielding. His fragile health would permit him to minister only to the small congregation at Kalaupapa. Were St. Philomena Church empty on Christmas, the onerous transgression would be Father Damien's, and his alone.

A dejected Father Damien was compelled to decline his bishop's invitation, promising to make the journey to Honolulu soon after Christmas.[31] He felt obligated to remain at his post and dispel the gloom of Moloka'i with the song and joy of the season, especially for the sake of the children and the hundred or so adults for whom this would be the last Christmas.

The Christmas celebration at Kalawao was a resounding success, aided by "beautiful" weather. Just prior to the midnight Mass, the young people "made the rounds of the village with two tambourines, waking everyone and crying, 'Merry Christmas!' This assured that St. Philomena was "packed wall to wall."[32] The lepers were happy, and so was Father Damien that he had not delegated his key role to his ailing confrere.

Two days after Christmas Father Damien carefully made his way up the *pali* trail to first visit the five Catholic parishes on Moloka'i before proceeding to Honolulu. Due to the numbness in his unfeeling left foot, he made his way much like a two-year-old toddler learning to climb stairs: step up with the right foot, then bring the ailing left foot up to meet it, brace the left foot, then step upward with the right, then repeat, repeat, repeat. Proceeding upward and downward this way doubled the time required to complete the trek. The most serious problems caused by the numbness in his foot were the multiple stone bruises, cuts, and puncture wounds owing to the loss of the normal protective pain reflex.

As he climbed and surveyed the beauty all around him, he prayed with his eyes open. Life, after all, was meant to be a continuous prayer. He asked that no one with whom he came in contact would contract leprosy. He was a leper, and as such he recognized that he posed a threat to the healthy. From this day forward he pledged to God that he would avoid any direct physical contact with a nonleper. God would understand and forgive.

16

The Year of the Nurses

I see God in every human being. When I wash the leper's wounds, I feel I am nursing the Lord himself. Is it not a beautiful experience?
—Mother Teresa (1910–1997)

BEFORE DAWN ON December 30, 1882, the interisland steamer from Molokaʻi with Father Damien on board docked in Honolulu. With a slight limp, the weary priest made his way down the gangplank and paused on the wharf for a few moments, thankful for the cessation of the rolling motion of the boat. Then he picked up his bag of belongings and began the long walk to the Cathedral of Our Lady of Peace and his temporary quarters. It would be good to celebrate the post-Christmas season in the relative calm of Honolulu and to enjoy several nights of uninterrupted sleep, a rare occurrence at the leper settlement.

No sooner had he reached his room and begun to disrobe than he was informed that a "neighbor" was dying in one of the area hospitals.[1] It is not known precisely who this neighbor was; nor is it known why Father Damien, a visiting priest, was asked to rush to her side. The implication is that either she was a member of one of his previous parishes or she was a leper. Damien dressed and hurried to the bedside of the lady, "who died at the moment" he finished giving her Extreme Unction. While attending to the funeral arrangements, he learned that two other Catholics in the hospital had died that same night. Magnanimously, he offered to conduct burial services for each of the three later in the day. By the time he completed the funeral arrangements, the hours for peaceful repose had passed. As he left the hospital he heard the cathedral bell pealing the invitation to morning

Mass, so he suppressed a yawn and hurried to join his peers. Following the Mass there was no time for even a brief nap because the remainder of his day was tightly scheduled. The only interruptions allowed
were for the three funeral services he conducted that afternoon.

The fatigue, the emotional stress, and the lack of sleep during the
previous forty-eight hours exacted their toll. Shortly before 4 A.M.,
Sunday, December 31, Father Damien awoke with a severe headache
and an upset stomach. So ill was he that he made his way to Bishop
Hermann's quarters to ask to be excused "from singing High Mass and
from preaching. He [the bishop] was gracious enough to do both."[2]

By early afternoon Father Damien had recovered sufficiently to
attend to the remainder of his assigned duties, which included ministering to the suspected lepers at the Kaka'ako Branch Hospital, an
assignment most members of the Hawaiian mission abhorred. As he
made his hospital rounds he was appalled by the abysmal conditions—
dirt, flies, and the absence of professional nurses. In a lengthy letter
written following his return to Kalawao, he disclosed to his brother
how he had urged Dr. Fitch, the medical director, to use his office to
persuade the government to enlist Bishop Hermann's help in recruiting Sisters of Charity to serve as nurses at the leper hospitals.[3] There
was no dispute that the Sisters of Charity were unsurpassed for their
nursing skills, and with Catholic fathers in attendance, there was a fair
chance that Catholic nurses could be recruited to serve in Protestant-
funded facilities. Dr. Fitch thanked the priest for the suggestion and
promised to pursue the matter with the Board of Health and Bishop
Hermann.

THE BOOM OF CANNON and exploding skyrockets awakened the city
of Honolulu on New Year's Day, 1883. Later that morning Father
Damien accompanied Bishop Hermann to the recently completed and
resplendent 'Iolani Palace for a meeting with Queen Kapi'olani and
Walter Murray Gibson. As prime minister and the minister of Foreign
Affairs, who still retained the title of president of the Board of Health,
Gibson had called the meeting to inquire how the leprosy program at
Kalawao might be improved. The queen listened intently to Father
Damien's suggestions, intrigued by his recommendation that Sisters of
Charity be invited to provide skilled nursing care in the government-
operated leper hospitals. Pleased with the Protestant Queen's interest

in Catholic nurses, Bishop Hermann expressed confidence that "some Sisters of Charity may arrive soon," although he had done nothing to explore the possibility.

The rest of the week passed rapidly for Father Damien. The knowledge that Sisters of Charity might soon be at his side nursing the lepers and overseeing the girls' orphanage revitalized his spirit and generated a torrent of energy dedicated to serve the lepers. His last morning was spent packing clothing that the Sisters of the Sacred Hearts had collected for the desperately poor lepers. In addition he packed a "generous supply" of women's and children's clothing, shoes, cloth, soaps, and other "necessities" that had been donated by Mr. Cartwright, a prosperous Protestant, with the written instruction that the gifts were to be distributed to the poor and needy without distinction as to religion or race. Father Damien wrote a thank-you note promising to do just that.

Upon his return to Kalawao, Father Damien promptly journeyed to Kalaupapa to hear Father Albert's confession, following which he informed the older priest of the Cartwright gift and the stipulated conditions for the distribution to the leper women and children. Father Albert nodded, his face as expressionless as a headstone without an inscription. Returning to Kalawao, Father Damien had begun to load his horse buggy with the portion of goods for Kalaupapa when he received this note from Father Albert: "Send me what belongs to this village. I will distribute it, excluding those public concubines who do not reside in Kalawao, and you can distribute there as you wish, and to whom you wish without my bothering you about it." Father Damien replied that he could not approve of excluding the "truly poor, even if they were living in concubinage."[4] By return messenger, he received Father Albert's retort: "In response to your letter of today, I have the honor to repeat that you can distribute as you wish in Kalawao; I do not concern myself with that."

The promise to Mr. Cartwright was a sacred oath, one that could not be violated. In an attempt to resolve the matter, Father Damien made a hasty return to Kalaupapa, where he found Father Albert to be immovable. Frustrated, Damien diplomatically asked for and obtained a list of names of those whom Father Albert judged to be deserving of Mr. Cartwright's generosity. The uneasy truce between the two priests was strained when he realized that Father Albert planned to exclude over half of the women and children living in Kalaupapa, persons he judged to be undeserving of charity. Refusing to debate the matter, Father Damien shipped Father Albert the appropriate amount of clothing for his chosen few, but let it be known that those who had been bypassed could come to Kalawao and receive their just share. Suspicious that Father Albert would complain to the hierarchy about the distribution of the gifts to the "unworthy," Father Damien wrote that "the poor of Kalaupapa came in great numbers to obtain the goods at my place."[5] The pledge of a Catholic Father, especially to a Protestant, was inviolate.

FATHER DAMIEN'S SUGGESTION that Sisters of Charity be invited to serve as nurses at the government-operated hospitals appealed to Walter Murray Gibson. There was no argument as to the competence of the Sisters of Charity, and with their vow of poverty the cost would be a pittance. The only outlay of money would be the required transportation costs, a convent in which to house them, and a small monthly subsistence allowance, a sum his strained budget could afford. After learning of Dr. George Fitch's enthusiastic endorsement of the idea, he asked the doctor to write a letter of support to accompany his formal request to Bishop Hermann.[6]

Bishop Hermann saw real merit in securing the nursing services of the Sisters of Charity. The presence of these gallant ladies would greatly enhance the Catholic mission in the Islands. Behind closed doors he discussed the logistics of recruiting with his new assistant, Father Léonor Fouesnel, the priest who had recently been transferred from his parish in Wailuku, Maui. This is the same Father Léonor who had been so openly critical of Father Damien's occasional faux pas. Together the two planned a campaign by which nurses belonging to a Catholic order would be recruited to serve in Hawai'i's fledgling hospitals. Both agreed that to recruit sisters exclusively for the leper hospitals was inhumane and out of the question.

It was decided that Father Léonor would visit the United States, where there were more than fifty Catholic orders with sisters who were trained professional nurses. The previous year this persuasive priest had gone to the United States and successfully recruited a cadre of the Brothers of Mary to teach at the boys' school currently under construction in Honolulu. Since English was the language of business, education, and the professions in Hawai‘i, the American sisters were the obvious choice.

THE ONGOING SCUFFLE between Father Damien and Father Albert as to the proper administration of the leper settlement continued unabated. Father Damien repeatedly implored Bishop Hermann to grant him the authority to overrule Father Albert in settlement disputes when, in his opinion, it was in the best interests of the lepers to do so. Father Albert strenuously objected to anyone dictating how he should act in matters clearly defined by Church law, especially when the judgment was forced upon him by a naive priest he considered totally ignorant of the finer points of Church law.

In an attempt to maintain the uneasy truce, the bishop officially divided the Kalaupapa Peninsula into two separate and absolutely independent parishes. To draw a smile and a blessing from Father Albert in the village of Kalaupapa, one had to be a Catholic and adhere to every tenet of Church law. Unlike Father André, Father Albert practiced no medicine. He appeared oblivious to the misery caused by the common illnesses for which medicinal therapies were available. Under no circumstance would he touch a leper or dress a leper's wounds. His focus was on spiritual well-being. In his eyes the recalcitrant, non-Catholic lepers in Kalaupapa were the true outcasts, the "unclean" who were destined for eternal damnation, persons to be shunned.

In his correspondence with Bishop Hermann, Father Damien wrote of his troubled relationship with Father Albert and of the problems arising from the division of the tiny Kalaupapa Peninsula into two parishes.[7] Bishop Hermann elected to ignore all of Damien's suggestions for remedial action. When, in early April, Father Damien queried his bishop about the progress of the recruiting program—"And the hospital Sisters? I have great need of them"—his bishop failed to give him a definitive reply.[8]

RUTH KE‘ELIKOLANI, the 300-pound Hawaiian princess who openly worshiped Pele, died on May 24, 1883. All of her land, one-ninth of the total landmass of the Kingdom of Hawai‘i, was willed to her cousin, Princess Bernice Pauahi Bishop, the wife of businessman and banker Charles Reed Bishop. This made the Bishops the wealthiest couple in all of Hawai‘i. Princess Bernice then appointed Rudolph

Meyer manager of the 46,500-acre ranch in west Moloka'i, which occupied the land division known as the Kaluako'i Ahupua'a but was popularly referred to as the Moloka'i Ranch.[9] This enormous responsibility forced Meyer to devote less time to overseeing the leper settlement. To remain in touch, Meyer initiated the practice of corresponding with Father Damien several times each week, using a runner to carry the brief inquiries and replies up and down the *pali* trail. Many of these letters have survived and they reveal how integral Father Damien was to the daily operation of the leper settlement—from overseeing the proper distribution of the weekly food allocation to the ordering of building supplies and the adjudication of disputes.

IN JUNE 1883, during her second term as provincial superior of the Sisters of the Order of St. Francis in Syracuse, New York, Mother Marianne Cope received a letter from Father Léonor Fouesnel stating that the king of Hawai'i had sent him to the United States on a mission of mercy "to look for Sisters, who would take charge of our Hospitals, and even of our schools, if it were possible." The letter continued, "I take, therefore, Reverend Mother, the liberty of addressing myself to you and begging you to assist us in our work."[10]

At her desk in the Mother House in Syracuse, Mother Marianne answered the request in a very positive manner. "I hardly know what to say. . . . Shall I regard your kind invitation to join you in your missionary labors, as coming from God? . . . My interest is awakened and I feel an irresistible force drawing me to follow this call. . . . Our Rev. Father Superior is at present in Europe, and without his approval I could not give you any hope of coming to your assistance although my heart and hands are more than willing."[11]

Encouraged by Mother Marianne's enthusiastic reply, Father Léonor extolled the virtues of Hawai'i in the exchange of letters that followed, carefully avoiding any mention of the leprosy epidemic the Islands were experiencing. "As far as nature is concerned, you will find a kind of earthly Paradise in the Sandwich Islands. . . . The government supports the hospitals and defrays all expenses. . . . The Sisters [will] direct the hospitals, the government will not interfere with their way of doing. . . . The Sisters will be helped and assisted by as many hands, as many servants as they would want, besides each Sister will receive from the government a salary of at least $20.00 per month."[12]

Anxious to consummate an agreement, Father Léonor journeyed to Syracuse and called upon the sisters in early July. Sister Leopoldina, a novice at the time of the visit, described the impassioned plea he made: "His story was sad, how he had gone from one community to another begging for workers, but not one community would accept the work. . . . His voice choked and tears were in his wonderful kind eyes as he told us of the sad need for sisters in the islands and of what little success he had until he came to us and now he said your good mother has given me great hope."[13]

Mother Marianne informed Father Léonor that the final approval as to whether the sisters of St. Francis might serve in Hawai'i rested in the hands of Father Joseph Lesen, the acting provincial minister of all the Minor Conventuals of St. Francis in the United States, who at the time was in Italy. In the meantime, Mother Marianne familiarized herself with the potential problems that an American nurse would face in Hawai'i—and in so doing learned the details of the leprosy epidemic. Rather than a deterrent, she viewed the prospect of caring for lepers as an intriguing and inviting challenge.

On July 12, while awaiting the return of Father Lesen, she wrote a letter to Father Léonor expressing her sentiments and openly addressing the issue of nursing the Hawaiian lepers: "I am hungry for the work and I wish with all my heart to be one of the chosen Ones, whose privilege it will be, to sacrifice themselves for the salvation of the souls of the poor Islanders. . . . I am not afraid of any disease, hence it would be my greatest delight even to minister to the abandoned lepers."[14]

Father Léonor returned to Hawai'i confident that the Franciscan sisters would soon follow. On July 31, he disembarked at Honolulu and hurried to show his bishop Mother Marianne's letters. As a reward for his recruitment achievements, Father Léonor was elevated to the position of vice provincial.

Upon his return to the United States, Father Lesen approved the venture and corresponded with Bishop Hermann to confirm the travel arrangements, the living accommodations, the sisters' monthly stipend, and the understanding that the sisters would remain members of the Order of St. Francis. By late fall all negotiations had been concluded; Mother Marianne and six sisters would go to the Hawaiian Islands. At the time it was Mother Marianne's intention to return to Syracuse and resume her duties as provincial superior of the Sisters of the Order of St. Francis, once she was satisfied that the Hawaiian situation was as promised.

JUNE 1883 PROVED to be another trying month for Father Damien. At the insistent request of Father Albert, he took the time to enclose the church cemetery at Kalaupapa with the same type of wild pig-proof picket fence as had proved so successful in Kalawao. With the assistance of the local blacksmith he even fashioned an ornate wrought iron entrance gate. When he showed his handiwork to Father Albert, anticipating that for once his confrere would be pleased, he was rudely chastised. The entrance gate did not meet with Father Albert's expectations. It lacked the aesthetic elegance a Catholic cemetery deserved, and his confrere demanded that the work be redone. The criticism and the demand for a new gate jolted Father Damien. After a moment of silent deliberation, the Belgian simply stated that he didn't have the time to devote to such a project. Father Albert vehemently demanded that he take the time—otherwise he would never again go to Kalawao to celebrate Mass in Father Damien's absence. Knowing that Father Albert would complain to Bishop Hermann, Father Damien wrote: "My confrere here is very difficult to satisfy. To the best of my ability I constructed his cemetery. However, its entrance doesn't please him. He wants it to be more beautiful, grander; but to accomplish what he demands the blacksmith wants four piasters, an amount he refuses to pay. The entrance and gate, as well as the craftsmanship of the blacksmith, are adequate and far better than he wanted. I do not have the will to begin again to make him another gate, no laila huhu loa, ia [that is why he is very angry]."[15]

Bishop Hermann responded in his customary manner by not taking sides in the cemetery gate controversy. As was his managerial approach, he again urged patience, brotherly love, and tolerance for the other's viewpoint. Father Albert wasn't appeased by this, and he continued to berate the aesthetics of his cemetery gate. Father Damien stood firm. Burials at one of the Catholic cemeteries were a common every-other-day occurrence, and there were aspects to funerals far more important than the perceived aesthetics of a cemetery gate. To alleviate grief and add a note of cheer to these all-too-frequent cheerless days, Father Damien introduced a native band to supplement the sacred music sung by one of his choirs. He wished to remind everyone that they were celebrating the return of a soul to God and eternal happiness.

DEEPENING POTHOLES in the badly deteriorated 2.5-mile road that linked the two leper villages were making the trek between them hazardous to those on foot as well as to the horses. Father Damien complained to both Rudolph Meyer and Dr. Fitch, who in turn presented the problem to the Board of Health. The board responded by allocating $300 for road repair, with the understanding that Father Damien would recruit the labor force and supervise the undertaking.[16] Father Albert shrugged his shoulders in disbelief. Road repair was manual labor, menial labor that fell squarely in the domain of the Sacred Hearts' brothers. With arched eyebrows he watched while Damien recruited a group of *kōkua* in late June and, with a pick and a shovel, join in the repair. No priest worthy of the name would dirty his hands by assisting with such a mundane project—certainly not a father of the Sacred Hearts. In his opinion, Father Damien's manual labor denigrated the priesthood.

BY YEAR'S END there were 743 lepers at the settlement—453 men and 290 women and children.[17] Of the three hundred admissions to the settlement in 1883, fifty were children, many of whom had no relatives or family friends among the leper population to shelter and nurture them. The welfare of these homeless children was of great concern to Father Damien. To better provide for them he continued to encourage the Sisters of the Sacred Hearts in Honolulu to collect clothing, and from his large garden and small chicken ranch he supplemented their diet with fruits, vegetables, and poultry products. Still, there were items such as soap, towels, linens, lanterns, dishes, bedding, and books that he needed and for which he requested funds.

In an appeal to Bishop Hermann in late August, Father Damien wrote: "I take the liberty of submitting to your Excellency the list of my orphan children whom I have adopted, begging you to help me to the measure of your resources in procuring for them what they need."[18]

There followed a list of the names of forty-four children, "eighteen born of Catholic parents and twenty-six born of non-Catholic parents."

The task of replying fell to Father Léonor, who alibied that the mission could not advance him additional money as the Church's discretionary funds were depleted. The children, Father Léonor reminded Father Damien, were the financial responsibility of the Board of Health, not the Catholic mission.

When Father Damien appealed to the Board of Health for funds to support the orphans, Walter Gibson informed him that the board's budget did not include money for orphans and, due to the financial stress the Kingdom was experiencing, additional funds could not be allocated. Father Damien was reminded that he would have to make due with the weekly food allotment and the annual clothing stipend provided for each leper.

Frustrated by the callous replies, Father Damien believed that he had no recourse but to appeal to private overseas donors, an action that disturbed Father Albert and raised the eyebrows of his bishop and the vice provincial. To the surprise of his superiors and to the embarrassment of the Board of Health, Damien's solicitation efforts were rewarded with generous donations from clergymen in Belgium, England, and the United States.

In July Father Damien informed his bishop that in addition to the monetary contributions from abroad, an American church had made a donation of a small organ for the St. Philomena Church. The plight of the Hawaiian lepers had captured the attention of the world.[19]

AT NOON ON November 8, 1883, the *Mariposa* with Mother Marianne and six sisters aboard rounded Diamond Head on the southern edge of O'ahu and was greeted by the ringing bells of Our Lady of Peace Cathedral, a prearranged announcement of the arrival of the sisters. Within minutes a large crowd assembled at the pier. Four royal carriages, each drawn by a prize team of prancing horses, inched through the crowd to the gangplank and stood waiting to transport the sisters to the cathedral where Bishop Hermann was waiting to celebrate Mass. Each carriage driver sat erect, proudly wearing a black top hat and a black dress coat with large brass buttons. After the gangplank was lowered and secured, Father Léonor, followed closely by Walter Murray Gibson, boarded the *Mariposa* to welcome the newcomers.[20] Conspicuously absent from the scene was the man who had first conceived of inviting Sisters of Charity to come to Hawai'i to serve in the leper hospitals—Father Damien. With a low bow, Gibson took the hand of each sister and said, "Aloha. Welcome to fair Hawai'i." Father Léonor then led the group to the carriages where he seated himself in the lead carriage and led the way to the cathedral by a deliberately circuitous route that toured the major streets of downtown Honolulu and passed by the newly completed 'Iolani Palace.

Bishop Hermann, dressed in purple vestments and flanked by the priests and brothers of the Congregation of Sacred Hearts, was standing in the cathedral's central doorway when the carriages arrived. Against a background of triumphant organ music, each of the sisters knelt and kissed the bishop's ring, following which each received his blessing. Then the Franciscan sisters were seated directly in front of the altar where they could be seen by all who crowded into the cathedral. Bishop Hermann preached "a very impressive sermon" during which "his voice choked and tears" ran "down his face" as he informed the congregation about the mission of mercy the sisters were about to undertake and "the many crosses" they would have "to bear."[21] The sisters sat erect with emotionless faces as they listened. Behind them in the shadows of the candlelit cathedral the silence was broken by an occasional sob.

During the first three days in Honolulu, the seven Franciscan sisters were quartered in the crowded convent of the Sisters of the Sacred Hearts that adjoined the cathedral. Their first visitors were King Kalākaua and Queen Kapi'olani, who called to thank the sisters for taking up a burden that no one else would assume. During the short visit the highly emotional queen began to cry. With tears streaming down her cheeks, she stammered in Hawaiian, "I love you! You have left your home and country to come to these far away islands to care for my poor afflicted children. I shall never forget you, and you are my Sisters and I shall always love you."[22]

When he learned of the cramped quarters in which the Franciscan sisters were living, Gibson moved the seven to the palatial Talula Hayselden mansion on King Street. The home, owned by Gibson, served as the Honolulu residence for his daughter Talula and son-in-law Fred Hayselden, who were elsewhere in the Islands. In typical Gibson fashion, the prime minister submitted a billing for the occupancy of the Hayselden mansion to the Board of Health for payment for the six weeks the sisters luxuriated in the spacious home, described by them as "a dream."[23] It featured all of the modern conveniences and was set back from the dirt street in an Edenic setting, where "the lawn and garden were so beautifully kept and the sweet air was always filled with perfume from the ever blooming flowers."[24]

While she appreciated the respite, Mother Marianne was anxious to visit the hospitals to which she and the sisters would be assigned. Gibson promised that he would personally escort them to the hospitals for an inspection tour once he could steal the time from his titanic administrative duties. As prime minister, minister of Foreign Affairs, and president of the Board of Health, his schedule was full.

True to his word, a few days later Gibson drove Mother Marianne and two of the sisters in his fine carriage to the branch hospital at Kaka'ako. As the carriage crossed the bleak salt flats upon which the branch hospital was built and passed by the security guards stationed around the perimeter fence, the Franciscan sisters had the impression that they were entering a prison compound. Inside the entrance gate, isolated by a low picket fence, was a two-story cottage that served as the administrative office and the home of Henry Van Giesen, the hospital superintendent. Between the administrative office and Van Giesen's home stood the dozen rectangular wooden buildings that served as the hospital wards for men and boys or women and girls. At the opposite end of the compound stood the notorious "death" building where the dying lepers were taken to breathe their last.

Leopoldina later recorded what Mother Marianne told her about the visit:

> A short distance from the office they entered a long narrow building made of rough boards and they were whitewashed. "This is the lepers' dining room," he [Van Giesen] said. Our gentle Mother and the Sisters stood staring—never in their lives had they met with such horrors, the dirt and swarms of flies that covered the long tables and benches. They were wondering if they had ever been cleaned. When they passed along a covered veranda at the end was the kitchen which was in a most frightful condition, thick with filth and flies. The slick handsome man having charge of the place was not ashamed—he seemed to think it was good enough for the lepers.
>
> They passed on to the wards, long buildings made of wide, rough boards and they were whitewashed. Long empty (devoid of furniture) wards with straw mattresses on the floor and dirty gray blankets. Some of the wards had carpenter horses with rough planks to put the mat-

tresses on. There were many children but they all looked alike, young and old. All seemed so despondent, their words so empty and cheerless. No tables, chairs or beds. The poor unfortunates were crouched on the floor with their knees drawn up to their chins and in every face utter despair. Not a smile from one of them. Most of them had thin little gowns barely enough to cover them.[25]

The contrast between the dirty, ill-equipped facility filled with despondent patients that the sisters were viewing and the spotlessly clean, brightly lighted St. Joseph's Hospital in Syracuse, New York, which they had left one month before, was striking. Van Giesen next led the way to a cluster of bungalows where the affluent lepers who were able to pay the appropriate fee to the king's treasury were permitted to remain indefinitely. Mother Marianne was told that as the number of permanent residents increased, Dr. Fitch envisioned establishing Kaka'ako as the main leper settlement. In Van Giesen's opinion, there was no need for the Kalawao facility. It was too remote and difficult to reach—and there was no resident physician to care for the lepers.

Mr. Van Giesen said, "Now let me show you the most interesting place," and he led them to a long, narrow building that extended so far out on the beach that the high tide brought the waves under part of the building. There were three rooms. "This first room," he said, "is where we have our dying lepers and when they die we put them in the second room for the benefit of the doctors. After the doctors have finished their work the remains [are] placed in this third room to await the coming of the cart and it is taken away to be buried. We never bring a sick leper in this house until they're hopeless and not one has ever recovered. It is sure death when they are brought in here and this poor man," pointing to the poor unfortunate on the floor, "will soon die. . . ."

While Mr. Van Giesen was speaking with Mr. Gibson and Mother, Sister bent over the dying man who was on the floor with only a dirty mat under him and a gray blanket to cover him. She tried to speak consoling words but he did not seem able to answer her. But she never could forget those sad pleading eyes as he looked up at her. [He] was a young man and how sad it was to see him so helpless and suffering without anyone to care for him. His large muscular arms thrown out on the bare floor and death agony in his ghastly face. There was a boy standing near and Sister asked him, "Where is his nurse?" This the boy seemed not to understand and then she asked him, "Where is the water? Does someone give him water to moisten his dry feverish lips?"

"No can geeve watah—Bimebye die."

"Does somebody give him milk or something to eat?"

"No can eat, s'spose come eenside dis place—Bimebye die."

"Does someone stay with him at night?"

A kind of sick look covered the boy's face and shuddering he said, "No can stop inside dis place—Bimebye die."

While Sister was telling Mother and Mr. Gibson what she had learned from the boy, the dying man's eyes were [fixed] on Mr. Gibson and the Sisters, a little gleam of hope appeared in his sad face. Mr. Gibson's kind eyes filled. He was horrified. "Oh," he said, "I had no idea that the sick were treated like this. Have this man removed at once to his room. Give him a nurse and plenty of milk as nourishment even if he should not get well. Never treat anyone like this again."[26]

Meanwhile, Father Damien was most anxious to meet Mother Marianne and the sisters, some of whom he assumed would be stationed at Kalawao because the need for their services was greater at the hospitals in the leper settlement than any place else in the Islands. Impatient, he wrote to Father Léonor inquiring when the introductory meeting might take place and when he might expect the sister-nurses to arrive. There is no copy of Father Léonor's reply. What is apparent is that the vice provincial had a different agenda for the Sisters of St. Francis. He announced his plan to station four of the sisters at the branch hospital at Kaka'ako and the remaining three on Maui to open the newly built but unoccupied government hospital for the general public. By so doing he could greatly enhance the Catholic influence in the Islands. Walter Murray Gibson concurred with this practical deployment of the nurses. For Gibson, the vision of the gentle sisters nursing the hideously deformed and loathsome patients at the leper settlement was a nightmare to be avoided.

Father Damien was devastated by Father Léonor's reply. His return letter to the new vice provincial, who seemed to be basking in the glory of his recruiting accomplishment, reflects his feeling of betrayal and lack of appreciation. He wrote:

My dear Father,

Just after I had dispatched my letter to you, Father Albert gave me the one you had sent in which you requested a reply.

Once again I find that you have little confidence in me, telling me that I should remain quiet and not complain, as if you held me to be unworthy and acting with impropriety. I reiterate that I have neither written, nor spoken, nor begged for the stationing of the Sisters here. I now realize that there is little prospect of having them here. In anticipation of a visit by the Mother Superior and one of the Sisters, in the company of your Reverence, I cleaned my house a little and would have lodged you in the portion of the village exclusively Catholic. As my presence may irritate you, I am willing to remain apart from them. Frankly, I did not realize that I had fallen so low in the opinion of my superiors.

Your very humble servant,
J. Damien of the SS.CC.[27]

17

Father Damien Denied

Be strong and of good courage; be not frightened, neither
dismayed; for the Lord your God is with you wherever you go.
—Joshua 1:9

FOR FATHER DAMIEN, the last weeks of 1883, culminating with the
biting rebuff from Father Léonor and the realization that none of the
Franciscan sisters would be assigned to the leper settlement at
Moloka'i, made a hollow mockery of the upcoming New Year's fes-
tivities. His lepers needed and deserved the most dedicated and skillful nurses; and his orphans, especially the girls, needed a mother's care.
But so be it. A resigned Father Damien seated himself at his small
wooden desk in the rectory and by the light of the flickering oil lamp
wrote the obligatory New Year's greeting to his bishop: "Accept, your
Excellency, my sincere wishes for a good year for you and for the work
which you direct."[1]

On Friday, January 4, 1884, Mother Marianne and the six sisters left the comforts of the palatial rented mansion in Honolulu and
moved into the cramped and poorly ventilated rooms of the stark
white, two-story, box-shaped convent situated at the opposite end of
the branch hospital complex from the administrator's bungalow.[2] It
required only three days for the sisters to settle in, and once Mother
Marianne received the signed contract from Gibson stating that they
were to "have unrestricted charge in the nursing care and administration of the patients," she and five of the six sisters attacked the dirt
and grime of the hospital buildings with brooms, mops, cleaning rags,
cakes of hard soap, and pails of water.[3]

Van Giesen frowned and shrugged his shoulders in silent resignation. He saw no need to scrub and polish the patient dormitories, wash all of the bedding and patient clothing, and upset the kitchen staff with ridiculous rules about using spotless utensils to prepare food that the sisters insisted be served on freshly washed dishes. Van Giesen reasoned that these inmates, these suspected lepers, were Hawaiian natives, not Caucasians. The facilities and the food were better than most of them had known when they lived in the squalor of thatched huts and ate poi and dog meat. Although Van Giesen believed that the soap and water approach of the sisters was a waste of time and effort, he was resigned to tolerate it in the name of peaceful coexistence.

By the end of the first week the sisters had introduced a reasonable semblance of hygiene—all achieved "with great vigor and irresistible good cheer."[4] Mother Marianne's goal was to convert the branch hospital into a hygienically clean facility stocked with the medicines and supplies that would enable the sisters to nurse the patients compassionately without concern for dirt, germs, and poor food.

The seventh Franciscan sister, Ludovica Gibbons, as instructed by Mother Marianne, remained behind at the convent, isolated from the infectious diseases present in the branch hospital. Her sole responsibility was to serve as the cook and the housekeeper. Mother Marianne adhered to the belief held by the more enlightened physicians of the day that food and drink contaminated with the leprosy bacilli were mainly responsible for the spread of the disease. To further protect themselves, the sisters wore freshly laundered work aprons over their habits and adhered to Mother Marianne's three cardinal rules for survival: fervent prayer, frequent hand washing, and the consumption of uncontaminated food and drink. During Mother Marianne's long tenure in the Hawaiian Islands, no Franciscan sister contracted leprosy.

Belatedly, Father Damien's superiors decided to give him the opportunity to meet Mother Marianne and the Franciscan sisters, and in mid-January he was invited to the dedication of the diminutive St. Philomena Chapel attached to the sisters' convent. Father Damien accepted the invitation and boarded the interisland steamer *Mokoli'i* after the delivery of the weekly food supplies. Since December he had been unable to scale the *pali* because the numbness in his left foot had progressed to the point that his sole was totally devoid of feeling. He could still walk safely on a flat, smooth surface, but climbing was hazardous.

Father Damien believed that there was a remote chance that his disability was due to the arthritic pressure on his sciatic nerve and not leprosy, but in either case the most practical means to travel to Honolulu was via the leper steamer.

On the morning of January 21, Bishop Hermann and his entourage of priests arrived at Kaka'ako a few minutes before the scheduled dedication of the St. Philomena Chapel. While the group awaited the arrival of Queen Kapi'olani, Father Damien was formally introduced to Mother Marianne and the six sisters, but no time was allotted for him to chat with them. A formal nod and a welcoming smile comprised the extent of the social exchange.[5] The brief introductions completed, Bishop Hermann pointed to where his accompanying priests were to stand during the ceremony, widely separated from the sisters. As he positioned the sisters, Queen Kapi'olani and her party, which included Walter Murray Gibson, arrived.

Curious patients, always remaining a discrete distance from the healthy visitors, gathered in small groups to watch the proceedings. Gibson stepped up onto a small podium where he addressed the assemblage, stating that it was the earnest desire of their majesties and the government to devise and carry out measures to alleviate the suffering of all Hawaiians. To accomplish this, ladies who devoted their lives to nursing and the care of the sick had come across the seas to administer to their needs, and "skilled physicians" had been sent for.[6] With a dramatic bow, Gibson then surrendered the podium to Bishop Hermann.

According to the newspaper account, a highly emotional Bishop Hermann had difficulty commencing his address.[7] Wiping away the tears from his cheeks, the bishop began by saying, "This is a supreme moment in my life!" He then proceeded to describe the merits of the sisters' mission and concluded by solemnly dedicating the tiny St. Philomena Chapel.

At the conclusion of the ceremony Bishop Hermann insisted that the fathers immediately return to Honolulu, frustrating Father Damien's desire to speak with Mother Marianne and plead for stationing some of the sisters at the leper settlement on Moloka'i. When he asked for the opportunity to meet with her, he was told that Mother Marianne and Sisters Renata and Antonella, accompanied by Father Léonor, were preparing to depart for Maui where the two sisters were to serve as nurses at the Malulani Hospital, the new government hospital in the town of Wailuku. It was apparent to Damien that neither Walter Gibson nor his own superiors wanted any interference with their plans for the Franciscan sisters.

Resigned to obey, Father Damien returned to Kalawao only to be confronted by a recurrent problem—a food shortage and hungry lepers. The rough wintry sea had prevented the offloading of the weekly food allotment during the week he had been absent, and the food shipment aboard the steamer that ferried him back to Moloka'i was 15 to 20 percent short of the required allotment. When two more weeks passed without a food delivery, Father Damien dispatched a *kōkua* to scale the *pali* and notify Rudolph Meyer of the emergency. Meyer replied, "I am truly pained to learn of the distress of the poor lepers, but I hope that the *Mokoli'i* will arrive Sunday or Monday with a quantity of provisions. It is a case of major storms; there were some days that the ship which makes the postal service could not leave, and consequently I was not able to send anything to Honolulu. . . . I cannot buy anything for the store, for there is no money, and I cannot even obtain a dollar to pay the bills on the food rations for this year nor for the half of last year."[8]

The hospitalized lepers with the more advanced disease picked at the substitute rations of salted salmon and rice, and often chose to go hungry. A diet deficient in both calories and protein invited a premature death when lepers were febrile with pneumonia or coping with infected skin ulcerations. By the end of the fourth week, starvation had doubled the number of funerals, and the coffin builders and the grave diggers worked long hours.

By early March calmer seas ended the food crisis, and the Board of Health refocused its attention on the overall effectiveness of the program to contain the leprosy epidemic. Members of the board were concerned about the alleged misuse use of the huge sums of money being expended. To obtain an independent evaluation, the board granted permission for a visiting physician, Dr. J. H. Stallard, M.B.L., a distinguished member of the College of Physicians, England, to inspect both the branch hospital at Kaka'ako and the leper settlement on Moloka'i. Dr. Stallard was struggling to remedy the inadequacies of the British Empire's program for the thousands of lepers in India and wished to learn about the Hawaiian experience. In return for the privilege of inspecting the leper settlement, Dr. Stallard agreed to submit a comprehensive report of his findings.

Accompanied by Dr. Fitch, Dr. Stallard began his investigation with a two-day tour of the branch hospital at Kaka'ako. The frankness of his report stunned the board:

> I was informed that this hospital was originally established for the purpose of segregating the recent and doubtful cases of leprosy which were to be submitted to careful medical treatment; and in case of cure, discharged. It was also intended that those on whom the disease became fully manifest, should be transferred to Molokai.
>
> In every one of these objects the hospital has proved a failure.
>
> The segregation has never been complete. . . . It is notorious that men have obtained access to the female wards, and that inmates have paid visits to their city friends without the knowledge of the superintendent. . . . But the most objectionable feature of Kakaako is the complete absence of any classification of the inmates; the practice of sending away the confirmed lepers has long since ceased. Apparently friends amongst persons high in authority are permitted to remain in spite of their condition, while those who have no friends are sent to Molokai, even before the hope of successful medical treatment has entirely passed away. . . . It is extraordinary to notice the absence of proper surgical instruments and appliances. On the occasion of my visit it was found necessary that a large abscess should be opened, and it was painful to observe that the instrument used by Dr. Fitch was taken from a post-mortem case, and that it cut through the tissues with great difficulty. . . . In conclusion, I am of the opinion that the hospital at Kakaako is totally unfit for the treatment of lepers.[9]

On March 5, Dr. Stallard, accompanied by Drs. Fitch and Arning, stepped ashore at the Kalaupapa landing wharf to inspect the leper settlement. With the kōkua and their children, the total number of persons in residence at the settlement numbered about a thousand. In his comprehensive report, Dr. Stallard made the following observations:

> I was most gratified at the cheerful and contented population, the entire absence of grumbling or complaint, the cleanliness of their persons and the comfort and tidiness of all their dwellings, the many neat little plots of onions, sweet potatoes, tobacco and flowers in front of many of their houses and above all, the general possession of a horse and little articles of personal adornment; everywhere we saw the appearance of happiness and freedom. All this contrasted most favorably with the confinement at Kakaako. . . . In the place of the wretched thatched huts,

resting on the damp ground, they have erected many comfortable dwellings of wood. They have brought in water from a neighboring stream; they have erected a hospital and the residence for a physician. They have encouraged those who have the means to build dwellings of a better class, and by allowing kokua they have greatly reduced the immorality which naturally resulted from separating 200 women from their husbands and forcing them to live in the same settlement with 300 men. . . .

But here my commendations end, all the natural advantages of Molokai have been destroyed by defective and incomplete administration. The excessive mortality alone condemns the management. . . . *This high mortality has not been caused by leprosy, but by dysentery, a disease not caused by any local insanitary conditions, but by gross neglect.* [Emphasis added.] The leper cannot stand up against starvation. He requires generous food, and he dies without it. . . . To supply those who are entitled to beef rations takes 5,600 lbs. per week, and from the beginning of the year . . . a deficiency in nine weeks of 26,526 lbs. . . . for three weeks out of nine there was no beef at all, and for two other weeks there was only a very partial supply, and that probably consumed by officials, whilst for three weeks only was the supply sufficient. During these times, the lepers were given salt salmon in lieu of beef, a food which has been universally condemned by the best medical authorities as entirely unfit for the use of lepers. . . .

It was my fortune to see the arrival of a cargo of lepers, and here also there was the same absence of proper management; no preparations had been made for their reception. They were simply "dumped" upon the "shore," and left to "shift" for themselves. Some of the young had happily been provided by the sisters at Kakaako with a letter to Father Damien, soliciting his interest in their welfare; but the rest, if not too feeble to walk, were left to shift for themselves.[10]

Dr. Stoddard concluded his report with the candid observation that unless there were a physician and professional nurses in residence, the medical care at the settlement would remain suboptimal.

The majority of the members of the Board of Health were offended by Dr.Stallard's report, which pointed an accusatory finger at them. To compound matters and add to the stress of appointed office, Queen Kapiʻolani asked to see a copy of the Stallard report as she was planning to visit the leper settlement during the coming summer months when the surf that pounded the Kalaupapa wharf was enjoying its seasonal calm.

The Stallard report confirmed Dr. Emerson's reservations about the utility of the Kaka'ako Branch Hospital. The facility had become a liability, a public disgrace, a haven for the affluent lepers able to contribute to the king's treasury. In Dr. Emerson's opinion, the hospital director, Dr. Fitch, was ill suited to his assigned task, biased as he was regarding the etiology of leprosy. With an impassioned plea, Dr. Emerson urged his fellow board members to close the branch hospital, dismiss Dr. Fitch, and concentrate on improving conditions at the leper settlement on Moloka'i.

After some hasty deliberation, the board elected to solicit a second "independent" opinion about the operation of the branch hospital and the leper settlement and asked Henry Van Giesen and Dr. Fitch to assess both facilities. Because both men were Gibson appointees, the prime minister was confident he could count on them to support the status quo.[11] When he read the reports submitted by Dr. Fitch and Van Giesen, he smiled. The status quo was adequate for the present. Dr. Emerson, however, was not appeased and continued to press for the closure of the branch hospital.

ON THE MORNING of March 19, Father Albert arrived in Honolulu unannounced and in a state of near collapse. His face was flushed with a high fever, and each time a deep booming cough doubled him over, he spit out a mouthful of thick, greenish phlegm. He had recognized that he was being stalked by pneumonia and had managed to stagger aboard one of the interisland steamers. When he was carried into the rectory in Honolulu, the fathers avoided him as if he had the black plague, fearful that he was harboring a dread form of leprosy. Drs. Fitch and Arning were summoned, and their clinical examination confirmed that the priest had pneumonia, the treatment for which was an extended period of bed rest—at the rectory. The fathers shuddered, but Dr. Arning assured everyone that Father Albert was not contagious, and that the ugly dermatitis could be treated at the same time as the life-threatening pneumonia.

A distraught Father Damien once again found himself the lone priest on Moloka'i. He wrote to his Bishop, "Will you see what you can do for the district of Moloka'i? I find it physically impossible to visit the entire district regularly. You know my foot will no longer permit climbing; there is no sensation in it so I cannot continue to climb the Pali. We have many dying here. Pray for me."[12]

Bishop Hermann replied that he was powerless to help. "The visit of Father Albert surprised us. It is disturbing because of the hole he has left you in at Molokai, and because of the disquieting fear of those of us here to contracting a contagious disease, a concern which, unfortunately, he does not share. As to a means to provide assistance for the rest of Molokai, where can I find someone? It may be impossible to find anyone."[13]

Dr. Arning took an interest in Father Albert's case and after prescribing several medicines for the treatment of the pneumonia, he carefully examined the priest for any overt signs of leprosy. Finding none, he focused his attention on the priest's long history of chronic, scaling dermatitis of the hands and face coupled with the alopecia (absence of hair) of the hairy surfaces of the body, including the eyebrows and beard. Then Dr. Arning astutely diagnosed psoriasis, a dermatitis that can mimic some of the skin manifestations of leprosy, and initiated a course of treatment that consisted of "heroic doses of arsenate of soda" and the external application of salicylate of bismuth ointment.[14] Father Albert obligingly but not enthusiastically began swallowing the huge doses of arsenate and coating his skin lesions with the ointment. To his immense relief and delight, as his pneumonia resolved, his skin lesions began to heal.

During his lengthy convalescence in Honolulu, Father Albert totally disrupted the serenity that generally pervaded the cathedral. Father Léonor was so irritated by Father Albert's behavior that he ventilated his frustrations in a letter to the superior general.

> We have had Father Albert here for a month, during which everyone has tried to escape from him because he pesters everyone. He has the air of a man who has been flayed. By the order of the doctor it is necessary that he be anointed and bandaged from head to feet twice a day. His anointing with an ointment with a disagreeable odor does not hinder him from going everywhere and touching everything, so that everything is greasy. The Bishop does his best to avoid him. The holy Father Modeste is obliged to change his place in Church, and he pursues me every day, repeating that the mission ought to take care of him. Thankfully, I believe the doctor is going to deliver us from him next week by returning him to Molokai.[15]

SPRING SMILED ON Moloka'i. April and May featured good weather and relatively calm seas. Shipments of food and supplies to the leper settlement arrived on schedule, and the necessary funds for critical purchases were forthcoming from the Board of Health. In late May, Rudolph Meyer informed Father Damien that Dr. Emerson had prevailed, and that the Board of Health was planning to discharge Dr. Fitch and abandon the branch hospital at year's end. To meet the need for additional housing for the anticipated influx of lepers, the board was shipping the materials with which to build an additional fifty all-wood houses.[16] Father Damien, in concert with Ambrose Hutchison, was to oversee the construction of the new houses.

The best news was that the board had allocated sufficient funds to entice a physician to reside full time at the leper settlement. Dr. Arthur Mouritz, a superbly trained physician with a knowledge of leprosy who had taken up residence in the Islands, was offered the post of resident physician. To the delight of the board, Dr. Mouritz, a bachelor, expressed an interest in the position and, finding the salary and housing arrangements to his liking, had agreed to move to Kalawao in the fall.

Meanwhile, Rev. Dr. Charles Hyde, the director of the theological institute for the training of young Hawaiians in the Protestant ministry, became concerned when a mysterious rash erupted on his feet that to him had the appearance of leprosy.[17] He had been assured by Dr. Fitch that leprosy was a fourth stage of syphilis and therefore noncontagious to moral Christians through casual contact. Confident that this information was accurate, Rev. Hyde had felt secure in commencing a program of weekly ministerial rounds at the Kaka'ako Branch Hospital, and on two occasions he had even dared to venture to the leper settlement on Moloka'i for brief visits, each time condescending to meet with Father Damien for a few minutes. Alarmed by the rash, he consulted several physicians who catapulted him into a state of near hysteria when they cautioned that Hyde's dermatitis might indeed be an early manifestation of leprosy and that a period of observation would be required to determine the true nature of the disorder.

Slowly, over several weeks, the dermatitis cleared, and a relieved Rev. Hyde became convinced that Dr. Fitch's view of the disease was the correct one. Confident that the only way leprosy was transmitted was through sexual intercourse with a leper, Rev. Hyde felt safe in resuming his weekly pastoral visits to the branch hospital, a practice he continued for several months until the Board of Health, at the insistence of Dr. Emerson, dismissed Dr. Fitch. In protest to the firing of his friend, he ceased ministering to the Protestants at Kakaʻako.

BY JUNE 1884, everyone in Honolulu stood in awe of the Sisters of St. Francis. Patients at the Kakaʻako Branch Hospital lauded the sisters' compassion and nursing skill. Reportedly, the sisters exhibited no fear or revulsion when cleansing and dressing the ugliest of skin ulcerations of those suspected to be lepers. To the Hawaiians, the sisters were "Angels of Mercy." Queen Kapiʻolani was proud of these courageous women, and chose to help them by sponsoring a series of charitable parties, theatrical performances, and musicals to raise money for their use at the branch hospital.[18]

Walter Murray Gibson was overwhelmed by the compliments he was receiving for his role in bringing the sisters to Hawaiʻi. He knew that if he could only double their number and assign them to area hospitals caring for the Native Hawaiians, his approval rating as prime minister would soar. So he wrote to Mother Marianne: "I am authorized by the Board of Health, and I pray you most of my own accord to invite other Sisters of your Order to come and assist you in your blessed work. Should you think it proper to invite as many as eight more at present, the Board will make the due provisions for their travelling expenses, and establishment here."[19]

Mother Marianne was pleased, but the number of Franciscan sisters available for service in the Hawaiian Islands was limited. Still, were she to add two sisters to her roster, she could consider assigning three sisters, including herself, to the leper settlement on Molokaʻi. She was fully cognizant of the danger but believed that by employing the known hygienic and disinfective techniques the leprosy bacillus could be rendered impotent.

ON JULY 19, Father Damien was informed by G. W. Parker, the secretary of the Board of Health, that Queen Kapiʻolani, accompanied by Princess Liliʻuokalani, planned to tour the leper settlement in two days.[20] Despite the short notice, Father Damien was elated. The queen's visit would provide the opportunity to demonstrate what had been accomplished in the three years since Princess Liliʻuokalani's visit and, more importantly, would focus her attention on the nagging problem of the mandatory incarceration of the children of lepers who as yet had not contracted the disease. And most importantly, should the queen consent to tour the hospital complex, he could dramatically point out the desperate need for professional nurses.

A relatively calm sea allowed Queen Kapi'olani and her party to land at the Kalaupapa wharf at 4 P.M. on July 21, 1884, and be welcomed by Ambrose Hutchison and Fathers Damien and Albert. The royal party, which included Dr. Arning and Walter Gibson, was escorted to a building where a large number of the patients were assembled. After the queen was formally introduced, she arose and spoke briefly in Hawaiian: "With love I greet you all. My heart-felt sympathy and that of His Majesty the King, your Father, is with you in your affliction. The King has sent his Sister to accompany me in this mission, to show his love for you. . . . The principal object of this mission to your Asylum is to know your condition, and to render such assistance as may be necessary for your comfort."[21]

The lepers were genuinely moved by the sincerity of the queen's remarks, and a series of designated responders stepped forward to outline the most pressing problems facing them.[22] The most eloquent of the presenters that day was Ambrose Hutchison, who took center stage, leading by the hand a ten-year-old girl who appeared perfectly healthy. While the royal party waited to learn the reason for the presence of the little girl, Hutchison continued to hold her hand as he summarized the merits of the key complaints of the previous responders regarding the problems with the food supply, the inadequate clothing, and the inherent horror of being placed in one of the hospitals in which there were no nurses and no doctor.

"The great want here," Hutchison began, "is the institution of more approved nursing facilities. . . . If two such provisions were added that of a resident physician and an efficient staff of nurses, the main source of objection would be removed, and then they might enter the hospital willingly instead of avoiding the place as they do now. Could some Sisters of Mercy be induced to come and remain among us, as is now the case at Kakaako, it would certainly be a blessing."[23]

Hutchison paused for a dramatic moment, then looked down at the little girl whose hand he was still holding. Slowly raising his eyes to meet those of the queen, he continued: "One thing I would like especially to call your Majesty's attention to, and that is among us are a number of children born of diseased parents, who themselves are *entirely free* from all symptoms of the disease [emphasis added]. Here is one of them, and there are here between fifty and sixty just such cases as this, and at various ages. These should be kept aloof from the diseased and properly cared for in a separate asylum, and not be allowed to remain where the chances are of so many of them becoming patients by contagion. I would urge upon the Queen and the Heir Apparent to have this matter attended to."[24]

Queen Kapiʻolani smiled at the little girl and nodded her head, a silent promise that she would do something to help the healthy children escape the risk of contagion. Then she rose and graciously thanked the several spokespersons for suggestions for improvement. Gathering her entourage, she next toured the village of Kalaupapa and inspected as many of the homes occupied by lepers as time permitted before proceeding on horseback to the main leper village at Kalawao. Arriving there at 7:30 P.M., the group had dinner and then retired for the night in the new house that had been built to provide safe accommodations for visiting physicians.

After breakfast the next morning, the royal party elected to visit the leper patients in the eight buildings that made up the hospital complex. In the first building the queen spoke with the nine male patients, who ranged in age from seven years to sixty. The sixty-year-old man was too weak to sit up, yet when asked by the queen what improvements should be made, he managed to blurt out several of the same complaints she had heard the day before: thin mats for beds on the rock-hard volcanic earth, not enough blankets to keep the patients warm at night, an insufficient supply of food that was often improperly prepared, and the desire for a resident physician who could prescribe for the intercurrent diseases such as dysentery and pneumonia. The dying man stated that the government physician from Honolulu came too seldom and his visit was so hurried that the patients derived little benefit.

It wasn't until Queen Kapiʻolani entered the last two buildings, which were designated for the dying patients, that the full horror of leprosy was unveiled. One blind leper, too horribly deformed to allow one to guess his age, was writhing in agony on his mat as the group stood helplessly by and stared down at him. To allay the agony of both the patient and the visitors, Dr. Arning reached into his small physician's bag for a narcotic drug, which he promptly administered. Then the group was ushered on to the mat-side of the next patient. Glancing back at the blind leper, the queen noted his pain had subsided sufficiently to allow him to relax and slip into sleep. Dr. Arning made the point that controlling the blind man's pain was an example of why there should be a resident physician at the settlement. Pain and infection were amenable to professional treatment. What the queen had just witnessed before Arning's intervention was an example of man's inhumanity to man.

In the second of the death buildings, a small girl, too weak to cry out, was mouthing the name of her mother through dry, cracked lips. She was suffering from simple dehydration, and Dr. Arning instructed one of the paid *kōkua* to moisten the girl's lips and give her sips of water every hour until she died. The absence of a nursing staff was unconscionable. The queen, her eyes filled with tears, nodded her agreement.

The queen smiled for the first time when she toured the boys' and girls' orphanages and schools, where forty-two young lepers were housed, fed, and taught. These children were either orphans or had been abandoned by their families. The two orphanages operated under the direct supervision of Father Damien, assisted by a Hawaiian woman named Kuilia, a nonleper, who was the matron for the girls' orphanage. Queen Kapi'olani was impressed with the cheerful atmosphere, the cleanliness, and the curriculum of study. What she was witnessing confirmed Princess Lili'uokalani's observation that the Catholic priest had made enormous contributions to the quality of life at the settlement, the finest of which was the care he provided the leper children.

Father Damien then led the party on horseback to Waikolu Valley, a distance of about 3.5 miles from Kalawao and 5 miles from Kalaupapa, where there was a deep pool of water that he proposed to utilize as the reservoir for the replacement water pipeline. He explained that this large pool had never gone dry during his sojourn at the settlement as it was continually fed by the tiny cascades of water splashing down the face of the *pali*. He pointed out that this natural reservoir lay in a fertile valley in which taro could be cultivated, along with other fruits and vegetables for use at the settlement. Cattle, too, could graze here and multiply, and could in time serve as the main source of beef and milk. The queen nodded her support for the proposed projects.

On the return to Kalawao, the queen insisted on stopping to visit the occupants of each of the outlying homes. In some of these she encountered dying lepers—lepers unable to care for themselves, but who steadfastly refused to submit to the horrors of the hospital. Father Damien and Hutchison reiterated the crucial need for a professional medical staff to provide compassionate care for the very ill and the dying. The queen, without first consulting prime minister Gibson, promised to help secure a doctor and nurses for the settlement.

Upon her return to ʻIolani Palace, the queen, with Princess Liliʻuokalani's assistance, prepared a list of recommendations for King Kalākaua. Each item listed was based on a suggestion made by Father Damien or Ambrose Hutchison:

1. As the supply of water was inadequate, a new pipeline should be constructed to transport water from the valley of Waikolu.
2. A full-time resident physician should be employed and quartered near the hospital complex.
3. The hospital accommodations should be increased to a 200-bed capacity.
4. If possible, Sisters of Mercy should be induced to serve as nurses at the hospital.
5. There should be an ambulance to provide for the transportation of crippled patients, and two spring wagons for the delivery of beef and pai ai to the lepers.
6. A small steamer capable of transporting 20-30 head of cattle, 50 cords of fire wood, and poi should be secured.
7. Lepers unable to care for themselves should be compelled to take shelter in the hospital.
8. Two buildings near Honolulu should be built: one for the care of children with incipient stages of leprosy; the second as an orphanage for healthy children born of leper parents.
9. The rations of food stuffs should be increased.
10. A moderately large herd of beef cattle and milk cows should be established on the pasture lands of the settlement.
11. The valleys of Waikolu and Waialeia should be cultivated for the growing of taro and other vegetables and fruits.[25]

Determined to do what she herself could manage, Queen Kapiʻolani decided to secure the necessary clothing for those lepers who were unable to provide for themselves. She wrote to Father Damien to learn just how many men and women fell into this category and was informed that there were 187 men and 93 women who lacked the wherewithal to purchase the minimum clothing for comfort and health. In the five surviving letters she wrote to Father Damien, we learn that she not only provided the clothing for the 280 lepers, but she also purchased a supply of basic household furniture, plus a variety of seeding plants.[26]

IN SEPTEMBER 1884, during one of Dr. Arning's infrequent visits to the leper settlement, the always inquisitive physician took Father Damien aside to inquire about the chronic "rheumatism" and sciatic nerve irritation that was troubling him.[27] Father Damien obligingly described the numbness he was experiencing in his lower left leg and foot, which other examining physicians, including Dr. Fitch, attributed to sciatic nerve compression from the arthritis in his lower back. The Belgian priest wasn't naive; he had long suspected that he had the early manifestations of leprosy. He had known at least a dozen lepers whose leprosy had first manifested itself with a numb extremity, but as long as there were no obvious skin lesions, there was room for doubt—or hope, depending upon one's point of view. Nevertheless, it had been his policy for nearly two years not to make direct physical contact with a nonleper for fear of transmitting the dread disease.

Dr. Arning asked permission to examine the priest's left leg and numb foot. With Father Damien seated, he examined the left foot. There was no obvious sign of muscle atrophy. When tested, all of the muscles had normal strength. Then Dr. Arning ran his fingers over the surface of the leg, palpating those areas where there were underlying major nerves. Ever so gently he ran his fingers over the knee. On the lateral or outside of the knee joint, just beneath the surface of the skin, he identified the normal bony protrusion that is the head of the fibula, the smaller of the two long bones of the lower leg. Then he eased his exploring fingers below and slightly behind the bony bulge where he felt a thin, ropelike structure beneath the skin—the swollen peroneal nerve! A normal peroneal nerve is not palpable. He rolled the ropelike structure beneath his fingers, making certain of his finding. A palpable peroneal nerve meant only one thing: *It confirmed that the Belgian priest was a leper!* Dr. Arning paused for a moment, said nothing, then had his fingers retrace their path and once again palpate the swollen peroneal nerve. There was no question as to the accuracy of his diagnosis. Next, he scrutinized the skin of Father Damien's face. The tiny reddish yellow spots on the priest's forehead and cheeks were compatible with leprosy. Carefully, he examined the small wartlike tumor on Father Damien's right earlobe. It too probably harbored millions of the infectious bacteria. In time, as the disease progressed, the skin lesions would enlarge and become obvious to everyone. The immediate problem, however, was how to tell the "hero of Moloka'i" that the next time he began to celebrate the Mass with his traditional opening words, "We lepers," he was speaking the truth, and that now he was one of them in body as well as in soul.

Whether Dr. Arning informed Father Damien of his findings at this time is not known. What is known is that he did inform Bishop Hermann that Father Damien was a leper. The bishop in turn told the vice provincial, who promptly wrote to the superior general: "Last week the doctor on Molokai told the Bishop in secret that Father Damien has leprosy, and at the same time I received a letter from Father Gulstan informing me that the poor saintly Father Gregoire (who does not know it) has the same. The only ones who know this are the Wailuku [Maui] physician, Father Gulstan, the Bishop, and me. . . . This news has overwhelmed us. What a plague this sickness is. . . . Nevertheless, he [Father Damien] can administer the sacraments to his poor unfortunate ones. I shall go to see him four times a year, to hear confessions (and to confess him, myself) and to say Mass.[28]

There is no evidence that Father Léonor ever once visited Father Damien at the leper settlement.

The forty-four-year-old priest from Belgium was a leper, but whether he knew it—or knowing it, believed he could not transmit the disease to another until such time as he developed skin ulcerations—is not known. For at least one month following Dr. Arning's examination, he continued with his normal routine of ministering to non-lepers outside of the leper settlement as if he were not a leper. Father Damien's superiors had medical confirmation that he was a leper and as such was potentially infectious to others, yet they did nothing to protect the healthy with whom he was coming in contact. To avoid any scandalous publicity, they concealed the truth and remained mute—and to protect themselves, they assiduously avoided any contact with him for the remainder of his life.

18

Damien, the Leper

And so I am sure of this: that God who began this good
work in you, will carry it on until it is finished.
—Philippians 1:6

APPARENTLY IGNORANT OF the fact that Dr. Arning had informed his superiors that he was a leper, Father Damien continued to visit Moloka'i's healthy parishioners living outside the settlement. To safeguard their well-being he made as little physical contact as possible. Handshaking, the customary method for one adult to greet another, was the one ritual it was impossible to avoid. Still, he rationalized, until an open skin sore appeared he probably could not transmit the disease. The admonition of Moses in the Old Testament not to touch the sores of a leper was the key to escaping the disease, and since he had touched countless hundreds of the hideous ulcerations, he was doomed.

The fact that Father Damien was a leper was also concealed from Rudolph Meyer, who dutifully continued to make his way down the *pali* trail every four to six weeks to inspect the leper settlement, insistent as always that no leper come within 6 feet of him or his mule. Upon completion of each inspection tour, Meyer would relax in the company of his friend and enjoy a cup of coffee while the two discussed any problem facing the settlement. When he rose to leave, Meyer always gripped the hand of the priest as he said, "Aloha, my friend."

During one of Rudolph Meyer's visits in the summer of 1884, the appointment of a new resident superintendent was explored. Both agreed that the new *luna nui*[1] should be a person with one of the milder cases of leprosy who was fluent in both English and Hawaiian, and so could competently attend to the day-to-day operation. When asked whom he would recommend for the post, Father Damien replied that he favored Ambrose Hutchison, the half-Hawaiian who had come to Kalawao in 1879 and who had served well as the assistant resident superintendent since his appointment the previous March. The young man was dedicated to improving the lot of the lepers, as witnessed by his recent dramatic presentation to Queen Kapi'olani on behalf of the healthy children trapped at the settlement. Meyer nodded his agreement, and Ambrose Hutchison was named the new *luna nui*.[2]

Over a second cup of coffee, Meyer described the shocking human experiment Dr. Arning had carried out on a convicted murderer. A Native Hawaiian named Keanu had been sentenced to be hanged for the bludgeoning death of the husband of his clandestine lover. In a formal letter to the Privy Council of State, Dr. Arning had requested that Keanu's death sentence be commuted to life imprisonment if the murderer would submit to an inoculation of tissue from a leper. The purpose of the experiment was to determine whether the implantation of a massive number of leprosy bacilli could induce leprosy in an otherwise healthy Hawaiian.[3] The Privy Council granted permission, and when offered the choice, Keanu chose inoculation to the hangman's noose. On September 30, Keanu reluctantly held out his right arm for the bite of Dr. Arning's scalpel and the painful insertion of leprous tissue that had been cut from the cheek of a young Hawaiian girl.[4] Following the operation, Keanu was confined to a cell in the O'ahu jail where Dr. Arning examined him every day, searching for the early clinical signs of leprosy. Meyer confided that several members of the Board of Health, including Dr. Emerson, were appalled by the abusive human research and were pushing for Dr. Arning's dismissal.

Saving the best news until last, Meyer, with a broad smile, announced that Father Damien was about to host a famous visitor. The Board of Health had granted permission for Charles Warren Stoddard, the first American journalist to visit the leper settlement after it had opened, to make a return visit. The internationally known correspondent was awaiting confirmation of his academic appointment as a professor of English at the University of Notre Dame and was planning to write a book based on his visits to the Hawaiian leper settlement. The Board of Health believed it was in their interest to permit the author to see the enormous improvements that had been made in the sixteen years since his initial visit. As they had done in 1868, the board assigned a government-appointed physician to escort Stoddard to the settlement for a one-week visit.

This was the same Charles Stoddard who had befriended the young Scottish novelist, Robert Louis Stevenson, in San Francisco in 1879 and introduced him to the novels of Herman Melville. In one of their evenings together, Stoddard had intrigued Stevenson with the account of his visit to the leper settlement and what he had subsequently learned about the "heroic Belgian priest" who had become its resident priest and part-time physician.[5] Stevenson was enthralled by the tale and had expressed an interest in one day meeting this priest, a man who had the courage to face an incurable disease—much as Stevenson was doing in his personal battle with pulmonary tuberculosis.

On Monday afternoon, October 6, 1884, Charles Stoddard, accompanied by Dr. George Fitch and the recently recruited Dr. Arthur Mouritz, boarded the SS *Likelike* in Honolulu bound for Moloka'i. Although Dr. Fitch's contract to serve as the chief physician at the Kaka'ako Branch Hospital and visiting physician to the leper settlement was not being renewed, he had agreed to host the visit of the famous author and the new physician. Fitch believed he had made major contributions to the control of leprosy in Hawai'i and wished these to be properly presented in Stoddard's upcoming book.

Tucked in a satchel slung over Stoddard's shoulder was a small leather-bound diary in which the author planned to record his candid observations of the visit for possible inclusion in his book. Stoddard had no intention of ever publishing his unedited diary, but twenty-four years after his death in 1933, 250 copies of his diary were printed for the Book Club of California.[6] From Stoddard's cryptic notations, the reader can picture the landing on the southern coast of Moloka'i, the overland ride to the *pali* for the descent to the leper settlement, sense the exhilaration and the danger when descending the treacherous *pali* trail, glimpse the horror of the leper hospital, gain a journalist's impression of the personalities of the people with whom Father Damien worked, and most importantly, meet and talk with Father Damien himself.

Once the *Likelike* churned out of Honolulu Harbor, Stoddard had his first opportunity to interview Dr. Fitch, whom he found to be loquacious, arrogant, and self-centered.[7] By contrast, Dr. Mouritz turned out to be an extremely well educated, well-read physician, reticent to talk about his accomplishments. Late that evening the trio disembarked at Kaunakakai on the southern coast of Moloka'i. Rudolph Meyer escorted them to a nearby cottage where the three could eat a light meal and rest until dawn.[8]

The next morning the group mounted horses and trotted overland to the edge of the *pali* overlooking the triangular-shaped Kalaupapa Peninsula.[9] Anxious to complete the trek that he had made eight to ten times a year since 1882, Dr. Fitch shouldered his backpack and shouted, "Come, let us be going!" Stoddard and Mouritz obediently followed. Stoddard wrote: "With staff in hand, approaching the precipitous trail, single-file, [we] took the first downward step. It was like plunging into space. . . . We were dropping, slipping, scrambling down a sharp flank of the cliff, that cut the air like a flying buttress. By a series of irregular steps we slowly descended, leaping from rock to rock. . . . It was every man for himself now."[10]

In his diary, Stoddard scribbled:

> I slipped and grew weary and weak legged and many a time wished the tiresome descent over. Wild goats slid showers of stones upon us. Huge birds soared under us and over us and made me dizzy. . . . Again and again we rested. . . . I wasn't sure-footed and, though amiable, was very weary and foot-sore. We were nearly two hours descending and when finally at the bottom—lo! The three horses which had been promised us by telephone while we were resting at Mr. Meyer's house were nowhere to be found. After another wait, which quite disgusted us, we had to foot it a mile and a half to Kalawao, where we arrived at last at about 3 P.M.[11]

"Faint and foot-sore," Stoddard trudged after the two physicians to the guest lodge on the outskirts of Kalawao, "a neat frame building, reserved for the exclusive use of the visiting physician and his friends." Grateful to have arrived, the trio deposited their packs, left orders for an early dinner, and then proceeded into the village proper. In Stoddard's words:

> The first glimpse of Kalawao might lead a stranger to pronounce it a thriving hamlet of perhaps five hundred inhabitants. Its single street is bordered by neat whitewashed cottages, with numerous little gardens of bright flowers, and clusters of graceful and decorative tropical trees.

. . . By the roadside, in the edge of the village, between it and the sea, stood a little chapel. . . . As we drew near, the churchyard gate was swung open for us by a troop of laughing urchins, who stood hat in hand to give us welcome. Now, for the first time, I noticed that they were all disfigured: that their faces were seared and scarred; their hands and feet maimed and sometimes bleeding; their eyes like the eyes of some half-tamed animal; their mouths shapeless, and their whole aspect in many cases repulsive. . . . The chapel door stood ajar; in a moment it was thrown open, and a young priest paused upon the threshold to give us welcome. His cassock was worn and faded; his hair tumbled like a school-boy's, his hands stained and hardened by toil; but the glow of health was in his face, the buoyancy of youth in his manner; while his ringing laugh, his ready sympathy, and his inspiring magnetism told of one who in any sphere might do a noble work, and who in that which he has chosen is doing the noblest of all works.

This was Father Damien, the self-exiled priest, the one clean man in the midst of his flock of lepers.[12]

In his diary, Stoddard added: "Father Damien, God bless him, received me with the utmost kindness, gentleness and courtesy."[13]

Damien invited the three visitors to have dinner with him, but was politely informed that Dr. Fitch's hired servants had already been instructed to prepare the evening meal with the clean food they had brought with them. The priest was not offended and, with a wave of his hand, dispersed the curious and growing congregation of lepers that now surrounded and stared at the newcomers. To lighten the mood Father Damien stepped into the church courtyard and, with a handful of corn in his outstretched hand, uttered a peculiar cry that was immediately answered by a whir of wings. Several dozen chickens descended "out of the air in clouds; they lit upon his arms, and fed out of his hands; they fought for footing upon his shoulders and even upon his head; they covered him with caresses and with feathers. He stood knee-deep among as fine a flock of fowls as any fancier would care to see; they were his pride, his playthings; and yet a brace of them he sacrificed upon the altar of friendship, and bade us go in peace."[14] Stoddard and the two doctors returned to the guest lodge for the evening meal, which was now a feast because of Father Damien's gift of the chicken.

On Wednesday, October 8, Stoddard wrote:

Slept very poorly; was afraid of waking the two doctors. . . . was about to start for chapel when Father Damien's carriage drove up to take me to Mass. I was doubly delighted, for it saved me the walk when I am lame and sore all over [from the *pali* descent], and it spared me the company of Dr. F___, who had volunteered to accompany me. . . .

As I entered, the natives were chanting a litany; I went to the altar rail and knelt; the priest was kneeling within it; shortly he came to me and said: "Will you please kneel there," pointing to a small, raised seat, quite apart from the others, in one wing of the transept. I was in a semicircular enclosure just large enough to surround me, and all the others in the church—altar boys and all save only the priest and I—were lepers.

I felt not the slightest fear; the place was dingy and dirty; the stations were tilted; the little interior painted in bad taste; the holy water font was a tin cup; some rosaries were scattered about, and a few torn catechisms. The priest's robes were singularly clean and beautiful, without being extravagant. The chalice was small, the altar decorations cheap and tawdry; the candles tilted all ways. The acolytes—two—wore no robes, though there were several of the scarlet ones hanging within the church.

Mass was said with great sweetness and deliberation and after it there was a brief instruction in the catechism. Then the priest said "Pau," "Finished" and the congregation, mostly children, hastened out of the place.[15]

When the two were alone in the churchyard, Stoddard asked when he might interview Father Damien. The priest promised to chat a few moments before breakfast and then throughout the day as circumstances allowed. Stoddard followed Damien to the small second-story balcony of the nearby rectory where both men seated themselves. Stoddard asked if he might smoke cigarettes during the interview. Father Damien nodded affirmatively and began to pack the bowl of his pipe with his homegrown tobacco. Next Stoddard opened his Moloka'i diary to a blank page and handed the book to Damien with the request that the priest write his name and the date and place of his birth at the top of the page. Father Damien complied and the interview began. In Stoddard's words, Father Damien answered "all the questions with great good sense and with much modesty."[16] Stoddard's notes of this first interview occupy the last ten pages of the diary and were the basis for much of the material in *The Lepers of Molokai*, which was published the following year by the Ave Maria Press at Notre Dame.

Stoddard inquired whether Father Damien had any recent photographs of himself, and the Belgian obligingly retrieved one from the small desk in the adjacent room. As he handed it to Stoddard he apologetically remarked that in the photo he looked "like a leper" because of the several suspicious spots on his face. Somewhat startled by the remark, Stoddard scrutinized the priest's face. A beard now covered and completely concealed the questionable areas in the photograph. The Belgian appeared so robust and energetic and full of life that Stoddard dismissed the possibility that Damien had contracted leprosy.

After answering a series of questions about his life at the leper settlement, Father Damien left the balcony and prepared a breakfast that consisted of "a pot of good coffee, some sugar on the top of a sea biscuit, and a jug of milk." After the meal Damien drove Stoddard to the visitor's lodge, where they were invited by Doctors Fitch and Mouritz to accompany them on hospital rounds.[17] Stoddard noted in his diary:

> I saw many horrible cases, especially one poor little fellow whose every pore was oozing stinking pitch and whose face had a kind of death mold on it half an inch deep—yet he felt no pain. Some of these lepers are filled with a kind of fever pain in all their bones and many of them have pains in their chests, but for the most part they do not suffer.
>
> Some chose to shake hands and these were in no wise refused. One man was in his last breath, his body was drawn up and old, his body and his face covered with a thick red blanket with a black stripe at each end of it. . . .
>
> In the same ward with him were a dozen others—awaiting death. None of these showed the slightest fear, or much appreciation of their situation. Dr. F___ was like a cheap showman; very loud, very wordy, and full of mock sentimentality. Whenever Father Damien tried to get a few words out of the natives, or to gain some little useful knowledge, or to help entertain the new doctor—the old one went away impatiently and called to us to come on. "I like to attend to business, that's the sort of person I am."[18]

In order to have more time in which to interview Father Damien, Stoddard accepted the priest's invitation to stay in the rectory during his stay. Both physicians strongly advised against this, urging that he sleep in the guest lodge where no leper was ever allowed to enter, but Stoddard chose to ignore the warning and moved his gear to the upstairs room in the rectory where his bed would be a mat on the wooden floor. The following morning as he eased himself into a sitting position on the mat, he discovered that his muscles were extremely sore and stiff from the stress of the *pali* descent. Finding himself alone in the rectory, he munched on biscuits left for him on the small desk and sipped from a bottle of claret while he recorded his thoughts and observations from the interview held late the night before. Then he left the rectory and walked to the chapel in anticipation of finding Father Damien there.

> As I neared the chapel one of the lepers mounted a horse and hastened away to call the Father—who was at work building with his boys. I went into the chapel—it was very quiet and peaceful—and having said my prayers, I opened the little American organ, a very good one, and began to play.
>
> Father Damien arrived as I was playing and came in at once to beg me to go on—natives had gathered to listen to me; a flock of unfortunates who were very polite and attentive. Father Damien began to read his office and requested me to continue at the organ, so he read it to the strains of "Trovatore." Then we adjourned to his house where he opened a bottle of claret—for on St. Bernard's day the bishop, whose fete it is, sent a case of claret to each of his priests. . . . more pleasant chat. How charming he is; how beautiful in his devotion, how sincere, how charitable. He showed me, but not until I had asked to see it, his decoration: Knight Commander of the Royal Order of Kalakaua. He brought me as a souvenir a white and gold chalice veil which for nine years he has used in saying mass in the leper chapel at Kalawao—how exquisite—only this morning he used it at Mass.[19]

Later that morning, while in the company of Dr. Mouritz, Dr. Fitch seized the opportunity to inspect the hands and face of the Belgian priest once again and search for any signs of leprosy. Finding no incriminating visual evidence of leprosy, Dr. Fitch pronounced the priest free of the disease he believed to be a late stage of syphilis. Turning to Dr. Mouritz, he asked the doctor to verify his findings. Dr. Mouritz obliged and carefully inspected the skin of the priest. Upon completion of his examination he remained silent. Years later, Dr. Mouritz published his observations: "The first meeting I had with Father Damien the dark copper color of the skin of his forehead attracted my attention; it was the visible proof of the invasion of the Destroyer [leprosy]."[20]

On October 22, 1884, less than two weeks after his return to Honolulu from Moloka'i, Charles Stoddard received notice of his appointment to the English Department of the University of Notre Dame as a professor of literature, a post he assumed the following February.

IN OCTOBER, Dr. Arning made a hurried visit to Kalawao for the purpose of reexamining Father Damien, this time in the presence of Dr. Mouritz. The peroneal nerve was still readily palpable and the skin lesions had progressed. With no apology, Dr. Arning told the priest that he indeed was a leper and that he had so notified his superiors. He assured Father Damien that his bishop wished him to continue in his present capacity as the resident priest and confine his ministry exclusively to the lepers. Since he was potentially infectious to all non-lepers, including frequent visitors like Rudolph Meyer, he was to avoid all physical contact with healthy persons.

Dr. Mouritz stood silently in the background while Dr. Arning informed Damien that his plight was not unique. Father Grégoire Archambaux, one of the priests serving on Maui, the supportive colleague who had boldly visited the leper settlement on multiple occasions to assist Father Damien, was now a suspected leper, and if the diagnosis were confirmed the French priest would be transferred to Moloka'i to replace Father Albert. Still, the situation was not completely hopeless. There were medicines, Dr. Arning assured Damien, that could ameliorate the symptoms of the disease, and he would provide him with a generous supply.

A stoic Father Damien thanked the two doctors and walked slowly to St. Philomena Church to meditate on the mysteries of existence and to pray for the strength to continue his mission to the lepers. For months he had harbored the knowledge that he probably was a leper, and for months he had prayed to have this frightful burden lifted from his shoulders. His Lord, the omnipotent Creator, had chosen to include him with the true apostles of the Church by crowning him with this horrible disease. It was an accolade from God, but a grotesque, cheerless tribute.

THE EXAMINATION OF Father Grégoire in Honolulu confirmed unequivocally that the priest was a leper. Father Léonor was beside himself. Leprosy was far more dangerous than he had believed it to be. Other priests in the Hawaiian mission had dressed the sores and skin ulcerations of lepers. Perhaps some of them were even now incipient lepers. Even he himself might have contracted the disease during a visit to at the Kaka'ako Branch Hospital. Pondering how to proceed, the provincial waited three days before officially informing Father Damien of Father Grégoire's diagnosis and grave prognosis.[21]

When Father Grégoire stepped onto the Kalaupapa wharf, Father Damien was there to welcome and console his colleague and friend of long standing, his new confrere. Standing nearly 6 feet tall, Father Grégoire was a powerfully built priest, dark complexioned with a full head of wavy black hair, whose black, bushy eyebrows were his most memorable facial feature.[22] On this day he was downcast, and tears welled up in his eyes when Father Damien gripped his arm and expressed his condolences.

Joining in the aloha welcome was Father Albert, silently grateful that Providence was providing him with an excuse to return to Tahiti and the Tuamotus. With two leper priests to serve the eight hundred lepers, there was no need for him to remain in the squalid surroundings of Moloka'i. Were he to depart before one of the two leper priests became disabled, he could avoid being trapped in the hell that was Kalawao.

His first night at the settlement, Father Grégoire was quartered in the rectory at Kalawao. Shortly after midnight, Father Damien was awakened from sleep by the loud wheezing and violent coughing of his confrere. When the wheezing and coughing continued for over an hour, Father Damien rose and went to Father Grégoire's room to investigate. He found the priest leaning forward on the edge of his bed, his curly black hair wet with perspiration, his face an ashen gray as he gasped for breath after each protracted exhalation of air through his tightly constricted bronchi. Father Grégoire was experiencing a severe asthmatic attack. In the flickering light of the oil lamp, Father Damien noted the ominous hue of the priest's cyanotic lips and the violent cough that failed to raise the thick, obstructing phlegm. He offered Father Grégoire sips of an herbal tea to relax the bronchi, but to no avail. The asthmatic attack lasted all night, and by dawn the priest who once boasted the most athletic physique in the mission sat haggard faced, exhausted.

At sunrise Dr. Mouritz was summoned, and he prescribed a trial of his favored asthma medication. But the medicine failed to prevent another night of wheezing and the struggle to breathe. The following morning an exhausted Father Grégoire took a few sips of his morning coffee, then excused himself and returned to his room to rest. Throughout the day Father Damien encouraged his wheezing friend to stay well hydrated. The worst thing an asthmatic could do, he had been taught, was to become dehydrated and allow the obstructing phlegm in the bronchi to become even more viscous. The third night Father Damien summoned Dr. Mouritz to witness an even more violent session, but the physician's attempts to abort the attack—or even lessen its severity—failed. Each succeeding night the asthma struck, and after several frustrating weeks of witnessing one nocturnal attack after another, Dr. Mouritz recommended to the Board of Health that Father Grégoire be transferred to the Kaka'ako Branch Hospital. He reasoned that something unique to the Kalawao environment was triggering Father Grégoire's life-threatening asthmatic attacks, incapacitating the priest and imposing a heavy additional burden on Father Damien.

The Board of Health was hesitant to grant this request and procrastinated. The majority of its members insisted that lepers go from Kaka'ako to Kalawao, not in the reverse direction. To permit a leper to return to the Honolulu area would set a dangerous precedent, but Dr. Mouritz persisted, warning the board that unless Father Grégoire were moved from Kalawao, the cause of the priest's death would be bronchial asthma, not leprosy.

While an exhausted, perpetually wheezing Father Grégoire was struggling to breathe, Father Albert was jubilant over the steady improvement in his once disfiguring dermatitis, an improvement he credited to Dr. Arning's treatment regime for psoriasis. With Father Grégoire now in residence, his presence at the settlement was no longer essential, so he requested that he be allowed to return to the Tuamotus. Bishop Hermann and Father Léonor found themselves in a quandary. To have the troublesome and often irritating priest return to the Tuamotu mission was a blessing much to be desired, but if the Board of Health were to allow Father Grégoire to leave the settlement, Father Damien would once again be the only priest on Moloka'i, a violation of Church law. Such a circumstance would force the mission to dispatch a healthy priest periodically to the leper settlement to hear Damien's confession. This would be untenable. Given the shortage of priests, the mission could not risk sacrificing another.

19

Damien, the Martyr?

Here, Lord, is my life. I place it on the altar today. Use it as You will.
—Albert Schweitzer

THE YEAR 1885 began ominously for Father Damien. The anesthetic spots on his face were increasing in size and number and taking on a reddish bronze hue. He knew that in time each spot would give birth to a nodule or ulcerate, for he had observed hundreds of similar spots on the skin of his lepers. The nodule on his right earlobe had grown to the size of a green pea and already was disfiguring his ear. While his beard covered the spots on his cheeks, those on his forehead announced to all observers that the foul disease of the unclean had invaded his body and in time would kill him. Waves of anxiety hurled themselves at his psyche, battering it with the same ferocity as did the waves that pummeled the rocky shoreline of the Kalaupapa Peninsula. He was a leper, and he pondered the consequences of the death sentence. Would the all-powerful, all-merciful God sustain him as the tentacles of leprosy slowly squeezed the life from his earthly body?

He turned to prayer for solace and guidance. When kneeling alone before the altar in St. Philomena Church, he sensed the closeness of God, and that closeness stilled the fear of the earthly tribulations that lay ahead. Prayer became the life raft that kept his psyche afloat and permitted him to continue his ministry to the lepers as if he were a well man.

To cope with the situation, Father Damien made changes in his daily routine. He allotted more time for prayer, prayer for the spiritual will and physical strength to continue to function as a priest to the lepers of Moloka'i. Then he dutifully swallowed the medicine Dr. Arning had prescribed. "It is possible," Dr. Arning had claimed, "to check the progress of leprosy by the persistent use of the following drugs: calcium sulphide, sodium salicylate, quinine, and guaiacol carbonate."[1] Twice a day he conscientiously applied the prescribed leprosy ointment to the reddish-bronze spots on his face and to the depigmented blotches that were appearing on his numb foot.[2]

Father Damien's superiors were shaken by the realization that leprosy could ravage their ranks. Without question Father Damien and Father Grégoire were confirmed lepers, and Father André had begun to question whether his elephantiasis was in actuality one of the more bizarre manifestations of leprosy. After conferring with Dr. Arning regarding the best way to prevent future contagion, Bishop Hermann met with his council and issued a declaration:

> The Fathers and the Brothers of the Mission ought, in the future, to avoid contagion, take necessary precautions, or simply use those indicated by the theologians and doctors, for example: to avoid touching the lepers, not to breathe their breath, not to use nor receive what has been used by them; when they confess, they ought (the ministers) breathe camphorated vinegar, etc., and if by accident, they have touched them, to wash themselves at once with a solution of carbolic acid or some other disinfectant.
>
> Those among us who are unhappily attacked by leprosy, ought in charity for their brothers, and their neighbors in general, avoid touching them as much as possible, never giving to others what they have used.[3]

To the astonishment of many, Walter Murray Gibson, in his capacity as the president of the Board of Health, granted Father Grégoire permission to return to his former parish in Lahaina, Maui, where his asthmatic attacks had been manageable. This was in response to Father Grégoire's independent petition to the board seeking permission to live where asthma wasn't life threatening. In open defiance of the segregation laws, Gibson had simply granted the priest's wish. The Protestants were incensed when such deference was shown to a Catholic priest, and the incident intensified the groundswell of opposition to Gibson's management of the Kingdom's affairs.

So it was in January 1885 that Father Damien helped a wheezing, dyspneic Father Grégoire into a longboat at the Kalaupapa wharf and waved good-bye to the confrere whom he respected and with whom he had good rapport. After a four-month struggle with asthma, the rectory at Lahaina would be Father Grégoire's new refuge. Once again Father Damien would be the lone priest on Moloka'i when Father Albert left.

To delay and possibly thwart Father Albert's pending departure, Father Damien wrote to his superiors, pleading with them not to sanction a move that would once again isolate him on Moloka'i. "I am crippled, probably for life. My foot, frightful as you yourself saw in Honolulu, is far from healed . . . the wound is scarred, and the inflammation and the swelling of the large nerve leading to the toe is unchanged. I drag my leg when I walk; when I go to or from the hospital, a mere five minute walk, I am exhausted and cry all night from the pain. . . . we must acknowledge that death is approaching little by little. Without being too preoccupied with my body, I must above all focus on my soul, which requires a good confessor."[4]

Bishop Hermann promptly interceded on Father Damien's behalf and wrote to the superior general requesting that Father Albert be instructed to remain at Kalaupapa indefinitely. The superior general declined to rescind his previous commitment to Father Albert, and a resigned Bishop Hermann wrote to Father Damien: "There is no way to retain Father Albert; he will leave day after tomorrow. He has already written me . . . that he will leave with or without my approval. I believe that he is wrong, but against such stubbornness, there is nothing I can do. So, make do with Father Gulstan and the other Fathers of Maui."[5]

As Father Damien made his customary medical and pastoral rounds following Father Albert's departure two days later, he pondered whether or not to inform his elderly mother and family members that he now was a leper. In the letter to his mother and family members he avoided any hint of the bleak fate that awaited him. After an apology for writing in French rather than Flemish "because although I have not forgotten our beautiful native language, the expressions do not come readily to mind after so long a time," he told how he had burned his foot the previous month.

Wishing to take a warm bath I had the stupidity to put my foot into almost boiling water causing the skin to burn and blister. After a month of care the wound has begun to heal. For fifteen days I could scarcely say Mass because of the pain. On Sunday I had to sit at the foot of the altar in order to preach. So, in the midst of my many sick parishioners, I myself played the sick man. Yet I try to carry my cross with joy, as did our Savior Jesus Christ. Since I cannot walk very well, I ordinarily travel by carriage. In a short time I will be healed; the inflammation has begun to subside and new skin is forming. . . . A doctor has advised me to go home and breathe my native air . . . what would become of my poor sick people? For the glory of the good God, and the safety of souls I will stay at my post. I hope until death.[6]

The blistered foot episode reveals just how far Father Damien's leprosy had progressed. He had resumed the nightly practice of soaking his feet in a basin of warm water to relax the muscles. On the evening of the accident, after he had filled the basin with boiling water, he had apparently been distracted before he had added the cool water to the foot basin. Then instead of immersing both feet simultaneously, he had lowered his numb left foot into the extremely hot water. With no feeling in the surface skin, he hadn't realized that he was scalding his foot until he stuck his right foot into the water. From the description of the skin blistering and the length of time it took for the second-degree burn on his left foot to heal, we know that the temperature of the water was near boiling and that the skin anesthesia of Father Damien's left foot was complete. His leprosy was advanced.

In his New Year's greeting to his older brother, he disclosed the worrisome news: "Leprosy is a contagious disease, and I believe I have nothing to complain about the protection which the good God has given me through the Holy Virgin and St. Joseph, as they have taken care of me for some time. With the exception of my left foot which during the past three years has lost most of its feeling, I am still as strong and robust as you saw me when I left in 1863. This [leprosy] is the secret poison which threatens to poison my whole body."[7]

The week following Father Albert's departure, Father Columban Beissel made his first voyage from Wailuku, Maui, to hear Father Damien's confession. He was one of the six new arrivals to serve the Hawaiian mission. All six had been trained in Louvain and had Father Pamphile as an instructor, so all six were acquainted with the career of the man now referred to as the "leper priest." During an intentionally hurried visit, Father Columban told Father Damien that

Father Léonor had directed him to make the journey to the leper settlement every other month to hear Father Damien's confession and, time permitting, to scale the *pali* and minister to the rest of Moloka'i's resident Catholics. Although Father Léonor had promised the superior general that he would personally visit the leper settlement four times a year to confess Father Damien, he rationalized that a priest stationed on Maui could accomplish the task more efficiently than could he. Thus he circumvented the inherent danger in ministering to a leper.

The Catholic efforts to aid and comfort the Hawaiian lepers continued to receive good press and the thanks of a grateful nation. Members of the Fort Street Congregational Church, Honolulu, calling themselves "the Missionary Children," unobtrusively and repeatedly donated money to aid Father Damien in his work on Moloka'i.[8] He had not solicited the funds, but he gratefully acknowledged the gifts and the Protestant donors. But the donations from the Protestants, while welcome and certainly useful, placed Father Damien in an awkward position. His superiors and some of his fellow priests felt that he was using the public's perception of him as the "martyr of Moloka'i" to garner both accolades for himself and money for "his" lepers, acts viewed as demeaning to the priesthood. There was a growing suspicion among his peers that he had discarded the robe of humility and donned the peddler's cloak to encourage the donation of money.

That same month, Mother Marianne announced her decision to return to the United States to resume her previous post now that she had completed her task of establishing efficient nursing operations at the two assigned hospitals. But one cherished goal had eluded her, a goal her spiritual being yearned to reach. She had an ardent desire to nurse the lepers at the Kalawao leper settlement, a desire frustrated by two men: Walter Murray Gibson, who genuinely believed that there was no place in the desolate ugliness of the leper settlement for a gentle sister immaculately dressed in a black habit; and Father Léonor, who insisted that the Catholic mission was best served by deploying the sisters in hospital settings serving large patient populations.

When Gibson learned that he was about to lose this brilliant hospital administrator, he dashed off a note pleading with her to reconsider remaining in the Islands: "Speaking for myself as President of the Board of Health I beg to say, that I should regard your leaving us as a great misfortune to the suffering people of this country, therefore I pray that you remain to Continue in charge of your mission of Mercy in these Islands."[9]

Yet public opinion was the compass that influenced the direction in which Gibson steered the Hawaiian ship of state, so he began to contemplate the applause he would garner should he open the door to the leper hospital at Kalawao for the Franciscan sisters. Should one of the sisters contract leprosy, however, public opinion would damn him. On the other hand, should the God of the Catholics protect the sisters at Kalawao as he had been doing at Kaka'ako and they escape Father Damien's fate, he would seriously consider becoming a Catholic.[10] Political expediency dictated that the role of the sisters in the Kingdom of Hawai'i be expanded to include not only the hospitals at Kalawao, but the orphanages as well.

SHORTLY AFTER DR. MOURITZ had established himself as the full-time resident physician, he was asked by a "government physician" to be present during a medical examination this physician wished to conduct on Father Damien. This unnamed physician stated that the priest had agreed to be examined, and he wanted a reputable witness present who could attest to the fact that the priest was also suffering from syphilis, should this prove to be the case. In Dr. Mouritz's book, *The Path of the Destroyer*, which describes the incident, the identity of the government physician is not disclosed, but it is reasonable to assume that the examining doctor was Dr. Fitch, the proponent of the theory that leprosy was the fourth stage of syphilis.

> On or about May 7, 1885, this certain physician stated to me whilst we were eating breakfast, "Dr. Mouritz, Father Damien will come to the dispensary at Kalawao at 10 o'clock, I want you to be there, we can then see how his leprosy is progressing. I also wish to specially examine him for evidence of other diseases. We will make a thorough examination." I assented.
>
> In due course and at the appointed time Father Damien arrived, serene and undisturbed. When asked to disrobe, he readily consented; we found sufficient proof that he was undoubtedly a leper, but nothing more.
>
> We searched his mouth, throat, and cervical glands, also carefully scrutinized his entire person and found absolutely NO TRACE of any other disease. . . . the "victim" of our examination did not seem to real-

ize the important bearing the discovery of any incriminating evidence might have on his future.[11]

By late May 1885, signs of the leprosy bacilli invasion of Father Damien's face became obvious to even the least observant. The skin of the priest's forehead became puffy and thickened and his eyebrows thinned.[12] The burn on the left foot from the scalding water accident healed without leaving a scar, but the numbness in the foot remained, making walking on uneven terrain difficult, especially so when an uncertain step began to precipitate a lancinating stab of sciatic pain shooting down the back of his leg. In June, the troublesome sciatic pain suddenly disappeared, and for the first time in several months Father Damien had hope that Dr. Arning's treatment regime was exerting a beneficial effect.

This hope was dashed in August, when the small leprous tubercle on the lobe of his right ear enlarged dramatically.[13] Each day Father Damien winced as he looked into a mirror, helpless to halt the enlargement and grotesque gnarled appearance of the earlobe, the "tubercular enlargement" of leprosy.[14] "The disfigurement of his person began in a general and marked manner." His eyebrows began to disappear, the lobe of his other ear became enlarged, and tubercular swellings "took possession of face, hands, etc." The knuckles and knees developed hard, enlarged knobs that later suppurated. Sores appeared on his hands and wrists and some on the neck. His eyes became "weak," and often the sclerae were red with engorged blood vessels.[15]

The major problem Father Damien experienced as his leprosy progressed was not the progressive disfigurement, but the debilitating fatigue. His routine physical tasks required more energy and strength than his disease would permit, and frustration resistant to prayer gripped him.

Charles Stoddard, now an established professor at the University of Notre Dame and unaware that the protagonist of his book was a confirmed leper, mailed Father Damien a copy of the manuscript for his book, entitled *The Martyrs of Molokai*, for review and any corrections the priest might choose to make. Father Damien was embarrassed by the author's saintly portrayal of him, and insisted that the word *Martyrs* be deleted from the title. Stoddard obligingly changed the title to *The Lepers of Molokai*, and the book went to press. As sales of the book soared in the United States, Canada, and England, "Father Damien" became synonymous with "hero" in Hawai'i. Indignation and jealousy infiltrated the ranks of the Sacred Hearts mission.

Stoddard and Father Damien continued to exchange letters after the publication of the book, and on October 5, Stoddard received a letter from Father Damien that staggered him—the priest confirmed he was now a leper! Father Damien's letter, written in English, revealed: "I have been attacked by the terrible malady. . . . The microbes of leprosy have finally become lodged in my left foot and in my ear. My eyelids [eyebrows] begin to fall [out]. . . . It is impossible for me to return to Honolulu any more because the leprosy has become visible. I remain calm and resigned, and I am even happier in my world. . . . The good God knows what is best for my sanctification, and in this conviction I pray daily, 'Thy will be done.'"[16]

Attendance at the two Catholic churches in the leper settlement increased, inspired by the leper priest who seemingly ignored the fatigue, the debilitating episodes of low-grade fever, and the progressive disfigurement while continuing in his role as a minister of God and a physician to the sick and weary. Lepers flocked to hear him preach. The Protestants, jealous of the surge in Catholic membership, were prompted to do more for those lepers who embraced the Protestant beliefs. If a leper priest could inspire a return to God, so might a renewed Protestant effort. To rejuvenate interest in the Protestant faith, the Siloama Chapel at Kalaupapa was enlarged to 45 x 25 feet.[17]

To promote the Protestant revival, the Reverend Doctor Charles M. Hyde, the senior educator at the Protestant seminary in Honolulu, visited the settlement for a second time. On September 2, 1885, the fifty-three-year-old minister, arrayed in his black doctoral robe with the three scarlet bands on each sleeve, participated in the rededication of the enlarged Siloama Chapel. Quartered in the disease-free visitors' house in Kalaupapa, eating food prepared by nonlepers, and avoiding all physical contact with lepers, Rev. Hyde rode overland to Kalawao to inspect the houses, the schools, the hospitals, and the orphanages. To his amazement he discovered that of the sixty orphans at the Moloka'i leper settlement, the forty-two with proven leprosy were housed in one of Father Damien's two orphanages. Rev. Hyde examined the structures and unreservedly praised the handiwork of the priest, although it was his firm conviction that the man whose work he was lauding was a "fallen" priest.[18] Resisting the temptation to be overly judgmental, the taller Protestant minister with the bushy eyebrows looked down into the disfigured face of the priest, which now lacked eyebrows, and promised to raise money with which to build a girls' home in Kalaupapa and an even larger boys' home in Kalawao.[19]

Upon his return to Honolulu, Rev. Hyde kept his pledge and spoke to both Charles Reed Bishop and Henry P. Baldwin, wealthy members of the Congregational Church, regarding the pressing need for larger orphanages at the leper settlement. Both businessmen responded with funds to construct, respectively, the Bishop Home for Women and Girls at Kalaupapa and the Baldwin Home for Boys at Kalawao.

IN RESPONSE TO Ambrose Hutchison's impassioned plea to safeguard the daughters of lepers, Queen Kapiʻolani oversaw the construction of an orphanage on the outskirts of Honolulu to serve as a haven and school for those who as yet showed no overt signs of infection. It was her initial intent to sequester fourteen girls in a disease-free environment where they could be nurtured in a more normal social setting until it was ascertained whether or not they had contracted leprosy.

Once the Kapiʻolani Home for Girls was ready for occupancy, the Board of Health notified Ambrose Hutchison that the fourteen believed to be disease free were to be relocated at the new Kapiʻolani Home in time for its dedication on November 9, 1885. After conferring with Father Damien, Hutchison made his selection, choosing girl orphans living in the home of a *kōkua* or a foster parent. None of the girls in Father Damien's orphanage were eligible for transfer because each one was a confirmed leper. The foster parents caring for girl orphans, however, objected vociferously because of the loss of the children's food ration and the child labor. Ambrose Hutchison ignored all objections.

As the sun was setting on the evening of October 29, 1885, the *Kīlauea* arrived, and the captain insisted that the fourteen girls board immediately so he might reach Honolulu by the next morning. Within two hours of the captain's order, the orphans, accompanied by either a foster parent or *kōkua*, made their way down the causeway leading to the wharf and the longboats. Father Damien, superintendent Hutchison, and Dr. Mouritz had all remained behind in Kalawao. Walter Murray Gibson later commented that had someone from the administration been present, the tragedy that ensued might have been averted.

One of the deportees was an eleven-year old girl named Abigail. She was accompanied by two foster fathers, Lohi'au and Momona, middle-aged lepers boasting powerful physiques. Both men were angered by her forcible removal, and both came armed with butcher knives. At the causeway the three were halted by a deputy sheriff and two police officers. In the darkness the officers failed to see the knives. Because lepers were never permitted to have contact with the crew of a longboat, the police directed Abigail to proceed to the wharf, but ordered Lohi'au and Momona to remain behind. Momona, who was carrying the little girl's trunk containing all of her earthly possessions, ignored the officers and belligerently pushed by them, trudging after Abigail. The deputy sheriff rushed after Momona and managed to stop him before he reached the wharf. When he attempted to wrest the girl's trunk from Momona, the lid of the trunk popped open and all of Abigail's possessions dropped into the sea. Furious, Lohi'au leaped forward with drawn knife and stabbed the deputy sheriff twice in the abdomen. Momona dropped the empty trunk, drew his knife, and stabbed the staggering deputy sheriff once more. The two police officers rushed forward to disarm Lohi'au and Momona, and both were savagely stabbed. During the fracas the sailors whisked the girls into the longboats and pushed off into the safety of the sea. Lohi'au and Momona brandished their blood-streaked knives and hurled curses at the fleeing sailors. Then they sullenly returned to their homes.

Onlooking Hawaiians summoned Dr. Mouritz, who sprinted to the wharf where he managed to arrest the hemorrhaging, then had the three stabbing victims carried to the visitors' house where he nursed them through the night. Despite his best efforts, the deputy sheriff and one officer died.

When the news of the murders reached Walter Murray Gibson, he was aghast. To honor the Queen, he had planned an elaborate dedicatory celebration for the Kapi'olani Home, and now the gruesome murders had cast a giant pall over the queen's gift to her nation. Somehow, he had to rectify the situation, and quickly. One week before the dedicatory celebration, Gibson, accompanied by R. J. Creighton, editor of the *Pacific Commercial Advertiser*, several members of the Board of Health, and a complement of police, left Honolulu on the tug

Eleu bound for the leper settlement. Upon arrival at the leper settlement, Gibson announced that he had come to investigate the stabbings and to determine if anyone in authority had been negligent. In an effort to appease the militant lepers assembled at the landing wharf, he emphasized that it had never been the intention of the board to remove a child from the settlement without first obtaining the express consent of the foster parents. "Three rousing cheers" from the lepers greeted this announcement.[20] Murder would not be tolerated, Gibson sternly declared, and he ordered Abigail's foster fathers arrested, handcuffed, and taken aboard the *Eleu* for transport to Honolulu and trial. After a short trial in Honolulu, Momona and Lohi'au were found guilty of murder and sentenced to ten-year prison terms.

As scheduled, the Kapi'olani Home for Girls was dedicated on November 9, the anniversary of the landing of the Franciscan sisters in Honolulu.[21] The ceremony began with the playing of the Hawaiian Anthem by the Royal Hawaiian Band, after which Bishop Hermann offered the dedicatory prayer. The assembly was next treated to "E Ola ka Mō'ī," sung by the fourteen girls who had been removed from Moloka'i. Gibson then delivered a long prepared speech that flattered Queen Kapi'olani for her generous gift of the school, prudently made no mention of the two murders, and concluded with the presentation of a huge picture of Queen Kapi'olani that was hung in the center of the auditorium.

Queen Kapi'olani, the lady patroness of the school, unlocked the main entrance door and handed the keys to Mother Marianne. When Mother Marianne bowed politely, the queen hung a ribbon around her neck bearing the medal that designated her as the latest recipient of the Order of Kapi'olani, the highest honor the queen could bestow. In the background the fourteen girls softly sang "The Hawaiian Lepers' Hymn." The ceremony concluded with the children singing "Home Maika'i" [Oh, Excellent Home!].[22]

THE LAST MONTHS of 1885 may have been the most depressing Father Damien experienced during his Hawaiian ministry. His forced confinement to the Kalaupapa Peninsula troubled him greatly in that the small Catholic parishes on the main island of Moloka'i were being neglected by the Church, and he was powerless to intervene. Most distressful was the thought that his life was ebbing away before he had

attained the level of spiritual growth and maturity that in his opinion
would allow him entrance into the coveted eternal life. Without regular and more frequent confession, he doubted he could reach his goal,
and his depression deepened. Adding to the emotional stress was the
grim fact that his stamina was diminishing. The carpentry projects that
had brought him so much joy in the past now became tests of will and
discipline over fatigue. The joy of being physically active had vanished.

In a short year-end letter to his mother, brothers, and relatives,
he emphasized his ongoing medical practice, but made no mention of
his leprosy. "On weekdays I visit my numerous sick, and I am busy
with my orphans, all of whom are lepers. It is more or less repulsive
to anyone's nature to be always surrounded by these unhappy children, but I find my consolation in them. At present I am more or less
a practicing physician, and like my patron, St. Damien, I try with the
grace of God to soften their frightful pains, and thus can point the way
to salvation."[23]

Father Damien wondered if the approaching New Year would be
his last on earth, and he pleaded with Bishop Hermann to rectify his
intolerable spiritual isolation.[24] Sensing there would be no favorable
response, he seated himself at his small table and by candlelight crafted
a plaintive letter to Father Pamphile, the one person who might possibly come to his aid.

> I have never been so isolated and excluded from all communication with
> my confreres as I have been since March when Father Albert left me. . . .
> As for me, I am just about the same; my health, since it is deteriorating
> because of the illness contracted in caring for the sick for almost 13
> years, does not allow me to continue my ministry among them as before.
> However, I have almost double the need as I did formerly. I have been
> very pained by the authorization that Reverend Father gave my col-
> league, Father Albert, to return to Tahiti. Since that time, contrary to
> an article in our Holy Rule, I am always alone. Good Father Columban
> comes every two or three months to hear my confession, but he leaves
> immediately. I have even been prevented by our Superior, Father Léonor,
> from going to Honolulu when I want to see a Father in the interval. I
> know well where this will end. I resign myself, however, to Divine Prov-
> idence, and find my consolation in my only companion who never
> leaves me,—our Divine Savior in the Holy Eucharist. It is at the foot of
> the altar that I often make my confession, and there I seek comfort in

my interior suffering. It is before Him, as well as before the statue of our Holy Mother that I sometimes complain, while asking them for the restoration of my health.[25]

Weeks passed before Father Pamphile received the letter. He read and reread it, remembering the boyhood pledges the idealistic Auguste and the youthful Jef had made to each other—brother priests like Saints Damien and Cosmas, standing shoulder to shoulder in the service of the almighty and all-merciful God. Time and circumstances had uprooted their idyllic dream. Tragically, only in make believe as young boys had they stood shoulder to shoulder as missionary priests. Now Jef was dying the most horrible of all deaths. He was alone and depressed, and being treated shabbily by the Church. The situation was insufferable. He, Father Pamphile, could not—would not—tolerate it. He would go to his brother's aid.

20

The Valley of the Shadow

*Yea, though I walk through the valley of the shadow of death,
I will fear no evil; for thou art with me; thy rod and thy staff,
they comfort me.*
—Psalm 23:4

HAVING MADE THE decision to come to the aid of his younger brother, Father Pamphile wrote to him offering to become a member of the Hawaiian mission for the purpose of serving as his confrere on Moloka'i. If Father Damien approved, he asked that the letter be forwarded to Bishop Hermann, the prelate with the regional authority to issue the formal invitation. Unfortunately, this letter has not survived. Apparently it was never placed in the Sacred Hearts archives by Bishop Hermann, who, when he learned of the proposed move, was adamantly opposed.

In 1885–1886, mail delivery between Hawai'i and Belgium via French ships was slow. From the time Father Damien wrote his plaintive letter to Pamphile in December 1885 until he received his older brother's offer to join him, six months elapsed. Never dreaming that Father Pamphile was preparing to leave his prestigious academic post and voluntarily join the ranks of the missionaries, Damien tenaciously continued with his daily routine, utilizing prayer buttressed by an intense desire to serve "his" lepers as the antidotes to his spiritual isolation, the increasing fatigue, and the physical pain.

A month after he had dispatched his letter to Father Pamphile, the Board of Health notified Father Damien that Walter Murray Gibson, the prime minister and president of the Board, was in the process of preparing a comprehensive report on leprosy. He wished to highlight the Hawaiian experience, supplemented by reports from Dr. Arthur Mouritz, Rudolph Meyer, and Father Damien. Gibson hoped to allay the fears of foreign investors and businessmen by showing that the leprosy epidemic in Hawai'i was under control, that all lepers had been segregated and were being well cared for.

In response to the Gibson request, Father Damien painstakingly prepared a forty-two-page handwritten document composed in clear, concise English.[1] When the English of this document is compared to the grammar and diction of the Damien letters written in English, it is obvious that someone assisted in the composition, most likely Dr. Arthur Mouritz. The report reveals just how far Father Damien's understanding of leprosy had progressed—from that of a naive young priest with no concept of the role of bacteria in disease to an appreciation of bacterial contagion with an understanding of the therapeutic agents available to ameliorate the illnesses to which the lepers were prone.

Dr. Mouritz's report was voluminous.[2] It began with a detailed history of leprosy in the Hawaiian Islands, leading to the establishment of the leper settlement on Moloka'i, and presented tables showing the number of lepers received at the settlement annually, tables comparing the mortality in the first and second decades of the settlement, and the geographical distribution of the cases of leprosy throughout the seven major islands. The report included a detailed medical history of Father Damien's leprosy and concluded with a short dissertation on the "disheartening" lack of efficacy of the available treatment modalities.

Rudolph Meyer, still smarting from the negative comments in Dr. J. H. Stallard's report of March 12, 1884, in which the excessive mortality experienced by the lepers was attributed to managerial mismanagement, mounted a stout defense of the Board of Health's leprosy segregation program and his role as the superintendent of the settlement.[3] He focused on the many physical improvements, the virtual absence of crime, and the positive role of the recently installed resident physician.[4] He proudly pointed to the replacement of all the thatched huts by substantial wooden houses, the all-wood hospitals where forty-three of the sickest lepers "are cared for, their food is prepared for them, they receive tea or coffee with sugar or milk," and a "new cookhouse" for the hospital, which "was clean and tidy, very different from what it used to be." Meyer stressed that the "Kalawao water supply has been much improved. . . . The food supply during the last two years, with the exception of the first few months, has been very regular. . . . For the preservation of law and order, a magistrate has been appointed. . . . With the exception of the one unfortunate case of manslaughter, committed at the Settlement in November last, crimes have been of rare occurrence. Since 1882 there has been but one case of burglary. . . . Drinking intoxicating beverages is forbidden, and persons found drunk are punished with 24 hours imprisonment. . . . Gambling is also forbidden at the Settlement, and guilty persons are punished."[5] Meyer's report argued convincingly that from an administrative standpoint, the leper settlement was well run.

Gibson studied the reports of Father Damien, Dr. Mouritz, and Rudolph Meyer, noting the emphasis on the seriousness of a contagious disease for which there was as yet no proven effective treatment. He frowned. To issue a comprehensive treatise on leprosy with these three addenda would do little to allay the public's anxiety. The three reports were briefly commented upon in a report to the legislature, then quietly filed in the Board of Health archives.

When King Kalākaua returned from his around-the-world tour in 1882, he told Gibson about a treatment that had been used in Japan for nearly a century—the *Goto treatment regime*. It consisted of two daily immersions in a hot bath containing herbs and taking herbal medicines after each meal, followed an hour later with the ingestion of a medicine made from the bark of a Japanese tree. Reportedly, the Goto regime was effective. Gibson, frustrated by the inability of American and European doctors to eradicate leprosy, decided to evaluate the efficacy of the Japanese approach and offered Gilbert Waller, an affluent American who had contracted the disease, the option of being treated in Tokyo by Dr. Goto rather than experience the trauma of lifetime incarceration at Kalawao. Waller chose the Japanese approach and, reportedly, the Goto regime arrested his leprosy. Following his return to the United States he wrote to Gibson, extolling the virtues of the Goto regime and urging that the Kingdom adopt it.[6] Gibson responded in 1885 by inviting Dr. Masanao Goto to come to the Kaka'ako Branch Hospital and conduct a clinical trial of his treatment program. Dr. Goto accepted, and after his arrival he immediately launched a small-scale study. Dr. Mouritz closely monitored the Goto treatment study and noted the improvement in the small number of patients in the trial. He then urged Father Damien to obtain permission to go to Kakaʻako for a trial of the new regime.

While he waited for permission, Father Damien continued his spiritual and medical practice ministry at the leper settlement. Resigned to the fact that his remaining days were numbered, he was determined to make each one as perfect and productive as possible. To accomplish this, he ideally needed the company of a spiritual confrere and the opportunity for regular confession. The brief and hurried visits by Father Columban every two to three months were a travesty. Were he allowed to visit the branch hospital at Kakaʻako for a trial of the new Goto treatment, he would have a confessor because he understood that Father Léonor visited the branch hospital each week.

For permission to leave the settlement Father Damien conferred with Rudolph Meyer, who unilaterally granted the required Board of Health permission. When Father Léonor was notified of the pending visit, the provincial objected, not only because of the physical threat he believed that Damien posed to members of the clergy, but because of the adverse publicity the Belgian's presence in the Honolulu area would undoubtedly generate. He wrote a stern note to Father Damien:

> There is still a rumor that you are planning to come here. Again, very dear Father, let me remind you anew of the decision taken by the Provincial Council [January 21, 1885], and not by me.[7] . . . If you choose to go to Kakaako you will be confined to the leper quarters where you could not say Mass, for neither Father Clement nor I would consent to say Mass with the same chalice and the same vestments which you would use, and the Sisters would not wish to receive Holy Communion from your hands. Your intentions, my dear Father, prove to us that you have neither the delicacy of feeling nor charity toward your neighbor, and that you consistently think only of yourself. This is pure self-centeredness, and I have come to the conclusion that your actions are not representative of either your heart or your head. . . . If the Japanese treatment should result in a cure, then you can come immediately, for it goes without saying my dear Father, we wish you to be cured if it is at all possible.[8]

Father Damien recognized that he had truly become one of society's outcasts—one of the undesirables, because he had dared to imitate Christ and minister to lepers—one of the "unclean," abandoned by his order.

On March 30, 1886, Father Damien was officially registered as a leper by the Board of Health.[9] In the *Record of Inmates at Kalaupapa, 1868–1900*, on page 100, leper # 2892 is listed as "Damien, Father." Dr. Arning had made the diagnosis in 1884 and made his findings known to the Board of Health. Why it took nearly two years to properly register Father Damien is not known.

CHARLES STODDARD'S *The Lepers of Molokai*, published in February 1886, was an immediate success in the English-speaking world. Before Father Damien had a chance to hold a copy of the finished book in his hands, he began to receive laudatory letters containing contributions from persons who admired his courageous ministry. In late March, copies of the book shipped by Father Hudson and Charles Stoddard reached him, one of which he sent to Bishop Hermann with a cover letter suggesting that the bishop might wish to promote the book's distribution because of the unadulterated praise of the Catholic mission effort.[10]

Bishop Hermann read *The Lepers of Molokai* with displeasure. Page after page extolled the virtues and the self-sacrifice of Father Damien to the exclusion of the many others who had toiled on behalf of the lepers of Moloka'i. To the uninformed reader, it would appear that nearly all of the improvements in the lot of the Hawaiian lepers had been the work of the lone priest from Belgium. He noted that the Board of Health's financial undergirding of the leper settlement was not mentioned, an omission which would no doubt incur the wrath of the Protestants, and that the Catholic Mission's contribution of priests and money was grossly understated. The book's bias disturbed Bishop Hermann to the degree that it further widened the ever-expanding fracture line in the rapport between Father Damien and himself. In the bishop's opinion, the professor from the University of Notre Dame, with Father Damien's help, had composed an exaggerated account of the priest's role in the leper settlement.[11] That Father Damien now had the audacity to suggest that the mission distribute the book, which would further extol his self-ascribed virtues, was outrageous. This priest had tossed all humility aside and assumed the role of Stoddard's fictitious Christian martyr. Equally annoying was the knowledge that contributions were being mailed directly to Father Damien for his exclusive use to further his work among the lepers.[12] There was a mission budget to balance, and now a disproportionate amount of money was being funneled to Moloka'i. Bishop Hermann quietly shelved the book, then knelt in prayer and asked for assistance in dealing with a priest who seemed out of control.

Prior to receiving his copy of *The Lepers of Molokai*, the bishop had submitted a summary of the work of the Hawaiian Mission to the directors of the Propagation of the Faith in which he cast the ministry of Father Damien in a very favorable light. The section of his report dealing with Father Damien was subsequently published in the *Catholic Mission* (Paris), then reprinted in the *Ave Maria* (Canada). This focused the attention of the Catholic world on the leper priest and added credence to the authenticity of Stoddard's biography.[13] Bishop Hermann feared that all of this furor was responsible for Father Pamphile's concern for his isolated brother's spiritual well-being. What the Hawaiian Mission didn't need, in the bishop's opinion, was the presence of two De Veusters.

Sensing that after reading *The Lepers of Molokai* the superior general would inquire about Father Damien's ability to function as a priest, Bishop Hermann wrote to reassure him that the situation was manageable. "Fathers Grégoire and Damien still conduct their sacred ministries. In general their health holds up well."[14] The bishop had no firsthand knowledge of the state of health of either priest. Lepers, after all, were outcasts a prudent bishop was wise to avoid.

Father Columban contradicted his bishop's assessment when he forwarded his observations to the superior general on the progression of Father Damien's leprosy.

Father Damien, who has definite leprosy, can still work in spite of the disease, but not without pain, and I believe that since the end of last year when the first symptoms of leprosy were unquestionable and visible, this disease has made rapid progress, and I have reason to believe that the greatest discomforts that this priest has suffered for a long time already, were not the precursor, but the leprosy itself. He can still say Mass, but he is suffering. He has insomnia, and now also experiences sharp pains in the other leg. The leprosy has attacked one of his ears which is filled with tumors and is painful when he lies down. His entire face has begun to swell, and lately one hand has begun to be attacked. However, he carries his fate with resignation, but not without apprehension concerning the time, perhaps not far off, when he will no longer be able to say Mass. . . . I make the trip to Molokai about every two months, and I am the only priest who goes to see Father Damien.[15]

In early June, Dr. Mouritz wrote to Bishop Hermann urging that he allow Father Damien to try the new Goto treatment with its baths and herbal medicines that was available at the branch hospital in Kaka'ako. He was "alarmed" by the "rapid change in his [Father Damien's] outward appearance," and he felt that the Goto regime might be of genuine benefit in slowing the progression of the disease.[16]

Father Léonor would have none of it. In a militant tone, he resolutely refused to permit Father Damien to leave the leper settlement. Convinced that a leper with advanced disease was highly contagious and that someone had to protect the Franciscan sisters, Walter Murray Gibson concurred with the provincial's decision. In his journal on June 10, Gibson noted, "Proposition to place Father Damien at Kakaako. I am opposed."[17]

Dr. Mouritz continued to recommend that Father Damien be allowed to commence the Goto treatment. Since the provincial was opposed, he suggested that the priest plead his case with a higher ecclesiastical authority. In desperation, Father Damien appealed directly to Bishop Hermann:

Last year . . . Having no confidence in our best European doctors to arrest the progress of this terrible sickness, I desired very much then to consult with Dr. Goto, but for reasons of prudence so as not to offend our wise ones, I kept this desire in my heart.

The absolute refusal, expressed in the tone of a gendarme rather than that of a religious superior, stating that if ever I showed myself in Honolulu, the entire mission would be placed under quarantine, gave me, I frankly admit, more pain than I have ever suffered since my childhood.

I responded to it by an act of absolute submission in lieu of my vow of obedience. . . . I have just learned today that Doctor Goto has really effected some good in the treatment of some lepers. Whatever it is, would he be able to help me by lessening the disease or curing it?[18]

June passed with no response from the bishop. His patience exhausted, Father Damien again wrote to Bishop Hermann on July 2. This time he received an affirmative reply and on July 11, he arrived at Kaka'ako to consult with Dr. Goto. After the treatment regime was explained, Father Damien commenced the twice daily hot-bath soaking, followed by the ingestion of the herbal medicines. His plan was to institute the program at the leper settlement upon his return should the Goto treatment prove beneficial.

Father Léonor wasn't the only person disturbed by Father Damien's apparent disregard for the safety of those with whom he would be in contact. Gibson was troubled, and he recorded in his journal on July 11: "Father Damien arrived at Kakaako. He is a confirmed leper—was advised not to come—but was determined to visit the sisters. I begin to doubt the genuineness of his religious devotion."[19]

Still, Gibson was courteous to the priest whom he had elevated to the position of the most famous leper in Hawai'i. Two days after Father Damien's arrival, Gibson called on him and noted in his diary: "I sent Father Damien some wine & many things for his use and comfort. S.M. [Mother Marianne] rewarded me with tender thanks. I called on Father D.—and still I have some misgivings—he talks too much."[20]

For the first time since the arrival of the Franciscan sisters, Father Damien had ample time to discuss his vision of the role of the sisters at the settlement, first with Gibson and then with Mother Marianne. The sisters, in his opinion, could best care for his orphans, especially the girls; and their nursing expertise would prove invaluable in the hospital setting. Gibson listened politely, but remained noncommittal. Mother Marianne, on the other hand, was most encouraging. With a gentle smile, she informed him that she and the sisters were prepared and anxiously awaiting the opportunity to serve at the settlement once the appropriate convent was constructed. The sisters, she insisted, could avoid contagion if they employed the standard hygienic practices used in the United States, prepared their own food, slept in uncontaminated housing, and had communion served by a healthy priest.

From a distance, Gibson observed the meetings between Mother Marianne and Father Damien and despaired of the influence the priest was exerting on the reverend mother. He recorded, "S.M. told me she was completely wearied out with Father Damien's talk—will be content when he returns to Molokai."[21]

Determined to abort the priest's stay at Kaka'ako, Gibson surprised Father Damien with an invitation to conduct an inspection tour of the leper settlement for the benefit of himself and a select group from the Board of Health. Father Damien had been in residence at the branch hospital for only four days, and even an abbreviated trial of the Goto regime required two weeks. Gibson argued that since Bishop Hermann had consented to accompany the group as a participant, Father Damien's presence was mandatory. Who better to conduct a tour of the settlement than the leper priest himself, and what better means to rid Kaka'ako of a dangerous nuisance?

Nonetheless, Father Damien's four days at Kaka'ako had been well spent. He had experienced firsthand the Goto treatment of leprosy and was encouraged by the discovery that in his case it had proved beneficial. The frequent hot baths cleansed the open sores and ulcers, dramatically reducing the unsightly skin inflammation and the repulsive malodor. With a supply of the herbal medicines and the resolve to build bathhouses at the settlement, he could now offer the Goto therapy to the lepers on Moloka'i.

Prior to the Gibson party's late-evening departure, the prime minister arranged for a brief visit between King Kalākaua and Father Damien. Gibson was a master at manipulating the press to demonstrate how earnest the king was in his efforts to improve the lot of his most destitute subjects. With the Americans accusing the king of financial irresponsibility and advocating annexation to the United States, the monarchy needed all of the good press it could garner.

The meeting was a staged media event, not the substantive meeting Father Damien had been promised. King Kalākaua was gracious in his remarks, but careful to maintain what he considered to be a safe distance from the priest. With Gibson serving as the master of ceremonies, Damien had little opportunity to say more than "Yes, your Majesty," or "No, your Majesty," before being ushered from the room.

The next morning the *Likelike* anchored off the shores of Kalaupapa. After an elaborate breakfast, the Gibson party, which included several newspaper correspondents, landed at the Kalaupapa wharf, where they were greeted by 90 of the 650 lepers and an equal number of *kōkua*. The party rode horseback to Kalawao and in front of the general purpose store conducted an open-air village meeting. In his introductory remarks, Gibson told the gathering of his recent meetings with their "noble priest" and invited anyone who had a complaint to state it.[22] This precipitated a deluge of grievances, charges, and countercharges. A highly disruptive session followed, the general tenor of which clearly revealed that many of the lepers felt that the Kingdom had failed to meet their basic needs. Kahului, one of the lepers, complained that the amount of *pa'i 'ai* supplied each week with which to make poi was not only insufficient, but of poor quality. Tax assessors, complained another leper, were taxing those who owned dogs. John Liefenasky, a native of Poland, shouted that the poor quality of the bread made from Oregon wheat was unacceptable for those of European extraction. Kalemanu, a former resident of Hilo, decried the fact that *kōkua* serving as nurses in the hospital were paid only fifty cents a month, the consequence of which was mediocre care at best.

Try as he might, Gibson lost control of the session and became alarmed as he noted the newspaper reporters scribbling every complaint, which would be duly reported in the press. In desperation, he turned to Father Damien to refute the charge that the nursing care provided by the *kōkua* was of poor quality. Speaking in a hesitating manner, Father Damien stated that he felt that the *kōkua* serving the hospital were doing so to the best of their limited abilities; however, what was needed were qualified professionals like the Franciscan sisters. Gibson must have winced as the assembled lepers cheered Father Damien's reply.

The avalanche of complaints occupied most of the morning, leaving no time to inspect any of the facilities at the settlement. At noon the Gibson party, minus Father Damien, made a hasty retreat to the *Likelike* for the return to Honolulu. In his diary for that disastrous Saturday, Gibson recorded: "An unsatisfactory reception by lepers at Kalawao—I feel that they have been prompted by the Opposition from Honolulu. Return to Honolulu by 6:30 P.M."[23]

Following the departure of the Gibson party, Father Damien enthusiastically showed Dr. Mouritz what he believed to be definite healing of several of his leprosy lesions. Dr. Mouritz nodded approvingly. The physician cautioned, however, that the twice daily bathing alone could be responsible for the observed improvement, and that Damien should continue the Goto regime for a longer period, before openly endorsing it. A week later, Father Damien was jubilant with what he judged to be continued improvement—both in appearance and strength. Anxious to share the same beneficial results with his lepers, he wrote to the Board of Health requesting fifty boxes of *Kai Gio Kioso Yoku Yaku* (bath medicine), fifty boxes of *Sei Kets-uren* pills, fifty packages of Decoction *Hichiyon* bark, and 10 pounds of sodium bicarbonate.[24] Next, he drew up plans for a bathing facility in which to treat one hundred lepers and submitted the drawings to Gibson for approval and funding. Gibson had no choice but to comply. His "hero of Moloka'i" was becoming an expensive asset.

In late July, Bishop Hermann received a letter from Father Damien in which he enclosed Father Pamphile's formal letter requesting an invitation to transfer to the Hawaiian Mission, specifically the leper settlement, for the purpose of serving as a confrere to his younger brother. The bishop squirmed as he read Father Damien's cover letter:

> Your Excellency,
>
> I am enclosing with this note a letter which my brother, Father Pamphile has addressed to you. It is probably through the publication of your letter that he was informed of the position in which I find myself. Without commenting, I leave it to you to judge the sentiments which he expresses.
>
> If your Excellency chooses to request of the Superior General the services of this priest who from his youth has always had a missionary's heart, he would be a fine acquisition for our dear mission. He is a profound theologian with good zeal for the ministry, knows English well, and above all is a good child of the Congregation. In 1863 and again in 1868, he received his obedience for the Sandwich Islands, but each time Father Wenceslaus retained him, under the pretext that he was essential at Louvain, where he still is today.
>
> Consider that there is no one else in the world that I would prefer to have, but I leave to you, your Excellency, and to the Superior General, to grant me the consolation of having my brother in Hawaii.
>
> Your very humble,
> Father J. Damien[25]

Sensing Father Pamphile's concern, displeasure, and frustration with the situation in which his younger brother was agonizing, the bishop assumed the role of the placating diplomat and rejected Father Pamphile's offer. To accept the politically influential Father Pamphile's offer would open the door to an investigation of his administration and its failures. Instead, the bishop chose to shift the blame for Father Damien's present isolation on the priest's inability to get along with a confrere. Then he closed by falsely stating that Father Damien was free to journey to Honolulu or Maui every week for confession.

My Reverend Father,

You have good reason to plead for your younger brother, Father Damien, because of his isolation, being the only priest living on the island of Molokai, and tainted with the very disease of those for whom he went to care. This dilemma also weighs heavily on my heart. If it were as easy to find a solution as it is to see the problem, the matter would have been corrected long ago. Father Albert left Molokai and has returned to Tahiti, partly because he was not able to get along well with Father Damien. Another of our priests would be able and would like to go there, but Father Damien does not want him for some reason. There is a third who would be able to stay at Molokai; but he has over-whelming repugnance. All of the other missionaries are essential for their own posts.

I thank you for offering yourself as you did. I appreciate the favorable references, and the advantages of having you. We have great need of new workers. However, I must leave the choice of personnel entirely to the judgment of the Superior General.

P.S. I forgot to tell you that Father Damien is not as miserable as you believe him to be. Father Columban goes to see him regularly every two months. In addition, your brother can communicate with Honolulu and Maui every week. He was recently here to consult a Japanese doctor whose treatment he is following at Molokai. His illness has not yet disfigured him much. He was very cheerful, and he was honored on the day of his departure by a visit from the King, his Prime Minister, and the Bishop. The Queen sent her compliments with the King since she was unable to come herself.[26]

When or just how Damien learned that Bishop Hermann had rejected Father Pamphile's offer to serve on Moloka'i is not known. Finally, after years of separation, his older brother now wished to join him; but the opposition on the part of his immediate superiors was preventing the reunion. Perhaps, Father Damien reasoned, it was best that Father Pamphile not join him in the contagious leper pit; for he, too, could contract the miserable disease. As he studied the reflection of his face in a mirror, noting the awful progress of the leprosy invasion, he debated the option of appealing Bishop Hermann's decision to the superior general. Once before in his career he had done so and received a favorable response. Perhaps he should risk a second appeal.

21

"I Am Brother Joseph. . . . I Have Come to Help"

We were not meant to do great things for God,
but small things with great love.
—Mother Teresa (1910–1997)

AS IF IN ANSWER to a prayer, a tall, lean American carrying a faded
duffle bag slung over one shoulder walked down the gangplank of the
freighter *Eureka* at dusk on July 23, 1886, and stepped ashore in Honolulu.[1] His thirty-day voyage from San Francisco had been uneventful
and often boring, but the passage fare was cheap. When the man
reached the main road that ran along the shore connecting the landing docks, he paused, glancing about for someone who would be
knowledgeable about the city. He approached a stevedore and in his
unusually soft voice asked directions to Our Lady of Peace Cathedral
on Fort Street.[2] The stevedore pointed the way and watched the
stranger with the quiet demeanor lift the duffle bag to his shoulder and
stride off.

The American located Fort Street and walked to the cathedral,
its outline a black silhouette against the starlit sky, its stained glass
windows weakly illuminated by candlelight, inviting. The cathedral's
main door stood open and from the entrance over a hundred flickering candles were visible in the main sanctuary. Except for a lone priest
kneeling at the altar rail, the sanctuary appeared empty. The American entered, knelt, and crossed himself, then slipped into one of the
rear pews for a moment of prayer. When he whispered "Amen" and

opened his eyes, the priest at the altar rail was looking his way. Leaving his duffle bag behind on the pew seat, the American stepped into the main aisle and approached the priest. "I am Brother Joseph Dutton from the United States," he said quietly. "I have come to help Father Damien at the leper settlement. Would you be so kind as to take me to your bishop?" The priest hesitated. There had been no announcement about a brother assigned to serve at the leper settlement. Then he motioned for the American to follow and led the way to Bishop Hermann's quarters.

Bishop Hermann had not been forewarned of Brother Joseph Dutton's coming, so there were many questions to be answered, beginning with who Dutton was, who had sent him to Hawai'i, what was his religious affiliation, and why he wished to work with the lepers. Brother Dutton explained that he wasn't really a brother of a religious order, but that it was his intention to serve the lepers in the capacity of a brother. His real name was Ira B. Dutton. At age twenty-one he had left Janesville, Wisconsin, to serve as a lieutenant with the 13th Wisconsin Volunteers in the Union Army. Following General Lee's surrender at Appomattox he had remained in the army for a short while before discarding his uniform and commencing his years of alcoholism and "ruinous" living.[3] Finally, disgust with his slovenly, sinful life led him to search for redemption. On April 27, 1883, his fortieth birthday, he had been received into St. Peter's Catholic Church in Memphis, Tennessee. As an act of penance, he had resolved to spend the rest of his life in service to God and his fellow man. "I have come here," Dutton reiterated, "to go to Moloka'i and spend the remainder of my life in work among the lepers."[4]

Bishop Hermann was intrigued. Brothers or their equivalent were needed at the leper settlement, and Father Damien had repeatedly implored him to allow them to come to Moloka'i to assist with his building projects and to teach at the boys' orphanage. Bishop Hermann had deliberately procrastinated, reluctant to send a brother into a leprous environment, and he had responded to each of Father Damien's requests for help with the simple half-truth—there was a dire shortage of brothers assigned to the Hawaiian Mission, and for the present all were needed elsewhere.

Bishop Hermann invited Joseph Dutton to sit down and describe in detail his life, his religious conversion, and why he had chosen to serve at the leper colony. The American replied that he would be happy to do so, and for the next hour the bishop listened to Dutton's life story.[5]

Ira Dutton's father Ezra was a farmer who also worked as a cobbler; his mother, Abigail Barnes, was a schoolteacher. When Ira was four the family moved from Stowe, Vermont, to Janesville, Wisconsin, where he received a fine formal education, attending Milton Academy and Milton College. Prior to the Civil War he had been one of the first to become a member of the Janesville City Zouave Corps, a national guard unit. When the Civil War erupted, the Janesville Zouave cadets became the 13th Wisconsin Volunteer Infantry. "On one occasion, while at Lawrence, Kansas, the regiment lost some 200 soldiers as a result of disease."[6] Witnessing dysentery and typhus kill more men than bullets had focused his attention on diseases and their treatment, an area in which he believed he could be of service to the lepers.

In Nashville, Tennessee, he met and courted a lady whom he married on New Year's Day, 1866. "My marriage . . . was a mistake; a very foolish act on my part."[7] The marriage failed, and after his wife left him in 1867, he began the "fierce and reckless" drinking of whiskey, "even up to July, 1876. Since that time I have been strictly an abstainer," he claimed.[8]

At age thirty-eight, he "began to prepare for Holy orders as an Episcopalian," but in studying the doctrines of the Catholic Church he decided Catholicism offered him the best opportunity for a penitential life.[9] Consequently, when he joined the Catholic Church at age forty, he took the name Joseph, after Saint Joseph.[10]

As "Joseph Dutton" he entered the Trappist Monastery at Gethsemane, Kentucky, perhaps the most severe and demanding order of the Catholic Church. For twenty months he led the monastic life of complete silence and hard physical labor, quartered in a 6-foot-square room with a 3-foot-wide wooden shelf for a bed. In this setting, he found that something was still lacking in his penitential pilgrimage—there was no element of service to his fellow men. "I wanted to serve some useful purpose during the rest of my life without any hope of monetary or other reward. The desire grew upon me with a forcefulness that is difficult to explain. The idea of a penitential life became almost an obsession, and I was determined to see it through."[11]

One day Dutton found and read *The Lepers of Molokai* by Charles Warren Stoddard, and without delay he journeyed to the University of Notre Dame to meet with the author. Stoddard graciously received Dutton and, after assessing his background, talents, and motivation, enthusiastically endorsed the plan to serve at the leper settlement. The professor even went so far as to assist with the travel arrangements for Dutton's voyage to Honolulu.

Bishop Hermann reflected for a moment, then informed the American that there was a problem. Stepping ashore at the leper colony as a volunteer was not a simple matter. One had first to obtain permission from the Board of Health, so he, the bishop, would do what he could to arrange a meeting with the board's president, Walter Murray Gibson. Gibson would have to give the official approval.

The next day Gibson received Joseph Dutton and politely reviewed the credentials of the American who had opened the conversation with the startling statement, "I have come here to go to Moloka'i and spend the remainder of my life in work among the lepers."[12] When Gibson broached the matter of compensation, Dutton was adamant in his resolve to accept no payment for his services. "Pay," he declared, "was entirely out of the question."[13] Gibson nodded that this was agreeable for the present, but that if in the future Dutton should find himself in need of money, the Board of Health would be happy to pay a stipend similar to the sum allotted to each of the Franciscan sisters. The two men shook hands, and Gibson issued the permit for Dutton to reside at the leper settlement. The best way for a stranger to reach the leper settlement, Gibson informed Dutton, was by the Mokoli'i, the interisland steamer reserved for lepers, and he indicated that it would be his pleasure to purchase the required ticket. With a hint of a smile, Dutton reached into his pocket and pulled out the ticket for the next voyage of the Mokoli'i. "Aloha, my friend," replied Gibson, and "God go with you."

On July 29, 1886, the Mokoli'i anchored off the Kalaupapa landing wharf and lowered a longboat to ferry Joseph Dutton to shore. While the sailors in the longboat struggled to row through the roll of the waves, Dutton scanned the small assemblage of people standing along the wharf and was able to make out the figure of a man dressed in black, sitting in a buggy drawn by a white horse.

After the longboat docked, Joseph Dutton proceeded directly to the black-robed priest seated in the buggy and introduced himself, trying not to stare at the priest's disfigured face. The priest in black studied the

American for a few moments, then said, "Welcome to Molokai, Joseph Dutton. I shall call you Brother Joseph." Years later, Brother Dutton recorded his recollections of that first meeting: "We climbed into the old buggy, and were off for Kalawao. . . . I was happy as we drove over that morning. The Father talked eagerly, telling how he had wanted Brothers here, but the Mission had none to spare as yet. So he called me Brother, as I had come to stay, and gave me at once care of the two churches. He was full of plans that morning, talking of what he wished for his lepers, the dreams he had always had."[14]

The maintenance of the churches at Kalawao and Kalaupapa was properly within the purview of a brother, and Brother Dutton's first assignment gave Father Damien the opportunity to observe the new volunteer in action. Brother Dutton knew he was on trial, but the skill and industry with which he completed his assigned tasks impressed his mentor. Father Damien found Brother Dutton imperturbable. Whatever he asked of the American, no matter how menial, the task was promptly and competently attended to and with never a complaint.

Most impressive was the ease with which Brother Dutton established a warm rapport with the lepers with whom he came in contact. He had a smile for everyone no matter how hideous their appearance, and he seemed oblivious to the objectionable odor emanating from many of the diseased bodies. Beginning the first evening and every evening after dinner, Father Damien tutored his new assistant in the Hawaiian language, and by the end of the first week Brother Dutton had acquired a working vocabulary of several hundred words. Within three months, he was reasonably fluent in Hawaiian.

Without being asked, the American added the cleaning and maintenance of the rectory to his list of duties, as well as the guest house where he was temporarily quartered. One morning he even had the audacity to prepare breakfast for Father Damien and himself, and during his second week at the settlement he requested permission to accompany Father Damien on his ministerial and medical rounds. During the hospital rounds, he expressed a desire to be taught the proper medical techniques for the care of the lepers' skin lesions. Were he to assume wound care as one of his major responsibilities, he could free Father Damien from the onerous chore, allowing the priest more time to devote to the more important spiritual matters. When asked to teach Brother Dutton the best techniques in wound care, Dr.

Mouritz was quick to initiate on-the-job instruction, and found the new brother an apt student. Dr. Mouritz wrote:

> Brother Dutton soon demonstrated that leprosy had no power to instil fear in his mind. For many months after his arrival, his daily routine, from daybreak to dark, was cleansing and dressing the sores, ulcers and other skin troubles; removing carious and necrosed bone—all of the type that leprosy inflicts on mankind. He was methodical and accurate in his work and quick to learn the rudiments of medicine and surgery. I started him dressing the wounds and sores of the leper proteges [orphan children] of Father Damien, and showed him (Dutton) the method of affixing dressings by properly applied bandages and other appliances. Within a very short time he had become so apt that he surpassed his teacher; in brief, "whatever Brother Dutton undertook to do he did it well."[15]

On July 1, leprologists Fitch and Arning left Hawai'i, both having worn out their welcome. Dr. Fitch boarded the ocean liner resolutely convinced that leprosy was a manifestation of the fourth stage of syphilis, a popular view then still held by many of the physicians practicing in Hawai'i. Dr. Arning, who believed leprosy to be a unique, highly contagious disease, was bitter because he had been fired for inoculating Keanu, the condemned murderer, with the leprosy bacilli. He considered what he had accomplished as brilliant—research that expanded mankind's understanding of leprosy, research that was misunderstood and unappreciated.

Following the departure of the two leprologists, Dr. Arthur Mouritz, the resident physician at the leper settlement, assumed responsibility for following Keanu's case. By the end of the year Keanu showed definite signs of leprosy; however, when Dr. Mouritz checked on the health status of Keanu's kinfolk, he discovered that several members of Keanu's immediate family were lepers. This raised the question as to whether Keanu had contracted the disease prior to Dr. Arning's inoculation of his right forearm—and completely negated the scientific value of the implantation experiment.

DURING THE YEAR that Brother Joseph Dutton joined Father Damien, King Kalākaua and his prime minister, Walter Murray Gibson, the two men most responsible for providing the leper settlement's

continuing operating funds, placed its future financial support in jeopardy. The business community, which paid most of the taxes and
which was comprised mainly of American expatriates, viewed the
actions of the overly ambitious king and the scheming Gibson with
increasing concern and suspicion. While the majority of the government's expenditures seemed well intentioned, the obvious fraud and
dishonesty involved in some of the transactions were intolerable.[16] To
add to the tension, King Kalākaua announced that since Hawai‘i was
well on her way to becoming a major Polynesian power, she needed
her own navy, and he promptly increased the national debt by pur-
chasing a British warship fitted out with brass cannons and Gatling
guns. Proudly, he named the ship *Ka‘imiloa*, "the far seeker," and dispatched her to tour the South Pacific and encourage the twenty-six
island nations to join Hawai‘i in a Polynesian federation with himself
as the supreme ruler. To American expatriots, the king appeared out
of control. Extravagance, fiscal irresponsibility, gambling, and alcohol
abuse were affecting his reason.

The rising discontent in the business community led to the formation of an opposition party, the majority of whose members were
haoles intent upon government reform. Before Christmas, 1886, the
irate members, led by Lorrin A. Thurston and Sanford Dole—both
elected legislators and both sons of the original Congregational missionaries—formed the Hawaiian League, a voluntary, secret organization whose purpose was to secure "efficient, decent and honest government in Hawaii." Within six months the league had more than four
hundred members, who pledged their lives, property, and sacred honor
to legislative reform, a pledge reminiscent of the one taken by the sign-
ers of the American Declaration of Independence 112 years earlier.
The Leagues' conservative members wanted to force Gibson's resignation, while the more radical members opted to overthrow the
monarchy and establish a republic, possibly seeking annexation to the
United States.

Although Gibson recognized that his status as the most powerful man in the kingdom was in jeopardy, he continued to increase the
financial support for the leper settlements at Kaka‘ako and Kalaupapa, using his position as the president of the Board of Health as an
excuse to spend an increasingly greater portion of his time in the company of Mother Marianne. He became infatuated with the mother

superior, and entries in his two surviving journals for the years 1886 and 1887 reveal that he was unquestionably in love with her.[17] During 1886, this sixty-four-year-old gentleman who was the most powerful and busiest statesman in the Kingdom, serving as prime minister, minister of the Interior, and president of the Board of Health, recorded in his diary over 119 separate one-hour sessions spent in the company of Mother Marianne.[18]

In the fall of 1886, the tense and beleaguered Gibson made one other move that would cost him dearly. Frustrated that his relationship with Mother Marianne couldn't proceed beyond the platonic stage, he began courting twenty-eight-year-old Flora St. Clair, an attractive widow who had recently settled in Honolulu. During this courtship he continued to meet regularly with Mother Marianne during the day and with Flora St. Clair after sunset. Toward the end of December, 1886, he proposed marriage to Mrs. St. Clair, and she accepted. Despite his fiance's insistence, Gibson refused to allow a public announcement of the engagement or set a date for the wedding. Flora St. Clair would not be trifled with. She vowed, "that ceremony will have to come off soon or I will raise—well, I'll make it warm for the old man, that's all."[19]

AUGUST SLIPPED AWAY, one long day after another, without a decision from the superior general regarding Father Pamphile's offer to transfer to the leper settlement. Anxious to resolve the impasse, Father Damien wrote to his brother, enclosing a second letter to be forwarded to the superior general. As always, the letter was delivered unsealed to Father Léonor for his approval and dispatch. It read:

> I sent your letter to Bishop Hermann, and the best for you as for me, is to let the ecclesiastical and religious authority decide if I shall have the consolation of seeing and working together with my brother, whom I am indebted to, after God, for having been chosen for the mission. You understand me without my saying all that I think. . . .
>
> I am too burdened with work to allow me to write you anymore, and to write the family. The government has charged me with the establishment here of a large hospital for the treatment, under my direction, of many hundreds of the sick. So, I work not only as a priest, but as a doctor and architect. Happily, my strength has returned a little. Best wishes to everyone at Louvain and at Tremeloo. Let us pray for each other. Soon ??[20]

The accompanying letter to the superior general was lengthy and carefully crafted, as if composed for possible publication in the *Catholic Missions*. While the body of the letter dealt with Father Damien's mission at the leper settlement and his personal battle with leprosy, it concluded with two short sentences pleading with his superior to permit his brother to come to his assistance. "Permission, please, my Very Reverend Father, for my brother Pamphile to come to help me. Article 392 of our Constitution is my advocate."[21]

On the same day he forwarded the letters to Father Léonor, Father Damien received a letter from Rev. Hugh B. Chapman, the Anglican minister of St. Luke's Church, Camberwell, in England, offering to raise money for the lepers.

> Reverend Father in Jesus Christ,
>
> I write you in all humility to offer you my profound and respectful sympathy, although I do not dare to say my pity, when I think that you carry the cross of a terrible suffering with which the Savior has honored you. It should be a source of real consolation to you, knowing that your courage has inspired some among us to follow your example, as far as God gives us the grace. . . .
>
> If money in any form can assuage the needs of those for whom you care, I will, upon receipt of a letter from you, collect 500 pounds and send it to you. . . . I am only a minister of the Church of England. . . . This letter is a feeble tribute of love for a man who has taught me the true significance of heroism. May God bless you and keep you in the hollow of His hand.[22]

Thankful that there were Protestants, like Dr. Wetmore, whose main goal was to be God's hands on earth, Father Damien penned a response. He was self-conscious about corresponding with an educated English Protestant who would note his grammatical and spelling errors, so he decided to depart from his usual letter-writing routine and first prepare a draft or two of his replies in the English language.

> Reverend Sir:
>
> Your highly appreciative letter of June 4 is at hand. Thanks to Our Divine Savior for having fired up in you, by the example of an humble priest fulfilling simply the duties of his vocation, that noble spirit of the sweet life of self-sacrifice. . . .
>
> Without the constant presence of Our Divine Master upon the altar

in my poor chapels, I never could have persevered in casting my lot with the lepers of Molokai, the predictable consequences of which now begins to appear on my skin, and is felt throughout the body. The Holy communion being the daily bread of a priest, I feel myself happy, well pleased, and resigned in the rather exceptional circumstance in which it has pleased Divine Providence to place me. . . .

Please allow me to pray daily for you and your brethren that we may all have one faith, belong all to the same <u>one true</u> Apostolic Church, and all become one in Christ Jesus, and thus obtain the same eternal crown in Heaven.

In regard to your intended collection in favor of the unfortunate lepers under my care, I would say that any amount, however small, will be received with gratitude for the relief of over 600 poor unfortunate lepers. Be it understood that I personally having made a vow of poverty, my wants are few. A draft from the Bank of England, on Bishop & Co., bankers in Honolulu, will be the simplest and the safest way for remittance. May the eternal blessing of God be with you, your family, and those who may contribute in any way to the relief of my poor sick people.

Yours affectionately in Our Lord,
J. Damien De. Veuster,
Catholic Priest for the Lepers

P.S. To give you some idea of our place, I send you by same mail a small book, "The Lepers of Molokai." May it be of interest to you and your friends.[23]

Upon receipt of Father Damien's letter, Rev. Chapman submitted it to the *Times* (London) for publication, along with a note of his own to inform the public that the proposed charitable fund-raising endeavor had the endorsement of the leading Catholic prelate of England, Cardinal Henry Edward Manning, archbishop of Westminster. Collecting money for the lepers of Moloka'i was to be a joint Catholic-Protestant project.

A few Protestants and a few Catholics were shocked at the notion of a cooperative venture and expressed their outrage in letters to the various English newspapers, to some of which Rev. Chapman was allowed to offer a rebuttal.[24] The attacks on Rev. Chapman and the counterattacks by his supporters aroused the interest of the English public in the Father Damien controversy.[25] People wanted to learn more about this Catholic priest, and the sales of Stoddard's *Lepers of Molokai* soared.

When Rev. Chapman tabulated the funds raised for the leper settlement, he counted 975 pounds sterling ($4,875), and he sent the
bank draft to Father Damien with the following note:

> I thank you for your fine letter of August 26th; more than all, for the
> prayers which you promise for those amongst whom I live and after
> that, those for myself. You will find enclosed a small sum which Chris-
> tians have charged me to send you and which they will thank you for
> accepting. The best way, they think, to do you a favor and to bring a
> smile to your lips, is to aid you to help your lepers. They leave you
> absolutely free to use this sum as you see fit. Your entire life is a guar-
> antee of the good use to which you will put it.
>
> You have the happiness of being loved and appreciated by your Car-
> dinal Archbishop towards whom I myself owe a great debt of gratitude.
> I beg you to salute respectfully, for me, your companion, Dutton. I
> thank God for him, and for the life he has chosen; well aware through
> knowledge of my own heart, how rare is such heroism.
>
> May this little flower of love which England sends you, spread about
> you its perfume. May it prove to you the affection of those who address
> you and who hope to meet you in heaven.

> Your friend who loves you,
> H. B. Chapman[26]

Pleased with the public's response to his request for contributions
to the leper fund, Rev. Chapman submitted a second appeal letter to the
Times (London), describing the plight of the lepers and their leper priest.
Again he emphasized that charitable contributions would be welcomed
from Catholics and Protestants alike. The *Times* accompanied the
Chapman letter with a lengthy article on Father Damien, written by a
seasoned journalist who presented a compelling story of the leper priest
"who has been 'doctor, nurse, and even in some cases undertaker and
grave-digger'—in fact, all things—for his stricken flock." In total, the
two fund-raising campaigns netted 2,625 pounds sterling (approximately $13,125), plus boxes of books and magazines for the lepers.

On December 28, 1886, the bishop was stunned to read in the
Pacific Commercial Advertiser an article reprinted from the *Boston
Post*:

> The affliction which has befallen Father Damien in his ministrations
> among the lepers, far from discouraging, has but stimulated the

Catholic missionary activity in this direction. Two priests from Paris and two more nuns from the Franciscan Convent in Syracuse, New York, which had previously sent six volunteers for the same work, have recently sailed for the leper mission in the Sandwich Islands. It is gratifying also to note evidence of appreciation of Father Damien's Christlike charity even outside the Church. The Rev. H. B. Chapman, Anglican Vicar, in Camberwell, England, has collected over $3,000 for the mission of Molokai, and M. Labouchere, of *Truth* lately forwarded to Cardinal Manning $1,500 received by him for the same purpose.[27]

Bishop Hermann believed that the Hawaiian Mission had been as generous in the support of Father Damien as the Catholic budget allowed. He did not appreciate the implication that the order had failed to provide adequately for Father Damien's needs.

As the prime minister and president of the Board of Health, Walter Murray Gibson was sensitive to the fact that the incoming donations implied a degree of negligence on the part of the board, and Gibson was certain that his political foes would use the publicity to his disadvantage, claiming that he had mismanaged the $170,516 appropriated for the lepers over the past twenty-four months. Granted, some might consider the annual clothing allowance of $6.00 per leper to be meager, but there was a limit to the money in the Kingdom's coffers.

OVER TWO MONTHS had elapsed since a priest had visited the leper settlement to confess Father Damien—an inexcusably long period. Additionally, there was no news regarding the decision as to Father Pamphile's offer to serve as his confrere. Feeling abandoned by his order, Father Damien turned to Joseph Dutton for companionship. Barring an emergency or an impending death somewhere in the settlement that would require Father Damien's presence, the two men would meet at sunset on the rectory's small porch and discuss the problems of the day. That finished, the conversation turned to life, God, and one's duty to his fellow man. Finally, Father Damien had a "good confrere."[28]

In a mid-September letter to Bishop Hermann, Father Damien wrote a brief progress report on Joseph Dutton. "Joseph Dutton is my good sacristan and occupies his free time in cleaning everything regarding the altar, etc. He is also my druggist for the Japanese treatment. He is of exemplary conduct and very pious. I have built him a little hermitage near the pu hala tree and the sacristy. An attached room will be used to lodge my confessor, when he comes; I have not had a confessor since my visit to Honolulu."[29]

THERE ARE VARIOUS accounts of the death of Anne Catherine De Veuster, Father Damien's mother, a lady of eighty-three years who had been in ill health for some months. One biographer attributes her demise to the shock of learning that her son was suffering from an advanced stage of leprosy and erroneously records April 6, 1886, as the date of her death.[30] Another simply states that on hearing of her son's leprosy, "the shock was great; it killed her. She died well and piously, clutching to her heart a picture of the Holy Virgin and a photograph of Damien."[31] Perhaps a more accurate account is that of Father Pamphile, who detailed the event in notes he furnished an early biographer, Father Philibert Tauvel:

> Three years ago (that is, in 1886) our mother was on her death-bed, when the Belgian papers announced the leprosy of my brother Damien. It is clear that they exaggerated his state, for among other things they said that his flesh was falling from him in rags. Someone imprudently read this account to my poor mother. She listened attentively, but resigned herself in her sorrow. "Well, then," she said, "we shall go to Heaven together." She died on the 5th of August, 1886, retaining all her faculties up to the last. On the morning of the day on which she died, she warned her grand-daughter, who was attending her, not to leave her for a moment; she passed the few hours that remained to her, keeping strictly to the order that she had settled for herself from the beginning of her sickness, that is to say, reciting her beads at stated times, making meditation, or listening to pious reading. About four o'clock in the afternoon, feeling her end approaching, she turned towards a picture of the Blessed Virgin, then to the portrait of my brother Joseph, making an inclination of the head to each; after which she gradually sank, and quietly expired.[32]

Weeks would elapse before Father Damien would learn of his mother's death. Brother Dutton was with him at the time he opened the letter from Father Pamphile informing him of her demise. He had been anticipating the sad news for some time, and after a few moments of silence, he turned to Brother Dutton and said quietly, "Pray for my good old mother that she may inherit eternal life."[33]

As FALL DRIFTED into winter, there was more rain, and the cooler wind off the ocean made those lepers with open skin lesions shiver. Father Damien pondered the awkward silence regarding his brother's offer to come to Moloka'i as mute testimony that the decision had been made in Paris not to risk the life of a healthy priest at the leper settlement. Without bitterness, Father Damien resigned himself to making his confession on bended knee, alone and before the altar.

The twice-daily Goto immersion in the hot baths seemed beneficial, although the baths sapped his strength. The numbness in his left leg was no better, and the lesions on his face had progressed, but he had regained the use of his right hand and could again swing a hammer and use a saw. But the joy of physical exertion had vanished. With Brother Dutton's assistance, he was able to resume his role as a builder of houses and churches. The construction of a small house for Brother Dutton hadn't been a problem, but he procrastinated when he faced the daunting task of enlarging St. Philomena Church. This would be a major undertaking, and he was fearful he lacked both the energy and the time to complete the project. Leprosy was a disease of Satan. It wrapped a person in a cloak of fatigue while it disfigured, slowly crippling and squeezing the life from its victim. His lepers needed him, and he thanked his Creator that despite the fatigue and the pain he still had the will to function as a priest and a part-time physician.

In the letter he wrote at year's end to Father Janvier Weiler, the secretary to the superior general, Father Damien described his busy activities during the Christmas season to demonstrate that his leprosy had not yet incapacitated him:

> Six months ago I was helpless and feeble; it was with difficulty that I said Holy Mass, etc. Today, thanks to the good God and the Holy Virgin I am renewed in strength and robust, although still a leper. I am strong again.
>
> Last Friday, Christmas day, I took my bath at five in the morning; at six I left for Kalaupapa, the other village, one league away; after the Mass and the instruction I went to the confessional until 11:30, being available for the young. After that I returned here, ate well enough and went again to the Confessional until seven, after having said my Breviary I took a cup of strong coffee, and at nine o'clock with all of my young people attending, went to Church to preside at the general examination of catechism which lasted until 11:30. At midnight I began High

Mass, with a sermon of a little more than half an hour. In the morning
I arrived at my other church with my sacristan, Joseph, the young American about whom Father Columban has spoken to you. And at five
o'clock I began my second solemn Mass with a sermon on another subject. After the Mass I performed a solemn baptism of some catechu-
mens, and at nine o'clock I said my third Mass here at Kalawao. . . .
Not being free to travel outside our establishment, I find it impossible
to go to see another confrere, and must wait with patience for the arrival
of a priest to hear my confession. . . . *It is this desertion by all the confreres of the dear Congregation which I find more painful than the sickness of leprosy* [emphasis added]. . . . while I wait for my confessor I
confess before the Blessed Sacrament.[34]

After sunset each day in the quiet of the St. Philomena sanctuary,
Father Damien would review the accomplishments of the day and
examine the challenging tasks looming before him. In the flickering
light of the altar candles, he would prayerfully repeat the words of
St. Paul: "I know how to be abased, and I know how to abound; in
any and all circumstances I have learned the secret of facing plenty
and hunger, abundance and want. I can do all things in Him who
strengthens me."

22

Death's Dark Shadow

*To come to the pleasure you have not, you must go
by a way in which you enjoy not.*
—St. John of the Cross

NEW YEAR'S DAY, 1887, was not a joyous one for Father Damien. As he dried his body after the first of the two 108-degree Goto baths scheduled for the day, he examined the leprosy nodules of various sizes that were protruding from his face, abdomen, back, arms, and legs.[1] The skin of his cheeks, nose, forehead, and chin had become excessively swollen and "deep copper-colored" blotches occupied the valleys between the hard lumps of swollen flesh, transforming his face into the mask of a medieval monster. The bridge of his nose had begun to collapse, and both earlobes had tripled in size and now dangled halfway to his shoulders. He had lost at least 35 pounds and his cassock hung on him like an oversized bag. His feet and ankles were so swollen that he couldn't lace his shoes, and when he walked he "tottered." Still, he was able to function as a priest, and for this privilege he thanked God.

When he returned to the rectory he placed twice the prescribed number of Goto herbal pills on his tongue and winced as he downed them with a cup of the bitter Japanese herbal tea, which stung the inside of his mouth and his throat. The tiny germs were now attacking the inside of his body as well as the outside. He had reasoned that by increasing both the immersion time and the temperature of the hot baths, plus doubling the dose of the Japanese medicine, he might still arrest the disease. But after trying this more intensive therapy for several weeks, he felt worse rather than better. In desperation, he consulted with Dr. Mouritz.[2]

Before rendering an opinion, Dr. Mouritz insisted he needed to determine for himself the current status of Father Damien's leprosy. Damien complied and soon found himself seated on the doctor's examination table where every inch of his body was carefully inspected. After Dr. Mouritz finished, he slowly shook his head and apologetically informed the priest that there were no additional medicines that would retard the progress of the rather advanced stage of his disease. There was nothing more, Dr. Mouritz counseled, that medicine could offer other than to warn him that intensifying the Goto regime was contributing significantly to the fatigue that he was experiencing. Slowly a disheartened Father Damien eased himself down from the examining table and departed, leaving the doctor to record his findings.[3]

Compensating in part for his increasing fatigue and difficulty in ambulation, the number of lepers to be served at the settlement had decreased almost in proportion to his waning energy. There had been only forty-three admissions to the settlement in 1886—an all-time low. The 101 deaths that had occurred during the past year had been manageable, and by year's end there were only 580 surviving lepers. Unsettling was the knowledge that there were more lepers running loose throughout the Islands than were segregated at the settlement.

On January 2, Bishop Hermann wrote to Father Damien, ostensibly to thank him for his New Year's "good wishes" and to confirm that his assignment at the leper settlement was renewed for another year. The communication contained no mention of the possibility of assigning a second priest to Moloka'i, nor was Father Damien's request for sisters to serve as nurses and orphanage matrons addressed. The primary thrust of the message was the bishop's growing displeasure with the awkward position in which the Hawaiian Mission now found itself as a result of Rev. Chapman's charitable fund drives to raise money for the exclusive use of Father Damien. The implications were obvious and unsavory. The bishop wrote:

> I am not jealous of the admiration which you are receiving from all sides for your heroism. Those who comment are not exaggerating too much, and I have often joined them in praising your efforts. It is for you to

understand—and this is not so easy—that you do not let the waiwai
[water] escape through a hole in the bottom of the pail. . . . If things
were known as they really are, it is highly unlikely that you would be
sent large sums of money.

Because I have a passion for justice to be done to everyone, even to
my enemies, the enemies of good, that I view with displeasure the fact
that the newspapers which admire you, exaggerate and distort the truth,
and fail to take into account what the government and others have
done. The mission has also done its part. It seems to me that they cannot praise you without making a serious error, at least indirectly by
doing an injustice to the others.[4]

Father Damien found the message hurtful; under the circumstances, he was doing his duty to God and the lepers as best he could.
It was the unsolicited publication of the bishop's laudatory report that
had caught the eye of the British public, not an act of his.

Unique problems continued to arise at the leper settlement that
required skillful intervention. A twelve-year-old girl believed to be disease free, the daughter of a woman with advanced leprosy, had been one
of the original fourteen girls selected to go to the Kapi'olani Home in
Honolulu in the hope that she would escape infection. Unfortunately,
shortly after her arrival at Kapi'olani she developed overt signs of leprosy and was promptly returned to the leper settlement. When the girl
stepped out of the longboat at the Kalaupapa landing wharf, she handed
Father Damien a note from Mother Marianne asking that he "watch
and look out for her." Damien assumed the responsibility and drove the
girl to her mother's house in his buggy. When he arrived, he found the
home environment deplorable. The girl's mother was extremely ill and
barely able to care for herself. Several men of questionable morality,
claiming to be relatives of the mother, were sharing the domiciliary and
seemed delighted to have the young girl quartered with them.

Concerned that the men might take sexual advantage of the girl,
Father Damien brought the matter to the attention of Ambrose
Hutchison, the resident superintendent, and asked that the girl be
transferred to the girls' orphanage once the mother died. Hutchison
agreed, provided the mother stated in writing that this was her wish—
but before the written statement was obtained, the mother died. Following the mother's funeral, Father Damien learned that one of the
relatives in the house, a man of Filipino-Spanish descent, now claimed

the girl as his mistress. Damien was disgusted and asked Ambrose Hutchison to transfer her to the orphanage immediately. While Hutchison recognized the unsavoriness of the situation, he insisted that in the absence of a signed statement from the now-deceased mother, he was powerless to remove the girl from the care of a relative. Father Damien scribbled a hurried note to Rudolph Meyer, informing him of the travesty, pleading that he use his authority to protect the girl.[5] A messenger, one of the healthy male *kōkua*, carried the message up the *pali* to Meyer's home. Meyer read the note and sent the *kōkua* scurrying down the *pali* to Father Damien with his reply. As superintendent of the leper settlement, Meyer was the ultimate magistrate, and he did as his friend the priest had requested. He directed Hutchison to escort the girl directly to the orphanage over the objections of the male relative. Despite his crippling disease, Father Damien continued to stand tall as the moral icon at the leper settlement.

January 19 was a very good day in the life of Father Damien. He received two letters from Rev. Chapman, in one of which was enclosed a certified bank draft for 975 pounds. Damien was ecstatic. The English Protestants had proved that they were capable of displaying Christian charity by joining with the English Catholics to aid his lepers. Knowing that Rudolph Meyer was planning a trip to Honolulu, he wrote to his friend:

> Dear Sir,
>
> At your last visit here I consulted you about what best to be done if any charitable contributions should arrive for our poor lepers. I now intend to follow your kind advice as I have just received a handsome sum of money for the comfort of the needy, and trying to profit from your presence in Honolulu, I take the liberty of requesting you to make some purchases for me. Trusting to your good judgement in this matter I am sure you will make some good advantageous bargains.[6]

There followed a detailed list of various fabrics—blue denim, dark-colored calico prints, red cotton prints—from which to make pants, shirts, and dresses for every leper in the settlement. A large quantity of sewing machine thread, 2 pounds of plain cotton thread, a generous supply of sewing needles of various sizes, a large stove and a smaller kerosene stove for the boys' orphanage, and wicks and glass chimneys for the kerosene lamps completed the shopping list.

That evening Father Damien drafted a thank-you letter to Rev. Chapman, informing him that the money had purchased the necessary fabrics and supplies with which to provide each leper with warm clothing for the approaching winter season.[7]

Instead of turning custody of the funds over to the Church, Father Damien asked permission of Bishop Hermann to deposit the funds directly in the bank in his name. He explained: "Since it is not a contribution solely from Catholics, but in large measure from Protestants, I suppose this could avert the distrust of the Catholic mission which has already surfaced in England by a few Protestants who were jealous and enraged by the actions of Reverend Chapman."[8]

The bishop granted the request but reiterated his concern over the public's misperception of Father Damien's role at the leper settlement: "According to the newspapers, the world is under the impression that you are the head of your lepers, as their provider, doctor, nurse, and grave digger, as if the government had done nothing. This is justly offensive to the King, Mr. Gibson, etc. It is possible that some jealous enemy seeks to prove to the world that you (so that we can be blamed) have extorted this money under false pretenses."[9]

In the next exchange of letters, Father Damien disclosed a proposal advanced by Rev. Chapman that would be viewed as a genuine threat and embarrassment to the Catholic Mission. The British had read in *The Lepers of Molokai* that there were no professional nurses at the leper settlement, so they were magnanimously offering to have Anglican sisters staff the hospital facilities. Since Father Damien's request to have the Franciscan sisters nurse the lepers on Moloka'i had been denied, he offered no objection to the British offer.

This development exasperated Bishop Hermann. Anglican sisters at the leper settlement would shatter the exclusivity of the Catholic Mission. Dressed in compassionate white, the Anglican sisters would garner the world's sympathy, eclipsing all that the solitary Catholic priest had achieved. In a sudden reversal of policy, Bishop Hermann wrote Father Damien.

> What I have always thought is that in time we would have Sisters at Molokai. . . . Mother Marianne ought to go to see the settlement; I have given her permission to do so. . . . If they want to assign a certain number to Molokai, I am not opposed to it, although the arrangements must be done properly, and with the consent of the Mother Superior. . . .

The difference between you and me is that you concentrate exclusively on the lepers while I am obliged to look out for all the mission. You see the end result while I must envision the means to achieve it. . . . Do not forget that we are in enemy country; they do not want to give compliments to anyone, and they seek to destroy the work that the Catholic mission achieves. . . .

After gold and incense, myrrh has not been to your taste, and you have spat it in my face with bile in your heart. Let us hope that there is no more left. For my part, I have never ceased to admire your heroism and to publicize it on every suitable occasion. If I have counted too much on your humility, I am sorry.[10]

From strangers, Father Damien received gold and incense; from his superiors, myrrh.

From Bishop Hermann's vantage point, there was no viable alternative. Before he would allow Episcopalian sisters to set foot on Moloka'i, he would sacrifice the Franciscan sisters. The dilemma this decision brought to the surface—and a major one—was that Mother Marianne was insistent that before she or any of the Franciscan sisters set foot on Moloka'i, a "healthy priest" had to be in residence at Kalaupapa. She would not allow a sister to receive communion from the hands of the leper priest.[11] Which of his priests was he willing to sacrifice along with the sisters?

WITH THE ARRIVAL of the cloth and sewing supplies Rudolph Meyer had purchased in Honolulu, Father Damien launched a sewing campaign, the goal of which was to provide each leper with warm clothing for the winter months. Meyer observed Damien hire persons to sew the articles of clothing for those lacking the required skills and for those too ill to do so. The result was that over five hundred lepers each received two articles of warm clothing.[12] The women recipients were given two shoulder-to-ankle-length dresses; the men each received a shirt and a pair of trousers. Meyer was relieved that Father Damien had "made no distinction as to the religion of the recipients."[13]

While Father Damien had achieved his goal of providing each leper at the settlement with "warm clothing," the publicity generated by the act had embarrassed the government and jeopardized the rapport between the Kingdom of Hawai'i and the Catholic Mission. Father Léonor, the provincial, complained to the superior general:

Now, my Very Reverend Father, here is an affair which we consider very serious. It deals with the subject of Father Damien. Because of the publication of some false information by him in England, he has received considerable gifts (23,621 fr) and others have come to him from America (5000 fr) (total 28,621 fr) without counting the additional gifts and provisions. The worst news is contained in a letter received by our only friend in the government, Mr. Gibson, the Prime Minister, that a group has been formed in London to come to the aid of Father Damien—a doctor and some Sisters of St. Joan (Episcopalian). He has led them to believe that the lepers lack everything, and that his immediate Superiors are opposed to him so that he must resort to fund raising (This last we saw printed in a newspaper). But my Very Reverend Father, all of this grows out of a proud head from the high praises—and is against the government which takes very good care of the lepers. . . . This brave Father passes himself off as the consoler, the provider, the physician, the coffin maker, the grave digger of the lepers, and he is none of these things. . . . and now he has become dangerous. Hardly had he had the donations in his hands when, without saying anything to anyone he made a gift of a complete wardrobe to every leper. This embarrassment to the government which came from the clothing distribution prompted a reprimand, a little sharp, from the Bishop to which he replied in a bitter manner, "After having received incense and gold from all, I did not expect that it would be my Superior from whom I would receive myrrh." And the Bishop replied, "but that myrrh you did not want, and you have spit in my face."[14]

A few days later Bishop Hermann expressed similar frustrations to the superior general. He prefaced his remarks thus: "Our celebrated hero of Molokai has received so many compliments (certainly well merited) from all sides, that he seems to be in danger of losing his balance, and his head which has perhaps always been a bit hard, is now more so."[15] The superior general patiently studied the complaints and charges of misconduct directed against Father Damien, but from his vantage point he judged the situation quite differently. The favorable publicity appearing regularly in the European newspapers pleased him. To better accomplish her earthly mission, the Church needed the inspirational uplift of a modern hero—a true Christian martyr—and in the Belgian priest, she had one. Father Janvier, the superior general's secretary, was instructed to write to Father Damien, to encourage him in his endeavors and to request additional information for publication in the *Catholic Missions*.

My Reverend Father,

I have received your good letter of last December 30 along with two copies of the book *[The Lepers of Molokai]*. Thank you very much. Our Reverend Father has also received your letter of August, handed him by Father Pamphile. . . . I will be very grateful if you would send a little article to be published, perhaps in the *Catholic Missions* or as an Appendix to the English book which I shall try to have published in French. . . .

If the Jesuits had a Molokai the news would never dry up, and the alms would flow like water.[16]

While Father Janvier's letter was refreshingly complimentary of his ministry to the lepers, it was clear that, contrary to the Rule of the Order, the decision had been made not to reassign Father Pamphile or a second priest to Moloka'i.

The following week Father Damien received a letter from Father Léonor demanding that he sign the enclosed Last Will and Testament, naming Bishop Hermann or his successor as the beneficiary of all charitable funds on deposit at the Bishop Bank. Obediently he signed his name to the will. The letter concluded with the reiteration of the provincial's policy of the strict censorship of all of Father Damien's correspondence, personal as well as Church related, "except to the Superior General, as is decreed in our Holy Rule."[17] This was nothing new. Since the first of his letters had been published, Father Damien had voluntarily submitted all of his correspondence, unsealed, for his superiors' approval.

In February the requested materials for the construction of the bathhouse complex to implement the Goto treatment for one hundred of the lepers were offloaded at Kalaupapa and promptly transported to Kalawao. With the assistance of Brother Dutton, Father Damien undertook the construction of what came to be known as the "Stone Valley Bathhouse." It consisted of two bathhouses with five bathrooms each, a boiler room, a dining hall, a cookhouse, six dormitories, and a dispensary. As the project progressed, it was apparent to Brother Dutton that Father Damien's increasing fatigue was seriously impairing his ability to perform manual labor. Each rise and fall of his hammer was slower, more deliberate, and required a maximum effort on the part of the priest.

IN AN EFFORT to limit the public relations damage to the government and the Board of Health caused by the publicity related to the continuing charitable donations from abroad, the secretary of the board wrote to Father Damien recommending that in the future all charitable funds be placed in the hands of his bishop, "who together with the Board of Health will use it, according to your wishes for the general good of our suffering brothers."[18]

Father Damien refused to comply and so notified Bishop Hermann. The money, he insisted, was donated for his exclusive use as God granted him the wisdom to do so. He would not compromise. The money was to remain in the Bishop Bank in an account in his name alone; but its use, he assured Bishop Hermann, would be guided by his superior's admonition: "Let your conscience dictate its use, in which case, you must consult with your Superiors as to how it is to be used."[19]

DURING THE TWELVE months ending March 31, 1887, there were only fifty-nine deaths at the leper settlement, a dramatic decrease from the average number witnessed in the previous five years. This was due in large measure to the better medical care now administered under the supervision of the capable Dr. Mouritz, who trained medical assistants such as Brother Dutton in wound care and encouraged the still competent Father Damien to assist in the treatment of common illnesses. Nonetheless, the leper census remained a low 593, due primarily to the continued reluctance of the government to enforce the segregation policy.[20] Tragically, 20 percent of the settlement's inmates were under five years of age— for the most part children of the incarcerated lepers. The majority of these youngsters did not as yet show overt signs of leprosy, either because of the long incubation period of the disease, or the tragic fact that while they were still healthy, they were trapped at the settlement where ultimate infection was inescapable.

WALTER MURRAY GIBSON'S continuing infatuation with Mother Marianne, his concern with King Kalākaua's extravagant spending, and his annoyance with Father Damien's solicitation of funds for the leper settlement were the major topics noted in his diary during the second and third weeks of February 1887.[21] He had no intention of ever permitting Mother Marianne to serve at the leper settlement. As long as she was quartered at the Kaka'ako Branch Hospital, he had ready access to "the love of his life."[22] Interestingly, during the time he was expressing his deep affection for Mother Marianne, Flora Howard St.

Clair—the young widow Gibson had courted for five months and to whom he had proposed marriage—was never mentioned in his diary. Determined to make Gibson pay for his dastardly subterfuge, the young widow hired an attorney and filled a breach of promise suit.

IN EARLY APRIL, Father Léonor responded to a letter of inquiry from the superior general regarding the remedial steps taken to improve Father Damien's access to a confrere and the status of the proposed deployment of the Franciscan sisters at the leper settlement.[23] The provincial stated incorrectly that the overworked Father Columban, who served five parishes on Maui, made the trip to the leper settlement "about every five weeks," when in fact the journey was undertaken only every two to three months. He falsely stated that two other priests—Father Grégoire, who was a confirmed leper and Father André, who was a suspected leper—absolutely refused to be stationed on Moloka'i because neither man could tolerate the dictatorial behavior of Father Damien, a priest with whom none could work. Father Léonor climaxed the letter with the disclosure that the mission was being forced to place the Franciscan sisters at the leper settlement, and he openly blamed Father Damien for the deadly predicament the sisters now faced: "The Franciscan Sisters will go there very soon; their sacrifice is every bit as great as that of Father Damien, for first of all, they are going to nurse the lepers, and most terrifying, they will be forced to take Holy communion from the hands of a leper. . . . We wish we could avoid this travesty, but how? It is the fault of Father Damien, who by his imprudent correspondence and even lies, has forced these poor women to make this sacrifice."[24]

The British public continued to be fascinated by the Father Damien story, the tale of a Christian martyr that rivaled that of their own David Livingston, the renown Scottish missionary who had explored Africa and made the "Dark Continent" known to the world. Edward Clifford, an affluent Englishman who was an accomplished artist, became intensely interested in Father Damien and, possessing the financial resources to visit the Hawaiian Islands, decided to do so during an upcoming world tour.[25] A visit to Moloka'i would provide him the opportunity to paint the now-famous leper priest. In anticipation of an affirmative response, he wrote a letter inviting himself to Moloka'i.[26]

Father Damien replied promptly, extending a cordial invitation to Clifford to visit the leper settlement. "Being myself subject to the segregation law, I cannot promise to go to meet you in Honolulu, but if you will let me know the time of your arrival, we will try to arrange comfortable transportation for you. . . . We must use prudence in the future, and not publish the letters of our donors anymore. If you please, not a word of this letter to the newspapers."[27]

DISPLEASED WITH THE adverse publicity generated by the monetary contributions Father Damien was continuing to receive from Europe and the United States, Walter Murray Gibson decided it was time to defend the good name of the Hawaiian Kingdom and discredit the thoughtless statements attributed to the Belgian priest. The best means for doing so, he believed, was in the pages the *Pacific Commercial Advertiser*, where the facts could be stated. He had used a newspaper to create a hero; now he would use one to topple the ingrate.

The *Advertiser* editorial staff, coached by Gibson, launched a stout defense of the Board of Health that featured a disclosure of the funds appropriated for the leper settlement: "During the last session of the legislature $100,000 was voted for the leper colony, and about $34,000 was spent during the last fiscal year for the same purpose. This seems to be an outlay generous enough for the lepers, and it seems that one ought to conclude that these expenditures are sufficiently high so that the lepers should lack for nothing. But according to Father Damien it is not so."[28]

The article cast doubt on Father Damien's assertion that the clothing provided the lepers was inadequate and demanded that there be a full accounting of the funds placed in the priest's hands for use at the settlement. On May 2, 1887, the *Pacific Commercial Advertiser* published a "Letter to the Editor" submitted by "A leper of Kalawao," a rebuttal many suspected was written by or at the instigation of the maligned Father Damien:

> Sir:
>
> In your publications of 11 and 25 April, there are articles concerning a subscription of 1000 pounds sterling for Father Damien and his flock of lepers, to be dispensed for his flock by him, and that, if it had really been received, the proper manner of spending the money according to the wishes of the donors would have been through the intermediary of the Board of Health.

But does the author of this article know the wishes of the donors? As for me, I do not believe so, for the desire of those subscribers was that the money was left entirely at the disposition of Father Damien, and it was distributed by him according as he judged appropriate, as the letters of Rev. Chapman demonstrate it seems to me that these gentlemen ought not interfere in the distribution of funds provided by private charity.

As this money, so generous, of 1000 pounds is spent in its totality, I will ignore the implications, but one thing is certain, as everyone knows, the sum of $6 accorded each leper for clothes and other needs, is not nearly sufficient. . . .

After all this, can anyone blame Father Damien for accepting a charitable gift from strangers, and even to ask for alms, since he knows that there is need and so much misery in his leper colony?[29]

Clearly, Father Damien's supporter had won the battle of words—but at the cost of irreparably damaging the rapport between Walter Murray Gibson and the Belgian priest.

DURING THE MONTHS of May, June, and July 1887, the tides of discontent among the haole planters and businessmen rose to the flood stage. When scrutinized, the government's financial accounts—including the moneys budgeted for the leper settlement—revealed dangerous leakage, graft, and extravagance.[30] It was common knowledge that in the early years of the leper settlement, its cattle had been purchased from the nearby Moloka'i Ranch, managed by Rudolph Meyer and owned by Charles Reed Bishop, the haole banker and philanthropist. For some undisclosed reason, in 1886 Gibson began buying cattle and sheep from the Parker Ranch on the distant island of Hawai'i, paying a much higher price for animals of no better quality than those available on Moloka'i. Contracts for government buildings, road improvement, and interisland transportation were seldom awarded to the lowest bidder. The American expatriots, the haole businessmen and planters who bore the brunt of taxation, vowed to resist the escalating extravagance even if it meant resorting to revolution.

On May 17, the *Hawaiian Gazette* published a story based on a series of affidavits by T. Aki, a prominent Chinese rice planter, and others who testified that Aki had paid $71,000 to a representative of King Kalākaua for the Kingdom's lucrative opium monopoly. Smoking

opium was one of the few pleasures enjoyed by the immigrant laborers working long hours on the plantations, and its absence would have
precipitated a labor crisis. The king had pocketed the $71,000 and
later sold the monopoly to a higher bidder.[31] Indignant haole planters
pointed to the theft and the king's refusal to return Aki's money as a
mandate for reform. The king's indebtedness was a national disgrace,
and the rumor that he might actually sell another of the Hawaiian
islands, as King Kamehameha IV had sold Ni'ihau to Mrs. Sinclair,
swelled the haole membership in the Hawaiian League and the Hawaiian Rifles.[32]

   To the delight of many who considered Walter Murray Gibson
the chief architect of the "failed" government, the *Pacific Commercial
Advertiser* headline on May 23 read "Breach of Promise Suit," naming the kingdom's prime minister as the defendant. Damages were laid
at $25,000.[33] Gibson's numerous political enemies were jubilant. The
St. Clair versus Gibson trial was scheduled for July, and if Gibson were
branded a scoundrel, the embarrassment to the king might force Gibson's resignation.

   Outright disgust with the management of the kingdom reached
its peak when King Kalākaua's highly controversial political venture,
the establishment of a Polynesian federation with himself as emperor,
fizzled. On June 15, 1887, the cannon-bristling steamer *Ka'imiloa*
reached Samoa on its mission to encourage those islands to become a
member of the proposed empire. The steamer's inebriated captain did
make port, where the Hawaiian crew mutinied and threatened to blow
up the vessel. This afforded the Germans, who—like the Americans, the
British, and the French—coveted Samoa, an excuse to dispatch a detach-
ment of marines to board the *Ka'imiloa*, restore command, and order
the steamer to return to Honolulu. This display of ineptitude sounded
the death knell for the short-lived Hawaiian Navy and the grandiose
plan to crown King David Kalākaua the emperor of Polynesia.

   The opium scandal and the *Ka'imiloa* debacle aptly demonstrated to the Hawaiian League that King Kalākaua was a monarch
lacking both integrity and sagacity, and in late June the group vociferously announced that if reform could not be achieved peacefully,
they were prepared to use armed force. Realizing that the badly out-
numbered palace guard could not protect him, the king appealed to
the United States for help. The United States minister met with King

Kalākaua and informed the frightened monarch that there was unanimity among the "tax payers" on several key issues: Gibson must resign; a new cabinet had to be appointed, made up of men who had the confidence of the business community; and in the future the king must remain aloof from all governmental proceedings. If he wished to wear the crown, Kalākaua would have to do so as a figurehead. The worried king acquiesced and informed Gibson and all his cabinet ministers that they had tendered their resignations.

Following a mass meeting of 2,500 angry members of the Hawaiian League on June 30, a Committee of Thirteen was appointed for the purpose of demanding that the king's new cabinet immediately write a new constitution relegating the monarch to the status of a figurehead.[34] To remain king, Kalākaua had to pledge not to use the influence of his throne for personal gain and to return the $71,000 owed T. Aki. In a futile attempt to salvage his royal powers, King Kalākaua summoned the ministers of Great Britain, France, Portugal, Japan, and the United States to inform them that the Kingdom of Hawai'i had been seized by a band of armed rebels. He told the diplomats that a few hours earlier the rebels had illegally arrested Walter Murray Gibson and charged him with the embezzlement of public funds, a crime punishable by hanging. The king pleaded with the foreign ministers to provide the military assistance to prevent the overthrow of his government. To his dismay all refused to help, and a distraught king was forced to accede to the demands of the Hawaiian League.

At 4 P.M. on the afternoon of July 6, the Hawaiian League presented King Kalākaua with the new constitution, which stripped him of most of his regal powers. All Gibson appointees, including the highly competent Dr. Arthur Mouritz, were immediately fired. In a plea bargain arrangement, the criminal charges against Gibson were dropped in exchange for his immediate departure from Hawai'i. The man most responsible for creating the "hero of Moloka'i" image—and who was in the act of erasing that image—hurried to pack his belongings. Dr. Mouritz rose above the politics of the day and magnanimously agreed to remain at the leper settlement until a replacement physician could be recruited.

SO FAR AS FATHER DAMIEN was concerned, the year's most encouraging news came in June when he learned of the arrival of a new mis-

sionary, Father Xavier Kuepper. At last, he reasoned, there was sufficient manpower to place a second priest on Moloka'i. His hope for a
confrere soared, and he wrote Bishop Hermann to inquire when he
might expect Father Xavier's arrival. A few days later he received his
bishop's chilly reply: "A new missionary, Father Xavier (Sylvester)
Kuepper has arrived. . . . We cannot force the new priest to share your
heroic life at the leprosarium as he has little interest in doing so. . . .
The isolation he would experience would soon discourage him.[35]

Father Damien, desperate for a confrere, wrote to protest the
bishop's decision. Bishop Hermann again refused: "Your good letter
of June 16 arrived yesterday. . . . I have not the right to send the new
missionary, Father Xavier, to the leper colony over his objection. He
does not wish to join you in your heroic exile. . . . Know that your
loneliness troubles me very much, but what can I do?"[36]

The bishop concluded his letter by stating that during the current
period of political unrest in the Islands, he would not permit any of
the Franciscan sisters to go to Moloka'i.

AT THE TIME King Kalākaua was despairing over the loss of his royal
powers, the majority of the lepers engaged in the Goto treatment were
despairing over the failure of the regime to ameliorate their disease.
One by one they dropped out of the program. This mass desertion also
influenced Father Damien. In an effort to limit the fatigue caused by
prolonged soaking in the hot water, he limited the bathing portion of
the treatment to one hot bath every other day. But the harm had been
done, and he failed to recover from his weakened state. The bridge of
his nose continued to sink, completely obstructing his swollen nasal
passages. A portion of the blocked nasal secretions drained into his
pharynx, causing a continual postnasal drip and a chronic, hacking
cough. The remainder of the nasal secretions dripped from what
remained of his nose, forcing him to wipe his nose with a handkerchief
every minute or so. When he walked, he limped, and a stout cane
became his constant companion to compensate for the increasing
weakness in the muscles of his left leg.[37]

Despite the increasing physical disability, Father Damien continued to fulfill all of the duties demanded of a healthy priest. Each day
after morning Mass, he climbed into his horse-drawn buggy and made
his house calls, toting the black bag filled with the medicines for the

relief of the common ailments affecting the lepers. He entered the Catholic homes as a priest and as a physician; he entered the homes of the non-Catholics with the same smile, but only in the role of a physician. Lepers confined to the hospitals and the three domiciliaries for the critically ill were now well cared for by Dr. Mouritz and his personally trained *kōkua* staff. One of these, Brother Joseph Dutton, under the supervision of Dr. Mouritz, dutifully continued to clean and dress the wounds of all of the orphans, a responsibility that consumed six to eight hours each day.

In September, Lorrin Thurston, one of the chief instigators of the recent revolution, was named minister of the Interior by the legislature, the most prestigious post in the new government. He in turn appointed the eminent physician Dr. Trousseau to the post of president of the Board of Health. Dr. Trousseau moved quickly to salvage and enforce the Segregation Law. No one was exempted from segregation, and he immediately directed that those lepers roving freely throughout the Islands be incarcerated. Dr. Trousseau also recognized that the supply of beef cattle for the settlement would have to be increased due to the anticipated influx of new lepers, so Rudolph Meyer was authorized to oversee the construction of a new *pali* trail suitable for supplying the settlement with cattle from the Moloka'i Ranch.[38]

After a few weeks of service, the elderly Dr. Trousseau asked that he be replaced as president of the Board of Health, and Dr. Nathaniel B. Emerson, the first physician to serve as a resident doctor at the leper settlement, agreed to accept the post. Dr. Emerson shared his predecessor's resolve to enforce the Segregation Law, and for the remainder of the year, the leper steamer *Mokoli'i* was busy offloading disgruntled lepers at the Kalaupapa landing wharf. The population of lepers at the settlement soared to 698 by year's end.[39] Father Damien's ability to serve the new arrivals was taxed to the limit. When he lay down on his mat to sleep, utter exhaustion closed his eyes.

No known leper was exempted, and this included the clergy. Thus it came as no surprise when the board directed that Father Grégoire, who was residing in near seclusion on Maui, be examined by Dr. C. A. Peterson, the physician hired to replace Dr. Mouritz. Dr. Peterson confirmed that Father Grégoire was afflicted with an advanced stage of leprosy and ordered the priest returned at once to the leper settlement, the place he had been forced to leave because of life-threatening bronchial asthma. Dr. Emerson ruled that the absolute necessity to segregate all lepers took precedent over the needs of any individual with a coexistent, life-threatening illness. If the leprosy epidemic were to be stemmed, segregation had to be strictly enforced.

On November 16, 1887, Father Damien slowly made his way to the Kalaupapa landing wharf to greet a forlorn Father Grégoire, who was so weak that he had difficulty stepping out of one of the longboats from the *Mokoli'i*. It was immediately obvious to Father Damien that the returning priest was suffering from near-terminal leprosy and so would be almost useless to the ministry. As he helped Father Grégoire into his buggy for the short ride to the rectory in the village of Kalaupapa, he learned that the ailing priest's main concern was not his approaching death, but the burden he would become when the life-threatening asthmatic attacks returned. As Father Damien looked into the sad eyes of the dying man, he remembered the robust, handsome priest with the broad smile who, on many occasions, had come to help him minister to the lepers. This was a man to be tenderly cared for, and he assured his colleague that should his asthma return he would never place him in one of the hospital buildings, but would quarter him in the large ground-floor room in the rectory in Kalawao where he would personally attend to his needs. Father Damien's sole consolation was that for a limited time he would have a confessor near at hand, even though that confessor was bedridden and dying.

As Father Grégoire had fearfully anticipated, within twenty-four hours of his arrival his asthma returned with a vengeance. As before, nighttime was the worst. A Hawaiian sunset was always the prelude to a violent asthmatic attack and sound, restful sleep was but a memory. Still, the wheezing priest made a valiant effort during the daylight hours to hear confessions and celebrate Mass at the Kalaupapa Church. When viewed in the candlelight before the altar, Father Grégoire's gaunt face, muscles taut in the struggle to breathe, was a pathetic, cadaverous sight.

23

Thy Rod and Thy Staff,
They Comfort Me

For this God is our God for ever and ever;
He will be our guide even unto death.
—Psalm 48:14

MOST OF NOVEMBER 1887 proved to be a grim and trying time for Father Damien. His crippling fatigue and difficulty walking, coupled with an episodic, debilitating fever, sapped most of the joy attendant to his daily activities. An act as simple as bathing or brewing coffee in the morning resulted in fatigue and the necessity to rest quietly for a few moments before moving on to the next task. No longer was he able to limit his sleep to four hours a night as he had done during his novitiate and the early years of his ministry. Now his illness dictated more rest. As each day proved more difficult than the previous one, the realization that he was now unable to attend to all of the spiritual needs of his lepers gnawed at his conscience. Without the assistance of a second priest, the Catholic mission at the leper settlement would continue to deteriorate.

Later that month, he received a packet from Father Lambert Conrardy, a Belgian priest who was currently serving as a missionary to the American Indians in Oregon, with whom he had sporadically corresponded for eleven years. The packet contained three documents: Father Conrardy's offer to join him at the leper settlement, the priest's resume, and a letter from Archbishop William Gross of Oregon stoutly supporting Father Conrardy's proposal of assistance. Archbishop Gross headed one of the American congregations that had recently contributed money for the lepers. As Damien read, his spirits were buoyed and he realized that God was listening to his impassioned prayers for help.

> How often I have thought about writing to you. It has been two years since I received your last good letter. I have read in the newspapers that the terrible malady has not spared you. The Divine Master who has given you the courage to help the lepers for so many years will certainly also give you the courage and the necessary resignation. . . .
>
> Do you think it would be advantageous were I to ask to be accepted in your mission? It seems that you are always alone. If I knew that I could be useful to you, I would choose to become a member of your Congregation,—to become a true priest is my aim, and it does not matter to me in which congregation so long as I can work in missions. . . . if you believe that my presence would be useful in helping you with your mission, I would be happy to place myself under the obedience of your Bishop so that he can see what kind of man I am, and then admit or reject me.[1]

The surviving correspondence reveals that twice before the two Belgian priests had explored the possibility of Father Conrardy serving at the leper settlement. Eleven years earlier Father Conrardy had taken the initiative and written to Father Damien after he had read one of the priest's letters that had been published in the *Annals of the Propagation of the Faith*. To Father Damien's surprise, Father Conrardy had offered to help at the leper settlement, citing Damien's lament over his isolation in a setting where there were too many lepers for one priest to care for. Father Damien had politely declined the offer because his countryman was not a member of the Congregation of the Sacred Hearts, and the Hawaiian mission was an exclusive project of the Sacred Hearts.

Father Damien had learned that Father Conrardy was a Belgian Walloon who had studied under the Jesuits and been ordained on June 15, 1866. He had previously served as a pastor at Stavelot, Belgium, and later in Hindustan for two years, where his ministry had been handicapped by repeated attacks of bronchial asthma.[2] In 1874, the year after Father Damien had become the resident priest at the leper settlement, Father Conrardy transferred to the United States to serve as a missionary to the American Indians. During his thirteen years of residency in Oregon, his asthma remained quiescent as he traversed the huge territory assigned to his care, a territory larger than the Kohala-Hāmākua District that had taxed Father Damien's strength.

In 1880, at a time when the prolonged absence of a confrere had precipitated a state of mild depression, a frustrated Father Damien had decided to accept Father Conrardy's earlier offer of help and mailed the priest an invitation to join him. A pleased but committed Father Conrardy was forced to decline, stating, "I could not leave my poor Indians, especially those on the reservation of Umatilla in the eastern part of Oregon."[3] Now the situation in Oregon had changed, Conrardy explained. The Jesuits had been given full control of the Indian mission in Oregon and were in the process of increasing the number of priests, sisters, and brothers. Father Conrardy had been given the choice of joining the Jesuit Order and remaining in Oregon or transferring to another mission post. Archbishop Gross, Father Conrardy's immediate superior, was encouraging him to join Father Damien.

It is not clear whether Father Conrardy's November offer was in response to a second invitation from Father Damien to come to his aid. In a July 1888 letter to a physician acquaintance, Father Conrardy claimed that "Father Damien had just written me, 'I beg you from the bottom of my heart to come to join me, to help me, and to replace me.'"[4]

Father Damien desperately needed assistance with his ministry. If all Sacred Hearts fathers, including Father Pamphile, were barred from the leper settlement, perhaps there would be no objection to a priest from another order. He promptly forwarded Father Conrardy's packet to Bishop Hermann with a cover letter pleading that his countryman be invited to serve at the leper settlement.

When Bishop Hermann received Father Damien's request, he carefully studied Father Conrardy's resume and the letter of recommendation from Archbishop Gross. He abhorred the intrusion of a Catholic priest from another order, but with two of his priests now confirmed lepers, what was he to do? Without question the priest described in the documents could become a valuable asset to the Hawaiian mission. He could assist and later care for the infirm Father Damien. Such a move would satisfy the superior general's concern over the lack of a confrere for Father Damien and at the same time protect the mission's priests from further contact with the infectious lepers. The major problem with the appointment of Father Conrardy was the priest's suboptimal education and his limited acquaintance with the Sacred Hearts modus operandi. Still, a second priest was needed at the leper settlement—and for the moment, Father Conrardy seemed the only viable candidate.

With some apprehension, Bishop Hermann decided to accept Father Conrardy's offer. Until his arrival, the two leper priests on the Kalaupapa Peninsula could confess each other, making unnecessary any future visits by Father Columban from Maui. So Bishop Hermann wrote to Father Conrardy, inviting him to join the Hawaiian mission as a secular priest at the leper settlement. He assured the Belgian that he could secure permission for this appointment from the prefect for the Propagation of Faith. The bishop forwarded a copy of this invitation to Father Damien.[5]

Neither Father Léonor nor the other Sacred Hearts' priests of the Hawaiian mission were pleased with the bishop's decision to allow an outsider to serve as a secular priest. The attention of the superior general and the world was focused on Moloka'i and the dying leper priest. By permitting an outsider to join Father Damien, it would appear that the Sacred Hearts Hawaiian Mission had not only abandoned one of their own, but that the Sacred Hearts priests were fearful of contracting leprosy. On November 28 and again on December 5, Father Léonor wrote to Father Damien stating that the superior general would certainly disapprove of a secular priest trained by the Jesuits serving at the leper settlement—and that if he were bishop, he would require Father Conrardy to complete a Sacred Hearts' novitiate before assigning him anywhere.[6]

While waiting patiently for resolution of the Father Conrardy offer, Father Damien labored furiously to complete the new dormitory for boys, and he expended his remaining charitable funds for the purchase of the essential winter clothing for the flood of incoming lepers. These funds were augmented by a Christmas contribution collected by Archbishop Gross of Oregon, and in a simple thank-you letter for the latest American contribution, Father Damien summarized how he had spent the funds to benefit the lepers. As always, he submitted the unsealed letter to his provincial for review prior to mailing. Father Léonor scanned what he considered to be a "thank-you note," and sent it on its way, never anticipating that the letter would be published.

Archbishop Gross promptly published Father Damien's letter in the *Catholic Sentinel*, which was circulated worldwide.

Your Excellency,

Your good letter of December 16 containing a check in the amount of $218.50 has been received. I thank your Excellency with all my heart, and each of the charitable donors. This sum gives witness to the generosity of your diocese and came just in time to pay a major portion of the supplies which I bought to distribute to the poor during the winter. I purchase only those things which are seldom provided, such as towels, calico, and quality shirts which the merchants give me at ten per cent discount. Our merchants in Honolulu save me many hundreds of dollars, and this helps me greatly in providing the necessities for those who are in need, having spent their six-dollar-a-year allowance for clothing.

We are well enough off with regard to good nourishment and lodging.

The number of lepers grows daily. They come to us from all points of our islands by order of the Board of Health, which does all in its power to make life comfortable for all the unfortunate lepers in our colony. The Ave Maria press, edited by Rev. D. E. Hudson of the University of Notre Dame, has published a small book entitled The Lepers of Molokai. On the last page of this little book you can see by some lines cited from my letter how I have been the past three years. Since then the disease has made some progress, slowly it is true, but to the point where it has now spread to my limbs and throughout my body. At present the sickness is only exterior, and I continue to be robust and able to attend to my duties.[7]

When Bishop Hermann received his copy of the Catholic Sentinel, he was disturbed because the letter dramatized the plight and struggle of a solitary leper priest and so encouraged future charitable contributions. Father Léonor's reaction was pure disgust. Bishop Hermann found himself in a quandary. If the interested American archbishop added Father Conrardy to his list of correspondents and then proceeded to publish the replies of both Father Damien and Father Conrardy, as apparently was his practice, the biased publicity could prove damaging to the image of the Sacred Hearts Hawaiian Mission. Father Conrardy would be heralded as the replacement Christian martyr of Moloka'i, garnering the credit for the Christian charity shown the lepers, overshadowing everything the Sacred Hearts had done. If, on the other hand, he now reneged on his permission for Father Conrardy to join Father Damien, he would soon be forced to station a Sacred Hearts priest on Moloka'i, a sacrifice he was reluctant to make.

SINCE DR. NATHANIEL EMERSON, the new president of the Board of Health, had initiated his relentless push for strict enforcement of the Segregation Ordinance, the *Mokoli'i* had dutifully transported an average of fifty lepers a month to the Kalaupapa landing wharf.[8] With each arriving group, five to ten children stepped ashore, each clutching a note written by Mother Marianne, requesting that Father Damien be their shepherd. With a smile and a warm greeting he always did so. In the Kingdom of God, children were special and were to be nurtured and protected. Thus the ministerial tasks before Father Damien became overwhelming. In addition to celebrating daily Mass and administering the sacraments, the increasing number of children required much of his attention, decreasing the time he could devote to the sick and the dying. A daily funeral became the routine. Fortunately, he was able to delegate a major portion of the responsibility for the care of the orphan boys to Brother Dutton, but the increasing number of orphan girls cried out for the Franciscan sisters. In a desperate effort to expedite matters, Father Damien circulated a petition among the lepers, requesting that the Franciscan sisters be invited to the leper colony to care for the orphan girls and the sicker of the female patients.

Rudolph Meyer, fully cognizant of the difficulties with which Father Damien was attempting to cope, kept his friend apprised of what he learned regarding the deployment of the Franciscan sisters: "As to the Sisters, they want to come, but they insist that a healthy priest accompany them to administer the Sacraments; but they are also needed at the Kapi'olani Home and at the Kakaako which has its own leprosarium. . . . Personally, I admit that it seems extremely harsh and unreasonable to demand that these poor women should go to live at the leper colony. It would be better if men were to come. But if the Sisters themselves really want to come, I do not think anyone would oppose it."[9]

WAVES OF DISCONTENT over the Father Conrardy appointment rose to tsunami height and battered the normally serene shores of the Sacred Hearts' Hawaiian Mission. To restore tranquility and correct what most considered a glaring mistake on his part, Bishop Hermann reversed himself and notified Father Damien via a letter that after careful reconsideration, Father Conrardy would be acceptable to the mission *only* if he first took a novitiate in Louvain, which would legitimize his entry into the Hawaiian Mission.[10] The bishop instructed Father

Damien to so notify Father Conrardy. Appalled by this reversal, Father Damien wrote his bishop:

> I have just received a letter directly from Father Conrardy (herewith enclosed) which has brought me great joy in the almost certain hope that this is a priest who, without any doubt, has a special vocation to be here with me, and who, when I shall be helpless, something that can happen any time now, would be able to keep the Catholic ministry going among the lepers.
>
> The last lines of your letter [to Father Damien], Monseigneur, have caused me great dismay, because your Lordship compels me to write him to the effect that he must first make his novitiate in Europe (which he cannot do). Besides, it is now that I need him most, and to get to the bottom of it, to write to him in this manner will spoil everything. Either he will stay in Oregon, or he will go to Mexico or elsewhere to the Jesuits.
>
> Therefore, I humbly beg of you to allow him to come as soon as possible. Once he is here and both parties, he and we, are satisfied, he could bind himself by temporary vows to your authority, such as the case with Joseph Dutton. . . . The circumstances in which I find myself being exceptional, why not come to my assistance in ways that are somewhat exceptional too?[11]

Father Damien's letter achieved its objective, and Bishop Hermann rescinded his stipulation that Father Conrardy first take a novitiate before joining the Sacred Hearts' Hawaiian Mission. In a short note to Father Damien he wrote: "Your letters of last week . . . have persuaded me to accede to your ardent desire. I have already written to Father Conrardy of my decision, and I added by way of a postscript my authorization for him to go directly to Moloka'i without first completing a novitiate. Understand that it is because of the status of your health that I have consented to deprive him of the advantage of religious training."[12]

DURING DECEMBER 1887, Father Grégoire's asthmatic attacks became so protracted that Dr. Peterson, the newly appointed government physician, advised Father Damien that Grégoire's death from asthma, not leprosy, was close at hand.[13] Father Damien promptly relayed this information to Bishop Hermann, who in turn delegated the matter to Father Léonor, the provincial. When Father Léonor realized that it was asthma, not leprosy, that was killing his priest, he called on Dr. Emerson at his home that very evening and petitioned the Board of Health to permit Father Grégoire to leave the leper settlement and return to the Kaka'ako Branch Hospital where his asthma had been relatively quiescent. Dr. Emerson was reluctant to honor such a request, as the board had previously done for Father Grégoire, fearing that it would establish a dangerous precedent. Other lepers would petition the board for permission to leave the settlement for reasons of health unrelated to their leprosy.

Father Léonor persisted, pleading for Father Grégoire's life, arguing that the priest would remain strictly segregated at the Kaka'ako Branch Hospital. After a lengthy debate, Father Léonor prevailed, and a compromise was reached. Dr. Emerson agreed to consult with other members of the all-Protestant board before rendering a final decision.

ONE JANUARY NIGHT in 1888, while Father Grégoire was experiencing one of his more protracted asthmatic attacks, a violent storm lashed the northern coast of Moloka'i, flattening the remaining thatched huts in the villages of Kalawao and Kalaupapa, lifting the roofs from a few of the wooden houses, and toppling St. Philomena's bell tower and steeple.[14] The next morning Father Damien, accompanied by Brother Dutton, surveyed the extensive damage. Brother Dutton had anticipated that the ailing priest, who had become a close friend, would be devastated at the sight of the fallen steeple—but no. To his surprise, he observed just the opposite. As Father Damien examined the remnants of the steeple, he saw himself like the steeple, broken and nearly useless. Were he able not only to rebuild the steeple but enlarge the church, he would not only salvage the structure, but he would be salvaging his waning usefulness. So Father Damien enthusiastically planned what he believed would be his last construction project—the dramatic doubling of the size of the St. Philomena Church and the rehanging of the deep-throated bronze bell.

A relieved Brother Dutton reminded Father Damien of the recent arrival of an Irish stonemason who had only minimal lesions of leprosy and who possessed the expertise to use slabs of volcanic rock with which to construct storm-proof walls for the new addition to the church. The use of stone, he pointed out, would add a touch of medieval charm to the structure and at the same time frustrate both the hurricane-force storms and the destructive jaws of Moloka'i's voracious termites.[15]

Without delay the project began. On most days Father Damien found time to work alongside Brother Dutton and the mason as they labored to double the size of St. Philomena. After donning his work clothes, Father Damien would carefully bandage his hands, which were now painful and swollen and covered with small ulcerations, the consequence of repeated minor trauma in areas where the skin had no feeling. The padding afforded by the bandages allowed him to grip his hand tools without undue discomfort, and he found he could still swing a hammer with accuracy sufficient to drive a nail—but with far less striking force than before. Spearheaded by Brother Dutton, a crew of *kōkua*, several lepers, and the expertise of the recently incarcerated stonemason, the work progressed steadily. Stone was cut from the makeshift quarry near the Kauhakō Crater in the center of the peninsula and carted to the building site, where it was used for the footings, the foundations, the flooring, and the exterior walls of the addition to the church.

Father Damien was pleased with the craftsmanship of the group effort. The architectural beauty of the emerging St. Philomena Church would surpass that of any church he had built in the past. In his imagination Father Damien envisioned the crowning touch to his creation: the giant bronze bell ringing majestically from the magnificent bell tower that he would build with wounded hands.

Observing the leper priest with the deformed face and the bandaged hands swing a hammer and lift slabs of volcanic rock into place was the emotional stimulus for the crews of carpenters trained during Father Damien's house-building program to labor long hours to replace the remaining thatched huts with substantial wooden houses. Within three months, the house-building project was completed—a tribute to the "master builder of Moloka'i."

AFTER HEATED DELIBERATION, the Board of Health granted Father Grégoire permission to leave the leper settlement and return to the Kaka'ako Hospital. Father Damien shook his colleague's hand for what he suspected would be the last time and helped him into a longboat at the Kalaupapa wharf. The following morning Father Grégoire, wheezing and gasping for air, arrived at the Kaka'ako Branch Hospital and was eased into a hospital bed.[16] Almost miraculously, within a few hours of Father Grégoire's arrival at Kaka'ako, the wheezing and chest tightness subsided and the priest began to breathe more normally. Exhausted by his ordeal, Father Grégoire fell into a sound sleep. When he awoke hours later he was breathing easily and announced that he was ravenous. The next two days were devoted to sleeping, eating, and saying his breviary.

The reason for Father Grégoire's severe asthmatic attacks while at the leper settlement is not known. The limited evidence suggests that an airborne inhalant unique to the Kalaupapa Peninsula was the precipitating trigger rather than an underlying psychosomatic factor.

Knowing that Father Damien would be anxiously awaiting word of his status, Father Grégoire wrote:

> Very dear and Reverend Father,
>
> Two days have passed since I have been here, and already my terrible asthma has left me as I predicted it would. I have become stronger; I do not cry any more; I eat well, and they take good care of me. . . . I cannot forget the distress which I have caused you. Please accept my sincere gratitude and always pray for your devoted brother in the Sacred Hearts of Jesus and Mary.
>
> Grégoire, Priest of the SS.CC.[17]

ON MARCH 22, the Board of Health responded to a request it had received the previous month from Father Damien for the wheels and axles with which to construct a horse-drawn cart for transporting supplies from the landing wharf to the boys' orphanage, which now housed over sixty. Dr. Emerson marveled at the continued dedication of the disabled priest. As a physician who had carefully avoided all physical contact with lepers, he had the highest admiration for the man who was deliberately sacrificing his life in order to help them. In place of the four wheels and two axles, a new horse cart was purchased. The minutes of the Board of Health meeting in April read simply, "A light, one horse cart to the settlement for the use of Father Damien in carting pai ai for the boys' establishment."[18]

At the April meeting of the Board of Health, Lorrin Thurston, the new prime minister, triumphantly entered the meeting hall and in a commanding voice read a letter from Charles Reed Bishop, the haole banker turned philanthropist:

Having been told that there are a number of young women and girls at the Leper Settlement on Molokai who have no proper protectors or guardians, and that it is the wish of the Government to provide such patients with houses separate from the general community of the settlement, and to place them under the immediate care of Christian women, either Protestant or Catholic, or both, I hereby request the privilege of paying for the cost of the houses . . . all to be erected under the direction of R. W. Meyer, Esq., and afterwards to be under the control of the Board of Health.

I wish to have it understood, if your Excellency grants my request, that in the control and treatment of the women and girls who may occupy the rooms to be provided, there shall be no interference, restriction, or discrimination on account of their religious faith.[19]

A motion to accept the philanthropist's offer was made, seconded, and unanimously approved. Rev. Hyde's promise to Father Damien that he would solicit funds with which to build a women's and girl's home at Kalaupapa had been kept.

Lorrin A. Thurston was ecstatic. In consultation with architects and building contractors, a plan for six all-wooden buildings to be constructed in the village of Kalaupapa was devised. The new complex would be called "The Bishop Home for Women and Girls." Two of the buildings would serve as hospitals for the most seriously ill, three would serve as domiciliaries for women and girls, and the sixth could serve as the convent for the Franciscan sisters, provided they could be induced to serve as nurses and supervisors.

In anticipation that Bishop Hermann would ultimately deploy the Franciscans at the leper settlement, Thurston extended an exploratory invitation to Mother Marianne.[20] In the negotiations that followed, Thurston further indicated that each sister would receive a monthly stipend of $20 along with a weekly supply of uncontaminated food. He communicated his offer to Bishop Hermann, who insisted that the government's offer be submitted in writing so that all concerned might study the proposition. To no one's surprise, Mother Marianne promptly accepted the challenge to nurse the lepers on Moloka'i with the proviso that a healthy priest be stationed at Kalaupapa expressly for the purpose of ministering to the sisters. She was adamant. No priest with leprosy would ever be allowed to touch the wine and the bread of the Holy Communion to be served to her sisters. Once a healthy Sacred Hearts' priest was stationed near the proposed Bishop Home, she and two of the sisters would be happy to serve the Lord on Moloka'i.[21]

This placed Bishop Hermann in an extremely awkward position. Two of his priests—possibly three if he counted Father André—had contracted leprosy from ministering to lepers in the Islands. Which Sacred Hearts' priest from among those remaining in the Hawaiian Mission could he ask to risk becoming the next victim? Father Conrardy would be stationed at Kalawao where direct physical contact with lepers would in time result in his infection, so he undoubtedly would not meet Mother Marianne's definition of a "healthy" priest. The bishop believed that he had no choice but to assign the post to one of the younger priests, someone who would adhere to his directive: under no circumstance make physical contact with a leper, a leper's possessions, or his food.

WHEN FATHER LOUIS-LAMBERT Conrardy arrived in Honolulu from San Francisco on Saturday, May 12, 1888, no one from the Sacred Hearts Mission was on hand to welcome him. As Brother Dutton had done, he asked directions to the Cathedral of Our Lady of Peace and made his way there to introduce himself to the bishop. Throughout the initial interview, Bishop Hermann seemed preoccupied and distant. When politely asked to do so, the bishop declined to introduce the newcomer to members of the Board of Health, so Father Conrardy was forced to take the initiative and make an appointment to introduce himself. Once he showed the board his letter of invitation from Father Damien, he was granted permission to proceed to the leper settlement.

Because most of the Sacred Hearts fathers and brothers resented the intrusion of a priest from another religious order, the newcomer was treated with a cold indifference. Father Conrardy did manage a conversation with Brother Bertram, who recorded in his journal that the inhospitality Father Conrardy was experiencing at the hands of the Sacred Hearts was "not bothering" him, for he was above such pettiness.[22]

Pained by his chilly reception but determined to proceed, Father Conrardy showed a newspaper reporter Father Damien's letter of invitation. The next day the Protestant newspaper, the *Hawaiian Gazette*, announced the fact to the world: "Father Conrardy, a Belgian priest,

has arrived from San Francisco to join Father Damien at the leprosarium of Molokai. All Christians, Catholic and Protestant, must
respect and admire the zeal and abnegation of this minister of Jesus
Christ, who in this way, voluntarily sacrifices himself for love of poor
suffering humanity, as before him, Father Damien has done."

Bishop Hermann was beside himself. The new priest had had the
audacity to make an unauthorized press release, permitting the
Hawaiian Gazette to create another Christian hero and martyr—and
the blame could be laid squarely at Father Damien's feet.

Following the press release, the inhospitality at Our Lady of
Peace Cathedral intensified. No one smiled, nodded, or spoke to
Father Conrardy. Undeterred, Father Conrardy left for Moloka'i on
the first available boat.

In contrast to the cool reception he had received in Honolulu,
Father Conrardy was warmly greeted by Father Damien and a large
contingent of lepers when he stepped ashore at Kalaupapa. The leper
priest smiled broadly and in fluent French he blessed the Walloon for
his courage and compassion for a brother priest. From the outset the
two men got along well. In the course of their daily endeavors, the fric-
tion that had marred the relationships between Father Damien and
Fathers André Burgerman and Albert Montiton never surfaced.

During the 2.5-mile buggy ride from the landing wharf to
Kalawao, Father Damien gave his new confrere an overview of the
leper settlement, detailed the status of his deteriorating health, and
introduced Father Conrardy to the Hawaiian language. The balance
of the morning was spent on a tour of the settlement and the formal
introduction to its inhabitants. After a lunch that was prepared by
Father Damien and that Father Conrardy hardly touched because of
a "nagging headache," the duo completed the tour of the Kalaupapa
Peninsula.[23] Father Conrardy was quartered in the larger of the two
rooms on the main floor of the rectory, the room reserved for drug
storage—the same room in which Father Grégoire had stayed when
incapacitated by asthma.

In a letter to Father Imoda at the College of St. Ignatius in San
Francisco, written a month after his arrival, Father Conrardy related
his initial impressions of the leper settlement and his concerns regarding contracting leprosy:

As for leprosy, I do not think that one can escape it here, if in fact the contagion comes from contact or breath. Although we do not live with them, it is necessary to come into contact with them in a thousand different ways. I believe that there is no other means of escaping but by living in faith.

We have now about eighty boys. I spend most of my time with them, and in addition, I live in the same house as Father Damien, who, as you know is a leper. This malady has a unique odor which is very disagreeable. The sight of it alone is absolutely repugnant.

At first the sight of poor Father Damien, whose ears, face, neck and hands are in a pitiful state, caused me to lose my appetite, and I suffered continuously from a headache. But now I have overcome both of these problems.[24]

The second month of Father Conrardy's sojourn at the leper settlement passed peacefully. He had come to serve, and serve he did in a subservient role as the supervisor of the boys' orphanage, a task he undertook without complaint or bickering. His motivation to risk death from leprosy was not because he coveted fame or the title of "Christian hero," but because of a genuine desire to serve God by imitating as closely as possible the martyrdom of Christ. In a letter written in July, he stated: "From the time I was twelve I prayed to become a martyr for the faith, but not seeing how I could sacrifice myself for Christ, I prayed daily to be stationed in the worst place in the world. That is why last December I refused a parish in South America near Buenos Aires where I had been offered a good parish at an annual salary of 1500 piasters. I fervently believed that life among the lepers would be worth more than all temporal comforts."[25]

Father Damien found in Father Conrardy the confrere he had waited so long for, but because of the priest's brazen publication of his letters, he was fearful that the bishop might insist that the new arrival leave the settlement and complete a regular novitiate. In an effort to counter such a move, he dictated a lengthy letter to the secretary of the superior general.

I informed you in my last letter of the critical situation in which Providence has seen fit to place me, far from all confreres and prevented from going to a confessor because of my malady. I wish anew to review with you my situation which has been improved due to the arrival of a compatriot priest, Father L. L. Conrardy. . . .

He has been here for over two months, living with me, leper though I am, as a very good confrere and companion. He performs many services in our large leprosarium, and most importantly, he helps me watch over and direct the 80 orphans who live with me. Being an accomplished scholar, he has already begun to speak the native Hawaiian tongue.

In daily endeavors he conducts himself as if he were one of us, living by the Vows of Poverty, Chastity, and Obedience, content and happy while living isolated from the world among the lepers. I take the liberty of addressing the Superior General, and through him the members of our Order, asking that they consult with each other to determine the best means to retain this good priest, and to obtain for him permission to be attached to us in some way . . . without obliging him to pass through a regular novitiate. . . .

I have great need of his services which each day become more indispensable.[26]

TO ADDRESS THE problem of ministering to the Franciscan sisters at the leper settlement, Bishop Hermann sent a circular letter to his missionaries, asking who among them would be willing to take up residence on the Kalaupapa Peninsula. Father Clément declined to respond, but all of the rest of the fathers replied affirmatively. Bishop Hermann pondered, then chose Father Wendelin Moeller because of his terse response: "My answer is in my Rules." This alluded to Article 241 of the Rules of the Congregation of the Sacred Hearts, which stated: "By the vow of obedience the professed religious engage themselves to do what the superior commands, and not to do anything he forbids." In the bishop's opinion, Father Damien had repeatedly violated Rule 241, and here was a priest who claimed to use Rule 241 as his spiritual compass.

AFTER SERVING AS the resident physician at Kalaupapa for only five months, Dr. C. A. Peterson tendered his resignation when twenty-two of the lepers petitioned the Board of Health to fire him. He was succeeded by S. B. Swift, M.D., who received an annual salary of $3,500. On July 1, 1888, Dr. Swift and his wife moved into the physician's house.

SEVENTY-YEAR-OLD Father Charles Pouzot, the venerable priest in Hilo who had introduced Father Damien to the practice of medicine, sought the aid of Dr. Arthur Mouritz who had reestablished his private practice on the Big Island after leaving the leper settlement. Father Charles' chief medical complaint was "repeated attacks of acute indigestion," an ailment that responded promptly to Dr. Mouritz's prescriptions. During the initial examination of the priest, however, Dr. Mouritz discovered "a more interesting condition . . . specific neuritis affecting the nerves of the left forearm and hand, due to leprosy, which was quiescent and had aborted, but it had left marked atrophic changes in the muscles, the typical hollow between the thumb and forefinger . . . defective sensibility of the hand and skin of the forearm; there were also atrophic changes in certain areas of the body, higher in color than the neighboring skin, and insensitive; thermo-anesthesia and symmetrical enlargement, or bulbing of the ulnar nerve above and below the elbow joint."[27] This documented that Father Charles was the third Catholic priest in Hawai'i to have contracted leprosy.

In 1894, the number of Sacred Hearts priests who had contracted leprosy rose to four when Dr. Mouritz had the opportunity to reexamine the sixty-year-old Father André Burgermann, the priest who had developed a peculiar skin disease initially thought to be elephantiasis. Dr. Mouritz confirmed the suspicion that Father André had a case of arrested leprosy with involvement of his forearm very similar to that of Father Charles. "In addition, Father André had ataxic symptoms, and the 'Lightning Shocks,' similar to Father Grégoire, together with incoordination, disturbances of sensation, and loss of reflexes."[28]

Of the four Catholic priests who had dared make physical contact with lepers to minister to them, and who subsequently became lepers, historians acknowledge only one "hero."

IN THE SUMMER OF 1888, Robert Louis Stevenson, the famous Scottish author, sailed from San Francisco in the luxurious 95-foot yacht *Casco*, bound for the South Sea Islands of the Pacific in search of a warm climate more favorable to his pulmonary tuberculosis. The emaciated author, who weighed less than a hundred pounds, was accompanied by his wife Fanny, his stepson, his mother, a cook, and a maid. Stevenson had begun to experience small pulmonary hemorrhages, and each time he coughed up blood his doctors reiterated their advice that he seek out a benign climate less stressful to his lungs.

A secondary goal of the Pacific odyssey was to meet the

renowned leper priest of Moloka'i. Stevenson had been interested in the career of Father Damien since the evening in 1878 when Charles Stoddard had mesmerized him with the tale of the humanitarian who was able with quiet courage to confront the most hideous, deforming disease known to mankind. When he later learned that the leprosy bacillus that was destroying Father Damien and the tuberculosis bacillus that was ravaging his own lungs not only killed their victims slowly, but looked remarkably the same when viewed through a microscope, he viewed Father Damien as a kindred spirit, almost a brother. If Father Damien managed to survive another eight to twelve months, Stevenson promised himself that he would greet the famous leper priest face to face.

24

Hawaiian Sunset

My peace I give to you.... Let not your heart be troubled,
neither let it be afraid.
—John 14:27

FATHER CONRARDY FOUND little difficulty in slipping into Father
Damien's daily routine. Within three months he had acquired a sufficient command of the Hawaiian language to allow him to assist Father
Damien with many of his ministerial tasks, freeing the time for the
leper priest to bandage his ulcerated hands and help with the enlargement of St. Philomena Church. After his Hawaiian language tutorial,
Father Conrardy attended to his personal correspondence, and his letters to Archbishop William Gross in Oregon were replete with his
observations and impressions of the leper settlement. To the conster-
nation of Father Damien's immediate superiors, Archbishop Gross
shared portions of his protege's letters with the Catholic community
by offering them to the press, and when the clippings from the American newspapers belatedly found their way to the desks of Bishop Hermann and Father Léonor, their reaction to Father Conrardy's somewhat biased accounts were predictable.

Bishop Hermann, frustrated and embarrassed by his inability to
control the newcomer, wrote to the superior general to solicit his aid:
"On the subject of Father Conrardy . . . If you have not yet given a
favorable response to Father Damien's wishes in this matter, I would
absolutely insist that Father Conrardy make a novitiate according to
the rule before he is definitely admitted into our mission. . . . the articles in the newspapers instigated by him, and a conversation of fifteen
minutes have sufficed to dispel the illusion. . . . In any case I have no

335

confidence in his alleged virtues; they do not rest on humility and they are not governed by obedience."[1]

Dr. Emerson was equally annoyed with Father Conrardy's reporting, especially those letters that ignored the substantial financial contributions of the board while criticizing its insensitivity to the fate of the lepers. He grimaced when Father Conrardy sensationalized the courageous work of the dying leper priest and credited the major improvements in the lives of the lepers not to the Board of Health nor the Kingdom of Hawai'i, but to the combined efforts of the two Catholic priests, thus focusing the spotlight of public acclaim on both Father Damien and himself. Dr. Emerson acknowledged that Father Conrardy was risking his life, a sacrifice he personally would not make, but the false impressions conveyed in the letters had to stop. Exasperated, the Board of Health sternly censured Father Conrardy for the continued publication of his self-aggrandizing letters that were critical of the policies of Kingdom.[2]

James Sinnett, a male nurse from St. Louis, Missouri, learned of the desperate need for nurses from one of Father Conrardy's letters published in a St. Louis newspaper, and in a letter to the Board of Health offered his service as a nurse at the leper settlement on Moloka'i. His motivation for volunteering was similar to that of Brother Dutton. He had led an adventurous, not too exemplary life, for which he now wished to atone by serving his fellow man. His talent was nursing, and his resume detailed his experience at Mercy Hospital in Chicago. If the Board of Health would provide passage money from the United States to Hawai'i, he volunteered to serve as a lay brother under the supervision of Father Damien.

Dr. Emerson recognized that a major weakness in the hospitals was the lack of competent nursing care. Ideally, six or more professionally trained nurses were needed. He reasoned that Brother Dutton had become a passable nurse under the tutelage of Dr. Mouritz. Perhaps James Sinnett would prove to be of genuine assistance, so he instructed the secretary of the board to correspond with Mr. Sinnett and ask for letters of recommendation from the doctors and the clergy in St. Louis. If Mr. Sinnett came well recommended, he announced that the board would pay his passage to Hawai'i. Within a few weeks, sterling letters of recommendation did arrive, and Dr. Emerson sent the passage money to Sinnett.

In response to Dr. Emerson's continued urging, the board voted to close the Kaka'ako Branch Hospital by the end of the year. This would free the sisters currently serving as nurses at Kaka'ako for reassignment elsewhere. In a conference with Dr. Emerson, Mother Marianne reaffirmed that she and two additional sisters were prepared to go to Moloka'i once the convent under construction was judged suitable for occupancy and a healthy priest was in residence in Kalaupapa. So that she might better manage the problems that the Franciscan sisters would confront, Mother Marianne went directly to Emerson and made application for a one-day visit to the leper settlement. Both the convent for the sisters and the housing at the Bishop Home for Women and Girls were reportedly under construction, and she wished to judge for herself the functionality of the Bishop complex. Additionally, she understood that Father Damien's health was deteriorating and that he might benefit from competent nursing care.

Dr. Emerson listened politely to Mother Marianne's request, marveling at the composure and raw courage she displayed. "Mother, you are indeed a brave woman to go there," he exclaimed, "but I shall not allow you to go alone. I shall go with you."[3] The stories about how terrified Dr. Emerson was of leprosy were legend, and Mother Marianne wondered whether this display of gallantry was because the doctor felt honor bound to protect a nurse, or simply because she was a woman she should not be allowed to journey unaccompanied into Hawai'i's little hell.

On a "gray, unpleasant" Wednesday evening in late September, Mother Marianne and her female companion from the convent, Olinda Gomes, were escorted by Dr. Emerson to a dingy-looking steamer, the *Lehua*, the only nonleper transport that made periodic voyages to Moloka'i and the Kalaupapa Peninsula.[4] High waves buffeted the steamer as she cleared the harbor, and within a few minutes the three passengers were seasick. There were no passenger staterooms aboard the *Lehua*, and the only sleeping accommodations provided were "little shelf bunks" lining two of the walls in the vessel's dining room. Dr. Emerson made his way to one of these and spent the night battling nausea. Mother Marianne desired more privacy than the group stateroom provided, so she and Olinda Gomes remained topside where the air was fresh and the splash of the waves against the steamer's hull drowned out the low rumble of the engines. Within an hour the two women were wet and cold from the ocean's spray. The forlorn nun in her ocean-soaked habit looked so pitiful that the ship's captain magnanimously offered the two ladies his small cabin for the night, the only room where privacy was assured.

A few hours before dawn the *Lehua* reached the Kalaupapa Peninsula and anchored about half a mile offshore where the sea was relatively calm, allowing the three weary passengers to doze for an hour after the miserable night of seasickness. As soon as the sun painted the eastern sky a pale pink, the captain, worried about an approaching storm, hurried the passengers down the rope ladder to the waiting long-boats with the warning that everyone wishing to depart the leper set-tlement that day would have to be back on board within three hours—or risk being stranded at the settlement for at least a week.[5]

Gathered at the wharf to welcome the visitors were a group of lepers headed by Ambrose Hutchison, who apologized for Father Damien's absence. He helped Mother Marianne into Father Damien's buggy, which he had borrowed to take her to Dr. Swift's home for breakfast. As they neared the resident physician's house, a gaunt and disfigured Father Damien galloped up to join the group, apologetic for not being on hand to greet them at the landing wharf, explaining that he had come as soon as he had finished celebrating early morning Mass at St. Philomena Church.

Dr. Swift's wife, an attractive, well-educated young lady resigned to face several years of isolation with her physician-husband and their young son, served a hearty breakfast to the visitors while Father Damien and the other lepers waited dutifully outside the protective picket fence. Following breakfast the group toured the Bishop Home for Women and Girls complex, which consisted of two dormitories, two small hospitals, a dining hall, the nearly completed convent, and a cookhouse and laundry. Mother Marianne was elated with what she saw and complimented Father Damien for having chosen so lovely a site for the Bishop Home complex.

Next on the tour were the two orphanages at Kalawao. Mother Marianne's reaction was muted, and she later informed the sisters at Kaka'ako that while Father Damien had done a fine job of providing shelter and food for the boys and girls, what was now needed was "a woman's touch."

The tour ended abruptly when a blast from the *Lehua*'s whistle summoned everyone to the departure wharf before the approaching storm battered Moloka'i's northern coast. Father Damien saw the visitors off and witnessed a surprising spectacle as the longboat carrying Mother Marianne and Olinda Gomes was tossed about by tall waves on its way to the *Lehua*. He saw Dr. Emerson stand up in the bow of the bobbing boat and, bracing his feet against the sides of the craft, spread both arms high overhead to hold his raincoat as a protective barrier against the spray from the incoming waves that would have soaked the two ladies. As he watched approvingly, he mused that there was much to admire in the behavior of the Protestant physician.[6]

OCTOBER WAS A MONTH in which Dr. Emerson exercised his authority to improve conditions at Kalawao and Kalaupapa while he closed the branch hospital at Kaka'ako. He authorized Rudolph Meyer to spend up to $500 to erect a dining hall for the residents of Father Damien's newest dormitory. Meyer was also instructed to determine whether the board or the Catholic Church had paid for the materials with which the boys' dormitories had been built. If the Catholic Church had provided any portion of the money or building materials, Meyer was to reimburse the Church, for it was the new policy of the Kingdom of Hawai'i to own all of the permanent structures at the settlement with the exception of the churches.

While the board appreciated the volunteer efforts of Father Damien and Brother Dutton, Dr. Emerson proposed that the two be paid a regular stipend for their invaluable secular services. He doubted that either man would accept the money, but he wished to make the gesture nonetheless as a means of saying "thank you" for their initiative with the building projects and their exceptional care of the orphans. Rudolph Meyer was authorized to pay Father Damien $25 a month for serving as the superintendent of the boys' home, and Brother Dutton was to receive a smaller monthly stipend for serving as the nurse for the eighty-eight orphan boys. Meyer later reported that while both men were pleased with the salary offer, neither took the money.[7]

The board's decision with regard to another request prompted the easiest vote of the year. Father Léonor wrote to ask that funds be appropriated with which to construct a separate house at the settlement for the exclusive and occasional use by Bishop Hermann or himself. Father Léonor was politely informed that the board "would endeavor to provide suitable quarters for the chaplain," but were not prepared at the present time to go to the expense of constructing a building that would see only occasional use. Father Léonor had never visited the leper settlement, and Bishop Hermann had done so twice—but only at the insistence of a member of the royal family.

In mid-October the dismantling of the Kaka'ako Branch Hospital complex began. Three wooden houses, a schoolhouse, the jail, and the fence that surrounded the Kaka'ako complex were disassembled and shipped by boat to the leper settlement. The girls' schoolhouse and several houses to be added to the Bishop Home complex were scheduled to be dismantled and transported the following month. To provide for a short-term receiving station for the exclusive quartering of lepers destined for Moloka'i now that the Kaka'ako Branch Hospital was closed, land was purchased in Kalihi upon which a small hospital was constructed. From 1865 to 1878, the original Kalihi Hospital had served as the holding hospital for the lepers.

FATHER DAMIEN'S LEPROSY continued to progress at a steady rate. As the nerves to his right hand succumbed to the invasion of the bacilli, he experienced increasing difficulty writing as a result of a frustrating combination of weakness and pain in his hand and fingers, plus numbness in his fingertips. This curtailed the length of any letter he composed. For longer letters, especially those requiring him to use English such as the ones written to Charles Stoddard or Rev. Chapman, he relied on Brother Dutton to take his dictation, correct the grammar, and polish the English diction.

One Sunday in October, while celebrating Mass, Father Damien staggered, then collapsed before the altar in St. Philomena Church.[8] The congregation gasped, then watched in paralyzed silence as Brother Dutton rushed to the side of the fallen priest, who was attempting to rise but could not. Brother Dutton noted that Damien was coherent, but flushed with a high fever. He helped the priest to his feet, then half-carried and half-dragged him to his floor mat in the rectory. The congregation realized that the inevitable demise of the leper priest was occurring right before their eyes. Calmly and with no hesitation, Father Conrardy stepped forward and resumed the celebration of the Mass. Within a week Father Damien's fever subsided, but a deep, paroxysmal cough developed that left him breathless, forcing him to sit until each paroxysm ended. Nonetheless, he managed to resume some of his normal activities, which included working on the addition to the St. Philomena Church, but now his movements were slower and more deliberate. Any physical labor required him to take frequent rest breaks. It was disturbing for those working with him to observe the tremendous effort it now required for him to complete the simplest of tasks.[9]

When Bishop Hermann and Father Léonor learned of Father Damien's collapse before the altar, they immediately instructed Father Conrardy to assume those duties Father Damien was unable to carry out. Then it was announced that Father Wendelin Moellers from Oʻahu was the "healthy" Sacred Hearts priest chosen to be stationed in the village of Kalaupapa to serve as the chaplain for the Franciscan sisters at the Bishop Home.

Suddenly, Father Conrardy, with all of his flaws, was viewed as indispensable. This forced Bishop Hermann to reverse himself once more and declare that Father Conrardy was proving of invaluable assistance at Kalawao now that Father Damien was too ill to carry out his priestly responsibilities. The bishop wrote: "He [Father Conrardy] has gained the affection and the admiration of the lepers by his compassionate manner and they would detest me were I to remove him now. Besides, he really does good. . . . The illness of Father Damien has made rapid progress; for some weeks he has not been able to celebrate Mass. Father Conrardy now provides all of the priestly services at the establishment. As he does not have contact with the rest of the mission, he is less dangerous to us than if he were to be forced out against his will."[10]

After Father Conrardy was assured by the bishop that he was in a position to render essential service to the Hawaiian Mission, he deliberately crafted another letter for publication in which he pictured himself as a martyr approaching the stature of Father Damien. This time he was careful not to offend the Board of Health and heaped praise on the Hawaiian government for providing so generously for the lepers. A month after its submission, the letter was published in the *Gazette* of Louvain:

> The government furnishes each leper with a pound of meat each day along with three pounds of poi, which resemble potatoes. In fact, the lepers are not badly off with regards to material goods. The government does very much for them, for the time they live,—about five to ten years.

. . . Father Damien has witnessed the population turn over three times. How many times will it be given me to see it renewed? Shall I become a leper myself? It is probable. Precautions are easy to recommend, but difficult to observe. . . .

I have not told you in this letter of the good Father Damien, who soon will be dead, a victim of his own charity. In England and America they refer to him as a martyred hero. It is my privilege to be with and to live with him. Leprosy does its damage; it travels to his eyes, his ears, his nose, his throat, his hands, his lungs!

The poor Father suffers a great deal. He is all disfigured; his voice is almost gone. If you could see him as I do, in his little room, lying on his bed on the floor, tears would come to your eyes to see a man who has accomplished so much for the thousands of lepers, reduced to so miserable a condition, and so little can be done to soothe him. . . . I live with him, and we eat together. My repugnance is overcome; I am in the hands of the good God.[11]

While the Board of Health may not have found fault with the letter, the Catholic clergy of the Hawaiian Mission would have despaired at Father Conrardy's lack of humility in his quest for praise.

THE TWO DAYS before Mother Marianne and Sisters Leopoldina and Vincent were to take up residence at the Bishop Home convent, it was apparent to all that Father Grégoire's illness was terminal. While his asthma was quiescent, he was febrile and experiencing excruciating pain caused by the badly infected skin ulcers that covered his body. Sister Crescentia, who was serving as his nurse, tiptoed to his bedside accompanied by Sister Leopoldina, one of the nurses chosen to go to the leper settlement, to ask that he bless this soon-to-depart nurse. The seventy-year-old missionary, once one of the handsomest and tallest of the Sacred Hearts fathers, roused himself and, while Sister Leopoldina knelt at bedside, he slowly raised his "almost lifeless hand" and in a "deep solemn voice" asked God to watch over the young lady who was about to risk contracting the disease that was killing him.[12]

Father Grégoire died the next day, the first of the Sacred Hearts priests in the Hawaiian Mission to succumb to leprosy. The following morning the Franciscan sisters attended the Requiem Mass for the repose of his soul offered by Father Léonor in the Chapel of St. Philomena at Kaka'ako. The press took little notice of Father Grégoire's death. In the obituary there was no mention of his numerous two-week-long visits to Moloka'i to assist Father Damien's ministry to the lepers, no mention of his fearlessness—some would say "carelessness"—in ministering to the lepers in his Maui congregations, and not even a whisper that this man deserved to be called a Christian martyr.

The day following the Requiem Mass, Mother Marianne arose after a restless night, suffering from one of her frequent bouts of an illness that retrospectively may have been pulmonary tuberculosis.[13] Mid-afternoon, the three Franciscan sisters, accompanied by Father Corneille Limburg—a Sacred Hearts priest serving on O'ahu whom Bishop Hermann had assigned to accompany the sisters until Father Wendelin Moellers could join them at Kalaupapa—boarded the *Lehua*, the same cramped interisland steamer Mother Marianne and Dr. Emerson had taken in September. On hand to bid the party farewell were Bishop Hermann, several of the priests serving on O'ahu, and Dr. Emerson of the Board of Health. Sister Leopoldina was impressed that of all those present, it was the Protestant physician who seemed the most grateful and at the same time the most concerned for their safety. "I have never forgotten his kind voice as he held my hand. 'May God bless you,' he said and turned quickly away."[14] At 5 P.M. the vessel departed the port of Honolulu with the three Franciscan sisters who would become the first professionally trained nurses to serve the one thousand lepers on Moloka'i—a daunting, nearly impossible task.

The *Lehua* anchored briefly off the Kaka'ako pier and took aboard twenty men and twenty women and children who were herded like cattle into a barricaded pen in the well of the main deck. Sister Leopoldina recorded (without punctuation) that the outcasts "were put in the cattle's place with no shelter and no bed poor creatures if they were sick and there was not as much attention paid to them as there would be to the sick cattle."[15]

Mother Marianne and her companions were shown the *Lehua*'s only sleeping accommodations, the narrow shelves in the stifling dining salon; but the three ladies chose instead to attempt to sleep on the open deck in camp chairs. It proved to be a long night. The waves increased in height, and within minutes the three sisters were leaning over the rail, seasick. Around midnight, a fine, chilling rain wet their faces and clothing. Toward dawn the rain ceased and the weary, water-drenched sisters could make out the silhouette of the towering *pali* that blocked the light from the stars.

With the sunrise the sea calmed, and the longboats had no difficulty landing the passengers. Father Conrardy and a welcoming committee of lepers were waiting to greet the newcomers. Mother Marianne's "lovely face was beaming with smiles[;] she looked so perfectly happy that it made us all feel at home," commented Sister Leopoldina. Once safely on the landing wharf, the arriving women and children surrounded the smiling mother superior, keeping a discreet two arm lengths from her habit, ever careful never to reach out and touch her. In her gentle voice Mother Marianne invited the girl lepers to follow her to the Bishop Home complex located near the Kalaupapa Church, and obediently, they trailed after her.[16]

Father Damien managed to leave his room where he had been confined by a fever for several weeks and ride to Kalaupapa in his buggy to welcome the sisters. Mother Marianne wrote:

> He conducted us to the orphanage of the leprous girls at Kalawao. "My children," he told them, "I shall die soon but you will not be abandoned. The Sisters whom you see have come to care for you. You will return with them to Kalaupapa." There was general regret. All the girls wept. Finally they accompanied the Sisters. There were two whom it was impossible to tear away from him. Clinging to his feet they cried, "Father, we want to stay here until your death." It was necessary to leave them and it was not until after his death that we went to search for them. This time they came willingly to Bishop Home, where they passed away shortly afterward.
>
> He took us also to visit the boys' orphanage and he showed us how to make their garments. At a later visit, he asked us, suddenly, "Will you take care of my boys when I am gone?" Three times he repeated the question. We promised him . . . and we have kept our promise.[17]

A few days after their arrival, Sisters Leopoldina and Vincent, while exploring the Kalaupapa Peninsula, decided on the spur of the moment to visit the dying leper priest, and hiked the 2.5 miles across the peninsula to Kalawao. Sister Leopoldina later recorded:

> We stopped at his little garden gate, and Father Damien was there to meet us. How thin and sick he looked. His face so ashy and yet he was

so cheerful and happy. I can still see him as he stretched his poor disfigured hands to heaven, thanking our Divine Lord that help had come.

"I knew I could not last long," he said, "and for many years I have been begging our Dear Lord to send someone to fill my place, and now I see He has answered my prayers. . . . I will not have to leave my flock alone. They will have better care than I could give them. Only I would like to finish my church. That will be my last work. Then I will be ready to say, 'Lord, I have finished the work you gave me to do.' Now come, Sisters, you must see my church. It is nearly finished," he said as he led the way.

His little old church was like a wing attached to the new concrete church which was partly finished. He clasped his hands together and said so pitifully, "Oh, if I can see my church finished, then I'm ready to go." His eyes glistened telling us how he had enjoyed the building of that wonderful church. The mason work he did mostly with his poor swollen hands. Every joint was twice the natural size. He was so pale and thin and looked so like death I could not keep the tears back. I could see at once he did not fancy tears. "Come," he said, "I will take you to the kitchen," and he stepped away as light as a bird. . . .

"Now, Sisters," he said, "I have had a clean woman prepare lunch for you."

"But, Father," I told him, "we cannot. Mother has forbidden us."

He looked so very sad, and then he said, "You go and take your lunch. I will make it right with Mother, and I will do the penance. The poor lady [the cook] did her very best, and she will be displeased if you do not accept it. You will be doing me a great favor. I am sure you will not refuse me."

What could I do? It would be cruel to disappoint the poor priest. . . . Of course, we could not enjoy the lunch. Sister Vincent was smiling all the time, and when we were alone she laughed heartily and said, "Oh, how glad I am that you are the oldest. If it is wrong you will have to answer for it."

"I cannot see the wrong," I said. "I feel that it would be wrong to hurt the feelings of the poor old sick priest and charity is the greatest of all virtues."

When we met him in the yard his face was burning. "I hope you have enjoyed your lunch," he said. "Do not let it worry you. I will tell mother all about it, and take all of the blame. I will answer for it."

The next day he [Father Damien] came rushing into the house, the only time he was ever in the house, and before he said "Good morning" or anything, he dropped on his knees at Mother's feet and begged pardon and said he wished she would give him a penance because he knew it was his fault. I do not know what answer Mother gave him, but she told us it gave her a shock. It was so unexpected to see the poor priest kneeling at her feet.[18]

Sister Leopoldina was assigned the task of cleaning and dressing the leprosy lesions of the women and girls housed in the Bishop Home, a task that occupied several hours each day. On one particularly warm morning, she took the women patients indoors to dress their wounds as she wished to shield them from "the blazing sun." While she was busy with this operation, Dr. Swift made one of his infrequent and always brief visits. When he saw what she was about he exclaimed, "For God's sake, Sister, what are you doing to have this crowd around you for hours? It is frightful; it must be stopped! . . . you are sure to be a leper, you cannot keep on like this, if you do before ten years have passed you are sure to be a leper. Remember what I tell you."[19]

Concerned about the prospect of becoming infected, Sister Leopoldina told Mother Marianne about the physician's warning and prediction of doom. "Mother," she said, "what will I ever do should I become a leper? I, too, would be barred away from the very life of my soul."

Without a moment's hesitation, Mother Marianne repeated her previous promise: "You will never be a leper. You must believe me. Neither you nor any of our Sisters will ever become a leper."[20] This utterance was prophetic. Not one of the scores of Franciscan sisters who have attended lepers in Hawai'i ever contracted leprosy.

ON NOVEMBER 27, James Sinnett, the male nurse from St. Louis, Missouri, arrived. Sister Leopoldina described him as "a tall, thin Irishman with narrow drooping shoulders and sunken chest. He had a long thin, pale face and an ugly little cough. He did great penance during his time here. He would not accept any bed but a plank. He was very neat and clean."[21]

"I shall call you 'Brother James,'" exclaimed a grateful Father Damien, and he immediately capitalized on James Sinnett's nursing expertise by assigning him to the boys' orphanage to assist Brother Dutton. The number of orphan boys in the two dormitories had increased to over a hundred, and the daily cleansing and dressing of their skin lesions was consuming most of Brother Dutton's time.

During the ten weeks before the complications of Father Damien's leprosy forced him to bed with terminal disease, Brother James noted with admiration the priest's struggle to continue to minister to the lepers and steal time to complete the work on St. Philomena Church: "I have seen Damien covered with dust and perspiration . . . as he toiled among the lepers at manual work beneath a tropical sky, or as he dragged himself from one death bed to another, or bound up the open sores of some poor diseased leper."[22]

Because Brother James also possessed a superior command of the English language, Father Damien accepted his offer to serve as his personal secretary when correspondence in English with flawless diction was desired. It was this same Brother James who became Father Damien's private nurse during his last weeks on earth.

From the safety of Honolulu, Bishop Hermann monitored the activities of Father Conrardy. To the superior general he wrote: "Here is my current assessment of the gentleman [Father Conrardy]. His troublesome letter writing before and for a short time following his arrival turned everyone against him. But his behavior at Molokai has reversed this first impression. He has learned the native language, and his friendly, but careless manner has made him very popular with the lepers. It appears that he positively is trying to contract leprosy. He has favorably impressed Father Corneille Limburg during his ten day stay; and Father Wendelin who has observed him for a month now is very satisfied with him. Therefore, I earnestly desire to retain him.[23]

TRUE TO HIS WORD, Edward Clifford, the artist-philanthropist, did journey to the Hawaiian Islands following his visit to India.[24] After obtaining official permission from the Board of Health, Clifford boarded the *Mokoli'i* at 5 P.M. on Monday, December 17, toting several cases of Gurjun oil, the latest treatment for leprosy, and a large wooden crate filled with presents for Father Damien from his English supporters, which included "a water-color painting of the Vision of St. Francis, by Mr. Burne Jones, sent by the painter."[25]

Clifford believed his most precious gift for Father Damien was the Gurjun oil for the treatment of leprosy. This oil, obtained from a fir tree grown in the Andaman Islands off the coast of Burma, was mixed with lime water to make an ointment as "soft and smooth as butter." The prescribed treatment, which had been reported to be curative for a group of lepers in a prison, consisted of rubbing the oil all over the body for two hours twice each day followed by drinking half an ounce of an equal amount of lime water and the oil. When Clifford had written to Father Damien about the use of Gurjun oil several months earlier, the priest had replied that he had actually tried Gurjun oil once before with no observable improvement, but so as not to offend his English guest, he agreed to try the remedy once again. Clifford later commented: "I think he had not much faith in the Gurjun oil, but at my request he began using it, and after a fortnight's trial, the good effects became evident to all. His face looked greatly better, his sleep became very good instead of very bad (he had only been able to sleep with his mouth open), his hands improved, and last Sunday he told me that he had been able that morning to sing Mass, the first time for months. One is thankful for this relief, even if it should be only temporary."[26]

Clifford was quartered in the guest house reserved exclusively for the "healthy" visitors. He had been thoroughly indoctrinated regarding the necessary precautions, and he had no intention of eating or drinking anything which lepers might have handled. He noted in his journal, "Father Damien would never come inside the guest house where I was staying, but sat in the evening on the steps of the veranda and talked on in his cheery, pleasant, simple way."[27]

The principal purpose for Clifford's visit to the leper settlement and Damien was to attempt to capture the essence of the man in sketches and paintings. If all went well, he planned to publish an illustrated account of his two-week visit.[28] On several occasions Father Damien posed for Clifford on the second floor balcony of the rectory while he read his breviary and answered questions about his ministry to the lepers. Clifford recorded in his journal:

> Some of my happiest times at Molokai were spent on this little balcony [second floor of the rectory], sketching him and listening to what he said. . . . I offered to give a photograph of the picture to his brother in Belgium, but he said perhaps it would be better not to do so, as it might pain him to see how he was disfigured.
>
> He looked mournfully at my work, "What an ugly face!" he said; "I did not know the disease had made such progress. Looking-glasses are not in great demand on Molokai!"[29]

DR. NATHANIEL EMERSON wanted the Board of Health to be an active participant in the upcoming Christmas celebration at the leper settlement. Two days before Christmas he notified Ambrose Hutchison, Mother Marianne, and Father Damien: "The Board of Health and other friends in Honolulu, send their Christmas greetings to you, and through you to all the afflicted ones at the Leper Settlement on Molokai. The Lehua or some other steamer will convey to you a quantity of gifts for the children, boys and girls at the Settlement, as an expression of their sympathy and aloha, and as a proof that they desire you not to be left out in the cold in the celebration of this glad anniversary. I would request you . . . to act as a committee to see that the various things are fairly and wisely distributed among the children. A Merry Christmas to you all, from your friend, N. B. Emerson."[30]

From Rudolph Meyer, Father Damien received a short Christmas greeting:

> I am enclosing a bank note for the clothes to be purchased for the orphan boys who are under your care. The amount was calculated for 100 boys, and solely for the boys. The clothes should be distributed gradually as the need arises. . . .
>
> We have collected a sizeable sum of money with which we have purchased all sorts of toys and other things which are to be distributed by the Christmas Committee of which you or Father Conrardy may be a part, if you wish it . . . .
>
> With my best wishes for a merry Christmas[31]

On Christmas morning, Clifford and Father Damien surprised each other with a gift. "I gave him [Father Damien] on Christmas Day a copy of Faber's hymns, which had been sent him by Lady Grosvenor's three children. He read over the childishly written words on the title page, "Blessed are the merciful, for they shall obtain mercy," and said very sweetly that he should read and value the book. . . . He was not a sentimental kind of man, and I was therefore the more pleased that he gave me a little card of flowers from Jerusalem, and wrote on it: 'To Edward Clifford, from his leper friend, J. Damien.' He also wrote in my Bible the words: 'I was sick, and ye visited me.'"[32]

December 31 was Clifford's last day at the settlement. Late in the afternoon he carefully placed his paintings and sketches into a long-boat at the landing wharf and bid good-bye to the priest who "gives himself no airs of martyr, saint or hero—a humbler man I never saw."[33] As the two men waved their final farewell, neither knew that the Robert Louis Stevenson party aboard the *Casco* had left Tahiti and was headed north, bound for Honolulu. At long last the famous author and the leper priest might meet.

Once in Honolulu, Clifford elected to remain and enjoy the sun and surf of Waikīkī Beach until he completed the manuscript describing his two weeks at the leper settlement. Upon his return to England, *Father Damien: A Journey from Cashmere to His Home in Hawaii*, was accepted for publication by Macmillan, London. The book unreservedly eulogized the saintlike career of the leper priest and was well received by the British public.

THE YEAR 1888 ended with 1,011 lepers incarcerated at the leper settlement. New lepers that had stepped ashore at the landing wharfs during the year numbered 571, and 236 resident lepers had been buried in wooden coffins, courtesy of Father Damien's coffin-building committee. The sight of a wild pig in the vicinity of the cemetery, a rare occurrence in 1888, was no longer a cause for dread and cursing as it had been in 1873, but an opportunity to seize the intruder and issue an invitation to friends and neighbors to attend a fine luau featuring a feast of pork cooked in an *imu*, the shallow underground oven of the Native Hawaiians.

25

Requiem for a Priest

Hold then Thy cross before my closing eyes;
Shine through the gloom, and point me to the skies;
Heaven's morning breaks, and earth's vain shadows flee;
In life, in death, O Lord, abide with me.
—Henry Francis Lyte

IT WAS OBVIOUS to all onlookers in December 1888 that Father Damien was in the terminal stage of leprosy. He was losing weight, and the exhaustion due to the intermittent high fevers and the anemia of chronic infection made every movement an effort. He walked slowly and stiffly, like an aged man, mouth open, taking gasping breaths, leaning heavily on his cane. Those few areas of his face still free from the advancing lesions of leprosy were pallid and thinner. He coughed often, always raising his hand to cover his mouth. Breathing through widely parted lips turned his attempts to smile into grotesque grimaces. The warm smile that consoled and gladdened was now only a memory.

Sister Leopoldina described Father Damien's last days in her journal:[1]

> I can never forget his last visit to the home [Bishop Home]. It was one of those dark, chilly, unpleasant days near the end of December, although we never have snow or frost here we have dark chilly unpleasant days during the fall and winter months, and those days are often accompanied with rain, wind, and frightful rough sea. . . .
>
> Of course, he would never go into the house. I can see yet as he was sitting on the veranda, his face and lips deathly gray, covered with purplish

351

red inflamed tubercles that are always accompanied with dreadful chills and high fever. During the damp fall months the lepers suffer more with those inflamed tubercles than they do during the hot summer. And I know that the saintly Father was suffering with that strong chilly wind moaning and howling as it swept the fine rain around the corners of the house whistling around him from all directions.

His voice was gone. He could speak only in a whisper. He looked so cold, his cassock so thin, and he had no coat. And yet, he was so happy and cheerful telling us that he had his church finished, and "I wish you would come to see it." Mother told him, "Father, when you send the cart, we will go."

He only remained a little while, and it was the only time he ever came without visiting the lepers in each cottage for they loved his cheerful manner. How they would flock around him for they knew he would have something interesting to tell them. . . . Poor Father, his last visit was only a few minutes and he was suffering so he could not visit them. I think no doubt he had a high fever.

The next day the cart came and again we went creeping over that horrid rocky unkept road. Father Damien was at the gate when we drew up. He rushed out to welcome us. When we entered the yard we were met by Mr. Dutton, and Father then led us to his new church. How happy he was! His manner was like a child who had received a great gift. He was so overjoyed about his new church and to think he had been able to finish it. He looked sick as he had the day before. His cassock was badly soiled with lime, cement, and paint. His priestly hands were a grayish purple and badly swollen. The joints of those sacred anointed fingers were twice their natural size and some of them with ulcers. . . .

"Now, Sisters," he said, "I have finished the work our Dear Lord has given me to do, and I am ready now to go home.[2]

Bishop Hermann and Father Léonor monitored the drama at the leper settlement and knew that Father Damien was dying, but neither had any intention of risking a visit to the leper settlement to comfort a brother in Christ. Leprosy was a deadly, contagious disease, a malady any prudent man avoided at all cost. The two priests in residence could attend to Father Damien's final needs. In the exchange of New Year's greetings, Bishop Hermann rationalized that his primary responsibility was directing the Hawaiian Mission, a burdensome task that precluded a visit to Moloka'i at "this time."[3]

In mid-January, a delegation from the Board of Health made a brief visit to the leper settlement to make certain that the Franciscan sisters were properly and comfortably situated. Assured that this was the case, they next checked on the progress of the construction of the new dormitory for boys; the number of male orphans now exceeded one hundred, and more were scheduled to arrive. Satisfied with the status of the dormitory, the delegation held an open meeting to hear any complaints the lepers might wish to lodge. They were disturbed to learn that drunkenness and social misconduct were again prevalent in the settlement now that Father Damien had been forced to discontinue his daily rounds. Reportedly the *kōkua* were the worst offenders, but an increasing number of lepers were joining the ranks of the disturbers of the peace. Another condition with potentially serious consequences was the shoddy restoration of the houses and buildings that had been moved from the Kaka'ako Branch Hospital.

Upon his return to Honolulu, W. G. Ashley, the board's secretary, wrote to Rudolph Meyer authorizing him to expel any *kōkua* who was guilty of misconduct or drunkenness.[4] Ashley further commented that Mother Marianne had confirmed that two of the houses that had been transported from the Kaka'ako were, in her opinion, unsafe for human occupancy. Ashley assured Meyer that the board held the contractors to be responsible for the poor workmanship and would see to it that the defective construction was promptly corrected.

ON FEBRUARY 12, 1889, a faltering Father Damien eased himself into the chair at his desk and wrote what proved to be his last letter to Father Pamphile. Not only did he have difficulty holding his pen because of the pain and weakness in his fingers, but his failing eyesight made it hard to see what he was writing.

To my dear brother, Rev. Father Pamphile,

Considering the nature of the disease from which, by the will of God I am suffering, I have abstained from writing to you as well as to the rest of the family for some time. But it seems to me that you all ought to write me at least as often as formerly, and even more.

Still I am always happy and contented, and though seriously ill, all I desire is the accomplishment of the Holy Will of the good God.

I have at my side a priest from Liege, Father Conrardy, and Father Wendelin is in the second village. Besides these I have here two Brothers, who help me in the care of a hundred orphans who are under my charge. There are more than 1000 lepers in the leper colony. We also have Sisters, three Franciscans in the hospital.

The English of London, Protestant as well as Catholic, are most sympathetic towards me and the work to which I have consecrated myself.

Say a greeting from me to all the Fathers and Brothers of Louvain as well as Gerard and Leonce and the entire family. At the altar, which up until now I have been able to mount daily (however, with a certain difficulty) I do not forget any of you, and in return, I pray that you pray for me who is dragging himself gently toward his tomb, that the good God fortify me and give me the grace of perseverance and a good death.

Your devoted brother in the SS. Hearts
J. Damien De Veuster[5]

THE LUMBER ARRIVED with which to build a small house for Father Conrardy, who had indicated that he had every intention of remaining indefinitely at the leper settlement as the successor to Father Damien. To remain in the rectory that had housed two leper priests was an invitation to an early death. Bishop Hermann and Father Léonor did not object. Fewer than 1 percent of the Catholic population in Hawai'i resided at Kalawao, and that 1 percent was dangerously contagious. For the immediate future they could tolerate Father Conrardy.

FATHER WENDELIN WAS 39 years old when he volunteered to serve as the "healthy priest" that Mother Marianne insisted be stationed at Kalaupapa. He stood 5 feet 6 inches tall and had a slim, malnourished appearance. His speech and movements were swift, giving the initial impression that he was a nervous, impatient priest. His peers jokingly referred to him as Father "Rapid Fire."[6] Although he was protectively quartered in Kalaupapa, well removed from the majority of the lepers, he had permission to go to Kalawao to minister to his brother priest, the dying Father Damien. When he did so, he faithfully did as he had been instructed, and never did he touch a leper. The wafer of Holy Communion was always dropped from a respectful height onto the tongue; and in the case of a dying leper, he had Father Léonor's dispensation not to touch the diseased eyes, hands, and feet.[7]

When Father Wendelin visited Father Damien for the first time, he obeyed Bishop Hermann's order and asked that the priest sign a codicil to his will naming Father Clément and himself executors, replacing Brother Dutton.[8] Damien, anxious to set his earthly affairs in order, signed the document and turned over $3,700—the balance of the charitable donations in his personal bank account—to Bishop Hermann. The distribution of his few material possessions Father Damien entrusted to Joseph Dutton, the man who had become his confidant. This left only one prize asset to protect—William, his faithful old horse, who had pulled his buggy so many times back and forth over the narrow, bumpy road between Kalawao and Kalaupapa. After signing the codicil to his will, he sold William, his saddle, and his bridle to Father Conrardy for the meager sum of 25 piasters. The bishop could have the charitable money. This was proper, for the bishop could be trusted to distribute it to benefit all of the lepers. William was another matter, and he saw to it that his aging horse would be properly cared for by a Belgian who shared the same love of animals as did he.

IN EARLY MARCH, the Board of Health issued a visitor's pass to Dr. Prince A. Morrow, a physician from New York City who was a specialist in infectious disease and an editor of an American medical journal, for the purpose of gathering the medical case histories from fifteen lepers, including that of Father Damien, for presentation at an international medical meeting addressing the role of microbes in human disease. Dr. Swift's medical records of the fifteen cases chosen for study were judged to be far too sketchy to be of genuine scientific usefulness, so the task of compiling more acceptable case reports was assigned to Brother Dutton.[9]

Accompanying Dr. Morrow was a photographer from Honolulu, William Brigham, whose assigned task was to take photographs of the fifteen lepers. Father Damien knew he was near death; nevertheless, he permitted the photographer to pose him.

One picture of Father Damien shows him seated on a two-tier bleacher, surrounded by sixty-three of his orphan boys. He is hatless, allowing all of the grim features of advanced leprosy to be seen. His face is grossly swollen. He is breathing through an open mouth, as his collapsed nose had obstructed his nasal airway. His right ear, enlarged three to four times its normal size, juts out from the side of his head at an ugly 45-degree angle. His right hand is heavily bandaged, and the arm is in a sling beneath the mantle of his cassock. The left foot, visible beneath the hem of the cassock, is also heavily bandaged. This was a priest barely able to amble from his rectory to the adjacent church.

For Brigham's close-up photo of his upper torso, Father Damien is wearing his battered, broad-brimmed black hat and squinting at the camera through his wire-rimmed glasses, which are perched on a sunken piece of flesh that once was the bridge of his nose. Too weak to stand motionless for the prescribed number of seconds to make the photograph, the priest is seated in a wooden armchair. The facial disfiguration is more clearly visible, revealing the loss of eyebrows. The right arm, still in a sling, is hidden beneath the mantle, while the left hand has been deliberately positioned on the arm of the chair closer to the camera's lens to magnify its misshapen features—multiple protruding tubercles, several of which are badly ulcerated; multiple joints swollen to twice normal size—a hideous spectacle.

A few days after the case reports had been mailed to Dr. Morrow, a dying Father Damien received a severe reprimand and a warning from Father Léonor. After listing the several items that Father Damien had requested and that were being shipped to Moloka'i, the provincial stated coldly:

> Now, my very good Father, I am going to say something which will give you pain, but you will see that we [the Sacred Hearts Congregation] are not the cause of it. A member of the Board of Health has informed us of their decision regarding the letters which are being dispatched to all corners of the world for the intention of making yourself known and admired at the expense of others. The next letter which is published will result in the Bishop being penalized. So you see then, that it is not only we who are displeased with you. Why this wish to distort the truth in order to speak highly of yourself and to receive sums of money? . . . He [Father Conrardy] wishes to remain, now that you have become powerless. It would be unfortunate if they should make him leave, for then we would have sacrificed another. Father Wendelin would not be able to do all of the work because of his health. Try then to correct him [Father Conrardy], and to do good in silence for the glory of God, without seeking the approbation of men. God will be able to give all the reward that you are seeking.[10]

Father Léonor also wrote to Father Conrardy, warning him that the board would expel him from the Islands were he to write additional letters containing any half-truths that would embarrass the board. Father Conrardy's response—apology or silence—is unknown. His letter writing to former colleagues continued unabated, and an occasional letter was published.

On March 18, Father Damien received a welcome congratulatory letter from the Reverend Mother Judith in Honolulu, one of the ten Sacred Hearts sisters who in 1863 had made the voyage with him to Hawai'i. The sisters were planning a day of celebration to commemorate the twenty-fifth anniversary of their safe arrival in the Islands.

> As tomorrow is the big day of jubilee of your arrival in the Islands, I am happy to send you my felicitation and to assure you that you will never be forgotten in the prayers of the entire community, and that you will not be forgotten by all of your companions of the voyage who will celebrate the Jubilee. Reverend Father, we ask the good St. Joseph to obtain improved health for you if it is the will of the Sacred Hearts, for we know that you do not desire anything else. . . .
>
> I received a letter from your good Brother Joseph who informed me that you were lacking bedclothes as well as some other things, which is why I am sending you another package similar to the one we sent last week.[11]

WHILE FATHER DAMIEN'S health was deteriorating, another event that would impact the Damien story was unfolding. On January 25, 1889, after a voyage of thirty days, the yacht *Casco* with the Robert Louis Stevenson party entered Honolulu Harbor. Physically, Stevenson felt better than he had in months and attributed the improvement to the relaxing sea voyage and the uninterrupted hours aboard the *Casco* to work on his latest novel, *The Master of Ballantrae*.

Stevenson was hailed as a celebrity, and within a few days of his arrival he called on King Kalākaua. The king, flattered to be recognized by so important a person, was jubilant when he discovered that the Scottish haole was a monarchist and a fine poker player. While sipping champagne and playing cards, Stevenson and Kalākaua enjoyed evenings together, exchanging Hawai'i's ancient legends for the poetry and novels in English and American literature. During one of these sessions,

Stevenson informed the king of his interest in meeting Father Damien and was told that all he need do was apply to the Board of Health for a permit to visit the priest at the leper settlement. If need be, the king promised to use his influence to see that his new friend was granted the permit.

Stevenson equivocated as he and his wife debated the advisability of his proposed visit to the leper settlement. Fanny understood her husband's desire to meet Father Damien face to face, but contended that the risk to the health of a man already crippled by pulmonary tuberculosis far outweighed any possible benefit.

Anxious to complete *The Master of Ballantrae* before venturing to Moloka'i, Stevenson rented a house on Waikīkī Beach about 4 miles from Honolulu, far enough removed from the capital to limit the number of the curious and the uninvited. A small shack adjacent to the main house became his workroom where he spent most of his days writing, dressed only in pajamas.[12] Occasionally when he coughed, the sputum was blood tinged, an ominous sign that his pulmonary tuberculosis was far from quiescent. As he labored on the manuscript, he pondered whether or not to go to Moloka'i. After several days of wrestling with the Brobdingnagian question, he decided to go—even if the visit might shorten his life.

ON FEBRUARY, 6, 1889, Keanu, the convicted murderer who had permitted Dr. Eduard Arning to transplant leprous tissue into his right forearm in 1884, was transferred from Honolulu to the newly constructed jail cell at the leper settlement. This was done on the recommendation of Dr. Mouritz, the settlement's former resident physician, who counseled that other prisoners in the close confinement of Honolulu Jail were certain to become infected should Keanu remain in Honolulu. Keanu was placed in the small, poorly ventilated jail cell at Kalawao where he languished until his death. During his prolonged incarceration, it is not known whether he ever asked for or was visited by a clergyman of either faith.

To prove to the world that leprosy could be transmitted by the inoculation of diseased tissue from a leper to a healthy person, Dr. Arning presented his data on Keanu to the First Congress of the Society of German Dermatologists. The initial response of the scientific community was favorable until it was disclosed that Keanu had been intimately exposed to leprosy in his family setting prior to the transplantation experiment. The informant was none other than Dr. Swift, the resident physician at the leper settlement.[13]

DURING THE FIRST two weeks of March, despite a debilitating fever with its attendant fatigue, Father Damien continued to drag himself to St. Philomena each day for prayer and meditation.[14] The cough that accompanied the fever and the weakness and that had initially been nonproductive now produced a thick, difficult-to-raise, greenish yellow sputum. Pneumonia, the angel of death for the aged and the infirm in the nineteenth century, was devouring Damien's lungs. After he became too weak to make the short trek to the church, he remained in the rectory, spending most of the day lying on the thin straw mat on the floor that served as his bed. Brother James assumed the role as Father Damien's personal nurse, and when the dying Belgian was too weak to resist, Brother James had the mat replaced by a hospital bed with a firm mattress, clean sheets, and a pillow, the first Father Damien had enjoyed since childhood.

On March 27, Brother Dutton rushed to Father Damien's bedside waving a letter that had just arrived from Father Hudson of the University of Notre Dame. He excitedly exclaimed that Father Hudson had purchased a large replacement bell for the new bell tower atop the enlarged St. Philomena Church. Father Damien struggled to sit up, and once sitting, managed a partial smile. Once the bell was in place, the St. Philomena Church project would be finished, and he could die a happy man. He then dictated a thank-you note along with the instructions for shipping the huge bell. Brother Dutton closed the letter with the promise to send Father Hudson the chalice Father Damien had used in his last Communion service.[15]

When notified by Dr. Swift that Father Damien's illness was in its terminal phase, Father Wendelin dutifully rode his horse to Kalawao each day to minister to his dying colleague. Following his visits he did as instructed by the bishop and carefully recorded his observations and the conversations he had with the dying priest: "Thursday, March 28, he began to stay in his bed. . . . From March 28 on he did not leave his room again. That day he arranged his temporal affairs. After having signed his papers he said to me, "How content I am to have given all to the Bishop, now I die poor; I have nothing of my own.""[16]

Once Father Damien was too weak to leave his bed, Father Conrardy and Brother James initiated a midnight ritual that brought St. Philomena to his bedside. Shortly before midnight Father Conrardy would go to the church accompanied by Brother James to get the Holy Sacrament. With Brother James leading the way, lighted taper in hand and ringing a hand bell for Father Damien to hear, the two slowly returned to the rectory and proceeded to bedside, where Father Conrardy administered the Holy Sacrament.[17]

Two weeks before Father Damien died, Father Wendelin wrote:

Saturday, the 30th, he prepared for death. It was truly edifying to see him; he appeared so happy. When I had heard his general confession I made my confession to him; afterwards we renewed our vows to the Congregation. The next day he received the Holy Viaticum. During the day he was cheerful as was his custom. "Do you see my hands?" he said, "All of my sores are closing; the scab is becoming black; this is a sign of death, you know. Look at my eyes, too; I have seen so many dying lepers, I cannot be mistaken; death is not far off. I have a great desire to see the Bishop [Bishop Maigret] once more, but the good God will call me to celebrate Easter with Him. May God be blessed in all!"[18]

On April 2, Father Damien received Extreme Unction from the hands of Father Conrardy. Later in the day when Father Wendelin visited him and knelt at his bedside to pray, Father Damien said confidently, "How good God is to have allowed me to live long enough to have two priests at my side to help me in my last moments, and the assurance to know that the good Sisters of Charity are here. It will be my Nunc Dimittis. The future for the lepers is assured; I am no longer necessary, so in a little while I shall go above."

"When you are there, Father," Father Wendelin said to him, "do not forget the orphans you leave behind."

"Oh, no," he replied, "If I have any influence with God, I will intercede for all those who followed me to the leper settlement."

Father Wendelin, sensing that he was at the bedside of an extraordinary priest, asked that Father Damien bequeath him his mantle as the Old Testament prophet Elijah had done for Elisha, to anoint the younger man as his successor.[19] Father Wendelin viewed himself as Father Damien's successor and wished to experience the symbolic transfer of authority.

Squinting into the sunlight, for bright light hurt his eyes, Father Damien replied, "Oh, what would you do with it? It is filled with leprosy. My blessing I will give you." With tears in his eyes, Father Damien blessed both Father Wendelin and the Franciscan sisters for whose coming he had prayed so long.[20]

Unexpectedly, Father Damien rallied, and for a few days he seemed stronger, and his appetite improved. Dr. Swift indicated that this improvement would be but a brief moment in time, a time in which the sisters and members of his congregation might kneel at bedside to say good-bye, and for the next few days there was a continuous flow of visitors to Father Damien's bedside.

While Father Damien was still lucid, Father Wendelin inquired as to where the priest wished to be buried. Without a moment's hesitation, Damien replied that his choice was to be placed at rest under the *pū hala* that had been his first shelter sixteen years earlier. Moloka'i was his home; he wished to remain forever in the churchyard where so many of his beloved "brothers, sisters, boys and girls" had been laid to rest. Father Wendelin promised it would be done as he wished, that a tomb would be prepared beneath the branches of the old *pū hala*. Father Damien smiled weakly and said, "This is another of my wishes that our Dear Lord has granted me."[21]

Two days before Father Damien's death, Rudolph Meyer coaxed his mule down the ever-treacherous *pali* trail to pay his final respects to the Catholic who had been such a good friend.[22] That same day Mother Marianne asked Sister Leopoldina to take the children to the valleys abutting the *pali* and gather flowers and ferns for the soon-to-take-place Requiem Mass and funeral service. She and Sister Vincent were going to Kalawao to receive Father Damien's last blessing and to see to the final arrangements for his burial.[23]

During his morning rounds on Saturday, April 13, Dr. Swift found Father Damien struggling to breathe. He noted that the priest's skin was hot and flushed, indicative of a high fever; and most disturbing was the observation that his feeble cough was unable to clear the congested airway. Dr. Swift removed his stethoscope from his small black doctor's bag and intently listened to the air being drawn into and then expelled from the priest's lungs. The normal breath sounds were absent, replaced by the ominous sounds of consolidated pneumonia. Death was near.

Turning to those present at bedside, Dr. Swift slowly shook his head. He instructed Brother James to give Father Damien another quinine tablet to lower the fever and suggested that the priest would be more comfortable in a semi-sitting position. Then he hurried from the rectory to his house and returned shortly with his camera, tripod, and glass photographic plates to take a deathbed photograph. He asked Brother Dutton to prop Father Damien up so he could photograph his face and hands. Brother Dutton dutifully obliged, gently placing two pillows behind the priest's shoulders and head. Dr. Swift's photograph reveals the stressed facial features of a man gasping for breath through an open mouth and the severely ulcerated fingers of both hands, which have been pulled from under the bedclothes and positioned so they would appear in the picture. Father Damien's forehead, nose, cheeks, and ears are swollen and misshapen. The death scene captured in the photograph is disturbing because of the agony present.

Father Conrardy knelt next to Father Damien's bed and read from his *Liturgia Horarum*: "From the realm of death deliver my soul, O Lord. Once I was dead but now I live—forever and ever. I hold the keys of death and the nether world. Come, let us return to the Lord; for he was torn, that he may heal us; he was stricken, and he will bind us up. After two days he will revive us; on the third day he will raise us up, that we may live before him."

Brother James was in constant attendance, doing what little he could to ease the pain and make Father Damien as comfortable as possible. When conscious, Father Damien was aware of the presence of two figures in the room, figures no one else could see. One figure stood at the head of his bed, the other at the foot. Father Damien pointed to the figures and spoke to them, but those present shrugged their shoulders and attributed Father Damien's hallucinations to a delirium caused by his high fever.

That evening Father Wendelin arrived and later recorded: "A little after midnight he received Holy Communion for the last time; he would soon see Him face to face. From time to time he lost consciousness . . . he recognized me, spoke to me, and we said our farewells.[24]

Father Wendelin left Kalawao at 1 A.M. for the return ride to Kalaupapa to celebrate the scheduled Mass later that morning. He wrote: "Monday, April 15, I received a note from Father Conrardy which told me that Father was in his agony. I hastened to return to him, but on the way a courier met me and told me of his death. He died quietly as if asleep, after having passed nearly sixteen years in the midst of the horrors of leprosy. The good shepherd had given his life for his sheep."[25]

When notified of Father Damien's death, Mother Marianne and Sister Leopoldina placed the burial supplies in Father Damien's buggy that had been brought for them and were bounced and jostled as William pulled them over the ruts and bumps of the narrow road that connected Kalaupapa with Kalawao. Sister Leopoldina recorded in her journal:

> When we reached the home there was dead silence everywhere. The poor boys were in little groups here and there like sheep without their shepherd. As they could not understand English and being strangers to them we could not fill their good Father's place.
>
> We were met by Father Conrardy. He was so overcome he could not speak and great tears were streaming over his thin pale cheeks. It seemed to me, Mother was never so beautiful. Her wonderful eyes were not filled with tears like mine. Her round velvet-like cheeks and the lovely peaceful smile on those full cherry lips was like bright sunshine in this gloomy place.
>
> She told Father Conrardy we wished to get to work, and we will see to Father Damien's remains after he is placed in his casket. Father led us to a clean place in the yard where they had put on two benches a rough board box in the shape of a coffin, and then we went to work. With skillful hands our Mother transformed that ugly box into a very beautiful casket. The outside she neatly covered with fine black serge and decorated it beautifully with silver headed tacks. The inside she padded and lined with white satin neatly pleated and edged with beautiful white lace. She lined the lid with white and covered it with black serge and decorated it with silver headed tacks. . . . Then the Fathers, after dressing the remains of the saintly priest in his beautiful white vestments, placed him in this pretty casket and carried him to his new church. . . . Mother was a real marvel. . . . Until late into the night she was trimming hats with crepe and making black sashes, for the next day was to be Father Damien's funeral.
>
> It was a most delightful morning, the bright sun and cool breeze from the mountains. Mother and Sister Vincent went in the little cart and the women and girls walked with me. . . . we enjoyed the long three mile

walk in the shade of the mountains and arrived in time for Mass. . . . Reverend Father Wendelin preached a very good sermon telling us how we should follow the example our good Father had given us. The church was well filled. The sermon, of course, was in native. . . . When the service was over we formed a procession for the funeral moving slowly around the side of the church where they had made a good large cement vault under the good old pu hala which had sheltered the saintly priest when he was young and strong.

It reminded me of our Holy Father Saint Francis and his Lady Poverty, but the good old tree was not clothed in rags, it was clothed beautifully in white. A vine had sprung up under the tree and the little tender vine had crept all around the long and drooping leaves and covered them with downy white flowers that had filled the air with sweet perfume. They placed the pretty casket in a strong rough box and slowly lowered the remains of the saintly priest down into his vault.[26]

Over the grave, the mission erected a large cross of black marble bearing the inscription:

> V.C.J.S.[27]
> Sacred to the Memory
> of the Rev. Father
> Damien De Veuster
> Died a Martyr to the Charity
> for the afflicted Lepers
> April 15, 1889
> R.I.P.

26

Accolades and a Preacher's Curse

*And while he was at Bethany in the house of Simon the leper,
as he sat at table, a woman came with an alabaster flask of
ointment of pure nard, very costly, and she broke the flask and
poured it over his head. But there were some who said to themselves indignantly, "Why was the ointment thus wasted?"*
—Mark 14:3–4

WHEN THE *Pacific Commercial Advertiser* announced that the Belgian priest had died from the complications of leprosy, there was a
spontaneous outpouring of adulation from the Hawaiians for the man
who had sacrificed his life to comfort their outcast family members
and friends, the lepers of Moloka'i. Several groups began collecting
money with which to erect a grand memorial to honor the life of
Father Damien. At Waikīkī, Robert Louis Stevenson read and reread
the obituary announcement, then turned to his wife Fanny and
remorsefully told her that the priest he had hoped to meet had died
while he was vacillating over the travel arrangements.

The following Sunday, Stevenson was startled to learn that the
Reverend Doctor Charles Hyde, a senior pastor of the Congregational
Church, a man in whose home he had been a dinner guest on several
occasions, was resentful of the accolades being heaped upon the "hero
of Moloka'i." Hyde was insistent that the leprosy that had felled Father
Damien was due to the priest's sinful indiscretion of sleeping with
Hawaiian women who were infected with syphilis. After all, Hyde contended, knowledgeable physicians like Dr. Fitch maintained that leprosy
was the fourth stage of syphilis, and he was convinced that Dr. Fitch was
right. Furthermore, Rev. Hyde decried the self-serving publicity the

Catholic Church was spreading throughout the Islands about the many contributions made by Father Damien. What the priest had accomplished, in Hyde's opinion, was insignificant in comparison to what the Board of Health and others had done for the lepers. Father Damien was a fallen priest who should be quietly forgotten, not praised.

Stevenson found himself in a quandary. The good name of the man he had held in high esteem was being defamed by a reputable clergyman. Had the priest led an exemplary life or not? That was the unanswered question. Stevenson felt compelled to learn the truth and rationalized that it wasn't too late to journey to Moloka‘i and interview those who had known the priest and witnessed both his accomplishments and possible immoral conduct. He discussed making a belated visit to Moloka‘i with Fanny, who rather reluctantly gave her consent. So Stevenson made application to the Board of Health for permission to visit the leper settlement for the stated purpose of including his observations in *The Eight Islands*, a collection of essays about Hawai‘i that he was preparing for publication. In his application to the all-Protestant Board of Health, he made no mention of his desire to investigate or comment on the Father Damien controversy.

The Board of Health deliberated on Stevenson's request for permission to visit the leper settlement, then denied it on the grounds that granting it would establish a dangerous precedent. Dr. Emerson envisioned that other journalists would make similar requests, destroying the effectiveness of the strictly enforced segregation policy. Stevenson, however, would not be denied. During one of his weekly poker sessions with King Kalākaua, he appealed the Board of Health's decision, arguing that the board had allowed other journalists and professionals to visit and later publish their observations—Professor Charles Stoddard and, most recently, the English painter Edward Clifford. Why the discrimination? His book, *The Eight Islands*, wouldn't be complete without mention of Moloka‘i and its lepers. King Kalākaua responded by personally intervening, and Stevenson was granted a one-week stay at the leprosarium.

IMMEDIATELY FOLLOWING Father Damien's death, there was a flurry of activity at the leper settlement. The first order of business was to inform Damien's family members, his close acquaintances, and the

Sacred Hearts hierarchy in Paris. It fell to Father Léonor to inform the superior general, and he did so in a lengthy, laudatory obituary that placed the blame for Damien's premature death on his careless physical contact with the lepers.[1]

When Father Pamphile received the official notification of his younger brother's death, he responded by composing a lengthy document in which he detailed the key events in the life of young Joseph De Veuster. Father Damien's pragmatic older brother appreciated that in order to ensure an uninterrupted continuation of his younger brother's work among the lepers, money would be required, and to insure this he would have to rekindle the public's interest in the "leper priest." He edited the document for the English press and sent it the *Times* of London. In the piece he told of the Belgian campaign to raise funds for a "Damien Institute," the purpose of which was to insure continuation of Father Damien's work at the leper settlement, provide a publication for the general public devoted to leprosy, and to establish college scholarships in Father Damien's name for those persons wishing to minister or nurse lepers.[2]

Father Pamphile believed that his younger brother's death had released him from his promise not to publish his letters, so when Father Kingdon, a Sacred Hearts priest, proposed to author a definitive biography, Pamphile gathered the letters he and the De Veusters had saved and turned over copies to Father Kingdon along with a lengthy account of Father Damien's childhood years. Father Kingdon's biography, *Life and Letters of Father Damien, the Apostle of the Lepers*, was published later in 1889 by the Catholic Truth Society, London.

The week following Father Damien's burial, Father Conrardy was suddenly stricken with abdominal pain, fever, and a cholera-like diarrhea. After several days of dehydrating diarrhea and high fever, he stabilized sufficiently to allow him to be transported to Queens Hospital in Honolulu where he languished for weeks, steadily losing weight and strength despite the intensive supportive therapies. In his absence the lepers turned to Father Wendelin for their spiritual needs, only to discover that they were once again relegated to the outcast status of the lepers of the Old Testament. Father Wendelin viewed them as the "unclean," the untouchables who were hazardous to health. He was Mother Marianne's "clean and healthy" chaplain, and he planned to remain so. There were no pastoral visits to the homes of the dying.

No one with a friendly smile made house calls to prescribe medicinal remedies for the common ailments that blighted the already poor quality of life of the lepers. Assiduously obeying his bishop, Father Wendelin avoided all physical contact with the lepers. He was a servant of the Almighty God, not a dresser of wounds nor a procurer of food and clothing nor a keeper of leprous orphans.

On April 30, 1889, the week after Easter, a solemn funeral Mass was celebrated in Our Lady of Peace Cathedral to commemorate Father Damien's death. The cathedral was packed. Whether Stevenson was in attendance is not known. Bishop Hermann pleased those present with an emotional and dramatic eulogy:

> We are assembled here to honor the memory of a man whose fame has spread over the whole globe.
>
> There is perhaps not a city, small or large, in the civilized world, where the name of Father Damien is not known and blessed by all sympathetic hearts. . . . But he has two more glorious titles which raise him above the rest of good men—he is a hero and a martyr of Christian charity. . . . Father Damien seems to me to have been a hero more glorious than he who falls on the battlefield, sword in hand. At about the age of thirty-four, in the full strength of youth and in perfect health, he offered to share the fate of those unfortunate ones, separated from their families and friends. He asked, as a favor, the permission to live at the lazaret, in order to console and to comfort, physically and morally, the suffering portion of humanity assembled there through inevitable necessity.[3]

DR. EMERSON, the president of the Board of Health, viewed the leper settlement as the responsibility of the government. Under no circumstances would he permit Bishop Hermann to turn the settlement into a Catholic showcase and shrine now that Father Damien was dead. The clergy were there at the pleasure of the board and, for the present, he would insist that all clergymen restrict their endeavors to the spiritual welfare of the lepers. The multitalented Father Damien had been a unique exception to this rule. From now on, only licensed physicians would be permitted to practice medicine. Should Father Conrardy recover from his illness and return to the settlement, the board would insist that Bishop Hermann find the resolve to either control the priest's letter writing or have him recalled. The priest's self-aggrandizing published letters, which consistently failed to give the board credit where credit was justly due, were a source of justifiable irritation.

From Dr. Emerson's vantage point, the Franciscan sisters were an asset to be nurtured. These women were well-trained American nurses who not only embraced the Christian virtues, but had the skill to oversee the orphanages while attending to the medical needs of the women and girls. To this end he promptly conferred with Rudolph Meyer and directed him to ask Mother Marianne about overseeing the proposed Baldwin Home for Boys in Kalawao. In addition Meyer was to learn how she felt about the future roles of Brothers Dutton and James at the orphanages. If either were unacceptable to her, he would be asked to leave the settlement.

Mother Marianne responded affirmatively to Meyer's inquiry, stating that the services of two additional sisters would be required to oversee the Baldwin Home for Boys. Additionally, the board would have to provide clean, uncontaminated quarters in Kalawao for the sisters who would serve there.[4] Mother Marianne then dutifully informed Bishop Hermann of her intention to transfer Sisters Crescentia and Irene from the branch hospital to oversee the boys' orphanage as soon as the proper quarters were provided.[5] With reference to the future roles of Brothers Dutton and James at the leper settlement, Mother Marianne agreed to employ the services of both men at the boys' orphanage but expressed doubt that Brother James would remain now that Father Damien was dead.

ON MAY 20, 1889, Dr. Emerson notified Rudolph Meyer of the board's decision to permit a visit by the famous Scottish author:

> The Board has granted to Mr. Robert Louis Stevenson, the eminent literary man, a permit to go to the leper settlement on a visit for the purpose of observing the working of things.
>
> Mr. Stevenson is a gentleman, and the Board has confidence that all he does will meet with the approval of the Board. Will you please to request Dr. Swift and the assistant superintendent to aid Mr. Stevenson and his fellow visitor, Mr. Strong, in all ways possible. Mr. Stevenson is in delicate health, and I am somewhat anxious about him.[6]

On the afternoon of May 21, 1889, Stevenson boarded the *Kīlauea Hou*. Standing on deck he witnessed the mournful arrival of

twelve lepers, who were directed by an armed guard to situate themselves in the confined area on the main deck reserved for transporting
cattle.[7] On the wharf, a small group of tearful spouses, children, and
friends expressed their grief in doleful *kanikau*, the traditional chants
of lament. Shortly before departure, two young Franciscan sisters,
immaculate in their black habits, boarded and went directly to their
stateroom below deck. Stevenson learned from the captain that they
were Sisters Crescentia and Irene from the Kaka'ako Branch Hospital,
the most recent Franciscan sisters to volunteer to serve as nurses at the
leper settlement. Stevenson, a Congregationalist, marveled at a faith
that could instill the courage in its followers sufficient to live and work
among the lepers.[8]

At sunset the *Kīlauea Hou* left the shelter of Honolulu Harbor
and began its battle with the buffeting waves of the surging ocean. On
the open deck, the twelve lepers huddled together in silence while their
guard followed Stevenson and the two sisters to the shelter of the staterooms. As he lay in his narrow berth that night, listening to the rhythmic slap of the waves against the ship's hull, the sounds coming from
the adjacent stateroom informed him the seasickness had claimed two
new victims—Sisters Crescentia and Irene.

At dawn, the tumultuous up and down motion of the steamer
woke Stevenson, who had slept very poorly. He slipped into his shoes
and made his way topside. In the distance he could make out the towering sea cliffs, the infamous *pali* that formed the northern coast of
Moloka'i and overlooked the flat shelf of land jutting out into the sea
on which the lepers lived.[9]

The *Kīlauea Hou* anchored offshore and lowered longboats to
transport the passengers to the dilapidated wooden landing wharf at
Kalaupapa. The first longboat transported the twelve lepers; the second conveyed Stevenson and the two sisters, pale and fatigued from
twelve hours of seasickness. As the longboat with Stevenson and the
sisters neared the wharf and the deformities of the lepers became clearly
visible, one of the sisters lowered her head and began to sob. Stevenson recorded his reaction: "My horror of the horrible is about my
weakest point; but the moral loveliness at my elbow blotted all else out;
and when I found that one of them was crying, poor soul, quietly under
her veil, I cried a little myself. . . . I thought it was a sin and a shame
she should feel unhappy; I turned round to her, and said something like

this: 'Ladies, God Himself is here to give you welcome. I'm sure it is good for me to be beside you; I hope it will be blessed to me; I thank you for myself and the good you do me.' It seemed to cheer her up."[10]

When the longboat with Stevenson was securely tied to the wharf, he stood up and looked into "hundreds of (God save us!) pantomime masks in poor human flesh."[11] Hands with missing fingers or wrapped in bandages reached out to assist him. Adroitly he backed away, keeping his hands deep in his pockets. "Every hand was offered: I had gloves, but I had made up my mind on the boat's voyage not to give my hand; that seemed less offensive than gloves."[12]

Avoiding all physical contact with the lepers, Stevenson managed to smile his way through the surrounding crowd of lepers and begin his trek to the guest house in Kalawao, 2.5 miles distant. As he trudged along the narrow road, he exchanged greetings with several neatly clad lepers he encountered, all of whom were on horseback. Riders with deformed faces and missing fingers mistook him for a new white leper, and the "alohas" from horseback were cheerful and said with a smile. As he proceeded, his image of lepers as perpetually sorrowful, misshapen creatures, dressed in dirty rags and crouching in shadows, began to dissipate—and with it, his fear of the disease.

About halfway to his destination Stevenson was hailed by another leper on horseback who introduced himself as Ambrose Hutchison, the resident superintendent. Hutchison was leading a second horse, which he offered for his famous visitor's use. Stevenson quickly accepted, for he was experiencing "crushing fatigue." Hutchison was a key person on the list of those whom he wished to interview. This man had been the resident superintendent for the past five years, and if Father Damien was a flawed priest, he would know and might possibly tell.

When Stevenson reached the guest house, he turned the horse loose in the garden and collapsed on the bed, where he slept until Dr. Swift woke him for breakfast. Too fatigued to venture out, he returned to bed and slept the rest of the day, awaking only long enough to eat the lunch and the dinner prepared by Mrs. Swift. Stevenson was an ill man.[13]

Stevenson's second day on Moloka'i was much more productive. After breakfast he mounted his horse and rode back across the low promontory from Kalawao to Kalaupapa to interview Mother Marianne, whom he believed would provide him with excellent, firsthand information.

Mother Marianne greeted Stevenson warmly and, after thanking him for the "beautiful new croquet set" he had shipped to the girl's orphanage the previous week, she agreed to answer his questions about the leper settlement and Father Damien. Stevenson found the mother superior to be a slender lady of medium height whose face at age fifty-one, framed in the immaculate white coronet and band, was remarkable for its beauty.[14] So captivated was he by the serenity she radiated, he resolved to capture the magnificence of the moment in a poem.[15]

When asked, Mother Marianne calmly recounted what she knew about the priest, information Stevenson jotted in his notebook. It was her conviction that Father Damien had worked a minor miracle at the leper settlement. He had treated the outcast lepers like brothers and sisters, with love and compassion. In addition to his spiritual ministry, he had served the lepers both as a physician and a carpenter. In so doing he had supplied the basic needs of the people—adequate food, water, medicine, clothing, and housing. Perhaps his greatest gift had been the care and compassion he had shown the children.

There were, however, minor flaws in the character of the leper priest, Mother Marianne confessed. He occasionally resorted to physical violence, such as destroying alcohol stills in order to maintain law and order. And he had been careless. *He had eaten food prepared by lepers!* Worse yet, he had repeatedly shared his pipe with the lepers. Truly, he was skillful with his hands. The problem was he didn't wash them as often as he should have so infection with the leprosy bacillus was inevitable.

After some refreshments the reverend mother gave Stevenson a tour of the Bishop Home complex, where he was allowed to visit with the seriously ill, ask questions, and take notes at bedside. Then she led him to the Bishop Home for Girls and introduced him to the seven orphaned girls residing there. Stevenson was awed by the atmosphere of cheerfulness, cleanliness, and comfort that pervaded the Bishop Home complex. Later that afternoon, with Mother Marianne looking on, Stevenson presented the new croquet set to the seven orphans. Since there was no one to teach them to play, he offered to become their tutor. The Dr. Jekyll side of his personality blossomed. He joked, laughed, and frolicked with the young girls.

Possibly the reversal in Stevenson's concern over the contagiousness of leprosy was due to Mother Marianne's revelation that by adhering to some simple hygienic rules, none of the sisters had contracted the disease. Father Damien had consistently violated these sound principles, and so had placed himself in harm's way. For whatever the reason, Stevenson took his hands out of his pockets and with abandon touched objects previously handled by the leper children.

That evening in the quiet of the guest house, Stevenson reviewed and expanded the notes he had taken. In an attempt to capture the essence of his impressions of the day's events, he composed an eight-line poem dedicated to Mother Marianne. This poem, judged not to be one of Stevenson's better compositions, was presented to Mother Marianne on the morning of May 23, 1889.

To the Reverend Sister Marianne, Matron of the Bishop Home, Kalaupapa

> To see the infinite pity of this place,
> The mangled limb, the devastated face,
> The innocent sufferers smiling at the rod,
> A fool were tempted to deny his God.
> He sees, and shrinks; But if he look again,
> Lo, beauty springing from the breast of pain! —
> He marks the Sisters on the painful shores,
> And even a fool is silent and adores.
>
> Robert Louis Stevenson [16]

During his seven-day stay, Stevenson spent most of his time interviewing the persons most familiar with Father Damien's ministry. In addition to the Catholics who held Father Damien in high esteem, Stevenson sought out those "who beheld him with no halo" and gathered information "from the lips of Protestants who had opposed the father."[17] Ambrose Hutchison was not reticent to detail what he had observed.[18] He essentially confirmed what Mother Marianne had told Stevenson. When questioned about Father Damien's alleged sexual encounters with leprous women, Hutchison replied that during his ten years at the leper settlement he had known of none, and had Father Damien been guilty of a sexual indiscretion, the few enemies he had would certainly have informed Hutchison and displayed the soiled linen to the world. While Hutchison considered Father Damien a "colleague-in-arms" whom he lauded for his efforts to improve the lot of the lepers, there was a negative side to the priest. The priest was a bit overbearing and dictatorial. When in the reverend father's view it was in the best interests of the leper community to do so, he imposed his standards of morality on everyone, the non-Catholics as well as the Catholics. He even had the audacity to ban the beloved hula on the grounds that the dance was a pagan religious ceremony, and from his pulpit he thundered that sex out of wedlock was a major sin.

When Stevenson attempted to interview Brother Joseph Dutton, his inquiries regarding Father Damien met with stubborn resistance, eliciting either a guarded answer or simply a shrug of the shoulders. Brother Dutton was fearful that because Stevenson was a Congregationalist, he might be allied with the Rev. Dr. Hyde and use any information he gave to desecrate the memory of his recently deceased colleague and friend.[19] Stevenson persevered and spent the morning shadowing Brother Dutton as he meticulously cleaned and dressed the skin lesions of the boy lepers, a task that sickened Stevenson. As he watched, he marveled at the joy Brother Dutton radiated, and the mood-elevating effect this had on the boys. For the next two mornings he repeated this shadowing, and by midweek he had established a healthy rapport with the man from Wisconsin. Between dressing changes, Brother Dutton began to mention the strengths and the weakness he had observed in the Belgian priest.[20] Father Damien had always assigned the highest priority to his spiritual ministry, but when time constraints threatened to compromise the spiritual ministry, secondary projects, like engaging in new home construction or dormitory maintenance, were either temporarily abandoned or turned over to Brother Dutton, his "right arm," for completion. Toward the end of the week, Stevenson was able to broach more delicate matters. When asked specifically about Father Damien's rumored sexual indiscretions, Brother Dutton confided that he and Father Damien had spent many evenings discussing the virtues and temptations inherent in the religious life. In the early years of his Hawaiian ministry, Father Damien had confided that the yearning to have sexual intercourse with one of the willing Hawaiian women had been a most difficult emotion to suppress.[21] On more occasions than he cared to enumerate, he had knelt in confession and asked forgiveness for his sexual fantasies, but—and Father Damien had been adamant about this—he had never engaged in the act!

When the time came for Stevenson to leave the settlement, he clapped Brother Dutton on the shoulder and said to the man whom he now considered a friend, "Don't worry, Brother Dutton. Your friend Damien is a man with all the grime and paltriness of mankind, but a saint and hero all the more for that."[22]

Stevenson completed his information gathering by sailing to Moloka'i's southern port, then riding overland to interview Rudolph W. Meyer.[23] He found the German rancher who was a devout Protestant to be an ardent supporter of Father Damien. Meyer considered the priest a personal friend—and most importantly, a friend to all of the lepers, irrespective of their religious beliefs. While he and the priest had occasionally disagreed on the best approach to solve a problem, once a project was undertaken Damien could be counted on to complete it. Father Damien had been Meyer's eyes and ears at the settlement, and for the past several years they had communicated several times a week with letters carried up and down the *pali* by runners. When Damien requested assistance, like the purchase of clothing or medical supplies, Meyer was always happy and honored to comply. When Damien alerted Meyer to an administrative problem at the settlement, he would advise the priest as to how he wished the matter handled and rely on him to do so.

An entry from Sister Leopoldina's journal completes the story of the Stevenson visit to the leper settlement: "Thursday morning as the steamer went, Mother told us Mr. Stevenson had gone, and that he told her he could not say good-bye. . . . The next morning when the steamer returned how surprised we were to receive from him a very grand $500 piano for the Bishop Home for Girls."[24]

On June 24, 1889, after a champagne farewell hosted by King Kalākaua, the Stevensons departed Honolulu on a chartered yacht, the *Equator,* bound for Samoa, in search of a still better climate for the writer's pulmonary tuberculosis. Stevenson had accomplished his mission to learn the truth about Father Damien. There was no reason to linger in Hawai'i.

During the voyage to Samoa, Stevenson completed his book, *The Eight Islands*, in which he included four essays dealing with leprosy, three of which focused on the Moloka'i leper settlement. In none of these did he disclose the wealth of information he had gathered regarding Father Damien.

DUE IN LARGE MEASURE to the books written by Charles Stoddard and Edward Clifford, coupled with the continuing charitable fund-raising

campaign for the Hawaiian lepers, Father Damien's name had become
a household word in England, synonymous with "hero," "martyr," and
"good Samaritan." In June, the Prince of Wales, the future King Edward
VII, outlined a proposal to honor the memory of Father Damien:

> The heroic life and death of Father Damien has not only roused the sym-
> pathy of the United Kingdom, but it has gone deeper. It has brought
> home to us that the circumstances of our vast Indian and Colonial
> Empire oblige us, in a measure at least, to follow his example. And this
> not for foreigners and strangers, but for our own fellow subjects.
>
> India . . . and our colonies with their unnumbered but increasing vic-
> tims to a loathsome disease that has hitherto baffled medical skill, have
> a far stronger claim on our aid than the poor natives of the Hawaiian
> Islands could ever have had on the young Belgian priest, who has given
> his life for them.
>
> To mark our debt to him, as well as our sympathy with his noble self-
> sacrifice, I have to propose to this Committee a memorial scheme that
> embraces a three-fold object: 1) A monument to Father Damien at
> Molokai; 2) The establishment of a leper ward, probably attached to
> some London hospital or medical school, to be called the Father
> Damien Ward, and the endowment of a travelling studentship or stu-
> dentships, to encourage the study of leprosy; 3) A full and complete
> inquiry into the question of leprosy in India, one of the chief seats of
> the disease, and where there are no adequate means of dealing with the
> disease.[25]

The spontaneous worldwide outpouring of admiration for the
priest to the lepers of Moloka'i continued unabated. The priest from the
small village of Tremeloo was viewed as a "hero for all time," a "true
saint." From within the ranks of the Congregation of the Sacred Hearts,
the question of sainthood surfaced. Father Pamphile's biographical
accounts of his brother's life, with the suggestion that Divine Intervention had played a prominent role—not only in protecting him from
harm in his early years, but in subsequently directing his ministry—
presented an undeniable portrait of a saint. In 1889, the Congregation
of the Sacred Hearts was a young order, numbering fewer than 360
professed members. No saint had risen from its ranks, so it was natural that the congregation's hierarchy entertained the possibility that
Father Damien might become their first saint.

A saint is a person who is *beatified*, or declared to be the lawful object of public veneration, as being in heaven with God. Sainthood honors a man or woman for heroism in the practice of virtue far beyond the ordinary minimum of goodness. In the Roman Catholic Church, only the pope has the power to confer sainthood, first with a beatification ceremony that may or may not be followed by canonization at a later date.

Father Marcellin Bousquet, the superior general of the Congregation of the Sacred Hearts, took the first step toward the beatification of Father Damien by initiating a formal inquest into the life of the recently deceased priest. All persons with firsthand knowledge of Father Damien were to be interviewed, and the gathered information was to be presented in testimonial statements or signed depositions. When informed of the inquest and instructed to undertake the Hawaiian Mission phase of the project, Bishop Hermann was astounded. Never in his wildest fantasies had he pictured Father Damien in the select circle of saints of the Church. There was little argument that Father Damien was a heroic figure, but he seemed a person too flawed to be considered seriously for beatification. And there was another problem with the assignment—a safety concern. Whoever conducted the interviews would necessarily have to spend considerable time at the leper settlement. Neither the bishop nor the provincial wished to undertake so dangerous a task, so the assignment to gather the required information was delegated to Fathers Corneille and Wendelin, the priests most recently in contact with key witnesses at the leper settlement. Father Conrardy was to be excluded.

To assist with the inquest, Bishop Hermann forwarded the standard nineteen-point questionnaire to serve as the framework upon which to assemble a detailed life history of the candidate. First and foremost, it was to be determined whether or not Father Damien's life demonstrated an impeccable love of God and his fellow man; and if so, to determine if God had responded with acts of Divine Intervention.[26] To assess the quality of the professed *love*, whether that love was exemplary enough to merit sainthood, the investigation was to determine whether the candidate had manifested the cardinal Christian virtues of *faith, hope, charity, prudence, justice, temperance*, and *fortitude*. As a priest, had Father Damien observed his vows of obedience, poverty, and celibacy? Had he been humble, avoiding the praise and esteem of others? Did pious men esteem him a saint while he was yet alive? In dying, had he borne the pain with patience and in complete submission to the Divine Will while following the prescriptions of the doctor? After his death, had the faithful gathered at his grave to pray for his intercession? Was his corpse incorrupt, did it remain so, and did a fragrance emanate from it? And the key determinant—was there reliable evidence of Divine Intervention as evidenced by a *miracle* after the death of the servant of God, through his intercession, which featured the return to health of a seriously ill person? And finally, was there any evidence by which God demonstrated that those interceding through the servant of God had been heard?

No sooner had Fathers Corneille and Wendelin undertaken the assigned task when they learned of an inflammatory letter deprecating Father Damien's ministry. In response to a query by Rev. H. B. Gage, a Protestant minister in California, requesting verification of the laudatory accounts of Father Damien's Christlike devotion to the lepers that were appearing in newspapers and magazines in the United States, the Rev. Dr. Charles McEwin Hyde of Honolulu had dashed off a short note:

Dear Brother,

In answer to your inquiries about Father Damien, I can only reply that we who knew the man are surprised at the extravagant newspaper laudations, as if he was a most saintly philanthropist. The simple truth is, he was a coarse, dirty man, headstrong and bigoted. He was not sent to Molokai, but went there without orders; did not stay at the leper settlement (before he became one himself), but circulated freely over the whole island (less than half the island is devoted to the lepers), and he came often to Honolulu. He had no hand in the reforms and improvements inaugurated, which were the work of our Board of Health, as occasion required and means provided. He was not a pure man in his relations with women, and the leprosy of which he died should be attributed to his vices and carelessness. Others have done much for the lepers, our own ministers, the government physicians, and so forth, but never with the Catholic idea of meriting eternal life.

Yours, etc.

C. M. Hyde[27]

Without first securing Rev. Hyde's permission to do so, Rev. Gage submitted the letter for publication in the *English Churchman*. The defaming epistle was quickly reprinted in newspapers, magazines, and Protestant church bulletins around the world.

Father Damien's supporters were shocked by this revelation. With the shattering of the saintly image of the world's latest hero, the Hawaiian project to erect a memorial to Father Damien came to a halt.

27

Response to the Curse

Blessed are you when men revile you and persecute you and utter all kinds of evil against you falsely on my account. Rejoice and be glad, for your reward is great in heaven, for so men persecuted the prophets who were before you.
—Matthew 5: 11–12

ON DECEMBER 7, 1889, the *Equator* with the Stevenson party reached Samoa, where Robert was astonished to read in a local newspaper that the project to erect a memorial to Father Damien in Hawai'i had been abandoned because a prominent Protestant minister had published a defaming letter about the priest. When he read the complete text reprinted in the *Sydney Presbyterian,* he turned to his wife and exclaimed, "Too damnable for belief!"[1] Infuriated, Stevenson shut himself in his study and composed "An Open Letter to the Rev. Hyde," a thirty-two page philippic in which he castigated the Rev. Hyde by detailing what he had learned about Father Damien during his visit to Moloka'i.[2] A few excerpts from one of literature's feistiest defenses of a man's good name follow:

Sir,

It may probably occur to you that we have met, and visited, and conversed; on my side, with interest. You may remember that you have done me several courtesies, for which I was prepared to be grateful. But there are duties which come before gratitude, and offenses which justly divide friends, far more acquaintances. Your letter to the Rev. H. B. Gage is a document, which, in my sight, if you had filled me with bread when I was starving, if you had sat up to nurse my father when he lay

380

a-dying, would yet absolve me from the bonds of gratitude. . . . If I have at all learned the trade of using words to convey truth and to arouse emotion, you have at last furnished me with a subject. For it is in the interest of all mankind and the cause of public decency that Damien should be righted, but that you and your letter should be displayed at length, in their true colors, to the public eye. . . .

You belong, sir, to a sect—I believe my sect, and that in which my ancestors labored—which has enjoyed, and partly failed to utilize, an exceptional advantage in the islands of Hawaii. The first missionaries came; they found the land already self-purged of its old and bloody faith; they were embraced, almost on their arrival, with enthusiasm. . . . In the course of their evangelical calling, they—or too many of them— grew rich. It may be news to you that the houses of missionaries are a cause of mocking on the streets of Honolulu. . . . when leprosy descended and took root in the Eight Islands, a *quid pro quo* was to be looked for. To that prosperous mission, and to you, as one of its adorn- ments, God had sent at last an opportunity. I know I am touching here upon a nerve acutely sensitive. I know that others of your colleagues look back on the inertia of your Church, and the intrusive and decisive heroism of Damien, with something almost to be called remorse. . . . But, sir, when we have failed, and another has succeeded; when we have stood by, and another has stepped in; when we sit and grow bulky in our charming mansions, and a plain, uncouth peasant steps into the bat- tle, under the eyes of God, and succors the afflicted, and consoles the dying, and is himself afflicted in his turn, and dies upon the field of honor—the battle cannot be retrieved as your unhappy irritation has suggested. It is a lost battle, and lost forever. . . .

For, if that world at all remember you, on the day when Damien of Molokaʻi shall be named Saint, it will be in virtue of one work: your let- ter to the Reverend H. B. Gage. . . .

That you may understand . . . we will (if you please) go hand in hand through the different phrases of your letter, and candidly examine each from the point of view of its truth, its appositeness, and its charity.

Damien was coarse.

It is very possible. You make us sorry for the lepers who had only a coarse old peasant for their friend and father. But you, who were refined, why were you not there, to cheer them with the lights of cul- ture? . . . and in the case of Peter, on whose career you doubtless dwell approvingly in the pulpit, no doubt at all he was a "coarse, headstrong" fisherman. Yet even in our Protestant Bibles Peter is called Saint.

Damien was dirty.

He was. Think of the poor lepers annoyed with this dirty comrade! But the clean Dr. Hyde was at his food in a fine house.

Damien was headstrong.

I believe you are right again; and I thank God for his strong head and heart.

Damien was not sent to Molokai, but went there without orders.

Is this a misreading? Or do you really mean the words for blame? I have heard Christ, in the pulpits of our Church, held up for imitation on the ground that His sacrifice was voluntary. Does Dr. Hyde think otherwise?

Damien had no hand in the reforms, etc.

All the reforms of the lazaretto . . . are properly the work of Damien. They are the evidence of his success; they are what his heroism provoked from the reluctant and the careless. . . . It was his part, by one striking act of martyrdom, to direct all men's eyes on that distressful country. At a blow, and with the price of his life, he made the place illustrious and public. . . . It brought money; it brought the Sisters (best individual addition of them all). . . . If ever any man brought reforms, and died to bring them, it was he. There is not a clean cup or towel in the Bishop Home but dirty Damien washed it.

Damien was not a pure man in his relations with women, etc.

How do you know that? Is this the nature of the conversation in that house on Beretania Street . . . racy details of the misconduct of the poor peasant priest, toiling under the cliffs of Molokai?

Many have visited the station before me; they seem not to have heard the rumor. When I was there I heard many shocking tales, for my informants were men speaking with the plainness of the laity; and I heard plenty of complaints of Damien. Why was this never mentioned? And how came it to you in the retirement of your clerical parlor?

But I must not even seem to deceive you. This scandal, when I read it in your letter, was not new to me. I had heard it once before; and I must tell you now. There came to Samoa a man from Honolulu; he, in a public house on the beach, volunteered the statement that Damien had "contracted the disease from having connection with the female lepers"; and I find a joy in telling you how the report was welcomed in a public house. A man sprang to his feet; I am not at liberty to give his name, but from what I heard I doubt if you would care to have him to dinner in Beretania Street. "You miserable little ____" (here is a word I dare not print, it would so shock your ears). "You miserable little ____," he cried, "if the story were a thousand times true, can't you see you are a million times a lower ____ for daring to repeat it?" I wish it could be told of you that when the report reached you in your house, perhaps after family worship, you had found in your soul enough holy anger to receive it with the same expressions; ay, even with that one which I dare not print. . . .

I will suppose—and God forgive me for supposing it—that Damien faltered and stumbled in his narrow path of duty; I will suppose that, in the horror of his isolation, perhaps in the fever of incipient disease, he, who was doing so much more than he had sworn, failed in the letter of his priestly oath—he, who was so much a better man than either you or me, who did what we have never dreamed of daring—he too tasted of our common frailty. "O, Iago, the pity of it!" The least tender should be moved to tears; the most incredulous to prayer. And all you could do was to pen your letter to the Reverend H. B. Gage!

Is it growing at all clear to you what a picture you have drawn of your own heart?[3]

On the afternoon of the day Stevenson completed his thirty-two-page draft of the open letter to Rev. Hyde, he read it to his wife Fanny, explaining that the subject matter was potentially libelous and should Rev. Hyde sue for damages, the Stevensons could be left penniless.[4] Without hesitation, Fanny encouraged her husband to publish the letter. He immediately did so, and twenty-five copies of the letter were privately printed by the Ben Franklin Printing Company, Sydney, Australia. The groundswell of sympathetic support for the priest to the lepers was immediate, and it provided the stimulus for the letter to be reprinted in newspapers and magazines worldwide. In Europe the philippic was reprinted in the *Scots Observer* on May 3 and again on May 10. In Honolulu the letter to Hyde first appeared as a supplement to the English edition of *Ka 'Elele Poakolu* on May 10, the seventeenth anniversary of Father Damien's arrival at the leper settlement.

The Stevenson refutation of the Hyde letter achieved its goal, restoring the impetus to honor Father Damien's memory with a memorial. The Hawaiians reopened their fund drive for a statue to be placed in Honolulu. The British followed suit, and Edward Clifford was chosen to design a large, white granite cross to be placed on Moloka'i. The inscription on the British gift read: "Greater love than this hath no man, that he give his life for his friend."

The Rev. Dr. Hyde found himself enveloped in a firestorm of public indignation. He read and reread the thirty-two-page rebuttal that

Stevenson had mailed him and reportedly quipped, "Stevenson is simply a Bohemian crank, a negligible person, whose opinion is of no value to anyone." Rev. Hyde maintained he had been slandered by Stevenson and that some persons were referring to him as the despicable Mr. Hyde of *Dr. Jekyll and Mr. Hyde*, a story Stevenson had written some years before. In a futile effort to defend his actions, he corresponded with his influential friends, reiterating that Father Damien was a victim of his own sexual indiscretions. Leprosy, after all, was a fourth stage of syphilis, a disease acquired via sexual intercourse.

Relentless in his quest to "feel the button off the foil and to plunge home," Stevenson issued a second privately published edition of thirty copies of the pamphlet printed by Messrs. Constable and Co., Edinburgh. He followed this with a third and larger edition published and distributed for sale by Chatto and Windus, London, in June 1890. In the negotiations regarding royalty payments, Stevenson informed the London publisher, "I do not stick at murder; I draw the line at cannibalism. I could not eat a penny roll that piece of bludgeoning brought me."[5] Mr. Andrew Chatto, the publisher, sent the author's share of the profits to the Leper Fund, an act that pleased Stevenson.[6]

Newspapers entered the fray, and the second of the Father Damien biographies written after the priest's death—*Vie du Pere Damien, l'apôtre des lepreux de Molokai [The Life of Father Damien, Apostle of the Lepers of Molokai]* by Father Philibert Tauvel—was published. The book was based on additional documents supplied to the author by Father Pamphile and cast Father Damien in a heroic light, stating categorically that the priest from Belgium had many of the attributes of a true saint.

Articles in the Hawaiian newspapers continued to debate the question of Father Damien's morality while pondering the silence of the Catholic Church on the matter. This forced a reluctant Bishop Hermann to respond. In an edition of the *Hawaiian Advertiser* in June 1890, which carried a letter from the *Liverpool Courier* written by Rev. Hyde confirming that the information in his original letter about Father Damien was entirely correct, Bishop Hermann countered with a short letter to the editor: "As head of the Catholic Mission here, a longer silence on my part would seem to credit this attack. I ask you to insert the following statement: 'I declare in the most peremptory and formal manner that there is absolutely no truth in the statements of Rev. Hyde against the moral purity of the late Father Damien.'"[7]

Hyde retaliated by taking careful aim at the Father Damien image and firing a sharp volley. On August 7, 1890, an article entitled "Father Damien and His Work for the Hawaiian Lepers: A Careful and Candid Estimate" appeared in the *Congregationalist*, the leading and most widely circulated magazine published by the Congregational Church. In the article he reaffirmed the validity of his previous statements in the Rev. Gage letter, but the piece did little to change the public's favorable assessment of Father Damien's accomplishments at the leper settlement.

The archbishop of Boston urged Bishop Hermann to comment on the original Rev. Hyde letter, which had been published in the *Boston Congregationalist*. Writing for an American audience, Bishop Hermann was more eloquent in his response:

The extract from the *Boston Congregationalist* is an infamous falsehood, and what is more, an atrocious calumny. It is the more injurious in that it is partly founded upon facts, which, through malicious misinterpretation and sectarian jealousy, are presented under a prejudicial light. The good works done by others do not, in the least, diminish the real merit of Father Damien. He consecrated his life to the welfare of the most unfortunate of human beings; he must justly be regarded as an extraordinarily heroic man. His visits to Honolulu did not amount to more than a total of six months during sixteen years. He was looked upon as the strongest moral authority and the most dependable and zealous resident on the Island, acting always as the confidential agent of the Board in full accord with Mr. Meyer. Physicians generally visited the Island; a small number receiving good salaries, rarely lived there longer than one year. He considered precautions as useless since his arrival, he was resigned to fall victim to the malady. Building chapels, erecting houses, making coffins, digging graves, cultivating the earth— could he be expected to observe the refinement of manner or to wear immaculate garments?

But I am amazed that anyone would attack his morals after his death, especially since, while living, I have never heard the purity of his life suspected. In the candor of his simplicity, he never deemed it necessary to take unusual precautions against evil interpretations of the rectitude of his life. It would seem that his accuser belongs to that class of people to whom prejudice systematically denies the merit of voluntary celibacy and who, therefore, do not believe in the chastity of priests in general. . . . It is extremely painful to learn that prejudice and sectarian jealousy can lead to such an extreme.[8]

WITH THE EXCEPTION of the deliberate exclusion of Father Conrardy, Brother James, and all Hawaiian lepers, Fathers Corneille and Wendelin interviewed in person or by mail all observers judged to be credible who had witnessed firsthand the ministry of Father Damien. The two priests amassed an impressive collection of signed depositions and testimonials.[9]

Following the receipt of all of the depositions and testimonials obtained by Fathers Corneille and Wendelin, Bishop Hermann was satisfied that the inquest into Father Damien's life was complete, and he submitted the package of information to the superior general. From his vantage point he still viewed the deceased Belgian as a courageous, even heroic priest—albeit quite imperfect. As to his vow of poverty, obedience, and celibacy, Father Damien had been guilty of collecting and distributing large sums of money he had solicited through questionable means, and he had not always obeyed his bishop. On the other hand, celibacy was the one vow he had not violated—of this Bishop Hermann was convinced.

Confident that the Rev. Hyde–Robert Louis Stevenson imbroglio was settled and would soon be forgotten and that Father Damien might well become the Congregation of Sacred Hearts first saint, Father Marcellin Bousquet, the superior general, championed the Cause of Father Damien and forwarded the collected data to the Vatican.

28

A Second Saint Damien

*To be able to continue this beautiful work of love and healing,
we need a saint to guide and protect us. Father Damien could
be that saint. Holy Father, our lepers and each one throughout
the world beg you for this gift—a saint and martyr of greater love
and a beautiful example of obedience to us religious.*
—Mother Teresa

DESPITE THE ACKNOWLEDGMENT of Father Damien's courageous
and self-sacrificing ministry, Bishop Hermann and Father Léonor,
Father Damien's immediate superiors, declined to support the proposition that his life exemplified exceptional merit. Both were of the
opinion that Father Damien's religious life was flawed. As for his intercession leading to a healing miracle after his death, they both contended that there would be none.[1]

In the first of a series of conciliatory letters to the superior general, Bishop Hermann wrote: "We know that it is your ardent desire
to make known the merits of Father Damien for the glory of the
Catholic Church in general, and for our dear Congregation in particular. I sincerely regret that I cannot satisfy your desire by extolling the
private virtues of our Christian hero. My funeral oration printed in the
newspapers, summarizes his public life; and Father Wendelin has
informed you about his holy death. As to his private virtues, one must
view them from a distance to appreciate them. He did exhibit some
superior virtues, but these were tainted with much that was imperfect.
I regard him as a true saint in some of his undertakings."[2]

Four months later, Bishop Hermann added: "The measures
which you propose on the subject of the celebrated Father Damien will

be taken, although we near him have been less enthusiastic than his admirers from afar. . . . In my funeral oration I believed that I should be brief and a bit reserved so as not to delve into his private life, which I believe to be holy, but not without considerable faults. His humility, his obedience, and his sweetness left much to be desired. I would be most insincere were I not to tell you this in confidence."[3]

The reservations regarding the exemplary life of Father Damien expressed by Bishop Hermann and Father Léonor did not deter the superior general. Satisfied that his assessment of the priest was the correct one, he proceeded with the Cause of Father Damien, confident that a healing miracle through intercessionary prayer would occur at some time in the near future.

The process by which a person becomes a saint in the Catholic Church is an arduous one, requiring on average a span of fifty years in which to review meticulously the religious life of the individual. It is a mammoth undertaking requiring evidence of *two* posthumous miracles as proof of the candidate's favored place in heaven. In 1924, depositions and letters were obtained from seven individuals who had observed Father Damien in action: Franciscan Sisters Leopoldina, Vincentia, and Crescentia; Ambrose Hutchison, the former resident superintendent; John Wilmington, a leper who had been at the settlement the last full year of Father Damien's residence; notes from Bishop Julliotte regarding the value of Brother Dutton's multiple testimonial statements; a letter from Brother Dutton to Father Reginald; and a lengthy supplement to Brother Dutton's original deposition.[4] To these data was added a major portion of Dr. Arthur Mouritz's book, *The Path of the Destroyer: A History of Leprosy in the Hawaiian Islands and Thirty Years Research into the Means by Which It Has Been Spread.*[5]

In 1935, the territorial governor of Hawai'i signed a law designating an annual sum of $3,000 to assure the preservation of the St. Philomena Church and the cemetery with Father Damien's grave.

In 1936, King Leopold III of Belgium asked the Territory of Hawai'i to exhume Father Damien's body at Kalawao and return it to Louvain for reburial. To expedite the process the king solicited the help of President Franklin D. Roosevelt. Ignoring Father Damien's deathbed request that he be buried next to St. Philomena Church beneath the *pū hala*, President Roosevelt honored King Leopold's request. On January 27, 1936, Father Damien's body was exhumed while dignitaries of the Church and the government watched. As the body was reverently placed in a casket of koa wood, an honor reserved for royalty and the affluent, resident lepers sang "Ke Ola" and "Aloha 'Oe," the traditional Hawaiian odes of farewell. The casket was flown to Honolulu where full official honors were paid to the remains and a solemn funeral Mass was celebrated in the Cathedral of Our Lady of Peace. From Honolulu, an American ship carried the casket to Panama where it was transferred to a Belgian ship that carried it on to Antwerp.

The body of the leper priest was given a tumultuous welcome by the King Leopold III, officials of the Belgian government, the Catholic clergy, and an enormous crowd. Funeral services were conducted in the cathedral and later, on the evening of May 3, a hearse carried the casket through Tremeloo to Louvain. Shortly before midnight Father Damien's casket was placed in a black marble crypt in St. Joseph's Chapel—the chapel whose chimney he had helped disassemble in 1861 and the chapel from which he had embarked seventy-three years earlier.

In 1938 beatification proceedings were formally begun. The Vatican's Congregation for the Causes of Saints, consisting of around twenty-five cardinals and bishops, commenced the investigation to determine whether Father Damien lived a life of heroic virtue. The process moved slowly, with years of additional research and study. Not until 1969 did the Roman Catholic Church initiate the first major step toward the canonization of Joseph De Veuster as Saint Damien. On July 7, 1977, Father Damien was declared "Venerable" by Pope Paul VI and his virtues "heroic," the last step before beatification. At this point, the debate over Father Damien's earthly existence was over, and the search for two posthumous miracles began. The first miracle would result in beatification and the title "Blessed"; the second miracle, canonization and "Saint." The Vatican standard for miracles is extremely high. A board of five doctors, notoriously exacting, must conclude that no reasonable medical explanation exists for a healing.

On May 7, 1984, the Cause of Father Damien received a major endorsement. Mother Teresa, winner of the 1979 Nobel Peace Prize, the Roman Catholic missionary in India who founded the Missionaries of Charity that operates schools, hospitals, orphanages, and leprosariums around the world, wrote to Pope John Paul II, nudging the pontiff to proceed with the beatification of Father Damien. In the mid-1950s, Mother Teresa had begun to help victims of leprosy. To assist her, the Indian government gave the Missionaries of Charity a 34-acre plot of land near the city of Asansol where a leper settlement called Shanti Nagar (Town of Peace) was established. Soon she was caring for over two thousand lepers, and the success of her venture led to the establishment of additional leper settlements in Asia and Africa. Mother Teresa believed that the lepers needed and deserved a saint to whom they could pray—and in her opinion, Father Damien was the prime candidate. She was not troubled by the absence of a documented miracle when she wrote to Pope John Paul II:

> Dear Holy Father,
>
> As you know we are working among thousands of lepers in India, Yemen, Ethiopia and Tanzania through mobile clinics and rehabilitation centers built on land given by different governments. To be able to continue this beautiful work of love and healing, we need a saint to guide and protect us. Father Damien could be that saint. Holy Father, our lepers and each one throughout the world beg you for this gift—a saint and martyr of greater love and a beautiful example of obedience to us religious. . . .
>
> I know a real (miracle), the removal of the fear from the hearts of the lepers to acknowledge the disease and proclaim it and ask for medicine—and the birth of hope of being cured. The change of hearts in people and governments toward the lepers—greater concern, less fear and ready to help—any time and all the time.[6]

In a letter faxed December 5, 1991, to members of the Congregation of Sacred Hearts around the world, Superior General Father Patrick Bradley announced that the Medical Commission of the Congregation for the Cause of Saints had accepted the unexplained medical cure of a French nun attributed to the intercession of Father Damien De Veuster.

The miracle was reported in the *Hawai'i Catholic Herald*:

> The cure happened in 1895 to a 37-year-old French, Sacred Hearts Sister named Sister Simplicia Hue. She became ill in February of that year with an influenza-like illness which soon escalated into a severe and intensely painful gastrointestinal disorder. Her condition deteriorated to the point where she suffered a discharge of bloody matter and could not eat. Bronchitis set in and by April she received Holy Viaticum and anointing facing the fact that she would soon die.

At this point, she began a daily novena asking Father Damien to intercede with the invocation: "Father Damien pray for us and cure me." Next to her death bed was Damien's picture. On the evening of September 11, worn out by pain, hunger, fever and fatigue she lost consciousness. On September 12 at 1:30 a.m. she awoke startled to find herself free of pain. Knowing she had been miraculously cured, she immediately cried out to the infirmarian, "Sister, I'm cured." Sister Simplicia lived another 32 years until her death in 1927 without any recurrence of this illness.[7]

Finally, the long wait was over. Pope John Paul II announced that the beatification ceremony for Father Damien would be celebrated in Brussels, Belgium, in June 1994, at the Basilica of Koelkelberg. Originally the ceremony was scheduled for Rome, but the Holy Father reversed himself and turned the beatification into a pilgrimage to the country of Father Damien's birth and Belgian grave. The Pontiff designated May 10, the date Father Damien landed at Kalawao, as his day on the universal liturgical calendar. Four hundred Hawaiians were among the thousands of the invited who assembled in Brussels for the event. Shortly before he was to leave the Vatican for Brussels, the Pope fell and broke his leg, forcing the ceremony to be rescheduled one year later on Pentecost Sunday, June 4, 1995.

Two days before the Beatification Mass, Mother Teresa arrived in Brussels. Finally, the Missionaries of Charity would have a saint to guide and help them in their ministry to the thousands of lepers throughout the world. On June 3, the tiny nun addressed an audience of three hundred students, faculty, and friends at Holy Spirit College. Standing at the podium she appeared stooped and frail, but she spoke slowly in a clear voice, extending an invitation to the students to do as Father Damien had done and serve mankind's more destitute: "Even today young people make big sacrifices to serve the suffering poor."[8] The students seated before her could do the same.

Pope John Paul II arrived that afternoon at Melsbroek Airport outside Brussels, braced for the anticipated mass demonstrations throughout Belgium in repudiation of his views on abortion. Ten years earlier in this predominantly Catholic country, a Mass outside the sixth largest basilica in the world would have drawn an enthusiastic congregation of over a hundred thousand. Now it was anticipated that as few as thirty thousand would honor the life of their Belgian hero.[9]

The Pope was apprised that security for the celebration would have to be tight because there were problems. Juan Fernandez Krohn— the Spaniard who had attempted to kill him in Portugal in 1982 and who had served several years in prison for the attempted murder—was in Brussels. On the previous day, before a large crowd, he had brazenly burned large pictures of the Pope and Father Damien. To further increase the tension and detract from the beatification ceremony, a protest group of the-right-to-choose abortion advocates was preparing to parade around the basilica, toting large placards expressing their disapproval of the Pope's views. Another group of protesters reportedly was planning to ring the basilica grounds and hand out condoms.

By contrast, the atmosphere in Hawai'i was one of exuberance and joy. The beatification of Father Damien dominated the front pages of the *Honolulu Star-Bulletin* and the *Honolulu Advertiser* for several days. Hawaiians were proud of their "hero of Moloka'i." The 102-member delegation from Hawai'i, which included several lepers with arrested disease, was given reserved seating in the front rows of the assemblage. Ten of the Hawaiians were to take part in the Mass and present gifts to the Pope ranging from a large calabash to a lei made with flowers from Moloka'i. Six Hawaiian hula dancers were scheduled to perform for the huge gathering once the Mass was concluded and the Pope had departed.

Before dawn on Pentecost Sunday, people in raincoats and huddled beneath umbrellas braved the downpour of rain and temperatures in the 50s to gather outside the basilica for the Beatification Mass. As for all public appearances by Pope John Paul II, security was tight. All roads leading to the basilica were closed, and mounted police exercised watchful surveillance over the rain-swept crowd awaiting the arrival of the pontiff. When the Pope's glass-enclosed vehicle came into view, the basilica bells announced his arrival and the crowd greeted him with cheers and waved white and yellow scarves above their heads. The Pope's vehicle slowly made its way through the crowd and paused briefly before the bronze statue of Father Damien erected in front of the basilica. While the pontiff gazed at the likeness of a young, robust Damien, the sun burst through the cloud cover for the first time that morning.[10]

The pope then proceeded to the 15-foot-high platform erected to serve as a makeshift altar for the Beatification Mass and looked out over the nearly thirty thousand people. In the front row he saw Mother Teresa, and the two exchanged a smile. Present in the audience were more than forty bishops and five hundred priests. The 102-member delegation from Hawai'i, all of whom were wearing colorful leis, waited expectantly.

As planned, the bishop of Honolulu, Francis X. DiLorenzo, formally asked the Holy Father to beatify Father Damien at the commencement of the Mass. In a solemn voice, Pope John Paul II declared:

The Church gives thanks to the Holy Spirit for Father Damien, because it is the Spirit which inspired in him the desire to devote himself without reserve to the lepers in the isles of the Pacific, in particular at Moloka'i. Today, by my mouth, the Church recognizes and confirms the exemplary value of Father Damien in the path of holiness. We praise God for having guided him to the end of his existence, by a path that was often difficult. The Church contemplates with joy what God can achieve by means of human weakness because "it is He who gives us holiness and it is a man who receives it."

Father Damien deployed a particular form of holiness in the course of his ministry; he was simultaneously priest, religious, and missionary. By this triple quality, he showed the face of Christ, pointing out the path of salvation, teaching the Gospel and being an untiring agent of the development. He organized the religious, social, and fraternal life on Moloka'i, an isle which at the time was excluded from the rest of society. . . .

My heart goes out to those who are today still afflicted with leprosy. With Damien, they now have an intercessor, because, before becoming sick, he is already with them, often referring to: "We, the lepers.". . . He became a leper. In the midst of other lepers, he became a leper for the lepers. He suffered and he died like them, believing in the resurrection of Christ, because Christ is the Lord! . . .

Blessed Damien, you allowed yourself to be led by the Holy Spirit, as a son obedient to the will of the Father. By your life and by your missionary work, you demonstrate the tenderness and the mercy of Christ for each human being, revealing to him the beauty of his inner being, which no disease, no deformity and no weakness can totally disfigure. By your action and by your preaching, you recall that Jesus took upon himself the poverty and the suffering of human beings, and that he revealed their mysterious value. Intercede with Christ, physician of bodies and souls for our sick brothers and sisters, in order that, in their fear and pain, they do not feel abandoned but, united with the risen Lord and his Church, they discover that the Holy Spirit comes to them, and thus they receive the consolation promise of the afflicted.[11]

The beatification Mass took place under the best weather of the day. With the beginning of the celebration of the Mass, the rain stopped and held off for about an hour, only to resume just after the pontiff declared Damien's beatification. Before the final blessing, while the Hawaiian choir sang a thanksgiving song in the Hawaiian tongue, Pope John Paul II presented a small casket containing Father Damien's right hand for reburial at St. Philomena, Kalawao, to Bishop Francis X. DiLorenzo, Father Bukoski, and to Edward Kato, a resident leper from Kalaupapa. By so doing he was granting Father Damien's deathbed wish that he be buried under the *pū hala* next to St. Philomena Church.

The hula dancing and the Hawaiian songs and chants—vestiges of the ancient Hawaiian culture that Father Damien as well as the Protestants had done their best to ban—were not supposed to be performed until the pontiff and all of the priests had left the stage. But when the pope lingered, talking with people, the security personnel—noting the return of the rain—motioned for the Hawaiian performers to proceed. As the performance began, the pope turned to watch as it was too late for him to exit without offending the performers. Observers reported that the pope "seemed transfixed by the dance" performed by six hula dancers, and "he was one of the first to clap at the end of the performance." Later, in a liturgy at the Cathedral of St. Michel et Gudule, the pope expressed gratitude to those who had made the trip from Hawai'i, saying he "especially appreciated the women who had danced."[12]

In a midnight service, timed to coincide with the Beatification Mass in Belgium, the Rev. Arsene Daenen celebrated Mass by the candlelight in St. Francis Church in the village of Kalaupapa. The resident lepers, all with arrested disease, were in attendance. The next morning the Protestants held Sunday worship in the tiny Siloama Church while the Catholics celebrated Mass in St. Philomena Church. Then the two groups merged for an interdenominational prayer service at Father Damien's empty grave adjacent to St. Philomena Church.

On June 5, 1995, the koa reliquary box containing Father Damien's right hand arrived at the Honolulu airport at 9 P.M. on

United Airlines flight 145 from San Francisco. It was taken by limousine to the Cathedral of Our Lady of Peace in downtown Honolulu for a 10:15 P.M. candlelight service. Throughout the months of June and July the reliquary box was displayed for public viewing at various churches and hospitals in Honolulu. On July 22 it was interred at the original gravesite adjacent to St. Philomena Church, where the sheltering *pū hala* had stood. The service was attended by the 150 residents from Kalaupapa, by 135 people who hiked down the steep *pali* trail, and by another 400 persons who were flown in by plane and helicopter. In the prayer of thanksgiving offered that day, God was thanked for the return of Father Damien to Kalawao.

The Vatican Congregation for the Cause of Saints continues to evaluate the legitimacy of miracles attributed to intercessory prayers to Father Damien. The canonization of Blessed Father Damien will require the discovery of another miracle attributed to his intercession.

LEPROSY PREMATURELY severed Damien's life at the midpoint, yet the priest lived long enough and achieved enough to allow some generalizations. Father Damien had a genuine love of God and served his Lord by ministering to people without regard to religion, race, sex, or affluence. Included in the spiritual ministry of this multitalented man was the practice of medicine, carpentry and building, music and laughter.

Damien was a man of high energy. He would drive himself to exhaustion to accomplish a goal. This obsession for achievement lighted his pathway during the dark months that preceded his death from leprosy.

Father Damien displayed remarkable religious tolerance toward all Christian denominations. He believed that one served God best by treating all persons—men, women, and children—as a mother, father, sister, or brother. He was the embodiment of the Good Samaritan not only to the Congregationalists, the Episcopalians, and the Mormons, but to those Hawaiians who continued to embrace the ancient religion of the Islands.

Damien was a humble man. He never sought the praise or accolades of men.

Father Damien did displease his superiors on multiple occasions, and he was guilty of periodically violating the rules of his order. When he did so, he did so knowingly, believing that he was doing what God would wish him to do. He was guided by his Lord's teaching: "The Sabbath was made for man, not man for the Sabbath."

Damien practiced medicine, believing it to be an integral part of his spiritual ministry. He decried human suffering and as a physician he could alleviate physical and emotional pain. In his medical practice he emulated the example of his patron saint, Saint Damien the physician, who led many to Christianity by the example of the Good Samaritan.

As a physician, I agree with Mother Teresa's assessment of Father Damien. His life was an example of extraordinary virtue. No additional miracle could add an iota of embellishment.

Perhaps Damien himself best summed up his life when he wrote, "I am the happiest of men for I serve the Lord through the poor and sick children rejected by everyone else."

Epilogue

SIX YEARS FOLLOWING Father Damien's death, **Father Pamphile De Veuster,** Father Damien's older brother, accepted a belated invitation to take his deceased brother's place at the leper settlement. He was 58 years old and had achieved his life's goal of being recognized as a premier biblical scholar. Accompanied by Bishop Gulstan, the successor to Bishop Hermann, he stepped onto the landing wharf at Kalaupapa on November 30, 1895, prepared to assume his brother's priestly responsibilities.

On the part of the Hawaiian Mission, there were dual reasons to issue the invitation. First, the world would applaud the courage of Father Damien's older brother who dared to follow in the footsteps of the "hero of Moloka'i." The second reason was purely political. Father Pamphile's presence would give the Hawaiian Mission the excuse to rid itself of its greatest nuisance, Father Conrardy, the overzealous Belgian priest who, after Father Damien's death, assumed the self-appointed role as his successor.

Father Pamphile never adapted to the gruesome environment of the leper settlement. Twenty-one months later he returned to Belgium and his beloved academic activities.[1]

When Father Pamphile assumed Father Damien's post at Kalawao in 1895, the Sacred Hearts Hawaiian Mission seized the opportunity to rid the leper settlement of **Father Louis-Lambert Conrardy,** the man whose mania for publicity could no longer be tolerated. The Board of Health, with Bishop Gulstan's tacit approval, ordered Father Conrardy to leave the leper settlement, which he did on December 27, 1895.

A few months later, Father Conrardy formally requested reinstatement. The minutes of the Board of Health for January 22, 1896, state: "Request of Father Conrardy to return to the leper settlement for the purpose of caring and nursing lepers not inmates of the Baldwin or the Bishop homes was read. In view of the fact that Father Conrardy had been officious and meddlesome and had indirectly defeated the wishes of the Board in several instances, it was voted to deny his request."

Father Conrardy refused to be brushed aside. He left for China in search of neglected lepers, whom he discovered in large numbers outside of Canton. Chinese officials frustrated his attempts to care for the outcasts, stating that only a doctor of medicine would be permitted to do so. Father Conrardy found no fault with this and returned to the United States to study medicine. Five years later, with his Doctor of Medicine diploma in hand, he returned to Europe to raise funds with which to build a leprosarium in China.

In July 1903, the Hawaiian Board of Health was startled to receive a second offer from Father Conrardy in which he volunteered to return to the leper settlement as the assistant resident physician. According to the minutes of the July meeting, "After a general discussion in which the past record of Dr. Conrardy—at that time 'Father' Conrardy—at the leper station was considered, his request was denied."

Undaunted, Dr. Conrardy returned to China in May 1908, and with the 150,000 francs he had solicited, he bought 20 acres on the island of Shek Lung, opposite Canton, and constructed a small village to which he invited seventy lepers. Within a few years he turned his Shek Lung establishment into a second Moloka'i. In time he received the support of the Chinese government, and his leper settlement swelled to serve seven hundred patients, aided by five nursing sisters and two priests. He died of pneumonia in August 1914, honored as "the example of those noble virtues that formed his characteristics: mortification, charity, energy."[2] If there is an unsung hero in the Father Damien story, it is Father Conrardy.

Because of the more favorable weather conditions on the western side of the Kalaupapa Peninsula, the leper settlement gradually moved to the village of Kalaupapa. Chilly, rain-swept Kalawao was officially abandoned in 1932. The discovery in the 1940s that the sulfone drug dapsone was an effective antimicrobial medication with which to treat leprosy ended Hawai'i's leprosy epidemic. Dapsone was curative, safe in pregnancy, and it was very inexpensive. In 1996 there were still sixty-seven patients remaining of those who chose to stay after quarantine was ended in 1969. They ranged in age from the mid-sixties to the late nineties. State law guarantees lifetime medical care to the lepers, and this has been expanded to include a completely equipped and staffed modern hospital, meals on wheels, and home care.

Because drugs have rendered the lepers noninfectious, there are no travel restrictions, and occasionally a visitor to Hawai'i may encounter one of the elderly lepers, who might be missing a finger or two, shopping in Honolulu.

All that is left for visitors to view in the original leper village of Kalawao are St. Philomena Church, Siloama Congregational Church, the ruins of the Baldwin Home Bakery, and a few pillars from the U.S. Leprosy Investigation Station. In 1980 President Carter signed a bill designating the Kalaupapa Peninsula as a National Historic Park.

The Native Hawaiian population continued its steep decline from a high of between 250,000 to 400,000 in 1778 to 34,436 in 1890 and 28,718 in 1900. Meanwhile, the total population of the Islands increased from 89,990 in 1890 to 154,001 in 1900. This demonstrates the havoc that communicable disease can inflict on a native population lacking natural immunity. Today there are fewer than five thousand full-blooded Hawaiians in the Islands.

Brother Joseph Dutton continued to serve at the leper settlement until, at the age of eighty-seven, deteriorating health made it necessary for him to be hospitalized in Honolulu. He was a prodigious letter writer and was as well known in his day as Father Damien had been earlier. In 1907, President Theodore Roosevelt acknowledged his years of selfless service by having the U.S. Naval Armada, which was circling the globe, salute the ex-Union officer with a volley of gunfire as it passed the Kalaupapa Peninsula.

In January 1931, the man from Janesville, Wisconsin, wrote, "I guess that I have come to the end of the trail; that my work is finished. I hope that God approves."[3] Brother Dutton died on March 26, 1931, one month before his eighty-eighth birthday. "Though unworthy, I wish to be buried at the feet of Damien"—his last request—was honored.[4]

President Herbert Hoover wrote: "I am deeply interested in the romantic story of Brother Joseph Dutton, whose life as a pioneer, soldier, and great humanitarian is so characteristic of our people in its variety, picturesqueness and idealism. His service to the lepers of Moloka'i crowned his life with a saintly glory. It is a privilege to pay tribute to his memory."[5]

Mother Marianne Cope continued to serve the lepers for the remainder of her life. In 1888 she resigned as the provincial in the United States when she took up residence at the Bishop Home in the leper settlement.

Mother Marianne died at the age of 81 on August 9, 1918, at the Sisters of St. Francis Convent in Kalaupapa. The cause of death was kidney disease and heart failure (tubular nephritis and mitral valvular disease). Her grave at Kalaupapa is marked by a beautiful monument, a high pedestal surmounted by a statue of St. Francis embracing the crucified Savior. In 1974, the Sacred Congregation for the Causes of Saints granted the Franciscan Sisters of Syracuse permission to gather and submit preliminary research on the life and virtue of Mother Marianne. Since 1980, the Historical Commission for the Cause of Mother Marianne, established by Bishop John Scanlan of Honolulu, has been collecting and submitting data to Rome.

The reign of **Queen Lili'uokalani** lasted only from 1891 to 1893, when she tried to increase the power of the monarch by abolishing the restrictions that had been placed on King Kalākaua. This precipitated an American-led revolution. The queen was deposed with the help of American troops who landed to keep the peace. A republic was established in 1894, with the hope that the United States would annex Hawai'i, but President Grover Cleveland tried instead to restore Lili'uokalani to her throne. He failed. In 1898, the United States annexed Hawai'i.

Lili'uokalani died in 1917. She is perhaps best known for her song, "Aloha 'Oe," the traditional farewell song of Hawai'i.

Robert Louis Stevenson, the famous author, returned to Hawai'i in 1893, and again he took up lodgings at Waikīkī. An avowed monarchist, he visited the deposed Queen Lili'uokalani but avoided all political involvement. Illness forced his return to Samoa, where he died of a stroke in 1894.[6] Father Damien lost his most flamboyant defender, but the words of the defender have been incorporated into each new Father Damien biography.

In 1893, **Rev. Dr. Charles M. Hyde** tried again to vindicate himself in staunchly maintaining that his view of Father Damien was the true and appropriate one by publishing a twenty-two-page pamphlet entitled "Father Damien and His Work."[7] In August 1895, Hyde dared to visit Kalawao for the dedication of the Henry P. Baldwin Home for Boys. He had been warned that if he ever set foot at the settlement, he would be pelted with rotten eggs. No eggs were thrown, and following the dedication ceremony he was magnanimously served dinner by the Franciscan sisters. Hyde lived until 1899, one year after the annexation of the Hawaiian Islands to the United States.

Many viewed **Mother Teresa,** winner of the 1979 Nobel Peace Prize, as a "living saint" for her fifty years of serving the poorest of the poor in her worldwide Mission of Mercy and Compassion. This champion of the Cause of Father Damien died following a heart attack at the age of 87 on September 5, 1997.

Rudolph Meyer died in Honolulu in June 1897, shortly after returning from an inspection of the leper settlement. At the time of his death, Meyer owned 2,988 acres of land on Moloka'i. Meyer's most notable saying to his sons was *"Mālama Ka 'Āina,"* "Save, perpetuate, and care for your land." Meyer's oldest son, Otto Samuel, remembered how the sons sat around the table in the evenings, talking about the old Hawaiians who were selling their land to foreigners or aliens. Meyer reportedly lamented, "The land is gone to the Caucasian missionary, the money is gone to the Chinese, the jobs have gone to the Japanese. Only the rocks are left to the Hawaiians."[8]

In November 1890, an ailing **King David Kalākaua** sailed for San Francisco for an extended rest and vacation. He had been diagnosed with Bright's Disease, a medical term used in the late nineteen century to designate serious kidney disease. Dr. G. W. Woods, the same physician who had visited the leper settlement in 1876, was one of his attending physicians in San Francisco. On January 20, 1891, the king died of a stroke. The USS *Charleston* returned the body to Honolulu for burial, and on the afternoon of the arrival of the casket, Princess Lili'uokalani, Kalākaua's sister, became Queen Lili'uokalani.[9]

Father Charles Pouzot continued to practice medicine among the Native Hawaiians on the Big Island, never shying away from the treatment of lepers. He had a neuritis "affecting the nerves of the left forearm and hand, due to leprosy," which was quiescent but left a numbness and marked atrophic changes in the muscles in the hand and skin of the forearm.[10] Father Charles also had atrophic changes in the skin over other areas of his body. A symmetrical enlargement of the left ulnar nerve above and below the elbow joint confirmed that the leprosy bacillus was residing in his body.

Dr. Charles Hinckley Wetmore died at his home in Hilo in April 1898, ninety days before Hawai'i was annexed by the United States. His daughter, "Dr. Frank," had assumed full responsibility for the medical practice, and in imitation of her father, never turned an indigent patient away.

After serving as the leper settlement's first resident physician for one year, **Dr. Nathaniel B. Emerson** established a private practice on O'ahu. In 1881 he married Dr. Sarah E. Pierce. From 1887 to 1890 he served as the president of the Board of Health, during which time a distraught husband of a leper attempted to shoot him. In 1905 he left private practice to became a police surgeon so he might devote more time to his historical research. His publications include a translation of David Malo's *Hawaiian Antiquities* and *Unwritten Literature of Hawaii*, a translation of the sacred songs of the hula, published by the Smithsonian Institution in 1909. He was a member of many professional, historical, and educational organizations, served for seventeen years as a trustee of Punahou School, and occupied his later years with research on Hawaiian folklore. He died on July 16, 1915, at the age of seventy-six while on a cruise between Alaska and San Francisco.[11]

In 1887, **Charles Warren Stoddard** left Notre Dame to join the faculty of the Catholic University in Washington, D.C., where he taught English literature for thirteen years. Then he returned to California and continued his writing, publishing multiple works of nonfiction and poetry, including *Footprints in the Padres* in 1903. He died in Monterey, California, in 1909.

After serving as a nurse to the lepers for forty-three years, **Sister Leopoldina Burns** retired to the St. Francis Novitiate in August 1928. She was transferred to the new St. Francis Convent, a memorial to Mother Marianne, when it opened in 1931; and she died in St. Francis Hospital, Honolulu, on June 3, 1942, at age 87. Her unpublished journals contained in fifteen notebooks housed in the archives of St. Anthony's Convent, the Mother House of the Third Franciscan Order Minor Conventual, Syracuse, New York, present a poignant history of the leper settlement.

Dr. Fitch died on June 4, 1904. His contention that leprosy was the fourth stage of syphilis proved to be false.

Dr. G. A. Hansen, the discoverer of the leprosy bacillus, died in 1912.

From Molokaʻi, **Father André Burgermann** was sent to Lahaina, Maui, where he labored many years until he became too feeble to continue as a parish priest. He never again engaged in the practice of medicine; but like Father Damien, his previous contacts with the lepers extracted a toll. Dr. Mouritz observed that he had "symptoms of leprous neuritis, almost identical with those of Father Charles Pouzot."[12] Father Andre died in Honolulu in 1907 at the age of 78.

Father Albert Montiton died in Spain in 1894.

In 1916, **Dr. Arthur Mouritz** published the first American book on Hawaiian leprosy, *The Path of the Destroyer*, a comprehensive treatise in which he presented in detail what he had observed and learned during his sojourn at the leper settlement on Molokaʻi. It is a brilliant historical text.

Leprosy Today

The number of leprosy cases worldwide has dropped dramatically in the past decade, from 10 to 12 million cases to 1.2–2 million. This decline is due to improved case detection, the use of short-course multidrug therapy, expanded BCG vaccination programs, and increasing global urbanization. Leprosy remains a disease of the rural poor. In 1995, five countries—India, Brazil, Bangladesh, Indonesia, and Myanmar—accounted for 76 percent of the estimated number of cases in the world. Up to 20 percent of cases occur in children under the age of ten. The incidence of leprosy in the United States has fallen from a peak of 360 cases in 1985—due mainly to the influx of immigrants from Southeast Asia—to an average of 150 cases per year.[13]

Direct human-to-human transmission is believed responsible for the majority of cases of leprosy. The development of clinical infection approaches 10 percent among close family contacts of untreated lepromatous patients; however, only a small fraction of those persons actually infected develop clinical disease.

Case finding and chemotherapy form the present basis for the control of leprosy, because infectiousness can be quickly suppressed with chemotherapy. Dapsone, a folate antagonist, is the mainstay of

therapy. It is quite inexpensive and safe in pregnancy. Years of dapsone monotherapy have led to the emergence of dapsone-resistant
strains of M. *leprae*. To counter this problem, multiple-drug therapy
is now recommended. The optimal duration of therapy is unknown.
In the United States, two or three drugs are administered for three to
five years, followed by lifelong dapsone therapy.

Notes

Codes are used throughout the notes to designate frequently cited sources. Unpublished sources are coded in full capitals (ARC.) and published sources in upper/lowercase letters (Bh.). For a key to these abbreviations, see the bibliography. All other sources in the notes are cited in full.

Prologue

1. *St. Anthony Messenger* 101:30–31, May 1994.
3. *The Lives of the Holy Martyrs and Hermits*. Pam.15. Tau.FD.2.

Chapter 1. Exile: Day One

1. Yze.186.
2. ARC. Letter from Bishop Maigret to Father Germain, June 19, 1873. Gre.26.
3. Bh.1886.64. David E. Stannard. *Before the Horror: The Population of Hawai'i on the Eve of Western Contact*. Honolulu: University of Hawai'i Press, 1989.
4. Joe.205–206.
5. HUT.
6. Bha.1886. Appendix M. "Special Report of Rev. J. Damien."
7. From a letter of Monsignor Maigret to Father Germain, procurator general. Catholic Missions, 1873, p.476.
8. Bh.1886.27–38,38.
9. Gre.58–59.
10. ARC. Letter from Bishop Maigret to Father Germain, June 19, 1873.
11. HUT. Gre.52–62.
12. Cah.24.
13. Cah.24–25.
14. *Pacific Commercial Advertiser*, May 10, 1873.
15. *Ka Nupepa Nuhou*, April 15, 1873.
16. HUT.
17. New Testament, Matt. 25:40 Revised Standard Version.

18. Bha.1886. Appendix M. "Special Report of Rev. J. Damien."
19. Ibid.

Chapter 2: Birth, Childhood, and Beyond

1. RAE. Shortly after Father Damien's death the Rev. Father Maurice Raepsaet wrote the *Life of Father Damien*, a biography based on Father Pamphile's biographical sketch of his brother. The manuscript was never published.

Pam. The first biography published after Father Damien's death was *The Life and Letters of Father Damien*, written in English by the Rev. Father Kingdon, S.J. Published in 1889, the work acknowledges Father Pamphile as an editor, is replete with quotations from his biographical sketch of his brother, and contains a collection of personal letters.

Tau.FD. *Father Damien, Apostle of the Lepers of Molokai*, composed in French by the Rev. Father Philibert Tauvel, a priest of the Congregation of the Sacred Hearts in Louvain, and published in 1890. This biography was based on additional documents supplied the author by Father Pamphile.

2. RAE., Pam., Tau.FD.
3. Pam.19.
4. Tau.FD.5.
5. Epidemic typhus is caused by *Rickettsia prowazekii*, a small, rod-shaped microbe, which is transmitted from person to person by the bite of a louse, *Pediculus humanus*. After successful invasion of a human body followed by an incubation period of 10–14 days, the disease usually begins abruptly with a severe headache, generalized aches and pains, and high fever with shaking chills. About the fifth day of the illness a rash appears. Fever may last two weeks. In the second week there may be delirium and stupor, progressing to coma and ending in death in 20 percent of those infected.
6. Pam.14–15.
7. Bun.29.
8. Pam.29.
9. Pam.21.
10. ARC. This undated letter was probably written in April 1858, shortly after Jef's arrival at Brains-le-Comte. Second letter from J. De Veuster to his parents on June 3, 1858, relates the torn trousers episode.
11. Pam.24.
12. ARC. Letter from J. De Veuster to his parents, July 17, 1858.
13. Pam.24–26.
14. Jor.16. Father Gerard Schellinger, former vice-rector of the American College at Louvain, related this interesting occurrence to Father Vital Jourdain, a Damien biographer.
15. Pam.25.
16. ARC. Letter from J. De Veuster to his parents, December 25, 1858.
17. ARC. Letter from J. De Veuster to his parents, January 1, 1859.

Chapter 3. The Sacred Hearts of Jesus and Mary

1. Officially, the canonical name of the order Damien had chosen to join was the *Congregation of the Sacred Hearts of Jesus and Mary and of Perpetual Adoration of the Most Blessed Sacrament of the Altar*. It was a young order, founded in 1800 and approved by Pope Pius VII in 1817. Its priests were known as Fathers of the Sacred Hearts or Picpus Fathers, after the Rue de Picpus in Paris where the Mother House was located. The founder of the congregation was Father Marie-Joseph Coudrin, a French diocesan priest who—at the risk of his life—had gone about in disguise during the French Revolution administering the sacraments to Catholics in hiding. In September 1792, while secluded in a barn after celebrating an undercover Mass, Father Coudrin had a vision of white-clad missionaries going to all parts of the world while a second group of religious knelt day and night praying for the missionaries and making reparation for mankind's crimes against the Blessed Sacrament. Some months later, when introduced to the Countess Henriette de la Chevalerie, he recognized her as one of the religious figures in his vision. Father Marie-Joseph promptly became the countess' spiritual mentor. Later, with her collaboration, he founded the Congregation of the Sacred Hearts on Christmas Eve, 1800.

2. "Damien" is the Belgian spelling of "Damian."

3. Pam.32.

4. Eng.21–22.

5. Eng.23.

6. Pam.32.

7. Pam.13.

8. Tau.23.

9. Ibid.

10. Ibid.

11. Pam.41. Jor.25–26. Bun.179–180.

12. Pam.40.

13. Pam.43.

Chapter 4. The Quest Begins: Hawai'i

1. Tau.28.

2. Pam.43.

3. Pam.44.

4. Ibid.

5. Pam.45.

6. Tau.30.

7. Pam.45. Jou.29–30.

8. ARC. Letter from Brother Damien to his parents, October 30, 1863.

9. ARC. Letters from Brother Damien to his parents, October 30,

1863, and March 22, 1864. Letter from Brother Damien to Father Pamphile, March 21, 1864.

10. Ibid.

11. Jou.32.

12. ARC. Letter from Brother Damien to Father Pamphile, March 21, 1864.

13. Ibid.

14. Ibid.

15. Ibid.

16. Ibid.

17. Ibid.

18. Kuy.II.124. Daw.ST.159.

19. Ruth M. Tabrah. *Niʻihau, the Last Hawaiian Island*, Chapter 10. Kailua, Hawaiʻi: Press Pacifica, 1987.

20. ARC. Letters from Brother Damien to his parents, April 25, 1864, and August, 1864.

21. Sta.8.

22. O. A. Bushnell. *The Gifts of Civilization: Germs and Genocide in Hawaiʻi*. Honolulu: University of Hawaiʻi Press, 1993.

23. Dia.214. Sta.

24. Joe.165–170.

25. Byzantine Liturgy, *Euchologion*.

Chapter 5. Puna: Father Damien's First Parish

1. ARC. Letter from Father Damien to the superior general, November 1, 1864.

2. Old Testament, 2 Kings 16:29–19:18 RSV.

3. Kam.98. N. P. Larsen."Medical Art in Ancient Hawaiʻi," 53rd Annual Report of the Hawaiian Historical Society. Honolulu, 1944.

4. E. S. Handy, M. K. Pukui, and K. Livermore. *Outline of Hawaiian Physical Therapeutics*. B. P. Bishop Museum Bulletin 126. Honolulu: Bishop Museum Press, 1934.

5. ARC. Letter from Father Damien to the superior general, November 1, 1864.

6. ARC. Letter from Father Damien to Father Pamphile, August 23, 1864.

7. ARC. Letter from Father Charles Pouzot to Father Modeste, August 21, 1864.

8. Hawaiian name for "Father Damien." *Makua* is "Father"; *Kamiano* is "Damien."

9. Jou.47.

10. ARC. Letter from Father Damien to Father Pamphile, August 23, 1864. Twa.77–81,85.

11. ARC. Letter from Father Damien to Father Modeste, August 15, 1864.

12. Yze.193.

13. ARC. Letter from Father Damien to Father Modeste, October 23, 1864.

14. ARC. Letter from Father Damien to Father Modeste, October 5, 1864.

15. Hal.202–217.

16. Hal.203.

17. Hal.229.

18. ARC. Letter from Father Damien to Father Pamphile, August 23, 1864.

19. ARC. Letter from Father Damien to the superior general, October 23, 1864.

20. Ibid.

21. DUT. "To Whom It May Concern," October 12, 1903.

22. ARC. Letter from Father Damien to the superior general, October 23, 1865.

Chapter 6. Kohala-Hāmākua: The Second Parish

1. ARC. Letter from Father Damien to the superior general, Oct. 23, 1865.

2. ARC. Letter from Father Modeste to the superior general, August 10, 1865.

3. ARC. Letter from Father Damien to Father Pamphile and the fathers in Louvain, October 23, 1865.

4. ARC. Letters from Damien to his parents, October 30, 1863, and March 22, 1864.

5. Mor.WH.11. Mor.30.

6. Richard A. Miller. "Leprosy (Hansen's Disease)." Chapter 126 in *Harrison's Principles of Internal Medicine*. New York: McGraw-Hill, 1991.

7. ARC. Letter from Father Damien to the superior general, October 23, 1865.

8. HUT.7.

9. Ibid.

10. ARC. Letter from Father Damien to his parents, January 15, 1867.

11. *Pacific Commercial Advertiser*: December 29, 1866; January 12, February 2 and 9, 1867; *Hawaiian Gazette*, February 6 and 13, 1867; *Report of the Board of Health*, 1868, pp. 2–4.

12. "The Lepers." An investigative report. *Hawaiian Gazette*, February 6, 1867.

13. ARC. Letter from Father Damien to Father Pamphile, October 1867.

14. ARC. Letter from Father Damien to Father Modeste, December 29, 1867.

Chapter 7. The Calm before the Storm of Molokaʻi

1. ARC. Letter from Father Damien to Father Modeste, January 28, 1868.

2. ARC. Letter from Father Damien to Father Modeste, February 13, 1868.

3. ARC. Letter from Father Damien to Father Modeste, March 24, 1868.

4. Kuy.II.105–107.

5. *Hawaiian Gazette*, April 15, 1868.

6. *Hawaiian Gazette*: February 12; March 11 and 18; June 10; October 21 and 28; November 4 and 18, 1868. *Pacific Commercial Advertiser*: March 14; October 10, 24, and 31; November 14 and 21, 1868.

7. ARC. Letter from Father Modeste to the superior general, August 26, 1868.

8. ARC. Letter from Father Gulstan to Brother Bernard, October 12, 1868.

9. Twa.L.54–55.

10. Twa.L.129.

11. Twa.L.175–176.

12. *Hawaiian Gazette*, August 6, 1868.

13. ARC. Letter from Father Damien to Father Modeste, August 25, 1868.

14. *Hawaiian Gazette*, January 13, 1869.

15. G. A. Hansen. "Forelobige Bidrag til Spedalskhedens Karakteristik" (Preliminary Contributions to the Characterization of Leprosy). *Nord med Arkiv* 1:1–12, 1869.

16. ARC. Letter from Father Damien to Father Modeste, July 9, 1870.

17. ARC. Letter from Father Damien to Father Pamphile, September 1870.

18. ARC. Letter from Father Damien to Sister Pauline, July 14, 1872.

19. ARC. Letter from Father Damien to Father Pamphile, July 14, 1872.

20. Kuy.II.262.

21. Gre.63.

22. Kuy.II.257.

23. *Pacific Commercial Advertiser*, July 8, 1873.

24. ARC. Described in detail in a letter from Father Damien to his superior general, August 1873.

25. MAI. May 1873.

26. Ibid.

Chapter 8. Exile: The First Weeks

1. ARC. "We lepers . . .": fourth paragraph of Father Damien's letter to Father Pamphile, November 25, 1873.

2. Ibid.

3. ARC. Letter from Father Damien to Father Marcelin Bousquet, superior general, August 1873.

4. Gre.57–61.

5. Bha.1886. Appendix M. "Special Report of Rev. J. Damien."

6. Ibid.

7. DUT. Father Damien's dictated description of the onset of his leprosy. Notes taken by Brother Joseph Dutton, March 10, 1889, Kalawao, Moloka'i.

8. *Ka Nupepa Nuhou*, May 13, 1873.

9. Bha.1886. Appendix M. "Special Report of Rev. J. Damien."

10. Ibid.

11. Mor.215–217.

12. Gre.85.

13. FD.5.

14. Bh.1886.62.

15. Mor.218–219.

16. Gre.53.

17. Bha.1886. Appendix M. "Special Report of Rev. J. Damien."

18. ARC. Letter from Father Damien to Father Modeste, May 12, 1873.

19. Bha.1886. Appendix M. "Special Report of Rev. J. Damien."

20. ARC. Letter from Father Modeste to Father Damien, May 20, 1873.

21. ARC. Letter from Father Damien to Father Modeste, May 20, 1873.

22. Mor.WH.59.

23. HUT.

24. ARC. Letter from Father Modeste to Father Bousquet, superior general, May 28, 1873.

25. Ibid.

26. Jor.101.

27. ARC. Letter from Father Damien to Father Modeste, May 27, 1873.

28. Gre.105–108.

29. Ibid.

Chapter 9. A Prisoner Forever!

1. Mor.217–218.

2. Mey.21–72.

3. Kae.7, 9. Letter 1, Peter to Emma, July 1, 1873.

4. Kae.

5. Kae.9. Letter 1, Peter to Emma, July 1, 1873.

6. In 1866, King Kamehameha V appointed Peter Kaeo to the House of Nobles.

7. The Board of Health established a fifty-bed hospital in the Kalihi District of Honolulu in 1865–1866. Following the establishment of the Kalaupapa leper settlement in 1866, Kalihi Hospital served as a way station for lepers en route to Moloka'i.

8. QE. Letter from King Kamehameha V to Queen Emma, Honolulu, January 18, 1868.

9. Editorial, *Pacific Commercial Advertiser*, July 8, 1873. Dr. Trousseau's views on Leprosy.

10. Kae.9. Letter 1, Peter to Emma, July 1, 1873. During his stay on Moloka'i, Peter Kaeo signed his letters to Queen Emma with the name of an

aristocratic ancestor, *Kekuaokalani*, a sacerdotal chief who had been chosen by Kamehameha I to be one of the two heirs to the Kingdom.

11. Kae.24. Letter 10, Peter to Emma, July 16, 1873.

12. Kae.30. Letter 12, Peter to Emma, July 20, 1873.

13. Kae.230. Letter 89, Peter to Emma, August 17, 1874. Twa.L.110–111. Seven years earlier, Mark Twain had observed William Ragsdale in action when he served as the chief bilingual interpreter for the Hawaiian legislature. Twain judged him to be an interesting enough politician—"a spice of deviltry"—to include him in one of his Hawaiian letters.

14. Kae.55. Letter from William Ragsdale to E. O. Hall, July 2, 1873.

15. Kae.16.

16. *Pacific Commercial Advertiser*, June 14, 1873.

17. Ibid.

18. MEY.

19. Kae.54. Letter 23, Peter to Emma, August 13, 1873.

20. Kae.55. Minutes of the Board of Health, August 15, 1873.

21. Ibid.

22. Kae.63–64. Letter 25, Peter to Emma, August 15, 1873.

23. Bha.1886. Appendix M. "Special Report of Rev. J. Damien."

24. ARC. Letter from the secretary of the Board of Health to Father Damien, September 1, 1873.

25. ARC. Letter from the president of the Board of Health to Bishop Maigret, November 4, 1873.

26. ARC. Letter from Father Modeste to the superior general, October 8, 1873.

27. Ibid.

28. ARC. Extract from a letter of Father Aubert, September 14, 1874.

29. ARC. Extract from a letter of Father Aubert, November 3, 1889.

30. Kae.141. Letter 54, Peter to Emma, October 27, 1873.

31. Vog.285.

32. Cli. Shortly before his death, Father Damien disclosed the secret behind his positive attitude to Edward Clifford, the English artist who visited him in 1887.

Chapter 10. Free at Last!

1. ARC. Letter from Edwin O. Hall, minister of the Interior and president of the Board of Health, to Charles R. Bishop, minister of Foreign Affairs, November 13, 1873.

2. ARC. Letter from Father Damien to his parents, November 25, 1873.

3. ARC. Letter from the Department of the Interior to Father Damien, December 18, 1873.

4. ARC. Letter from Father Damien to Father Pamphile, November 25, 1873.

5. Ibid.

6. ARC. Letter from the superior general to Father Damien, August 21, 1873.

7. Kuy.II.259, 261–262.

8. Kae.84. Letter 37. Emma to Peter, September 2, 1873.

9. Gre.98.

10. HUT.1–5.

11. ARC. Letter from Father Pamphile to Father Damien, May 1873.

12. Gre.99.

13. ARC. Letter from Father André Burgermann to Father Damien, February 24, 1874.

14. ARC. Letter from Father André to the superior general, Kalua'aha, January 6, 1875.

15. ARC. Letter from Father Damien to Father Modeste, March 16, 1874.

16. Kae.184. Letter 71, Peter to Emma, April 14, 1874.

17. *Pacific Commercial Advertiser*, April 8, 1874.

18. Kae.242. Letter 91, Peter to Emma, September 16, 1874.

19. ARC. Letter from Father Damien to Father Modeste, April 19, 1874.

20. ARC. Letter from Father André to the superior general, January 6, 1875.

21. ARC. Letter from Father Gulstan to Father Damien, July 2, 1874.

22. ARC. Letter from Father Damien to Father Pamphile, November 25, 1873.

23. ARC. Extract from a letter of Father Léonor, July 22, 1874.

24. Ibid.

25. ARC. Letter from Father Damien to Father Modeste, June 21, 1874.

26. ARC. Letter from Father Damien to Father Gabriel Germain, December 8, 1874.

27. ARC. Note from Father Damien to Father Modeste, August 1874.

28. ARC. Extract from a letter of Father André to the superior general, Kalua'aha, January 6, 1875.

29. DUT. Father Damien's dictated description of the onset of his leprosy. Notes taken by Brother Joseph Dutton, March 10, 1889, Kalawao, Moloka'i.

30. ARC. Letter from Father Damien to Father Pamphile, December 8, 1874.

31. Dut.SM.79.

32. ARC. Letter from Father Damien to his mother and family members, December 8, 1874.

Chapter 11. Like the Christ: Priest, Physician, Carpenter

1. ARC. Letter from Father Modeste to the superior general, May 10, 1875.

2. ARC. Letter from Father Damien to Father Germain, March 1876.

3. ARC. Letter from Father Modeste to the superior general, September 14, 1875.

4. Mey.76–77.

5. ARC. Letter from Father André to the superior general, September 1, 1875.

6. Kae.317. Letter 122, Emma to Peter, May 10, 1876.

7. *Pacific Commercial Advertiser*, June 28, 1876.

8. Kae.281–282.

9. *Pacific Commercial Advertiser*, May 4, 1878.

10. Bh.1886.78.

11. Ibid.

12. Wod. All of the quotations by Dr. Woods are from his published account: *Reminiscences of a Visit, in July, 1876, to the Leper Settlement of Molokai, Having Special Reference to Rev. Father J. Damien De Veuster.* Birmingham, England, John Gately, 1895.

13. Ibid.

14. Ibid.

15. Ibid.

16. Ibid.

17. Ibid.

18. Kae.230. Letter 89, Peter to Emma, August 17, 1874.

19. Wod.

20. Ibid.

21. ARC. Letters from Father Damien to his parents and Father Pamphile dated October 30, 1863, March 21, 1864, and March 22, 1864.

22. Wod.

Chapter 12. "We Lepers . . ."

1. DUT. Father Damien's account of his leprosy, dictated to Brother Joseph Dutton, March 10, 1889, Kalawao, Moloka'i.

2. Ibid.

3. Eng.153–154.

4. Bh.1886.80.

5. Ibid.

6. *Analysis of the Taxation of the Hawaiian Kingdom for the Year 1881.* Honolulu, 1882.

7. ARC. Letter from Father Damien to R. W. Meyer, March 20, 1877.

8. Letter from R. W. Meyer to C. T. Gulick, June 14, 1877. Correspondence, Board of Health, Archives of Hawai'i, Honolulu.

9. *Hawaiian Gazette*, December 12, 1877.

10. ARC. Letter from Father André to Father Damien, November 26, 1877.

11. ARC. Letter from R. W. Meyer to Father Damien, November 29, 1877.

12. ARC. Letter from R. W. Meyer to Father Damien, December 7, 1877.

13. ARC. Letter from R. W. Meyer to Father Damien, December 19, 1877.

14. Letter from Father Damien to Samuel Wilder, January 25, 1878. Board of Health Letter Book.

15. ARC. Letter from Father Damien to Father Modeste, February 25, 1878.

16. Board of Health, Archives of Hawai'i.

17. ARC. Letter from Father Modeste to the superior general, February 27, 1878.

18. Mor.234–235.

19. *Hawaiian Gazette*, August 7, 1878.

20. *Pacific Commercial Advertiser*, June 22, 1878.

21. Bh.1886.80–92.

22. Ibid.

23. Gre.101.

24. Pam.16.

25. MEY.

26. ARC. Letter from Father Damien to R. W. Meyer, April 25, 1878.

27. ARC. Letter from Father Damien to Father Lesserteur, August 21, 1878.

28. ARC. Letter from Father André to Father Damien, December 17, 1878.

29. ARC. Letter from Father Damien to Father Modeste, December 21, 1878.

30. ARC. Letter from Father Damien to Father Bousquet, superior general, February 4, 1879.

Chapter 13. Hutchison, the Survivor; Emerson, the Courageous Physician

1. Hut.1–5.
2. Ibid.
3. Ibid.
4. Ibid.
5. Hal.304–305.
6. Ibid.
7. Bh.1886.96–97.
8. HUT.3–5.
9. Bh.1886.94–95.
10. *Pacific Commercial Advertiser*, August 2, 1879.
11. HUT.23–24.
12. Letter from the minister of the Interior to J. H. Napela and Ephraim Kanoe, June 14, 1879. Interior Department Book 16, p. 225. Archives of Hawai'i.

13. HUT.

14. HUT.20–21.

15. Ibid.

16. A. Neisser. "Zur Aetilogie der Lepra" (The Etiology of Leprosy). *Breslauer arztl. Zeitschr.* 1:200–214, 1879.

Chapter 14. His Finest Works

1. ARC. Letter from Father Damien to Father Pamphile, January 31, 1880.

2. Mor.76.

3. Pam.105.

4. Gre.128.

5. ARC. Letter from Father Damien to Father Pamphile, January 31, 1880.

6. *Pacific Commercial Advertiser*, February 21, 1880.

7. Ibid.

8. Sto.LM.80–85.

9. ARC. Letter from Father Damien to the Mormons, February 1, 1880.

10. ARC. Letter from Father Regis to the superior general, July 5, 1880.

11. Ibid.

12. ARC. Letter from Father Regis to the superior general, February 9, 1880.

13. Letter from Father Damien to Dr. Emerson, July 13, 1880. Board of Health, Archives of Hawai'i.

14. HUT.

15. Ibid.

16. Ibid.

17. ARC. Letter from Father Gulstan to Father Damien, August 23, 1880.

18. ARC. Letter from Father Charles to Father Damien, October 1880.

19. ARC. Letter from Walter Murray Gibson to Father Damien, 1880.

20. Bh.1886.100–106.

21. Ibid.

22. *Hawaiian Gazette*, December 1, 1880.

23. Kuy.III.223–224.

24. Ibid.

25. Gre.130.

26. Bh.1886.107–113.

27. DUT. Father Damien's account of his leprosy, dictated to Brother Joseph Dutton, March 10, 1889, Kalawao, Moloka'i.

28. ARC. Extract from a letter of Father Modeste to the superior general, May 10, 1875.

29. ARC. Extracts from a letter of Father Regis to the superior general, August 20, 1879.

30. ARC. Extracts from a letter of Father Regis to the superior general, April 21, 1880.

31. Jou.160–161.

32. HUT.28.

33. ARC. Letters from Father Damien to Bishop Hermann Koeckemann, December 6 and 31, 1881.

Chapter 15. A Medal of Honor and a Crown of Thorns

1. *Hawaiian Gazette*, September 21, 1881; *Pacific Commercial Advertiser*, September 24, 1881.

2. Ibid.

3. Ibid.

4. Ibid.

5. Hawaiian for "Father Damien." *Makua* means "Father."

6. ARC. Letter from Princess Lili'uokalani to Father Damien, September 20, 1881.

7. *Hawaiian Gazette*, September 21, 1881.

8. ARC. Letter from Bishop Hermann to the Associates of the Holy Childhood, October 21, 1881.

9. HUT.56.

10. ARC. Letter from Father Damien to Father Pamphile, December 13, 1881.

11. Ibid.

12. Bh.1886.113.

13. Board of Health Report, 1884.

14. ARC. Letter from Father Damien to Father Pamphile, December 13, 1881.

15. Bh.1886.117–119.

16. ARC. Letter from Father Damien to Bishop Hermann, December 6, 1881.

17. ARC. Letter from Bishop Hermann to Father Damien, December 20, 1881.

18. Cah.21–23.

19. Daw.ST.224–225.

20. Joe.215–217.

21. Kuy.III.88.

22. G. A. Hansen. "Bacillus leprae," *Nord. med. Arkiv.* 12:1–10, 1880; "Bacillus Leprae," *Virchow's Archiv.* 79:32–42, 1880; "The Bacillus of Leprosy," *Quart. J. Microscop. Sci.* 20:92–102, 1880.

23. Bh.1886.122–124.

24. ARC. Letter from Father Damien to Bishop Hermann, August 31, 1882.

25. Ibid.

26. ARC. Letter from R. W. Meyer to Father Damien, November 22, 1882.

27. ARC. Letter from Father Damien to Walter M. Gibson, November 1882.

28. DUT. Father Damien's account of his leprosy, dictated to Brother Joseph Dutton, March 10, 1889, Kalawao, Moloka'i.

29. L. E. Watson, ed. *Light from Many Lamps.* (New York: Pocket Books, 1976):161.

30. ARC. Letter from Bishop Hermann to Father Damien, December 18, 1882.

31. ARC. Letter from Father Damien to Bishop Hermann, December 21, 1882.

32. ARC. Letter from Father Damien to Father Pamphile, January 18, 1883.

Chapter 16. The Year of the Nurses

1. ARC. Letter from Father Damien to Father Pamphile, January 18, 1883.

2. Ibid.

3. Ibid.

4. ARC. Letter from Father Damien to Bishop Hermann, February 8, 1883.

5. Ibid.

6. Bh.1886.139–140. Letters from Walter Murray Gibson and Dr. Fitch to Bishop Hermann, January, 1883.

7. ARC. Letter from Father Damien to Bishop Hermann, February 22, 1883.

8. ARC. Letter from Father Damien to Bishop Hermann, April 3, 1883.

9. Mey.29.

10. Han.42–43.

11. Han.45.

12. Han.47.

13. BUR.

14. Han.72.

15. ARC. Letter from Father Damien to Bishop Hermann, June 14, 1883.

16. Interior Department Book 22, p. 64, January 8, 1883.

17. Gre.98.

18. ARC. Letter from Father Damien to Bishop Hermann, August 30, 1883.

19. ARC. Letter from Father Damien to Bishop Hermann, July 2, 1883.

20. Han.94–97.

21. BUR. Book One.

22. BUR. Book One. Han.104.

23. BUR. Book One, Chapter 1.

24. Ibid.

25. BUR. Book One, Chapter 2. Han.121–128.

26. Ibid.

27. ARC. Letter from Father Damien to Father Léonor, November 22, 1883.

Chapter 17. Father Damien Denied

1. ARC. Letter from Father Damien to Bishop Hermann, December 31, 1883.

2. Han.133.

3. Han.134.

4. Han.137.

5. Han.149.

6. *Pacific Commercial Advertiser*, January 22, 1884.

7. Ibid.

8. ARC. Letter from R. W. Meyer to Father Damien, February 21, 1884.

9. Dr. Stallard's report to A. S. Cleghorn, March 12, 1884. Mor. 313–315.

10. Ibid. Mor.315–319.

11. Bh.1886.140–143, 145–146.

12. ARC. Letter from Father Damien to Bishop Hermann, March 20, 1884.

13. ARC. Letter from Bishop Hermann to Father Damien, March 25, 1884.

14. Mor.250–251.

15. ARC. Letter from Father Léonor to the superior general, April 30, 1884.

16. ARC. Letter from R. W. Meyer to Father Damien, May 26, 1884.

17. Hawaiian Mission Children's Society Library, Honolulu. Letter from Rev. Dr. Hyde to the American Board of Commissioners for Foreign Missions, February 15, 1884.

18. *Pacific Commercial Advertiser*, June 24, 1884.

19. Letter from W. M. Gibson to Mother Marianne, July 15, 1884. Archives of St. Anthony's Convent, the Mother House of the Third Franciscan Order Minor Conventual, Syracuse, New York.

20. ARC. Letter from G. W. Parker to Father Damien, July 19, 1884.

21. "Report of her Majesty Queen Kapiolani's Visit to Molokai by H. R. H. Princess Liliuokalani, July, 1884." Mor.295–312.

22. Mor.296–297.

23. Mor.300.

24. Ibid.

25. Mor.308–311. "Report of her Majesty Queen Kapiolani's Visit to Molokai by H. R. H. Princess Liliuokalani, July, 1884."

26. ARC. Letter from Queen Kapiʻolani to Father Damien, October 15, 1884.

27. Mor.379.

28. ARC. Letter from Father Léonor to the superior general, September 23, 1884.

Chapter 18. Damien, the Leper

1. *Luna* in Hawaiian means "chief officer," "foreman," or "superintendent"; *nui* means "principal" or "greatest."

2. ARC. Letter from R. W. Meyer to Father Damien, September 23, 1884.

3. Mor.326.

4. Mor.152–156.

5. Sto.Dia.iv–viii.

6. Sto.Dia.

7. Ibid.

8. Sto.Dia.2–3.

9. Sto.LM.19.

10. Sto.LM.21, 32–33.

11. Sto.Dia.4–7.

12. Sto.LM.35–39.

13. Sto.Dia.8–10.

14. Sto.LM.39.

15. Sto.Dia.13–15.

16. Sto.Dia.16.

17. Sto.Dia.16–17.

18. Sto.Dia.17–19.

19. Sto.Dia.30–31.

20. Mor.231.

21. ARC. Letter from Father Léonor to Father Damien, October 28, 1884.

22. Mor.252.

Chapter 19. Damien, the Martyr?

1. Mor.380.

2. ARC. Letter from Father Damien to Father Pamphile, January 31, 1885.

3. ARC. Council of the Reverend Provincial of the Catholic Mission of the Sandwich Islands Resolutions, January 21, 1885.

4. ARC. Letter from Father Damien to Bishop Hermann, February 25, 1885.

5. ARC. Letter from Bishop Hermann to Father Damien, April 13, 1885.

6. ARC. Letter from Father Damien to his mother and family members, February 2, 1885.

7. ARC. Letter from Father Damien to Father Pamphile, January 31, 1885.

8. Mor.249.

9. MM. Letter from Walter Murray Gibson to Mother Marianne, February 19, 1885.

10. Adl.

11. Mor.235–236.

12. Mor.379.

13. Ibid.

14. DUT. Father Damien's account of the development of his leprosy as dictated to Brother Joseph Dutton, March 10, 1889, Kalawao, Moloka'i.

15. Ibid.

16. ARC. Letter from Charles Warren Stoddard to Father Hudson, editor of the review *Ave Maria*, October 1885.

17. Gre.118.

18. C. M. Hyde. "Father Damien and His Work for the Hawaiian Lepers: A Careful and Candid Estimate." *The Congregationalist*, August 7, 1890.

19. ARC. Witnesses and Depositions Section. "Witness of Dr. Mouritz on Father Damien," by Father Maurice Desmedt, pp. 27–28.

20. "Visit of His Excellency Walter M. Gibson," November 2, 1885. Revised report of the *Pacific Commercial Advertiser*. State Archives of Hawai'i.

21. Dedication of the Kapi'olani Home, November 9, 1885. State Archives of Hawai'i.

22. Ibid.

23. Letter from Father Damien to his mother, brothers, and relatives, November 25, 1885.

24. ARC. Letter from Father Damien to Bishop Hermann, December 30, 1885.

25. ARC. Letter from Father Damien to Father Pamphile, November 26, 1885.

Chapter 20. The Valley of the Shadow

1. Mor.cx–cxxiii. Appendix M. "Special Report from Rev. J. Damien, Catholic Priest at Molokai." March 1886.

2. Mor.Appendix K.

3. Bh.1886.140–143.

4. Report of R. W. Meyer, April, 1886. Mor.Appendix N.

5. Ibid.

6. Hansen's Disease File, Archives of Hawai'i. Letter from Gilbert Waller to W. M. Gibson, January 1, 1885.

7. On January 21, 1885, the Provincial Council published a declaration that a priest infected with leprosy should not make physical contact with an uninfected person. See Chapter 19.

8. ARC. Letter from Father Léonor to Father Damien, February 8, 1886.

9. HUT.119.

10. ARC. Letter from Father Damien to Bishop Hermann, March 31, 1886.

11. ARC. Chapter 3.

12. ARC. Letter from Father Damien to Sister Gabrielle, March 25, 1886.

13. ARC. Bishop Hermann's report to the directors of the Propagation of the Faith, 1886.

14. ARC. Letter from Bishop Hermann to the superior general, May 28, 1886.

15. ARC. Letter from Father Columban to the superior general, July 2, 1886.

16. ARC. Letter from Dr. Mouritz to Bishop Hermann, June 5, 1886.

17. Gib.52.

18. ARC. Letter from Father Damien to Bishop Hermann, June 16, 1886.

19. Gib.58.

20. Gib.59.

21. Ibid.

22. *Hawaiian Gazette*, July 20, 1886. *Pacific Commercial Advertiser*, July 19, 1886.

23. Gib.59.

24. Hansen's Disease File, Archives of Hawai'i. Letter from Father Damien to Sec. Hayselden, July 21, 1886.

25. ARC. Letter from Father Damien to Bishop Hermann, July 21, 1886.

26. ARC. Letter from Bishop Hermann to Father Pamphile, July 28, 1886.

Chapter 21. "I Am Brother Joseph. . . . I Have Come to Help"

1. Dut.Mem.64.

2. Gib.53.

3. DUT.

4. Dut.Mem.65.

5. Dut.Mem.

6. Dut.Mem.39.

7. Dut.Mem.46.

8. Dut.Mem.48–49.

9. Letter from Joseph Dutton to Father Hudson, May 10, 1909. Brother Joseph Dutton File, Rev. Daniel E. Hudson Papers, University of Notre Dame Archives, Notre Dame, Indiana.

10. Dut.SM.179.

11. Dut.Mem.60–61.

12. Dut.Mem.65.

13. Ibid.

14. Ibid.

15. Mor.285–286.

16. Joe.216–218.

17. Adl.112, 116, 119, 124, 128, 131.

18. Adl.3–99.

19. Joe.223.

20. ARC. Letter from Father Damien to Father Pamphile, August 1886.

21. ARC. Letter from Father Damien to the superior general, August 26, 1886.

22. ARC. Letter from H. B. Chapman to Father Damien, June 4, 1886.

23. ARC. Letter from Father Damien to H. B. Chapman, dated August 26, 1886, as reprinted in the *Times* (London), October 16, 1886.

24. Jor.208.

25. Jor.210.

26. Jor.276.

27. *Pacific Commercial Advertiser*, December 28, 1886.

28. Letter from Father Damien to Father Hudson, November 23, 1886. Brother Joseph Dutton File, Rev. Daniel Hudson Papers, University of Notre Dame Archives, Notre Dame, Indiana.

29. ARC. Letter from Father Damien to Bishop Hermann, September 15, 1886.

30. Jor.258.

31. Daw.HM.165.

32. Tau.FD.136–137.

33. DUT.

34. ARC. Letter from Father Damien to Father Janvier Weiler, December 30, 1886.

Chapter 22. Death's Dark Shadow

1. Mor.246–249.

2. Ibid.

3. Ibid.

4. ARC. Letter from Bishop Hermann to Father Damien, January 2, 1887.

5. Alexander Meyer Collection, Moloka'i. Letter from Father Damien to R. W. Meyer, January 13, 1887.

6. Alexander Meyer Collection, Moloka'i. Letter from Father Damien to R. W. Meyer, January 19, 1887.

7. ARC. Letter from Father Damien to Rev. H. B. Chapman, January 20, 1887.

8. ARC. Letter from Father Damien to Bishop Hermann, January 20, 1887.

9. ARC. Letter from Bishop Hermann to Father Damien, January 24, 1887.

10. ARC. Letter from Bishop Hermann to Father Damien, February 5, 1887.

11. ARC. Letter from Bishop Hermann to the superior general, February 15, 1887.

12. Alexander Meyer Collection, Moloka'i. Letter from R. W. Meyer to Father Damien, February 16, 1887.

13. ARC. Extract from a letter of R. W. Meyer to Father Damien, February 21, 1887.

14. ARC. Letter from Father Léonor to the superior general, February 8, 1887.

15. ARC. Letter from Bishop Hermann to the superior general, February 11, 1887.

16. ARC. Letter from Father Janvier Weiler to Father Damien, February 11, 1887.

17. ARC. Letter from Father Léonor to Father Damien, February 14, 1887.

18. ARC. Letter from F. H. Hayselden to Father Damien, February 15, 1887.

19. ARC. Letter from Bishop Hermann to Father Damien, April 3, 1887.

20. Bh.1888.

21. Adl.123–127.

22. Ibid.

23. ARC. Letter from Father Léonor to the superior general, April 1887.

24. Ibid.

25. Cli.FD.4.

26. ARC. Letter from Edward Clifford to Father Damien, April 7, 1887.

27. ARC. Copy of a letter from Father Damien to Edward Clifford, May 12, 1887.

28. ARC. *Pacific Commercial Advertiser*, April 25, 1887.

29. ARC. *Pacific Commercial Advertiser*, May 2, 1887.

30. Daw.ST.226–227.

31. Joe.218.

32. Tab.89–100.

33. *Pacific Commercial Advertiser*, May 23, 1887.

34. Joe.219.

35. ARC. Letter from Bishop Hermann to Father Damien, June 12, 1887.

36. ARC. Letter from Bishop Hermann to Father Damien, July 18, 1887.

37. DUT. Father Damien's account of the development of his leprosy as dictated to Brother Joseph Dutton, March 10, 1889, Kalawao, Moloka'i.

38. Mey.91.

39. Minutes of the Meetings of the Board of Health, 1881–1889. State Archives of Hawai'i, Honolulu.

Chapter 23. Thy Rod and Thy Staff, They Comfort Me

1. ARC. Letter from Father Conrardy to Father Damien, November 4, 1887.

2. Jor.296.

3. ARC. Letter from Father Conrardy to M. M. G., a physician in New Haven, Connecticut, July 19, 1888.

4. Ibid.

5. ARC. Letter from Bishop Hermann to Father Damien, November 28, 1887.

6. ARC. Letters from Father Léonor to Father Damien, November 28 and December 5, 1887.

7. Letter from Father Damien to Archbishop Gross, January 10, 1888, published in the *Catholic Sentinel*.

8. Hal.305.

9. ARC. Letter from R. W. Meyer to Father Damien, December 10, 1887.

10. ARC. Letter from Bishop Hermann to Father Damien, January 23, 1888.

11. ARC. Letter from Father Damien to Bishop Hermann, February 2, 1888.

12. ARC. Letter from Bishop Hermann to Father Damien, February 13, 1888.

13. Joseph Dutton, May 1908, in Joseph Dutton file 1890–1912, MS 266.2, D95, Hawaiian Historical Society Library.

14. Ibid.

15. Ibid.

16. ARC. Letter from Father Grégoire to Father Damien, March 17, 1888.

17. Ibid.

18. Board of Health Minutes, March 22, 1888. Archives of Hawai'i, Honolulu.

19. Letter from C. R. Bishop to L. A. Thurston, April 13, 1888. Archives of Hawai'i, Honolulu.

20. Letter from L. A. Thurston to Mother Marianne, May 21, 1888. Internal Deptartment Letters, Archives of Hawai'i, Honolulu.

21. Letter from Mother Marianne to Bishop Hermann, September 15, 1888. Roman Catholic Chancery, Our Mother of Peace Cathedral, Honolulu.

22. Journal of Brother Bertram, May 13, 1888. Pacific Marianist Archives.

23. ARC. Letter from Father Conrardy to Father Imoda, June 27, 1888.

24. Ibid.

25. ARC. Letter from Father Conrardy to a physician in New Haven, Connecticut, July 17, 1888.

26. ARC. Letter from Father Damien to Father Janvier, July 26, 1888.

27. Mor.253.

28. Mor.254.

Chapter 24. Hawaiian Sunset

1. ARC. Letter from Bishop Hermann to the superior general, July 29, 1888.

2. ARC. Letter from the Board of Health to Father Conrardy, September 10, 1888. Board of Health Records, State Archives of Hawai'i, Honolulu. Vol. 11, Board of Health Letter Book, pp. 42–43.

3. Han.282.

4. Han.282–284.

5. Han.286.

6. Han.288.

7. Letter from R. W. Meyer to W. G. Ashley, secretary of the Board of Health, November 7, 1888. Archives of Hawai'i, Honolulu.

8. ARC. Letter from Brother Bertrand to Father Jacques Bund, October 15, 1888.

9. DUT.

10. ARC. Letter from Bishop Hermann to the superior general, October 9, 1888.

11. ARC. Letter from Father Conrardy to a friend, November 7, 1888. Published in the *Gazette* of Louvain.

12. Han.292.

13. Han.292–293.

14. Han.294.

15. Ibid.

16. ARC. Report of Father Corneille to the superior general, December 1, 1888.

17. Jor.365.

18. BUR. Chapter 28, pp. 25–30.

19. Han.303.

20. BUR. Chapter 30, p. 4.

21. BUR. Chapter 23, p. 9.

22. Yze.214. J. Sinnett in the *Catholic Advocate*, March 18, 1891.

23. ARC. Letter from Bishop Hermann to the superior general, December 18, 1888.

24. Cli.FD.4.

25. Cli.9.

26. Cli.8.

27. Cli.12, 73.

28. Cli.7–8.

29. Cli.12.

30. Letter from N. B. Emerson to the Christmas Committee on Moloka'i, December 23, 1888. Fayetteville Archives.

31. ARC. Letter from R. W. Meyer to Father Damien, December 25, 1888.

32. Cli.52–53.

33. Ibid.

Chapter 25. Requiem for a Priest

1. BUR. Chapter 23, p. 1.
2. Ibid.1–6.
3. ARC. Letter from Bishop Hermann to Father Damien, January 2, 1889.
4. Letter from W. G. Ashley to R. W. Meyer, January 20, 1889.
5. ARC. Letter from Father Damien to Father Pamphile, February 12, 1889.
6. Yze.212.
7. ARC. Letter from Father Léonor to the superior general, November 20, 1888.
8. ARC. Codicil to the will of Father Damien, February 28, 1889.
9. DUT. Letter from Brother Dutton: "To Whom It May Concern," October 12, 1903.
10. ARC. Letter from Father Léonor to Father Damien, March 11, 1889.
11. ARC. Letter from Mother Judith to Father Damien, March 18, 1889.
12. Joe.226–227.
13. Mor.134.
14. BUR. Chapter 23, p. 10.
15. Letter from Brother Dutton to Father Hudson. University of Notre Dame Archives, Indiana.
16. ARC. Details on the death of Father Damien submitted by Father Wendelin.
17. ARC. Letter from Brother James to Edward Clifford, July 24, 1889.
18. ARC. Details on the death of Father Damien submitted by Father Wendelin.
19. Old Testament, 2 Kings 2:1–18 RSV.
20. ARC. Letter from Father Wendelin to the superior general, April 17, 1889.
21. Ibid.
22. Mey.85.
23. BUR. Chapter 23, pp. 11–15.
24. ARC. Letter from Father Wendelin to the superior general, April 17, 1889.
25. Ibid.
26. BUR. Chapter 23, pp. 19–21.
27. V.C.J.S. stands for "Vivat Cor Jesu Sacratissimum!" (Live Forever the Most Sacred Heart of Jesus!)—the motto of the Congregation of the Sacred Hearts of Jesus and Mary.

Chapter 26. Accolades and a Preacher's Curse

1. ARC. Letter from Father Léonor to the superior general, April 22, 1889.
2. *Times* of London, June 29, 1889.

3. Jor.377.

4. Letter from Mother Marianne to R. W. Meyer, May 2, 1889. Sisters of Saint Francis Archives, Syracuse, New York.

5. Letter from Mother Marianne to Bishop Hermann, May 16, 1889. Sisters of Saint Francis Archives, Syracuse, New York.

6. Board of Health records, State Archives of Hawai'i. Vol. 11, Board of Health Letter Book, p. 844.

7. Rls.III.147–148.

8. Rls.III.151–154.

9. Ibid.

10. Rls.III.148.

11. Ibid.

12. Ibid.

13. Rls.III.149–150.

14. Han.11.

15. Rls.TH.178.

16. Ibid. In 1984, while visiting St. Anthony's Convent, the Mother House of the Third Franciscan Order Minor Conventual in Syracuse, New York, I was permitted to hold the signed original for a few moments.

17. "Father Damien." In *The Collected Works of Robert Louis Stevenson*, Thistle Edition, vol. 4, p. 94. New York: Charles Scribner's Sons, 1897.

18. HUT.

19. Mor.285.

20. DUT.

21. Ibid.

22. DUT.; Rls.TH.140.

23. Rls.TH.56.

24. BUR. Chapter 24.

25. Jor.379–380.

26. ARC. Fundamentals of the Questionnaire Set Up by the Promotion of the Faith.

27. Rls.TH.150–151.

Chapter 27. Response to the Curse

1. McG.105.

2. Rls.TH.147–167.

3. Ibid.

4. McG.108. The booklet first appeared on March 27, 1890.

5. Rls.III.312.

6. McG.108.

7. Letter from Bishop Hermann Koeckemann to the editor of the *Honolulu Advertiser*, June 7, 1890.

8. Jor.347.

9. ARC. "Le Pere Damien—Vie et Documents." Part V: "Inquest, Testimonies, Depositions." Rome Archives, Congregation of the Sacred Hearts, 1966.

Chapter 28. A Second Saint Damien

1. ARC. "Le Pere Damien—Vie et Documents." Part V: "Inquest, Testimonies, Depositions," p. 1.

2. ARC. Letter from Bishop Hermann to the superior general, August 22, 1889.

3. ARC. Letter from Bishop Hermann to the superior general, December 13, 1889.

4. ARC. "Le Pere Damien—Vie et Documents." Part V: "Inquest, Testimonies, Depositions," pp. 117–201.

5. Mor.

6. *St. Anthony Messenger* 101:30–31, May 1994.

7. Patrick Downes. "Damien of Moloka'i, Servant of Humanity." *Hawai'i Catholic Herald*, March 27, 1992.

8. *Honolulu Star-Bulletin*, page D-1, June 5, 1995.

9. Francis, D'Emilio. "Belgians fail to pack house for papal ceremony." Associated Press. June 4, 1995.

10. Greg Wiles. "Damien walks in the ranks of the Blesseds." *The Honolulu Advertiser*, p. A-1, Sunday, June 4, 1995.

11. "Servant of God, Damien De Veuster, SS.CC., Blessed Servant of Humanity." Pope John Paul II's Beatification Homily, Pentecost Sunday, June 4, 1995. Sacred Hearts Home Page, Internet.

12. Greg Wiles. "Papal hospitality at Damien rite." *The Honolulu Advertiser*, pages A-1–2, June 5, 1995.

Epilogue

1. Yze.230.

2. Han.360.

3. Dut.Mem.235–236.

4. Gib.116.

5. Letter from Herbert Hoover to Father Hanz, May 14, 1932. Archives of St. Jude's Church, Beloit, Wisconsin.

6. Joe.228.

7. Hawai'i State Archives, Honolulu.

8. Mey.127.

9. Kae.40–41.

10. Mor.253.

11. Hal.305. Susan N. Bell. *Unforgettable True Stories of the Kingdom of Hawai'i*, pp. 104–105. Van Nuys, California: Delta Lithograph, 1986.

12. Mor.254.

13. Richard A. Miller. "Leprosy (Hansen's Disease)." Chapter 172 in *Harrison's Principles of Internal Medicine—14th Edition*. New York: McGraw-Hill, 1998.

Glossary

'ai pa'a. Cooked taro pounded into a hard mass not mixed with water, sometimes preserved in ti-leaf bundles.

ali'i. Chief, chiefess, monarch, aristocrat, noble, ruler, king, queen, commander.

aloha. Love, affection, compassion; greeting, salutation; to love, be fond of; to show kindness, mercy, pity. Hello! Good-bye! Farewell!

kahuna. Priest, sorcerer, minister, expert in any profession (whether male or female).

kahuna 'anā 'anā. Sorcerer who practices black magic; a priest who prays a person to death.

kahuna lapa'au. Medical doctor, healer.

kahuna pule. Priest, minister, parson.

kama'āina. Native born.

kanikau. Chant of mourning.

kōkua. Helper, assistant; help, aid, assistance.

lei. Lei, garland, wreath; necklace of flowers, leaves, shells, ivory, feathers, or paper, given as a symbol of affection.

luna. Foreman, headman, leader, supervisor.

luna nui. Chief officer or foreman, head overseer.

mea aloha. Loved one, beloved.

ma'i. Sickness, illness, disease, sick person, patient.

ma'i Pākē. Leprosy. *Lit.,* Chinese disease.

pa'i 'ai. Hard-pounded but undiluted taro.

pali. Cliff, precipice.

pū hala. Pandanus or screw pine *(Pandanus odoratissimus).* A tree with many branches that are tipped with long, narrow, spine-edged leaves; its base is supported by a clump of slanting aerial roots.

Bibliography

Listed here are the major sources of information and quotations in this biography. The abbreviations preceding each item in the notes identify the reference listed below. Unpublished sources are coded in full capitals. Published sources are coded in upper and lower case. Thus, DUT. designates Ira Dutton in unpublished manuscript, while Dut. designates Ira Dutton in print. Listings are alphabetical by code, usually an abbreviated surname. Asterisks denote items of particular importance to this study. All other sources, including minor books, periodical articles, and documents, are cited in full when they appear in the notes.

Unpublished Material: Journals, Diaries, Letters, and Manuscript Collections

*ARC. Provincial Archives of the Congregation of the Sacred Hearts, Louvain, Belgium. Contains copies of all remaining Father Damien letters, correspondence to and regarding him, and the three-volume manuscript of the "Inquest, Testimonies, and Depositions" taken following Father Damien's death.

*ARH. State Archives of Hawai'i, Honolulu.

*BUR. Burns, Sister M. Leopoldina. "The Journals of Sister M. Leopoldina Burns." Undated manuscript consisting of fifty-six chapters in fifteen notebooks housed in the Archives of St. Anthony's Convent, the Mother House of the Third Franciscan Order Minor Conventual, Syracuse, New York. Permission was given by the director of the Cause of Mother Marianne Cope, Sisters of the Third Franciscan Order, to use and reference *A Song of Pilgrimage and Exile* (Hanley and Bushnell), and to quote from the unpublished journals of Sister M. Leopoldina Burns.

*DUT. Dutton, Ira B. "Joseph Dutton Papers, General Group 1905–1929." Division of Archives and Manuscripts, State Historical Society of Wisconsin, Madison, Wisconsin.

*HUT. Hutchison, Ambrose. "In Memoria of Reverend Father Damien Joseph De Veuster." Unpublished manuscript, State Archives of Hawai'i, 1930.

*MAI. Maigret, Bishop Louis. "Diary." 3 vols., Bishop Museum, Honolulu.

*MEY. Meyer, R. W. "Report of R. W. Meyer, Agent of the Board of Health at the Leper Settlement, Moloka'i, April 1886." Manuscript, State Archives of Hawai'i, Honolulu.

*MM. Cope, Mother Marianne. "Diary" and letters, 1884–1889. Roman Catholic Chancery, Syracuse, New York.

RAE. Raipsaet, Rev. Maurice. "Life of Father Damien." Congregation of Sacred Hearts, 1889.

Published Works

Abb. Abbott, Isabella A. *La'au Hawai'i: Traditional Hawaiian Uses of Plants.* Honolulu: Bishop Museum Press, 1992.

*Adl. Adler, Jacob, and Gwynn Barrett. *The Diaries of Walter Murray Gibson, 1886–1887.* Honolulu: University Press of Hawai'i, 1973.

Arn. Arning, Dr. Eduard. *Copies of the Report of Dr. Eduard Arning to the Board of Health.* Honolulu: *Hawaiian Gazette*, 1886.

*Bir. Bird, Isabella L. *Six Months in the Sandwich Islands.* Honolulu: University of Hawai'i Press, 1966.

Bee. Beevers, John. *A Man for Now.* New York: Doubleday, 1973.

*Bh.1878. *Report of the Special Sanitary Committee on the State of the Leper Settlement at Kalawao.* Honolulu: n.p., 1878.

*Bh.1886. *Leprosy in Hawaii: Extracts from Reports of Presidents of the Board of Health, Government Physicians and Others, and from Official Records.* Honolulu: Daily Bulletin Steam Printing Office, 1886.

*Bha.1886. *Appendix to the Report on Leprosy of the President of the Board of Health to the Legislative Assembly of 1886.* Honolulu: P.C. Advertiser Steam Print, 1886.

*Bh.1888. *Report of the Special Committee on the Leper Settlement at Kalawao, Molokai.* Honolulu: Gazette Publishing, 1888.

Bun. Bunson, Margaret R. *Father Damien: The Man and His Era.* Huntington: Our Sunday Visiting, 1989.

Bus. Bushnell, O. A. "Dr. Edward Arning: The First Microbiologist in Hawai'i." *Hawaiian Journal of History* 1:3–30, 1967.

*Bus.GC. Bushnell, O. A. *The Gifts of Civilization: Germs and Genocide in Hawai'i.* Honolulu: University of Hawai'i Press, 1993.

Cah. Cahill, Emmett. *Yesterday at Kalaupapa.* Honolulu: Mutual Publishing and Editions Limited, 1990.

*Cli. Clifford, Edward. *Father Damien: A Journey from Cashmere to His Home in Hawaii.* London: Macmillan, 1889.

*Cli.FD. Clifford, Edward. "Father Damien." *The Damien Institute Monthly Magazine* 5, 1899. Clifford's published account of his visit to Moloka'i.

Coc. Cochrane, R. G. *A Practical Textbook of Leprosy.* London: Oxford University Press, 1947.

*Daw.HM. Daws, Gavan. *Holy Man: Father Damien of Molokai.* New York: Harper & Row, 1973.

*Daw.ST. Daws, Gavan. *Shoal of Time: A History of the Hawaiian Islands.* Honolulu: University Press of Hawai'i, 1968.

*Dut.Mem. Dutton, Ira B. *Joseph Dutton: His Memoirs.* Ed. by Howard D. Case. Honolulu: Star-Bulletin Press, 1931.

Dut.SM. Dutton, Charles J. *The Samaritans of Molokai: The Lives of Father Damien and Brother Dutton among the Lepers.* New York: Dodd, Mead, 1932.

Eng. Englebert, Omer. *The Hero of Molokai: Father Damien, Apostle of the Lepers.* Translation by B. T. Crawford. Boston: St. Paul Editions, 1954.

Far. Farrow, John. *Damien the Leper.* New York: Sheed & Ward, 1937.

Fee. Feeny, Patrick. *The Fight against Leprosy.* New York: American Leprosy Missions, 1964.

Gib. Gibson, Emma Warren. *Under the Cliffs of Molokai.* Fresno: Academy Library Guild, 1957.

*Gre. Green, Linda W., *Exile in Paradise: The Isolation of Hawai'i's Leprosy Victims and Development of Kalaupapa Settlement, 1865 to the Present.* Denver: Branch of Planning, Alaska/Pacific Northwest/Western Team, U.S. Department of the Interior, National Park Service, Denver Service Center, 1985.

Gui. Guinto, Ricardo S., et al. *An Atlas of Leprosy.* Tokyo: Sasakawa Memorial Health Foundation, 1983. Excellent pictorial presentation of diagnostic signs.

Gus. Gussow, Zachary, and George S. Tracy. "Stigma and the Leprosy Phenomenon: The Social History of a Disease in the Nineteenth and Twentieth Centuries." *Bulletin of the History of Medicine* 44:425–449, 1970.

Gut. Gutmanis, June. *Kahuna La'au Lapa'au.* Aiea, Hawai'i: Island Heritage, 1992.

*Hal. Halford, Francis John. *9 Doctors & God.* Honolulu: University of Hawai'i Press, 1954.

Han.HP. Handy, E. S. Craighill. *The Hawaiian Planter, Volume 1: His Plants, Methods and Areas of Cultivation.* B. P. Bishop Museum Bulletin 161. Honolulu: Bishop Museum Press, 1940. Reprinted 1971 (New York: Kraus Reprint).

Han.NP. Handy, E. S. Craighill, and Elizabeth Green Handy. *Native Planters in Old Hawai'i: Their Life, Lore, and Environment.* B. P. Bishop Museum Bulletin 233. Honolulu: Bishop Museum Press, 1972.

*Han. Hanley, Sister Mary Laurence, and O. A. Bushnell. *A Song of Pilgrimage and Exile.* Chicago: Franciscan Herald Press, 1980. Permisssion was given by the director of the Cause of Mother Marianne Cope, Sisters of the Third Franciscan Order, Syracuse, New York, to use and reference *A Song of Pilgrimage and Exile* and to quote from two letters written by Mother Marianne.

Has. Hansen, G. A. "Causes of Leprosy." *Norsk Laegevidensk* 4: 76–79, 1874. The classic work on leprosy.

*Has.L. Hansen, G. A., and C. Looft. *Leprosy: In Its Clinical and Pathological Aspects.* Translated by N. Walker. Bristol: John Wright, 1895. One of the first leprosy textbooks by the discoverer of the leprosy bacillus.

*Hat. Hathaway, J. C. "Leprosy in Hawaii." *Hawaii Medical Journal* 29:429–437, 1970. Excellent overview of the history, clinical features, and treatment of leprosy.

Haw. Hawai'i Audubon Society. *Hawai'i's Birds.* Honolulu: Hawai'i Audubon Society, 1993.

*Haw.LH. Hawai'i (Kingdom) Board of Health. *Leprosy in Hawaii.* Honolulu, 1886.

*Hyd. Hyde, C. M. "Father Damien and His Work for the Hawaiian Lepers: A Careful and Candid Estimate." *The Congregationalist,* August 7, 1890.

Ins.4. *The Damien Institute Monthly Magazine* 4, 1898. Birmingham, England: John Gateley.

Jac. Jacks, L. V. *Mother Marianne of Molokai.* New York: Macmillan, 1935.

*Joe. Joesting, Edward. *Hawai'i: An Uncommon History.* New York: W. W. Norton, 1972.

Jop. Jopling, W. H., and A. C. McDougall. *Handbook of Leprosy.* Oxford: Heinemann, 1988.

*Jor. Jourdan, Vital. *The Heart of Father Damien.* Milwaukee: Bruce, 1955.

Jud. Judd, Gerrit P. IV. *Dr. Judd, Hawaii's Friend.* Honolulu: University of Hawai'i Press, 1960.

Jud.H. Judd, Laura Fish. *Honolulu: Sketches of the Life Social, Political, and Religious, in the Hawaiian Islands from 1828 to 1861.* Honolulu: Star-Bulletin Press, 1928.

*Kae. Kaeo, Peter, and Queen Emma. *News from Molokai: Letters between Peter Kaeo and Queen Emma, 1873–1876.* Ed. by Alfons L. Korn. Honolulu: University Press of Hawai'i, 1976.

Kam. Kamakau, S. M. *Ka Po'e Kahiko: The People of Old.* B. P. Bishop Museum Special Publication 51. Honolulu: Bishop Museum Press, 1964.

Ken.HS. Kent, Harold W. *Dr. Hyde and Mr. Stevenson.* Tokyo: Tuttle, 1973.

Ken.CB. Kent, Harold W. *Charles Reed Bishop: Man of Hawaii.* Palo Alto: Pacific Books, 1965.

*Kuy.II. Kuykendall, Ralph S. *The Hawaiian Kingdom.* Vol. 2. *1854–1874: Twenty Critical Years.* Honolulu: University of Hawai'i Press, 1953.

*Kuy.III. Kuykendall, Ralph S. *The Hawaiian Kingdom.* Vol. 3. *1874–1893: The Kalakaua Dynasty.* Honolulu: University of Hawai'i Press, 1967.

*Law. Law, Anwei, and Richard A. Wisniewski. *Kalaupapa National Historical Park and the Legacy of Father Damien (A Pictorial History).* Honolulu: Pacific Basin Enterprises, 1988.

Lin. Lindsley, Alfred. "Aikualani: The Story of a Leper." *The Hawaiian* 1:403–444, 527–549, 1895.

Luc. Lucas, Lois. *Plants of Old Hawaii.* Honolulu: Bess Press, 1982.

Lud. Ludlow, J. L., M.D. *A Manual of Examinations upon Anatomy, Physiology, Surgery, Practice of Medicine, Chemistry, Obstetrics, Materia Medica, Pharmacy and Therapeutics.* Philadelphia: Henry C. Lea, 1867.

McB. McBride, L. R. *The Kahuna: Versatile Mystics of Old Hawaii.* Hilo, Hawai'i: Petroglyph Press, 1983.

McG. McGaw, M. M. *Stevenson in Hawaii.* Westport, Connecticut: Greenwood Press, 1978.

*Mey. Meyer, Charles S. *Meyer and Molokai.* Alden, Iowa: Graphic-Agri Business, 1982.

*Mil. Miller, Richard A., "Leprosy (Hansen's Disease)." Chapter 172 in *Harrison's Principles of Internal Medicine—14th Edition.* New York: McGraw-Hill, 1998.

*Mor. Mouritz, Arthur A. *The Path of the Destroyer: A History of Leprosy in the Hawaiian Islands and Thirty Years Research into the Means by Which It Has Been Spread.* Honolulu: Star-Bulletin Press, 1916.

Mor.WH. Mouritz, Arthur A. *A Brief World History of Leprosy.* Honolulu: A. Mouritz, 1943 (revised ed.).

Mra.HM. Mrantz, Maxine. *Hawaiian Monarchy: The Romantic Years.* Honolulu: Aloha Graphics and Sales, 1974.

Mra.WH. Mrantz, Maxine. *Women of Old Hawaii.* Honolulu: Aloha Graphics and Sales, 1975.

Mul.HJ. Mullins, Joseph G. *Hawaiian Journey.* Honolulu: Mutual Publishing, 1978.

*Pam. Father Kingdon and Father Pamphile De Veuster, ed. *Life and Letters of Father Damien, the Apostle of the Lepers.* London: Catholic Truth Society, 1889.

*Rls.III. Stevenson, Robert Louis. *The Letters of Robert Louis Stevenson.* Vol. 3. Ed. by Sidney Colvin. New York: Charles Scribner's Sons, 1911.

*Rls.FD. Stevenson, Robert Louis. *Father Damien: An Open Letter to the Reverend Doctor Hyde of Honolulu.* Sydney: Ben Franklin Printing, 1890.

*Rls.TH. Stevenson, Robert Louis. *Travels in Hawaii.* Ed. by A. Grove Day. Honolulu: University Press of Hawai'i, 1973. This volume is a collection of the writings of Robert Louis Stevenson in, from, and about Hawai'i. It includes his correspondence from Hawai'i, his famous letter in defense of Father Damien, his essays detailing his visit to the leper settlement, and excerpts from his journal.

Rok. Rokstad, Ingvald. "Gerhard Henrich Armauer Hansen." *Internat. J. Leprosy* 32:64–70, 1964.

Ryr. Ryrie, G. A. "The Psychology of Leprosy." *Leprosy Review* 22:13–23, 1951.

*Sch. Schmitt, Robert C. *Demographic Statistics of Hawaii: 1778–1965.* Honolulu: University of Hawai'i Press, 1968.

Ski. Skinsnes, V. "A Self-Imposed Exile: The Life of Brother Joseph Dutton." In *Brother Joseph Dutton, A Saint for Vermont.* Ed. by R. Halpern. Stowe, Vermont: Blessed Sacrament Church.

Sta. Stall, Edna Williamson. *Historic Homes of Hawaii.* East Aurora: Roycrofters, 1937.

*Stn. Stannard, David E. *Before the Horror: The Population of Hawai'i on the Eve of Western Contact.* Honolulu: University of Hawai'i Press, 1989.

*Ste. Stewart, Richard D. "Leper Priest of Moloka'i: The Father Damien Story." A dissertation submitted in partial fulfillment of the requirements for the degree of Doctor of Philosophy (English) at the University of Wisconsin–Milwaukee. UMI number 9821973. Ann Arbor: UMI Dissertation Services, 1997. This 1,021-page dissertation contains major portions of each letter referred to in the text of this biography. A Father Damien letter referenced in a given chapter in this biography is found in a chapter of the same number in the dissertation.

*Sto.Dia. Stoddard, Charles W. *Charles Warren Stoddard's Diary of a Visit to Molokai in 1884, with a Letter from Father Damien to His Brother in 1873.* San Francisco: Book Club of California, 1933.

*Sto.LM. Stoddard, Charles W. *The Lepers of Molokai.* Notre Dame: Ave Maria Press, 1893.

*Sum. Summers, Catherine C. *Molokai: A Site Survey.* Pacific Anthropological Records No. 14. Honolulu: B. P. Bishop Museum, 1971.

Tab. Tabrah, Ruth M. *Ni'ihau: The Last Hawaiian Island.* Kailua, Hawai'i: Press Pacifica, 1987.

Tau. Tauvel, Father Philibert. *Vie du Pere Damien, l'apôtre des lepreux de Molokai.* Bruges: Desclee De Brouwer Et C, 1890.

*Tau.FD. Tauvel, Father Philibert. *Father Damien, Apostle of the Lepers of Molokai.* Translated from the 1890 French version. London: Art and Book, 1904.

Tho. Thompson, Vivian L. *Hawaiian Myths of Earth, Sea, and Sky*. Honolulu: University of Hawai'i Press, 1966.

Twa. Twain, Mark. *Mark Twain in Hawaii*. San Francisco: Sacramento Union, 1866.

*****Twa.L.** *Mark Twain's Letters from Hawaii*. Ed. by A. Grove Day. Honolulu: University Press of Hawai'i, 1979.

Vog. Vogelsang, Th. M. "Gerhard Henrik Armauer Hansen, 1841–1912." *International Journal of Leprosy* 46:257–332, 1978. Original work published in Norwegian by Gyldendal Norsk Forlag, Oslo, 1968. Translated by author; edited, amended, and expanded by Anwei V. Skinsnes.

*****Wod.** Woods, G. W. *Reminiscences of a Visit, in July, 1876, to the Leper Settlement of Molokai, Having Special Reference to Rev. Father J. Damien De Veuster*. Birmingham, England: John Gately, 1895.

Who. World Health Organization. *WHO Expert Committee on Leprosy*. Fourth Report. World Health Organization Technical Report Series No. 459. Geneva: WHO, 1970.

*****Yze.** Yzendoorn, Father Reginald. *History of the Catholic Mission in the Hawaiian Islands*. Honolulu: Star-Bulletin Press, 1927.

Index

About the Author

RICHARD STEWART is a semi-retired professor of the Medical College of Wisconsin and continues to be an active teacher. A graduate of the University of Michigan Medical School and Medical Center, he is a specialist in both internal medicine and medical toxicology. He led the medical team that invented and successfully tested the hollow fiber artificial kidney, which was used by 142,000 Americans last year.

Stewart has a Ph.D. in English literature and considers American histroy and medical mysteries his primary avocation. For several years he served Milwaukee's classical music station WFMR as director and co-host of a program exploring the influence of medicine and disease on the lives of famous people. It was this interest that prompted his 15-year investigation into the life and career of Father Damien De Veuster.

CPSIA information can be obtained
at www.ICGtesting.com
Printed in the USA
FSHW012140080421
80304FS